HEALTH PSYCHOPHYSIOLOGY:
Mind–Body Interactions in Wellness and Illness

HEALTH PSYCHOPHYSIOLOGY:
Mind–Body Interactions in Wellness and Illness

Steve Suter
California State College,
Bakersfield

LEA LAWRENCE ERLBAUM ASSOCIATES, PUBLISHERS
1986   Hillsdale, New Jersey   London

Lawrence Erlbaum Associates, Inc., Publishers
365 Broadway
Hillsdale, New Jersey 07642

Library of Congress Cataloging-in-Publication Data

Suter, Steve.
   Health psychophysiology: Mind–Body Interactions in
   Wellness and Illness

   Includes index.
   1. Medicine and psychology.   2. Psychology.
Physiological.   3. Mind and body.   I. Title.
R726.5.S84   1986   610'.1'9   85-15907
ISBN 0-89859-605-X
ISBN 0-89859-672-6 (pbk.).

Printed in the United States of America
10   9   8   7   6   5   4   3   2

This book is dedicated to my parents
Doris and Spike Suter

Contents

Preface

Health Psychophysiology is an introduction to this new field for students with no special preparation in biology, psychology, or medicine. The text looks at humans as psychophysiological beings, exploring the implications of this perspective for understanding and improving our health. It is intended to help fill the gap between supermarket-check-out-stand-type discussions written for health-care consumers and advanced presentations on narrow topics for researchers and practitioners. The first kind are interesting, but usually extremely speculative with little scientific substance. The material in advanced texts is not accessible to non-specialists.

The major topics covered here, such as pain, stress, relaxation, self-regulation, positive health, optimum performance, and a number of specific disorders — indeed the field of health psychophysiology itself — reflect the relatively recent convergence of biological and psychological research. Because many readers will not be familiar with the perspective of this book, I have included some orienting comments in chapter 1 that would otherwise have been found in this preface.

Health Psychophysiology was written with advanced undergraduates in psychology, nursing, or related fields, in mind, but it should also provide a solid foundation for graduate students who will pursue specialized study in this field. Because of general interest in the topics discussed in this text, it could support popular elective courses for students in non-health fields.

ACKNOWLEDGMENTS

Many individuals contributed to this project. Penelope Sholes Suter and Brendan Maher reviewed all of the chapters. David Cohen, Karen Naifeh, Dick Noel, and Ed Sasaki commented on individual chapters from an early draft. Technical computer support was always available when needed from Michael Fleming and Phil Whitney of the California State College, Bakersfield Computer Center, and from Jen-Lin Chen of the Psychophysiology laboratory, NASA/Ames Research Center. Many library personnel were extremely helpful, especially David Kosakowski, Jim Segesta, Lorna Frost, and Johanna Alexander at the California State College, Bakersfield Library, Barbara Kornstein and Sonia Kaufman at the UC-Berkeley Education/Psychology Library, and Pam Jamiko at the Life Sciences Library of the NASA/Ames Research Center. Photography is by Reza Azarmsa and original graphics are by Lillian Bell. Finally, I am sincerely grateful for the exceptional eye-hand coordination and steady nerves of Robert Hayes, ace driver for Peerless Stages and the East Bay Commute Club, on whose run between Berkeley and Mountain View, California I drafted about half of this textbook.

Steve Suter

1 Introduction to Health Psychophysiology

A person is a psychophysiological being—a synthesis of mind and body. When health is considered from this starting point it becomes apparent that illness and wellness must result from interacting biological and psychological forces. Interesting new questions arise as to how illness develops; alternate methods for recovering and maintaining good health become plausible. These are the topics of this book.

It may be useful to discuss some labels, by way of orientation. *Medicine*, in this book, refers to the activities of medical doctors (M.D.s). They are always referred to as *physicians*, to avoid any confusion with Ph.D. doctors like myself. Most physicians see patients, and are therefore considered health care *practitioners*. There are many non-medical practitioners, such as dentists, optometrists, physical therapists, and some psychologists. The author, incidentally, is not a practitioner, but a researcher and teacher specializing in human psychophysiology.

For many years, some of the disorders and concepts discussed in this text were considered under the rubric of *psychosomatic medicine*, "the study and treatment of bodily symptoms of psychological origin." This term is avoided here because, it falsely suggests that health problems can be sorted into those that are psychosomatic problems and those that are not. In fact, there probably is no such thing as a purely somatic (bodily) health problem.

Behavioral medicine is a more recent term that refers to the use of certain nontraditional techniques, such as biofeedback, for health problems that had been treated customarily with the traditional medical interventions of surgery or drugs. This usage has seemed peculiar to me ever since

1

the term was introduced in the early 1970s. There is practically no behaving involved in the self-regulation methods, such as biofeedback, nor are these procedures usually intended to change the patient's behavior. Behavioral medicine is not used here.

Holistic health is another recent addition to the health vocabulary, and refers to an alternative approach to health whose basic premise is that health is a function of the whole person—mind and body. This concept is endorsed in this text. As argued later in this chapter, the Western model of health is shifting toward a more holistic view. Holistic health might have found its way into the title of this text, except that the term, at present, is an umbrella for an astonishing assortment of interventions, along with their promoters, whose only common characteristic appears to be their rejection by traditional medical practitioners. With mixed feelings because of the identification of psychophysiology with holism, the holistic health label is used sparingly in the rest of this text.

A new term is introduced here, one that is intended to be sufficiently encompassing but without the excess baggage of existing labels—*health psychophysiology*, the science concerned with the psychophysiological analysis of illness and wellness.

THE EMERGING PSYCHOPHYSIOLOGICAL PERSPECTIVE

Science progresses in great leaps. Every so often there is an upheaval so fundamental that it alters what scientists take for granted and changes the kinds of questions that scientists ask—something like a scientific revolution (Kuhn, 1962). The old puzzle no longer seems worth solving, and it is set aside; rules are laid down for a grand new puzzle and researchers begin to work on it. From the 1920s into the 1960s behaviorism dominated scientific psychology. The puzzle was to analyze and explain behavior from an outside-the-organism point of view. With the decline of behaviorism, many scientists, including some former behaviorists, have taken up a new puzzle—attempting to understand the person as a mind-body phenomenon. One sign is the birth of scientific periodicals dedicated to psychophysiological research. Led by *Psychophysiology*, a bi-monthly introduced in 1964, more recent arrivals, and their birthdates, are: *Biological Psychology* (1973), *Journal of Holistic Health* (1975), *Biofeedback and Self-Regulation* (1976), *Journal of Holistic Medicine* (1980), *Journal of Clinical Neuropsychology* (1979), several with tongue-twister titles—*Neuropsychobiology* (1975) and *Psychoneuroendocrinology* (1975), and a very simple one—*Stress* (1980).

The media bring news to the general public of scientific developments that must seem more like science fiction than real science. Newspapers and TV report such things as: (a) children learning to control their own brain activity and avoid epileptic seizures (chapter 5); (b) evidence that fake pain killers, placebos, may relieve pain via the same biochemical changes in the brain as do the real pain killers such as morphine (chapter 4); and (c) the likely dependence of many diseases, from cancer to heart disease, on psychological factors, such as personality characteristics (chapters 3 and 7). Advertisements in magazines describe the healthful benefits of hanging upside down, sitting under pyramids, or floating in dark tanks of water. The mind and body no longer seem so independent.

Graduate Study in Psychology and Associated Fields (American Psychological Association, 1984) lists about 40 graduate programs, most of them recently developed, offering doctoral level training in such areas as biopsychology, psychobiology, biological psychology, behavioral medicine, clinical psychophysiology, health psychology, human psychophysiology, neuropsychology, and medical psychology. Holistic health clinics spring up almost overnight in every major United States city.

THE CHANGING MODEL OF HEALTH

The developments just described are linked to important changes in our concept of health, understanding of illness, and approaches to treatment. The contemporary model of health is changing in five major ways: (a) the target of treatment; (b) the time of treatment; (c) the role of the patient; (d) the treatments of choice; and (e) the goals of treatment.

Target of Treatment

Until recently, the Western model of health dealt almost exclusively with discrete diseases, and individual organs of the body. Although this model has enjoyed many successes, and continues to be useful in some cases, contemporary thinking is shifting toward a psychophysiological concept of health, with illness and wellness seen as conditions of a whole person.

Modern medicine grew out of important discoveries in the 19th century. Perhaps the most important was confirmation of the ancient germ theory of disease, the idea that certain maladies are discrete conditions caused by tiny living creatures. Soon, the new science of bacteriology began to identify some of the agents of specific infectious diseases. Near the end of the century immunization procedures were introduced, for example, for diphtheria and tetanus (in 1890), and for tuberculosis (in 1908). Because of its success with infectious diseases, the disease concept has become one of the cornerstones of traditional Western medicine. However there are some problems with the disease concept.

It is a tempting conceptual trap to think that the infectious agent explains why we get sick. The fallacy of this type of reasoning has been known for many years. Consider the observations of this 19th century physician (Creighton, 1891), discussing the causes of leprosy:

> Such special causes may be present in a country generally, among the poor of all the towns, villages and hamlets, and yet only one person here and there may show specific effects that are recognisable as a disease to which we give a name. Unless there be present the aiding and abetting things, the special factor will hardly make itself felt. . . . These aiding things are for the most part the usual concomitants of poverty and hardships, wearing out the nerves far more than is commonly supposed and producing . . . an excessive amount of nervous affections among the poor. But among the poor themselves, as well as among the well-to-do, there are special susceptibilities in individuals and in families. (p. 112)

If bacterial agents alone were responsible for infectious diseases, we would be sick all the time—the bacterial agents of many infectious diseases are always present in and around the body. There must be additional factors. One of the most important considerations is the condition of the immune system (chapter 2), whose function is highly sensitive to psychophysiological variables, especially stress (chapter 3).

Ironically, the success of the disease model in combating infectious disease has helped shift health patterns, so that we are now faced with health problems for which the disease model is inappropriate and even counter-productive. Table 1.1 lists the five leading causes of death in the United States. Heart disease heads the list. The odds of dying of a heart attack or a related ailment have tripled since the turn of the century, in spite of the development of many drugs, such as the beta-blockers (chapter 2), and surgery techniques, such as the coronary artery bypass procedure (chapter 7). Cancer is second, and it too has tripled as a cause

TABLE 1.1
Leading Causes of Death: United States, 1983
(National Center for Health Statistics, 1984)

Rank	Cause	Rate per 100,000	Percent of all deaths
1	Heart Disease	327.6	38.1
2	Cancer	188.6	21.9
3	Cerebrovascular disease	66.8	7.8
4	Accidents	39.0	4.5
5	Lung Diseases	28.4	3.3

of death since 1900, in spite of the introduction of chemotherapy and radiation treatment methods. The third leading contemporary cause of death is cerebrovascular disease, the death of brain cells due to interruption of their blood supply because of a clot or a hemorrhage; deaths due to stroke have increased only slightly in the past 80 years. Together, these three conditions account for 68% of all deaths in this country. In contrast, for the years 1900-1904, tuberculosis and pneumonia were the leading causes of death in the United States (Bureau of the Census, 1906).

In the more technologically advanced countries, infectious diseases are no longer the greatest health problems. It is suspected, although difficult to prove, that this shift in health patterns reflects more than the decline of infectious disease, and that modern civilization, with its polluted air and water, and stressful living conditions, has contributed to an absolute rise in the *diseases of civilization*. Equating civilization and industrial development, the term reflects the much higher rate of stress-related disorders in the more highly developed parts of the world. For example, the death rate in the United States for heart disease is about 10 times the rate in Mexico; the cancer death rate is four times the Mexican rate; deaths due to stroke are about five times higher in the United States. Middle-aged males in the United States have one of the lowest life expectancies in the industrialized world.

The disease model does not transfer well to conditions such as essential hypertension (high blood pressure) and coronary heart disease (chapter 7). There is a tendency to look for a discrete cause, for something like the bacterial agent of an infectious disease. None of the major disorders discussed in this textbook can be understood in terms of single, discrete causes. For example, the long list of contributors to essential hypertension may include diet, smoking, lack of exercise, personality characteristics, and stress. There is a hereditary component. The risk of hypertension is related to age, race, gender, and geography.

Another reason that the disease analogy is inappropriate is that it tends to nurture hope for a "magic bullet" cure, like an immunization procedure or an antibiotic drug. People continue to smoke cigarettes while counting on a cure for cancer that may be just over the horizon. Because there are multiple causes of the psychophysiological disorders, effective treatment will have to speak to these causes.

Time of Treatment

About 4,500 years ago, the Yellow Emperor of China is said to have written:

> Hence the sages did not treat those who were already ill; they instructed those who were not yet ill. They did not want to rule those who were

already rebellious; they guided those who were not yet rebellious. . . . To administer medicines to diseases which have already developed and to suppress revolts which have already developed is comparable to the behavior of those persons who begin to dig a well after they have become thirsty, and of those who begin to cast weapons after they have already engaged in battle. Would these actions not be too late? (Veith, 1972, p. 105)

More health care dollars are being spent digging wells and casting weapons against future use. Health care is shifting away from a model that was primarily curative, addressing ailments that had already developed, and in the direction of a more prevention-oriented perspective. This has been prompted, in part, by recognition that "an ounce of prevention is worth a pound of cure" in the case of many psychophysiological disorders. Curative medicine has begun to show diminishing returns in reducing mortality and lengthening life expectancy, in particular in bringing expensive technology to bear on health problems such as heart disease.

To a very great extent, our major illnesses are now diseases of choice— we choose to watch TV rather than to exercise, to smoke cigarettes, to poison the environment in which we must live, and to live and work in highly stressful circumstances. "Affluence is not an unqualified boon and while it has certainly enabled us to avoid some diseases, for example those due to nutritional deficiency, it has opened the door to others arising, for instance, from unwise behaviour and over-indulgence in one form or another" (Department of Health and Social Security, 1976, p. 31).

The most familiar examples of preventive medicine are really aimed toward enhancing the effectiveness of curative medicine. They involve the early detection of health problems at a stage when they can be treated more successfully. This is the rationale behind various health screening measures, such as community blood pressure assessment programs. The periodic health examination—the yearly physical—popularized in the United States in the 1920s and 1930s by the American Medical Association, is intended to detect ailments before they have become obviously symptomatic. Cancer is treated much more successfully if the malignancy is detected and treated early.

Not much of our limited health resources are yet devoted to maintenance of good health. Of the 4,475 medical residency positions provided by the University of California system in 1980-81, not one was in preventive medicine. The Graduate Medical Education National Advisory Commission predicts an over-supply of physicians by 1990, but a shortage of preventive health physicians (Torrens, Breslow, & Fielding, 1982). Prevention efforts have mainly attempted to alter public attitudes about harmful health habits. An example is the nationwide publicity about the health hazards of smoking cigarettes, including the 1964 Surgeon General's Report and federal legislation prohibiting TV advertising and requiring warnings about health hazards on tobacco products. Apparently as a consequence of this campaign, in 1978 the percentage of adults who smoked cigarettes was at its lowest point in 30 years. However, 33% of all adults continued to smoke, in the face of convincing evidence that it can lead to a slow and very painful death, demonstrating that public awareness of risk factors is not sufficient to prevent the diseases of choice.

The U.S. federal government officially recognized health maintenance as a nationwide problem in the Surgeon General's report on health promotion and disease prevention, *Healthy People* (Public Health Service, 1979). This document established specific national goals in terms of reductions in death rates or days of disability due to particular health problems. For example, one goal was a 35% reduction in infant mortality by 1990. A second report in 1980, *Promoting Health*, spelled out some of the steps that will have to be taken in order to attain these improvements in health (Public Health Service, 1980). Perhaps in the next decade, promotion of good health will become a familiar everyday feature of health care.

Role of the Patient

With the new emphasis on treating the whole person and on prevention, individuals are being encouraged to play a more active role in the healing process and in maintaining good health. This reflects a change away from the traditional medical model in which patients were expected to assume a passive/dependent role and be cured by the physician.

Several forces have prolonged the passive role of the patient. One is the ignorance of many individuals about their health. For example, a majority of adults in a nationwide poll believed that diabetes is caused by eating too much sugar (Department of Health, Education, and Welfare, 1968). Many persons consider TV medical melodramas and TV advertising to be important and factual sources of information about health. Physicians are perceived as powerful authorities with access to a mysterious body of knowledge. The objects of this veneration, the physicians themselves, have not always discouraged these attitudes. Some physicians are guilty of an authoritarian communication style in which treatment is administered without explanation—it is no misuse of terms when we commonly refer to these communications as "doctor's orders!" Information may be withheld to suspend the patient in optimum ignorance (Rushmer, 1975), a condition in which the patient is most easily controlled. Decisions about whether or not to provide medical information to the patient are sometimes viewed by the physician as problems of "patient management." The net effect can be to make an already stressful experience even more so.

A variety of interventions that actively involve the patient in the health recovery process enhance healing following illness and surgery. Even something as simple as providing accurate information about what is going on is beneficial. For example, in one study (Johnson, Morrissey, & Levanthal, 1973) patients were given different preparatory instructions before an endoscopy examination, which required throat swabbing to accomplish local anesthesia, insertion of an intravenous device, and then sliding a tube down the throat into the stomach. One variable measured was the amount of Valium, a muscle relaxant and antianxiety agent, needed for adequate sedation. The patients who had been told what to expect in terms of the procedures or what they would be feeling required less Valium during the procedure than did the patients given no such information. Similarly, children who were about to have a cast removed with an electric saw experienced less distress (facial grimaces, crying, screaming, etc.) as rated by observers, when they were given advance information about what they would experience, as compared to children who were given no advance information (Johnson, Kirchoff, & Endress, 1975). The relationship between stress, helplessness, coping, and illness is considered in chapter 3. The patient has probably played a more active role in the healing process all along than had been imagined. The capacity of humans for self-healing is now practically universally accepted, based on: (a) understanding of the self-healing functions of the immune system (chapter 2), (b) recognition that "placebo effects" (chapter 4) represent self-healing, and (c) the obvious fact that we frequently get well without any treatment whatsoever.

Treatments of Choice

The traditional treatments, surgery and drugs, which speak only to the biological dimension of the person, are now supplemented by a wider range of treatments addressing the whole psychophysiological person. The most conspicuous additions to the treatment arsenal are the self-regulation techniques—biofeedback (chapter 5), progressive relaxation (chapter 5), hypnosis (chapter 6), autogenic training (chapter 6), and meditation (chapter 6).

Surgery became a routine intervention in the middle of the last century following the introduction of general anesthesia (in 1846) and antiseptic procedures (in 1865). What had been a grisly nightmare to be endured only as a last resort, could now be undertaken with some confidence. Routine surgery was an important force in determining the physiological and organ orientations of modern medicine. Recent technological advances include the introduction of laser surgery, making possible, for example, brain surgery with no bleeding; cryosurgery, the use of rapidly achieved very low temperatures to destroy tissue; and microsurgical techniques necessary for delicate operations such as cataract removal to improve vision.

The great benefits of modern surgery are accompanied by some problems. There is some mortality associated with even such routine procedures as tonsillectomy, along with a low risk of death from general anesthesia itself. Certain operations have been overprescribed. Radical mastectomy—breast removal in cases of localized cancer—and the widespread use of lobotomies in mental patients from the 1930s into the 1950s, come to mind. Surgery has been employed when an alternative treatment is available that does not share the risks or side-effects of surgery. A good example would be the use of "sympathectomy" in cases of vasospasm when self-regulation procedures are able to control these attacks in some cases (chapter 8). In our laboratory, a woman faced with a sympathectomy learned to curtail her vasospasms through biofeedback training and the surgical procedure proved to be unnecessary. Another overprescribed procedure is surgical shortening, or recession, of eye muscles to reposition the eye where the eye has deviated from proper alignment. The correction achieved surgically is often imprecise, and visual training methods are available that successfully remedy the condition for many individuals.

There were no consistently useful drugs employed in Western medicine until 1935 when the first sulfa compounds were developed that could cure bacterial infections. These were soon followed by antibiotics such as penicillin and streptomycin. Drugs became the treatment of choice in psychiatry in the middle 1950s when tranquilizers and antipsychotic agents such as chlorpromazine (Thorazine) were introduced for use with mental patients. As a direct result, from 1956 to 1969, while the population of the United States rose by 20%, the number of persons in mental institutions declined by 35% (Julien, 1981). Pharmacological treatments have alleviated great suffering, but, as with surgery, there are areas for concern.

Real drugs do not work like the cartoon drugs shown in TV commericals that speed directly to where they are needed to produce a discrete therapeutic result with no side effects. In reality, most drugs used therapeutically are distributed throughout the body and have many consequences that have nothing to do with the intended treatment effect. In psychiatry it is not unusual to prescribe four or five kinds of medication at once, in an attempt to simultaneously juggle various side effects.

Advertising agencies market the products of pharmaceutical companies to their customers (physicians) with the same positive attitude formation techniques used to sell automobiles and deodorants to the general public.

An advertisement in a 1983 issue of a major psychiatry journal shows an old violin with the caption, "Some things are hard to improve upon. Like a Stradivarius . . . and (the antipsychotic drug being sold)." Below, in small print, is a list of more than 50 adverse reactions to this drug including hypotension or low blood pressure ("sometimes fatal"), cardiac arrest, jaundice, nausea, constipation, headache, inhibition of ejaculation, eczema, skin pigmentation, blurred vision, and insomnia. Also listed is "persistent" *tardive dyskinesia*, a typically irreversible side effect of antipsychotic drugs seen in 15% to 20% of all patients in mental institutions. Symptoms include involuntary lip smacking, jaw movements, sucking, chewing, thrusting of the tongue, and drooling (Berger & Rexroth, 1980). Some Stradivarius.

Drug side effects are not always this devastating, and must be weighed against the beneficial effects of the drug, as with the extremely noxious side effects of cancer chemotherapy agents. Nonetheless, side effects are sometimes sufficiently severe so as to reduce compliance in taking the medication, a serious problem in the pharmacological treatment of essential hypertension. Patients who do comply are sometimes made miserable by unwanted side effects. In such cases alternative treatments should be welcomed.

Drug therapy can have unfortunate psychological side effects when they imply that the health condition under treatment must be: (a) of biological origin, and (b) beyond the patient's control. This is one of the controversial aspects of the widespread stimulant treatment of hyperactive children (chapter 9). Even if the child manages to avoid these pitfalls, others may not. A practitioner who worked with hyperactive children commented: "One 12-year old, after four years of drug therapy, asked me if his teacher and parents *had* to know that medication was being stopped. He was fairly certain of his behavior, but was afraid of others'" (Restrom, 1976, p. 108).

Psychological side effects are important considerations in administering drugs for the psychological manifestations of stress. Each year in the United States about 45 million prescriptions are filled for diazepam (Valium) and nearly as many for chlordiazepoxide (Librium). These antianxiety agents and muscle relaxants are the most frequent drug-related cause of visits to hospital emergency rooms (Julien, 1981). In many cases, pharmacological treatment does not help the patient cope with the sources of stress and may even mask serious interpersonal problems.

Several philosophical considerations support the search for alternative treatment methods. Specifically, the feeling of personal responsibility, and the ability to act autonomously may be intrinsically desirable—ends in themselves. Plainly, some kinds of health care are more compatible with these goals than others. Drugs are highly incompatible, while the self-regulation methods, which extend personal control, are especially congruent with these values.

Goals of Treatment

In addition to curing illness, health care practitioners and consumers have begun to explore the upper reaches of the illness-wellness continuum. Everyone has experienced positive states that are far beyond the absence of illness. It may be possible to cultivate wellness as an enduring condition, as well as "peak experiences" and "peak performance" as momentary states. Thus, besides the traditional goals of curing and preventing illness, treatments are being developed whose goal is wellness, or positive health. The physiological, psychological, and behavioral aspects of wellness are considered in depth in chapter 10.

MIND AND BODY

This chapter begins with the observation that a person is a psychophysiological being. The concept of a person as a psychological entity and a biological organism—mind and body—needs to be discussed.

If we limit our study to only the biological or psychological person, we fail to perceive what a person is. The possible consequences of a narrow view is illustrated in an old Sufi teaching story about the blind persons and the elephant that has been told in many versions: There was a city in which all of the inhabitants were blind. One day visitors set up camp outside the gates of the city. They are said to have a fearsome beast, called an elephant, in a large tent. Four of the blind townsfolk are delegated to investigate this creature, and report back. They do so. The first person reports that an elephant is a straight, hollow thing like a stovepipe; the second argues that, instead, an elephant is like a large thick rug. The third blind person says that an elephant is really like a strong rope, while the final investigator is certain that an elephant is like a set of mighty pillars. In touching only the trunk, ear, tail, or legs of the elephant, each of the blind persons has been misled.

A device first used by the existential psychologist Viktor Frankl (1969) and more recently by Donald Bakal (1979) also illustrates the importance of maintaining a broad perspective in trying to grasp the nature of a human being (see Fig. 1.1). Imagine spotlights, one up above and one off to the right, each casting a shadow of a cylinder onto a translucent screen. Let the cylinder represent a human being, and the two shadows the biological and psychological aspect of a human being. Picture a stationary

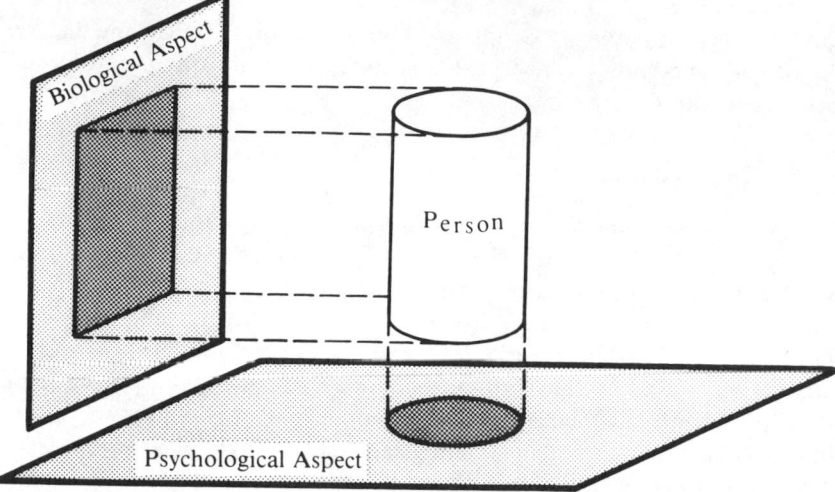

FIG. 1.1 If a person were a cylinder. Biological and psychological perspectives. From "Reductionism and Nihilism" (p. 404) by V. E. Frankl, 1969, in A. Koestler and J. R. Smythies (Eds.), *Beyond Reductionism*, London: Hutchinson. Copyright 1969 by The Hutchinson Publishing Group. Adapted by permission.

observer situated behind each screen, each one trying to understand the cylinder from its shadow. However, the cylinder is neither a circle nor a rectangle, nor is it even a circle plus a rectangle. Similarly, a human being is neither a body, nor a mind, nor a body plus a mind—not a machine with a ghost in it. Our essence becomes apparent in the interaction of mind and body, thus the subject matter of psychophysiology.

The Mind-Body Problem

The mind includes qualities of *consciousness* and the sense of *self*. It is composed of an ongoing stream of mental events such as visual perceptions, thoughts, and emotions. When we wake up in the morning, our familiar sense of personal identity is there to greet us. The *concept* of mind, at least, is not dependent on a physical body. Most of us have even experienced ourselves as a "disembodied spirit" in dreams.

However, as we have seen, a person is not a disembodied spirit. Human beings do not just experience; we sweat, bleed, and move about, existing as elements of the physical universe. We are biological organisms composed of living cells organized into tissues and organs comprising a physical body whose height and weight can be measured.

The mind-body problem is how to fit these two aspects of the person together. How can these two utterly different attributes, mind and body, be reconciled? To take examples from health psychophysiology, how can people warm their hands just by thinking about it? How can an asthmatic choke and wheeze at the sight of a plastic flower? Mind-body theories offer alternative frameworks within which to interpret these more specific questions. This section poses some mind-body questions, and reviews explanations that have been put forward.

The mind is not part of the physical universe. If it were made of physical "stuff" there would be no special difficulty in talking about causal relationships between mind and body. But the mind is not made of anything—an idea has no physical substance. The mind does not take up space, and hence is not located anywhere. We should be careful not to confuse the *mind* and *brain*, as happens so frequently when these terms are used informally. One can weigh the brain or look at its cells under a microscope, but one cannot take a thought and weigh it or study its details under magnification. A scientist can observe the brain in action by recording its electrical activity. But this would reflect activity of the physical body; it would not display a person's thoughts.

The mind-body problem is not traditionally introduced in psychophysiology textbooks. This is partly because it is a difficult topic, but also because, historically, it has been a favorite topic of philosophers, not scientists. This is changing. As one philosopher has observed (Bunge, 1980, p. 30), in recent years "While psychologists bored the tunnel from one end, neuroscientists tried to reach the mind from the other." In addition, philosophers are paying more attention to scientific evidence that might reflect on their mind-body theories, whereas scientists are becoming more sophisticated about their mind-body assumptions. This convergence of science and philosophy is yet another manifestation of the emerging psychophysiological perspective, and has been prompted by the phenomena described in this text, which suggest that something of great interest is lurking in this mysterious realm. In becoming acquainted with the mind-body problem, the student will become more familiar with the limits of present knowledge, and better able to evaluate statements with mind-body implications. We briefly survey the major contemporary mind-body theories, shown schematically in Table 1.2.

Mind-Body Theories

Two theories attempt to resolve the mind-body problem by denying, in one case, the existence of the mind, and in the other, the body, in effect creating a non-problem. Surprisingly, neither of these approaches is easily refuted.

Idealism

According to this theory only the mind exists. The physical world is not out there. Because all of our knowledge of the physical universe is in the form of perceptions, which are mental events, it is conceivable that the

TABLE 1.2
Types of Mind-Body Theories

Theory	Symbol	
Idealism		(Only the Mind Exists)
Materialism		(Only the Brain Exists)
Animism		(Mind Controls Brain)
Epiphenomenalism		(Brain Controls Mind)
Interactionism		(Mind and Brain Interact)
Emergent Dual Aspect		(Mind is Part of Brain)

Note. Adapted from *The Mind-body Problem: A Psychobiological Approach* (p. 9) by M. Bunge, 1980, NY: Pergamon Press. Copyright 1980 by Pergamon Press. Adapted by permission.

physical objects that we assume are the basis of our perceptions, do not exist—they might be "all in our minds." This stance has appealed to many writers attempting to understand the altered states of consciousness induced by psychedelic drugs. The stream of consciousness is changed by these drugs so profoundly that it becomes difficult to believe in an external fixed reality.

Idealism is central to Christian Science, a religion and system of health care based on the writing of Mary Baker Eddy who, nearly 100 years ago, claimed to have become privileged to the principles that Jesus is said to have used to heal the sick and raise the dead, that mind is God, and is both perfect and infinite. Healing is accomplished by bringing the unreal material body into harmony with the mind through prayer. The Church of Christ, Scientist, trains and accredits healers who then accept fee-paying patients. Although external physical reality cannot be proven to exist, it is often extremely useful to operate as if it did. This can be seen in the unfortunate cases involving children of Christian Scientist parents who have died when traditional medical treatments have been withheld.

Materialism

This theory maintains that only the body exists. The only reality is the physical world of atoms and molecules; the mind is an illusion. This idea reached its zenith in the 17th and 18th centuries, shortly after science had acquired the necessary principles to explain the movement of objects, and the world had become mechanized with the first physical gadgets—pulleys, pumps, clocks, and levers that really worked.

To watch machines whir and move was entertainment; some gardens in Europe were equipped with moving statues for the amusement of guests. Human movement was explained as the result of fluids pumped about in the body under pressure. William Harvey had offered a clever explanation of the circulation of blood based on a pump and a system of tubing. Perhaps a person could be understood as a machine, as *only* a machine. Materialism is strengthened by the circumstance that we individually have access to our own mind, only. The troublesome introspective evidence that one really does seem to have a mind is usually explained as a misperception. The materialist position is often attributed to the behaviorists John Watson, and later, B. F. Skinner, who thoroughly disapproved of studying or theorizing about the mind. However, these psychologists never seriously claimed that mental phenomena do not exist, merely that they were unimportant or even misleading in efforts to predict and control behavior. Neither idealism nor materialism is a useful framework for psychophysiology. Three *dualist* theories are considered next. All of the dualist mind-body theories propose that both mind and body exist, and as separate entities. The theories differ as to how the two elements are related.

Animism

According to animism the mind controls the body without being affected by the body in any way. Thus, the electrical activity that can be recorded from the brain is *caused by* mental activity, but nothing in the brain can cause a mental event. Because the mind does not depend on the body, this position allows for a soul that can survive after the death of the biological person, including the "transmigration" of the soul in which it takes up residence in another organism, and the existence of ghosts and other disembodied spirits. This theory is not popular among psychophysiolgists due to the overwhelming evidence that events in the brain have experiential consequences.

Epiphenomenalism

This theory is just the opposite of animism. Bodily events cause mental events, yet the mind has absolutely no influence over the body. The mind is an *epiphenomenon*. This unfamiliar term refers to an event that is considered a secondary phenomenon that accompanies another event and is thought of as caused by it. One of the most bizarre examples of an epiphenomenon can be found near the end of a Kurt Vonnegut novel (Vonnegut, 1971), when all of human history is reduced to this status. The reader discovers that distant alien beings initiated life on Earth and have orchestrated everything since, for the sole purpose of delivering a spare part to one of their explorers whose spaceship had broken down elsewhere in our solar system. The mind is an epiphenomenon because mental activity is secreted by the brain, rather like a fire giving off smoke or an automobile engine giving off noise. However, the smoke cannot cook food and the noise does not move the vehicle, nor does the mind control the brain. We might feel mentally in control, but this is because the brain, which is actually in charge, occasionally gives off a puff of mental activity that is perceived as "will." The French astronomer LaPlace is supposed to have replied to Napoleon's question concerning the role of God in his explanatory system: "Sire, I have no need of that hypothesis." Similarly, science may have no need for mental activity as a causal agent.

Interactionism

The interactionist view is that mind-body causality goes in both directions. Certain bodily activities are controlled by the mind, whereas some mental events have physical causes. This was the attempt of the 17th century French mathematician and philosopher René Descartes to provide a reasonable explanation of the nature of man without offending existing theological doctrines concerning the soul. The mind houses the soul and is responsible for all voluntary actions; the rest of human behavior is to be understood in purely physical terms. Animals, lacking minds, can be explained using strictly physical principles. Of the six mind-body theories, this theory is most consistent with everyday experience. It maintains that the mind really is in charge when one chooses to do something, yet pangs of hunger do originate in the stomach, just where they seem to. This theory, however, is not widely accepted today by philosophers, and especially by scientists, for several reasons. One difficulty is in fathoming how causation might be exercised between the mind and body, one being immaterial the other being physical. Descartes himself argued that the mind was somehow able to move a pea-sized structure on the bottom of the brain (the pineal gland) to and fro; this directed the flow of animal spirits into different channels to produce various movements. A second difficulty is that interactionism requires two sets of explanatory principles, mental and physical, although it must be admitted that if this is the true nature of the human being, then science will just have to put up with this complication.

Dual-Aspect Theory

This mind-body theory exists in many variations, and will be termed the *emergent dual-aspect* theory here. The mind is not a separate entity caused by the brain, but is one property of the brain. The mind might be regarded as "the way the brain perceives itself." A major scientific advantage of this approach to the mind-body problem is that it requires only one set of explanatory concepts. But why does the brain possess mind? That is, why is it conscious, whereas a typewriter or a mushroom is not? One argument is that mind is a property of sufficiently complex systems, and the human brain is such a system. Notice that mind does not reside in any of the individual elements comprising the brain, but that it is a property that emerges when they are taken together. Also, note that if the elements of the system need not be alive, then a sufficiently complex machine could possess a mind.

This introduction raised more questions than it answered because it dealt with the limits of knowledge. Hopefully the student has become sensitized to lurking mind-body assumptions and aware of some of their implications, but has not become intimidated by the subject matter of this text. In fact, researchers and practitioners in psychophysiology spend most of their time working on much more concrete problems, and the content of this text reflects this. There are only occasional references to mind-body problems in later chapters. For ease of communication, this text adopts the comfortable and familiar interactionist assumption and terminology throughout, speaking of mind and brain as separate entities.

2 Basic Anatomy, Physiology, and Methodology

This chapter is a survey of human anatomy and physiology, and the methods used to study the workings of the human organism for students with little background in biology and for those who wish to review. Many of the concepts and technical terms introduced here are used later in the text.

THE NERVOUS SYSTEM

The *nervous system* is a complex communication system that receives information from its environment (that includes the body enclosing it), makes decisions, and initiates responses in the form of muscular contractions and glandular secretions. Information about past experience is selectively called up from storage to help direct these activities. The mental world depends on the nervous system, but, as discussed in chapter 1, the fundamental nature of this relationship is still being debated.

Neurons

The principle functional unit of the nervous system is the nerve cell or *neuron*. Each of these billions of individual cells is specialized to transmit information encoded electrically in the form of *nerve impulses*. The major structures of a neuron are the *dendrites*, the *cell body*, and the *axon*, as shown in Fig. 2.1. The complexly branching dendrites are the input side of the neuron through which it is influenced by other neurons. The cell body contains the nucleus of the cell, which takes care of metabolic requirements. Nerve impulses typically originate in the cell body, and are

18

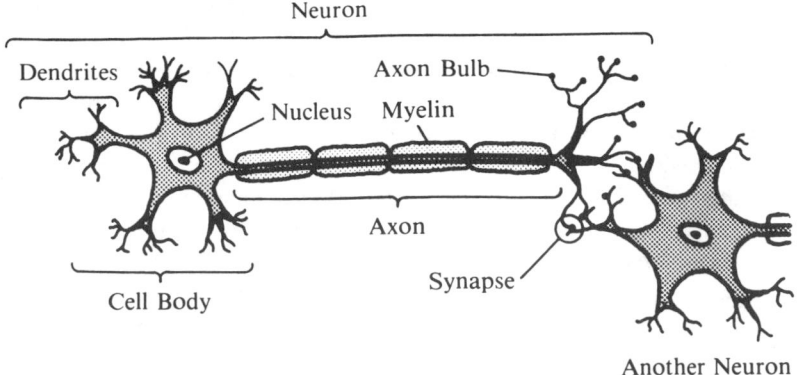

FIG. 2.1 The major features of a neuron.

conducted down, usually, a single axon, the output side of the neuron. The axon usually branches at the end where the neuron establishes functional contact with other neurons.

Neurons in various parts of the nervous system are organized somewhat differently depending on their function. The task of neurons in sensory and motor pathways is to transmit nerve impulses quickly from one part of the body to another, for example, from sensory receptors in the skin to the brain, or from the spinal cord to the skeletal muscles. They tend to have very long axons, some of them several feet in length, which are covered with *myelin*, a white fatty substance that insulates axons from one another, and lowers neural conduction time. For this reason *nerves*, which are simply bundles of axons, are white in appearance, as are the neural tracts running up and down the spinal cord. This myelinated, or "white matter," is also found inside the brain where neural pathways conduct information from one part of the brain to another. There are other areas of the nervous system, especially the surface of the brain, that are composed of closely packed cell bodies with extremely short unmyelinated axons, whose dendrites are so elaborately developed as to resemble dense bushes. These areas of "gray matter" are centers specialized for complex intercommunication among large arrays of neurons.

The membrane covering the neuron acts like a filter with respect to electrically charged molecules known as *ions*. By keeping certain ions inside and others outside, the membrane maintains the outside positively charged, with respect to the inside. The nerve impulse, more technically the *action potential*, is created when the filtering action of a localized section of the membrane temporarily reverses, or "depolarizes," allowing positively charged sodium ions to rush in through the membrane. This electrical charge is, itself, quickly reversed, but it progresses down the axon. A series of recording electrodes situated along the axon would indicate a wave of negativity lasting a few thousandths of a second moving down the axon at speeds up to several hundred meters per second.

Several rules hold for action potentials. The greater the diameter of an axon, the faster it conducts action potentials. Also, action potentials follow the *all-or-none* principle. Within a given neuron, action potentials are always the same size, and are conducted at the same speed. Any stimulus that is sufficent to cause the neuron to "fire," that is, to produce an action potential, will result in a full-sized action potential. Therefore, a neuron must encode its messages, not in different sized nerve impulses, nor in variations in conduction speeds, but in different rates of firing.

Synaptic Transmission

In the human nervous system, action potentials do not ordinarily stimulate other neurons. A tiny gap, the *synapse*, separates output and input processes between neurons. Neural transmission across the synapse is usually chemical. The fine branches of an axon may synapse with the cell body of other neurons, with dendrites, or even with other axons. Because neurons typically have a great many dendrites and axon branches, it can be seen that the interconnections among neurons are complex indeed. An individual synapse is diagrammed in Fig. 2.2.

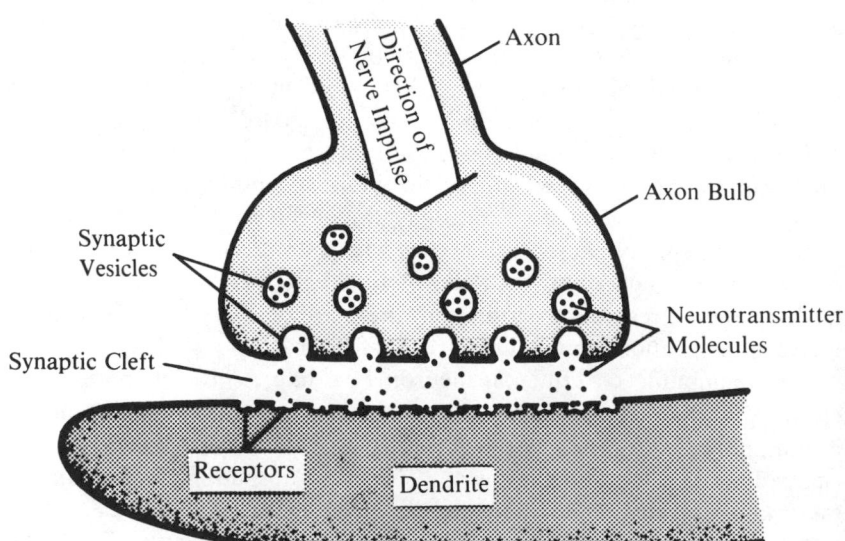

FIG. 2.2   A synapse.

When an action potential reaches the *axon bulb* it causes a small amount of a *neurotransmitter* substance to be released from *synaptic vesicles*, where this chemical is stored. The neurotransmitter diffuses across the *synaptic cleft* to the postsynaptic neuron where it is detected by receptors embedded in the postsynaptic membrane. Excess neurotransmitter molecules in the synaptic cleft are quickly taken back up into the synaptic vesicles for re-use, or broken down and destroyed, clearing the synapse to respond to the next action potential. The entire process, from arrival of the action potential to stimulation of the detector in the postsynaptic neuron, takes only a few thousandths of a second. Among invertebrates and lower vertebrates, "electrical synapses" are common. These are very narrow synapses across which the electrical current flows directly from one neuron to the next. This type of interneuronal connection is rare in the mammalian brain, and its function is not understood (Shepherd, 1983).

Returning to common chemical synaptic transmission, the chemical message across the synapse may have an excitatory or inhibitory effect on the postsynaptic neuron, depending on the type of receptor. When some receptors are stimulated they generate an *excitatory postsynaptic potential* which is a change toward the firing threshold of the neuron; other receptors create an *inhibitory postsynaptic potential* that makes it more difficult for the neuron to fire. In contrast to the all-or-nothing nature of action potentials, postsynaptic potentials are "graded" in magnitude and summate both spatially and temporally. Thus, the firing rate of a neuron at any given instant is directed by an ongoing argument between excitatory and inhibitory postsynaptic potentials.

There is a growing list of neurotransmitter substances. *Acetylcholine* (ACh) is the chemical messenger at the interface between skeletal muscle fibers and motor neurons. ACh is also the neurotransmitter in the parasympathetic division of the autonomic nervous system (to follow). *Norepinephrine* is used in the synapses of major parts of the sympathetic division of the autonomic nervous system and in the brain where it is used in circuits that radiate to every part of the cerebral cortex. *Serotonin* and *dopamine* are also major brain neurotransmitters, as are *glutamic acid* and gamma-amino-butyric acid *(GABA)*. *Substance P* is an important neurotransmitter in spinal pain pathways. Hundreds of neurotransmitters may eventually be discovered.

Neuromodulators, a class of natural biochemicals, do not function as neurotransmitters, yet have important "modulating" effects on neurochemistry. Some neuromodulators influence chemical events at the synapse whereas others are able to stimulate special neural receptors that are not located at synapses. Important neuromodulators include the *endorphins* (see chapter 4), which diminish the perception of pain, and the hormones testosterone and estrogen.

Many drugs influence the nervous system by facilitating or interfering with synaptic transmission. A brief discussion of how some drugs affect ACh gives an idea of the complex neurochemistry at the synapse. Botulism toxin, found in spoiled food, blocks the release of ACh from the presynaptic neuron. Black widow spider venom has the opposite effect, causing continuous release of ACh into the synaptic cleft regardless of the firing rate of the presynaptic neuron. Curare is a powerful paralytic substance first used by South American Indians on their blow darts. Curare acts as a "false transmitter," resembling the ACh key enough to fit into the ACh receptor lock, yet is sufficiently different so that it is not deactivated by acetylcholinesterase (AChE), the enzyme that normally destroys ACh to clear the synapse. The net effect is that curare interferes with ACh synapses. Nicotine resembles ACh so closely that it mimics the synaptic effects of ACh. Finally, some nerve gases and many insecticides, such as Malathion, operate by interfering with AChE so that the postsynaptic potentials at ACh synapses persist for great lengths of time.

There has been considerable interest in the neurochemical analysis of psychological disorders. Using schizophrenia as an example, fairly convincing cases can be made for disturbances in norepinephrine, serotonin, and the endorphins, however, the leading single candidate is dopamine, specifically, excessive dopamine activity. Amphetamines, cocaine, and methylphenidate (Ritalin), in sufficiently large doses, can produce symptoms resembling those of schizophrenia. All of these drugs intensify dopamine action, although in different ways. Dopamine, when injected into schizophrenic patients, immediately exacerbates their symptoms (Davis, 1974). The drug most often used to treat schizophrenia is chlorpromazine (Thorazine), which blocks dopamine receptors.

Matthysse (1974) has offered a provocative theory about dopamine and schizophrenia. He observes that with too little dopamine activity, as in Parkinson's disease, voluntary movements become very difficult to initiate. Too much dopamine activity can result in excessive and repetitive movements, as seen in the "choreiform movements" of some psychotic patients. This suggests that there is a dopamine-based circuit that acts like a gate to carry out orderly selection among a large number of "subthreshold" motor commands from the cerebral cortex, allowing only a useful subset of them to become expressed as movement. Matthysse's idea is that dopamine circuitry may function the same way with respect to thoughts and emotions. Perhaps there is normally a jumble of irrelevant subthreshold cognitive material; however, only a small portion of it is "disinhibited" by the dopamine gate to actually reach consciousness. In the schizophrenic, excessive dopamine action allows the entire confusing welter of extraneous and half-formed thoughts to emerge into consciousness.

Organization of the Nervous System

For discussion purposes the human nervous system may be divided into the *central nervous system* (CNS) and the *peripheral nervous system*. The CNS includes the brain and the spinal cord. The only contact the CNS has with the world around it is through the peripheral nervous system, which includes all neural tissue outside the bony protection of the skull and spine. *Afferent*, or *sensory* neural pathways conduct information toward the CNS. The CNS influences the body it lives in via two major *efferent* pathways that conduct neural messages away from the CNS. The *somatic* system conducts CNS impulses to the glands and the skeletal muscles, with which we execute voluntary movements. The *autonomic nervous system* (ANS) provides neural control of visceral functions such as circulation and digestion. The ANS can be divided into the *sympathetic nervous system* (SNS) and the *parasympathetic nervous system* (PNS), which have different influences on the organs they innervate. A few aspects of nervous system structure and function that are essential to health psychophysiology are discussed next.

The Central Nervous System

The major functions of the spinal cord are to collect together afferent fibers from sensory receptors and route them to the brain, and to disperse efferent fibers originating in the brain to the glands and muscles. The spinal cord has some degree of independence from the brain and contains a number of simple *spinal reflex* neural circuits; the "knee jerk" reflex to a tap on the knee is an example. Incoming information about pain may be gated to some extent at the spinal level.

The brain is organized in a layered arrangement (see Fig. 2.3). The inner core is the most primitive and phylogenetically oldest, in the sense that the same structures performing the same functions are seen in many lower species. This is the *brainstem* that includes: (a) the *reticular activating system*, a diffuse network of neurons projecting to the cerebral cortex that regulates alertness by activating widespread areas of the brain; (b) the *pons* which participates in motor coordination and initiates REM sleep; and (c) the *medulla oblongata* which helps integrate ANS-controlled functions such as circulation, breathing, and digestion. The *cerebellum* is the major motor coordination center and is responsible for postural adjustments, maintaining muscle tone, and organizing voluntary movements.

Enveloping the inner "life support system" is a layer of neural structures engaged in somewhat less basic functions including perceptual organization, emotions, motivation, and memory. The *hypothalamus* is only about the size of a pea, but it plays an important executive role in

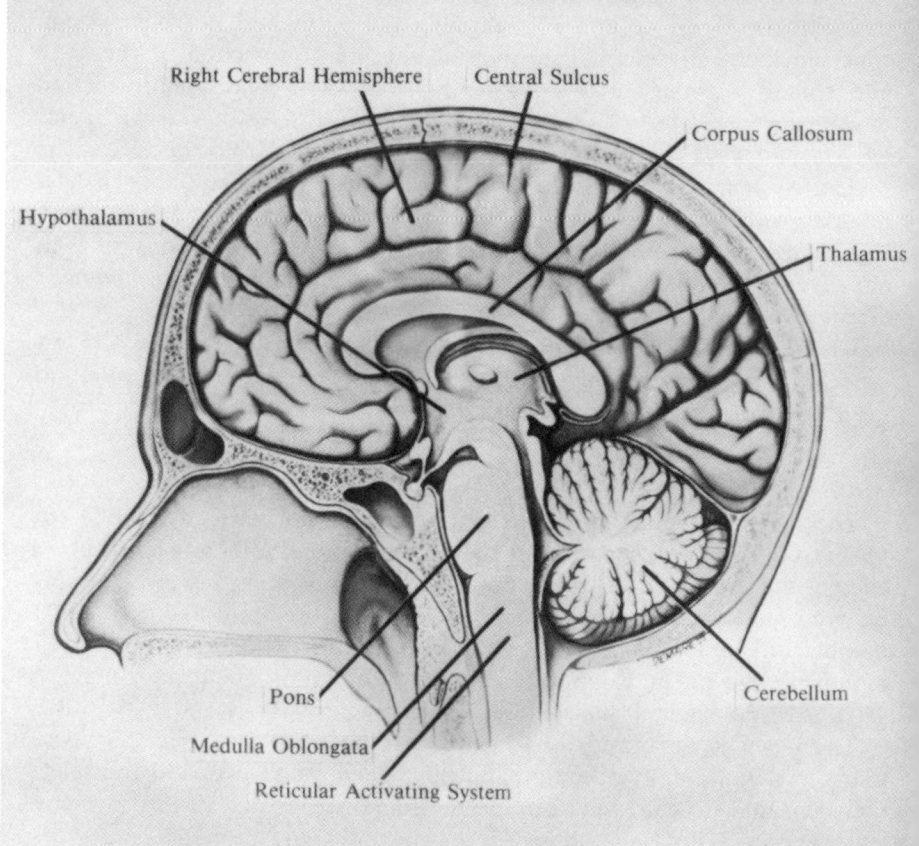

FIG. 2.3 Some important inner structures of the brain. A section through the middle of the brain is shown. From *The Human Nervous System* (2nd ed., p. 4) by C. R. Noback and R. J. Demarest, 1975, New York: McGraw-Hill. Copyright 1975 by McGraw-Hill. Adapted by permission.

such complex actions as eating, drinking, and sexual behavior. The hypothalamus oversees the metabolic needs of the body, helping to regulate endocrine and ANS functions. There is a *thalamus* in each side of the brain, just above the hypothalamus. The thalamus is primarily a relay station for sensory pathways on the way to the cerebral cortex, and participates in the direction of attention to sensory input. Emotions, and some aspects of memory, are served by a complex arrangement known as the *limbic system* that wraps around the brainstem and extends into the frontal and temporal lobes of the cerebral hemispheres. The limbic system includes the *hippocampus, amygdala, septum,* and pathways interconnecting them to many other brain regions.

The outermost brain layer is the *cerebrum,* whose two *cerebral hemispheres* are covered by a highly convoluted or folded surface known as the *cerebral cortex* (see Fig. 2.4). The cerebrum is necessary for the purposive thinking, planning, and logical reasoning that appears to distinguish humans from other species.

The surface of each hemisphere is divided into several lobes as shown in Fig. 2.4. In addition to the *frontal, temporal, parietal,* and *occipital*

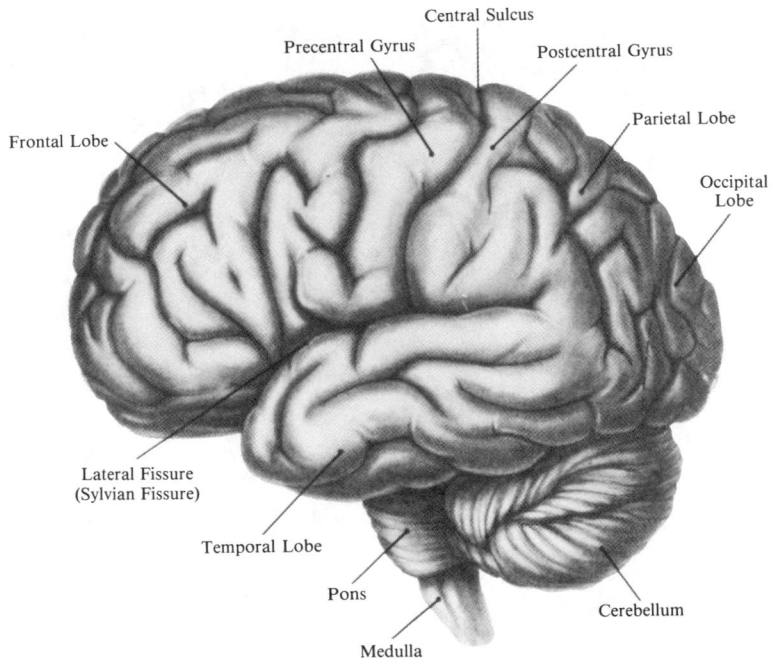

FIG. 2.4   The lobes of the cerebral hemispheres. From *Physiology of Behavior* (2nd ed., p. 112) by N. R. Carlson, 1980, Boston: Allyn and Bacon. Copyright 1980 by Allyn and Bacon. Adapted by permission.

lobes, the lower inner surface between the hemispheres is sometimes referred to as the *limbic* lobe.

Like other areas of the brain, the cerebral cortex is locally specialized to carry out specific functions. Some of these functions are shown in Fig. 2.5. The senses of audition, vision, and touch have sensory "projection areas" located in the temporal, occipital, and parietal lobes, respectively. The *visual cortex* is organized like a map of the visual field, although disproportionately greater cortical space is devoted to the small central area of the visual field where vision is most detailed. The *somatosensory* cortex in each hemisphere, subsuming the sense of touch, is laid out like a map of the opposite side of the body. Language is supported by two cortical areas. *Broca's area*, located in the frontal cortex, is necessary for language production, including speech; *Wernicke's area* is situated between the auditory and visual areas, and is essential in the decoding or understanding of language. These centers are located in the left hemisphere for the great majority of individuals, including left-handers.

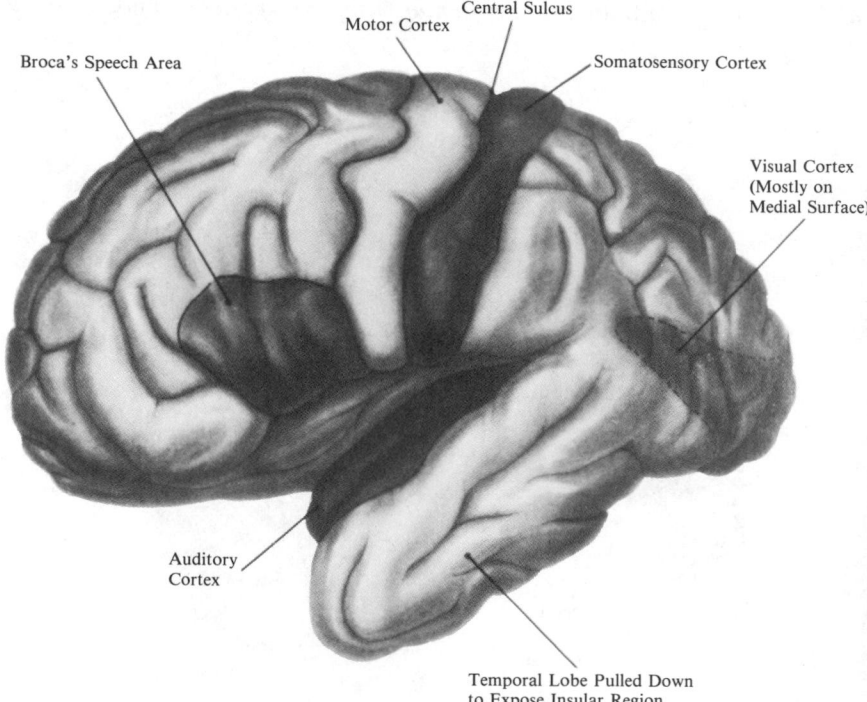

FIG. 2.5 Some specialized functions of the cerebal cortex. The left hemisphere is shown. From *Physiology of Behavior* (2nd ed., p. 114) by N. R. Carlson, 1980, Boston: Allyn and Bacon. Copyright 1980 by Allyn and Bacon. Adapted by permission.

Voluntary motor commands originate in the *motor cortex* of the frontal lobes. Some cortical activities are arranged more diffusely. Areas subsuming perceptual organization and memory extend across wide regions of the parietal and temporal lobes, whereas widespread areas of the frontal lobes appear to be devoted to purposive cognition.

The Autonomic Nervous System

Common expressions refer to autonomic nervous system (ANS) involvement in emotion: we "blush with embarassment," get "cold feet," and turn "pale with fear." A spectacular sunset, our favorite song, or the sight of a special person can cause "goose bumps," more scientifically, "piloerection." Just as the ANS influences emotional experience, including emotional disorders, psychological factors contribute to disorders of organs regulated by the ANS, including stress-related disorders such as heart disease. New treatment methods incorporate trained voluntary control of ANS functions. It is important that the student of health psychophysiology be familiar with the basic structure and function of the ANS.

The ANS plays a major role in regulating bodily processes that are ordinarily beyond control of the will. These include the beating of the heart, the motility and chemical secretions of the digestive tract, the size of the pupils of the eye, the secretion of tears, saliva, and nasal mucus, the contraction and dilation of blood vessels, and a number of other functions that are listed more completely in Table 2.1. The ANS typically operates beyond awareness and without conscious direction; it is, in this sense, "autonomous."

Most organs are controlled by only one of the two ANS divisions; when the SNS and PNS both innervate an organ, they have opposing effects (see Table 2.1 and Fig. 2.6). For example, the SNS causes the heart to beat faster and more forcefully, and the bronchia of the lungs to dilate, enabling more rapid absorption of oxygen. In contrast, neural activity in PNS nerves causes heart deceleration, and constriction of bronchia. The smooth muscles and glands that are innervated by both divisions, such as the heart, lungs, bladder, and pupils of the eye, are somewhat like a car being driven with both the gas and brake pedals depressed at once. At any moment the speed of the car is determined by the balance of gas and braking; either depressing the gas pedal or lifting the brake will make the car speed up. In the same way, when the heart beats faster, this may be due to increased SNS action, decreased PNS action, or both.

The SNS mobilizes the physiological resources of the organism for emergencies, whereas the PNS has to do with the routine day to day workings of the body, returning bodily functions to resting levels following SNS activation. The role of the ANS in stress and psychophysiological relaxation is considered more fully in chapter 3.

TABLE 2.1
Parasympathetic and Sympathetic Effects on Various Organs

Organ	PNS Effect	SNS Effect
Eye		
Iris	Decrease pupil size	Increase pupil size
Ciliary muscle	Contraction for near vision	Relaxation for distant vision
Lacrimal gland	Secretion	Excessive secretion
Salivary glands	Secretion of copious watery saliva	Scanty secretion—rich saliva
Lungs	Contraction of bronchioles and blood vessels	Dilation of bronchioles and blood vessels
Heart		
Stroke volume	Decreased	Increased
Heart rate	Decreased	Increased
Blood vessels		
Skin	Dilation	Constriction
Skeletal muscle	Constriction	Dilation
Viscera (except heart and lungs)	Dilation	Constriction
Stomach and intestines		
Wall	Increased motility	Decreased motility
Sphincters	Inhibited	Stimulated
Glands	Increased secretion	Decreased secretion
Liver	Increased bile secretion	Decreased bile secretion
Pancreas	Increased secretion	Decreased secretion
Adrenal medulla	Little effect	Epinephrine secretion
Bladder	Stimulates wall, inhibits sphincter	Inhibits wall, stimulates sphincter
Sweat glands	Normal function	Stimulates secretion

Note. From *The Nervous Body* (pp. 30-31) by C. Van Toller, 1979, U.K.: Wiley. Adapted by permission.

Beyond their antagonistic relationship, the two divisions of the ANS differ in several other respects. The effect of neural activity in the SNS is more prolonged and anatomically diffuse as compared with the briefer and more localized action of the PNS. There are several good reasons for this.

First, there is an important anatomical difference between the two ANS branches. Notice in Fig. 2.6 that the SNS is a two-stage system. SNS *preganglionic* neurons exit the spinal cord and synapse in either of two *sympathetic ganglion* chains that flank the spinal cord; from there, *post-*

PARASYMPATHETIC
DIVISION

SYMPATHETIC
DIVISION

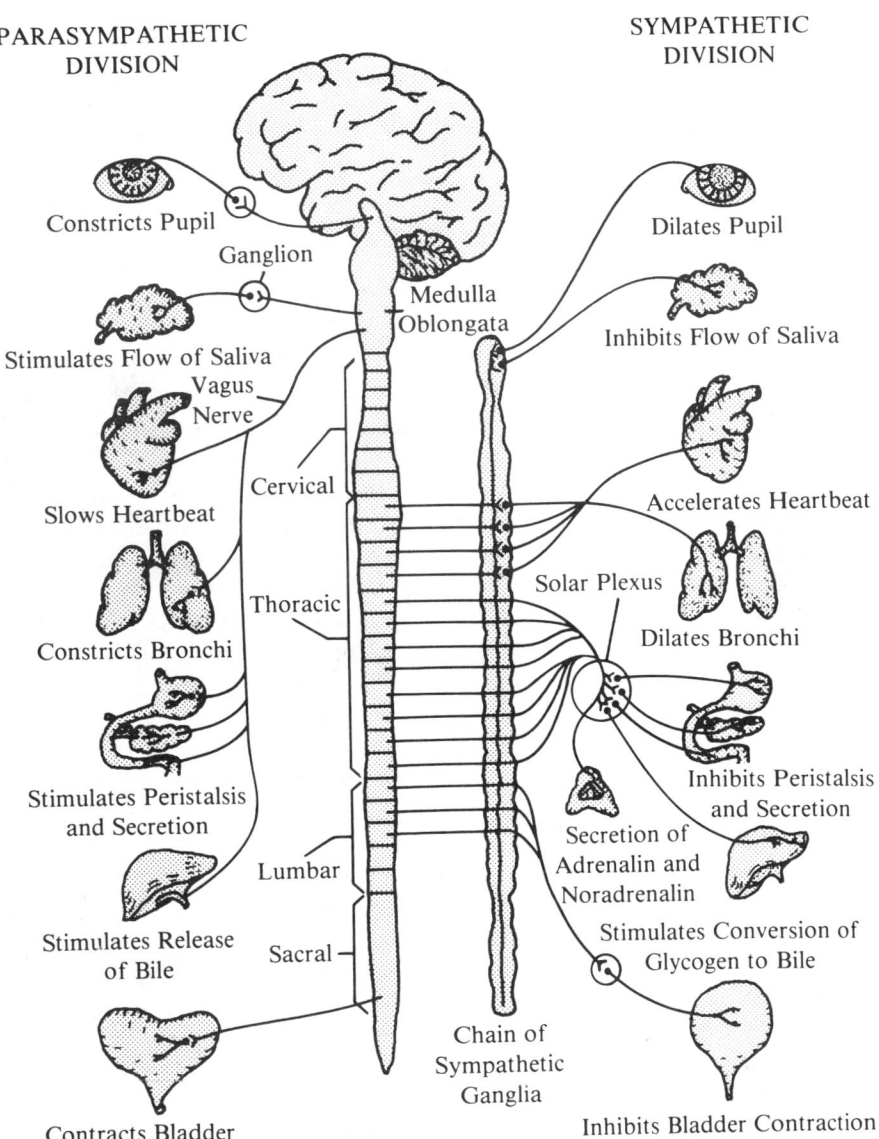

FIG. 2.6 Anatomy and function of the sympathetic and parasympathetic divisions of the autonomic nervous system. From *Introduction to Psychology* 58th Edition by Rita L. Atkinson, Richard C. Atkinson, and Ernest R. Hilgard. Copyright 1983 by Harcourt, Brace, Jovanovich. Reproduced by permission of the publisher.

ganglionic fibers proceed to their target organs. This arrangement permits coordinated SNS action via the interconnections within the sympathetic ganglia. However, PNS ganglia are located near their organs and are not interconnected.

Secondly, the neurotransmitter for the PNS is ACh, most of which is broken down within a fraction of a second after its release into the synaptic cleft (Guyton, 1982). The SNS pre-ganglionic fibers are also cholinergic, however the post-ganglionic SNS neurons use norepinephrine as the primary neurotransmitter. Norepinephrine is not broken down as quickly as ACh. The sweat glands are exceptions, innervated by the SNS, but with ACh post-ganglionic synapses as if they were controlled by the PNS.

Thirdly, as shown in Fig. 2.6, there is an SNS pathway to the adrenal medulla where nerve impulses cause release of epinephrine and norepinephrine into the blood stream to circulate throughout the body. Epinephrine is the chemical precursor of norepinephrine. These chemicals exert the same effects as direct neural stimulation for several minutes as they circulate (Guyton, 1982). The surge of epinephrine and norepinephrine that accompany SNS activation causes widespread potentiation of SNS effects. There is no parallel phenomenon for the PNS. The redundant neural and chemical mechanisms for SNS activation may have evolved as a safety factor.

The SNS influences its target organs via two types of adrenergic receptors, which Ahlquist (1948) designates α and β receptors. The α receptors are most sensitive to norepinephrine, and mediate primarily smooth muscle contraction such as vasoconstriction, which reduces the diameter of the blood vessels and is the major mechanism through which blood pressure is increased. The β receptors are much less sensitive to norepinephrine and produce mainly inhibitory responses such as vasodilation and bronchodilation, with an important exception—excitation of the heart muscle. Biochemical studies have shown that there are subtypes of both α and β receptors (Stiles & Lefkowitz, 1984). The concept of adrenergic receptor types based on the sensitivity of synapses to different chemicals has had many practical applications, including a family of "β-blocker" drugs that are widely used in the treatment of hypertension and heart disease.

Although the ANS goes about its business without conscious direction, it is elaborately interconnected with and guided by the brain. The hypothalamus contains a number of centers that provide executive control of ANS functions. The hypothalamus itself receives inputs from many limbic system structures that are involved in motivation and emotion. The general balance of SNS/PNS activity is established within the hypothalamus, a process that has been called *autonomic tuning* (Gellhorn, 1967). Descending neural commands are further coordinated by circuits in the brainstem, some of which have been traced in detail. There are neural mechanisms at this level that constitute feedback circuits to help regulate specific ANS functions. For example, the *baroreceptor reflex* involves stretch receptors on the walls of major arteries that transmit nerve impulses to the brain stem when high pressures are detected; the brain stem baroreceptor circuit then inhibits descending SNS messages to the heart and blood vessels.

Studying Nervous System Function

Some of the procedures used to study the nervous system are complex. However, all of them are undertaken with straightforward aims in mind. These are to: (a) determine the effects of natural or experimental damage or disturbances in the nervous system; (b) observe the effects of stimulation of the nervous system; or (c) obtain direct measurements of activity in selected parts of the nervous system.

Although the following discussion emphasizes the study of brain function, many of the following procedures can be used to investigate other parts of the nervous system. Electrical recordings of brain activity can be obtained without too much difficulty. This is not true for the ANS, which is anatomically diffuse and buried deep inside the body. For these reasons ANS activity is usually inferred from responses of the organs innervated by it. One commonly used measure is *electrodermal responding*, which reflects changes in the electrical characteristics of the skin. These responses, formerly labelled *galvanic skin responses* (GSR), include "skin resistance," "skin conductance," and "skin potential." Electrodermal responding is correlated with changes in sweat gland activity, controlled primarily by SNS nerves. Measurement of other important ANS responses is discussed later in the chapter.

Damage/Disturbances

In 1861, the idea that different cognitive functions are associated with localized brain regions was being hotly debated. That year, a young French surgeon named Paul Broca reported a pivotal case study to the Society of Anthropology in Paris. He described an old man with a long history of paralysis on one side of his body (*hemiplegia*), and inability to speak, which Broca termed *aphemia*, but is now know as *aphasia*. Broca's post-mortem examination revealed an area of damaged brain tissue, a *lesion*, on the surface of the left frontal lobe. Four years later, after Broca had seen the same pattern in a series of patients, he concluded:

> I have been struck with the fact that in my first aphemics the lesion always lay, not only in the same part of the brain, but always the same side—the left. Since then, from many postmortems, the lesion was always left-sided.

One has also seen many aphemics alive, most of them hemiplegic, and always hemiplegic on the right side. Furthermore one has seen at autopsy lesions of F3 on the right side in patients who had shown *no* aphemia. It seems from all this that the faculty of articulate language is localized in the *left* hemisphere, or at least that it depends chiefly upon that hemisphere. (Broca, 1864, cited in Critchley, 1970, p. 63)

As previously mentioned, the region of the left frontal cortex that underlies spoken language is now commonly known as Broca's area.

Specific parts of the nervous system may be destroyed in research animals, usually by surgical methods, to clarify the role of the lesioned tissue in the intact organism. For example, in one experiment the pons in the brainstem was lesioned in cats (Jouvet, 1973). As do humans, cats have periods of rapid eye movement (REM) sleep, when the eyes begin to dart back and forth, there is EEG desynchronization, and the skeletal muscles are extremely limp. It is during REM sleep that humans, and we might imagine, cats, dream. The cats with the lesioned pons showed physiologically normal sleep except they had no REM periods. These data, and supporting results suggest that the pons is a neural pacemaker that switches on periodically during sleep to initiate dreaming.

With advances in neurochemistry, researchers have, with increasing confidence, turned to biochemical manipulations and assay methods to make inferences about the nervous system. These methods, including chemical blocking and enhancement of events at the synapse, have supported neurochemical theories of psychosis and led to the discovery of opiate receptors in the human brain (see chapter 4).

Electrical Stimulation

Neural circuitry can be coaxed into action by applying an electrical current from an external source through stimulating electrodes. The researcher may learn something about the neural tissue in question by carefully noting the behavioral effects of the stimulation, or sometimes the experiential effects from self-report in humans. Neurons can be made active by using fairly weak current applied merely to the skin or the scalp. The penlight battery powering an ohmmeter is sufficient to cause visual flashes when the ohmmeter leads are touched (for test purposes) to electrodes in good contact with the scalp over the visual areas of the brain. Surface electrodes are sometimes used to administer electrical pulse trains to spinal pathways in an attempt to control chronic pain (see chapter 4).

It is not always possible to use surface electrodes to deliver electrical current to neural structures for research purposes because of uncertainty about which neural tissue is actually being stimulated. Implanted or depth electrodes that are in physical contact with their neural targets can be used to achieve more precise, discrete neural activation. Implantation is sometimes necessary in clinical applications.

A series of studies by the Canadian neurosurgeon, Wilder Penfield, illustrates the value of direct electrical stimulation (Penfield, 1975). Beginning in the 1930s, Penfield used an exploratory procedure with epileptic patients in which a substantial section of skull was first removed under local anesthesia. Then a handheld electrical probe was employed to deliver small electrical currents to selected locations on the exposed surface of the brain. The clinical purpose was to discover the brain region that was the origin or *focus* of the seizure condition (see chapter 9). In order for Penfield to obtain subjective reports of each stimulus and note any behavioral effects, the patient was fully conscious. By stimulating different sites, a kind of functional mapping of the brain surface was accomplished.

Careful stimulation of the motor areas of the cerebral cortex produced movements (that were experienced as involuntary). Sensations of touch were perceived to arise from various body locations when the cortical somatosensory areas were activated. For some reason, epileptic foci are frequently located in one of the temporal lobes. Penfield always examined their surface especially closely. Here, the effects of stimulation were much more complex—rather than simply sensory or motor phenomena, Penfield saw what he termed "psychical" effects. In some cases successive stimulations of a given location yielded the same "memory" or "flashback." For one patient, stimulation of a specific temporal site invariably caused an experience in which he was at a baseball park observing a small boy sneak in under a fence to watch the game. Another patient was in her kitchen listening to the voice of her child, who was outside playing. A third, on each of the 30 instances that Penfield probed the point, heard an orchestra playing the same melody, which she could hum (Penfield, 1975). Some locations for certain patients yielded different "memories" across repeated stimulations. Penfield's work with brain stimulation in conscious humans has been influential in shaping modern concepts about the relationship between the brain and the stream of conscious experience, including memory.

Another important insight into brain function, based on electrical stimulation, originated by accident in a rat experiment conducted in late 1953. James Olds, assisted by a graduate student, Peter Milner, had planned to see if stimulation of the brainstem, which should have an alerting effect, facilitates learning (Olds, 1973). However, they were worried that the stimulation might prove "aversive"—a stimulus the organism will work to avoid or escape—which would complicate matters. Tiny electrodes were duly implanted in a rat. When the animal had recovered from surgery, the researchers placed it in a test enclosure. Electrical stimulation was delivered whenever the subject went to a particular spot in the box. To their amazement, the animal became keenly interested in this peculiar little corner of its world where such remarkable things happened in its brain—it came back for more, again and again.

Olds and Milner (1954) went on to investigate rewarding electrical brain stimulation more systematically by arranging a "self-stimulation" procedure whereby a brief train of pulses was delivered automatically whenever the test animal pressed a small lever (see Fig. 2.7). They found that rats will press a lever at rates up to several thousand responses per hour for brain stimulation reward, and prefer it to food or even sex; rats will run across an electrified shock grid to get to a lever that they can use for self-stimulation. In retrospect, the stimulating tips of the electrodes must have been misplaced by several millimeters in the original rat. The electrode placements that will support self-stimulation are located nearer the middle of the brain, and include especially the septal region and portions of the hypothalamus. Olds and Milner (1954) refer to these brain areas as "pleasure centers."

Measuring Nervous System Activity

Near the end of the 18th century, Luigi Galvani showed that the mysterious, invisible force through which the nerves direct the muscles, creating behavior, is electricity. Nearly 100 years later the first electrical recordings of brain activity were described by Henry Caton (1875) in a brief paper, "The Electric Currents of the Brain." In summarizing his studies of the brains of rabbits and monkeys, Caton (1875) reported:

> In every brain hitherto examined, the galvanometer has indicated the existence of electric currents. . . . Feeble currents of varying direction pass through the multiplier when the electrodes are placed on two points of the external surface, or one electrode on the grey matter, and one on the surface of the skull. The electric currents of the grey matter appear to have a relation to its function. . . . For example, on the areas shown by Dr. Ferrier to be related to rotation of the head and to mastication, negative variation of the current was observed to occur whenever those two acts respectively were performed. (p. 278)

The Electroencephalogram. The electrical power in brain signals decreases rapidly with distance from the neural tissue of origin. Had sensitive electrical amplification methods existed in 1875, Caton's work would have led directly to practical, noninvasive measurement of brain activity in humans. Indeed, his remark about currents from "two points on the

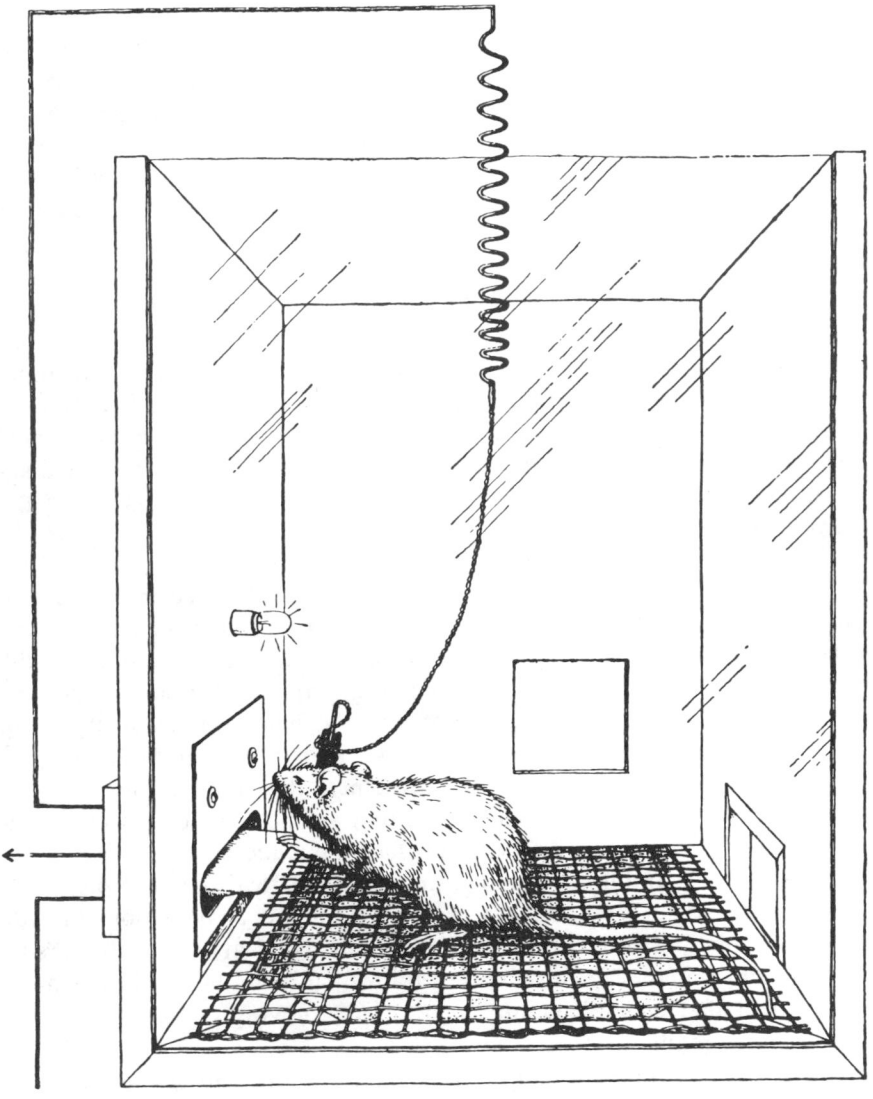

FIG. 2.7 Olds' self-stimulation circuit. When the rat presses the lever it triggers an electrical stimulus to its brain. The lever-pressing responses are recorded automatically. From "Pleasure Centers in the Brain" by J. Olds, 1956, *Scientific American, 195*, 108. Copyright 1956 by W. H. Freeman and Company. Reprinted by permission.

external surface" seems to mark the discovery of the electroencephalo-gram. As it turned out, adequate technology was not available until 50 years later when vacuum tube amplifiers were developed for the radio. It was with such a device that Hans Berger (1929) finally demonstrated that faint electrical signals that he called "brain waves," could be detected from recording electrodes attached to the human scalp. The characteristics of the waves were related to ongoing mental activity. Most noticeably, a large slow pattern he called the *alpha rhythm*, dominated the recording when the subject was relaxed with eyes closed; a faster, smaller, irregular pattern, designated as the *beta rhythm*, emerged during various kinds of mental activity. Within a few years, Berger's *electroencephalogram* (EEG) had become a standard clinical diagnostic tool in assessing human brain function in connection with head injuries, epilepsy, and possible tumors.

Nervous system electrical activity may be recorded from implanted electrodes. In humans this is only done when, in connection with diag-nosis or treatment, it is necessary to obtain information concerning the function of structures inside the brain. Very fine electrodes can be implanted to detect the impulses of a single neuron. Some clincans, for their convenience, routinely insert the tips of needle electrodes beneath the scalp which creates adequate electrical contact between tissue and electrodes without skin preparation. But most often one or another of the kinds of surface electrodes shown in Fig. 2.8 are filled with an electrode creme or paste that is a good conductor, and held securely to the scalp with sticky tape, a head band, or a glue-like substance. The resulting EEG signal is then conducted by wires to equipment that amplifies it and filters out electrical components of the signal that are not part of the biopoten-tial of interest. In the EEG these "artifacts" include 60 Hz "noise" from electrical wiring and flourescent lighting, and electrical activity from skele-tal muscle activity including eye movements. Recent innovations include special miniaturized devices that amplify the signal at the recording site, which improves the signal to noise ratio of the recording, and telemetry equipment that enables monitoring of freely-moving organisms because no wires are required.

The EEG is usually displayed as a trace on an oscilloscope, or a pen recording on a roll of chart paper that moves at constant speed under a pen whose complex up/down deflections represent the moment to moment changes in voltage of the amplified EEG signal. Sometimes simultaneous recordings are taken from different electrode placements and displayed on a *polygraph* that contains multiple recording channels and pens, usually 8 or 16.

The EEG varies in frequency and amplitude. The total height of any deflection is its amplitude. Every deflection of the pen, that is, every wave in the EEG, is produced by the summated activity of a great many neu-

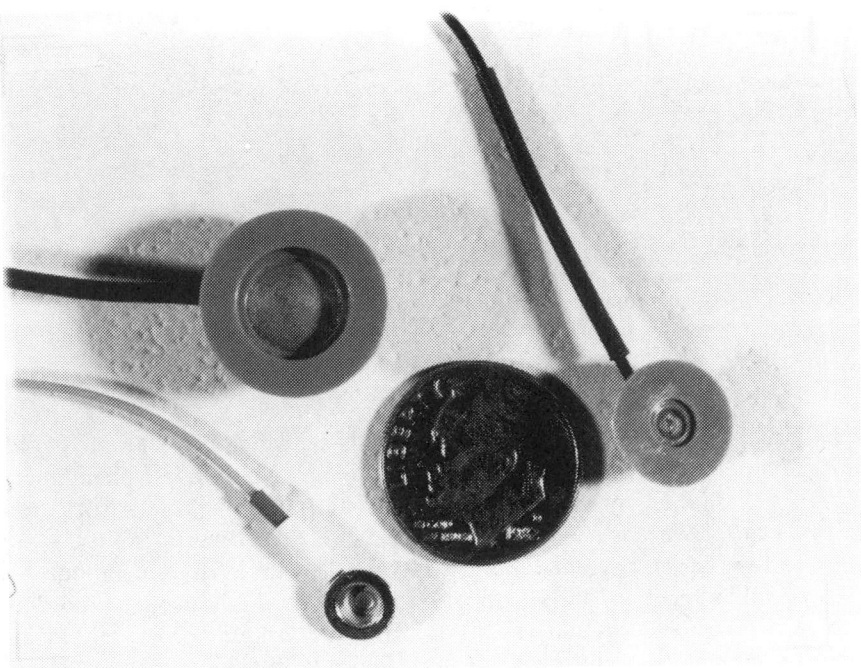

FIG. 2.8 Surface EEG recording electrodes: (a) standard disc, (b) miniature disc, (c) miniature gold cup.

rons. The more neurons creating a wave, the greater the amplitude of that wave. The degree to which the EEG reflects massed simultaneous firing of neurons is its *synchronization*. The greatest synchronization and largest EEG amplitudes are seen in the EEG during an epileptic seizure. Fig. 9.1 shows a polygraph recording of the EEG during a seizure. The EEG has become so synchronized as to display "spikes" rather than waves.

Desynchronization occurs when many of the neurons whose actions compose the EEG fire at different rates, presumably because they are engaged in different activities. The alpha rhythm reflects primarily synchronization, while the beta rhythm, with its small, fast, irregular waves, shows desynchronization. The shift from synchronized to desynchronized EEG is sometimes referred to as "alpha blocking." This phenomenon is illustrated in Fig. 2.9, which displays an EEG recording taken from the visual cortex while a participant alternately opened and closed his eyes. The alpha rhythm is often interpreted as the resting, background rhythm of the conscious human brain.

The frequency of the EEG is number of waves per second, or the cycles per second of the waveform (Hz). Most of the EEG activity that

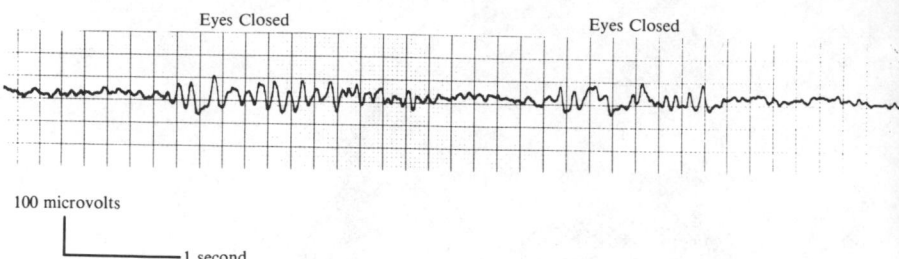

FIG. 2.9 A recording from our laboratory showing synchronized EEG with abundant alpha from the visual cortex when the eyes were closed, as compared to EEG desynchronization when the eyes were opened.

presently can be interpreted is approximately between 5 to 200 microvolts in amplitude, and from 1 to 50 Hz in frequency. Many EEG phenomena have been defined by their frequency and amplitude characteristics, and given names. We have already mentioned the beta rhythm (about 14-30 Hz) and the alpha rhythm (about 8-13 Hz). The theta rhythm (about 4-7 Hz) is still larger than alpha, and is found in normal adults on the borders of sleep. The delta rhythm (about 1-3 Hz), the largest normal EEG pattern, is found only during the physiologically deepest stage of sleep. Representative examples of delta, theta, alpha, and beta activity are shown in Fig. 2.10. Notice that in general, the slower the frequency, the larger the amplitude. A number of other EEG characteristics have been studied enough to have acquired names. Some of these are discussed later in the text.

Beginning students sometimes ask whether EEG equipment will "read their mind." This would be a great boon to the study of consciousness, but the answer is no. First, EEG equipment "reads" the brain, not the mind. Second, despite many thousands of published EEG studies, there are still many unanswered questions concerning how the brain produces the EEG, and its proper interpretation with respect to brain function. Still less is known about the connection between the EEG and the mind. We are far from establishing precise correlations over time between the ongoing stream of consciousness and the EEG. An analogy has been offered that may help clarify the reasons for this (Margerison, St. John-Loe, & Binnie, 1967). The EEG researcher is like a blind person listening outside the walls of a great factory. The task is to arrive at an understanding of the workings of the factory, based on an analysis of only the distant muffled roar of the machinery. In some ways it is surprising that EEG researchers are able to make anything of this distant muffled roar of the brain.

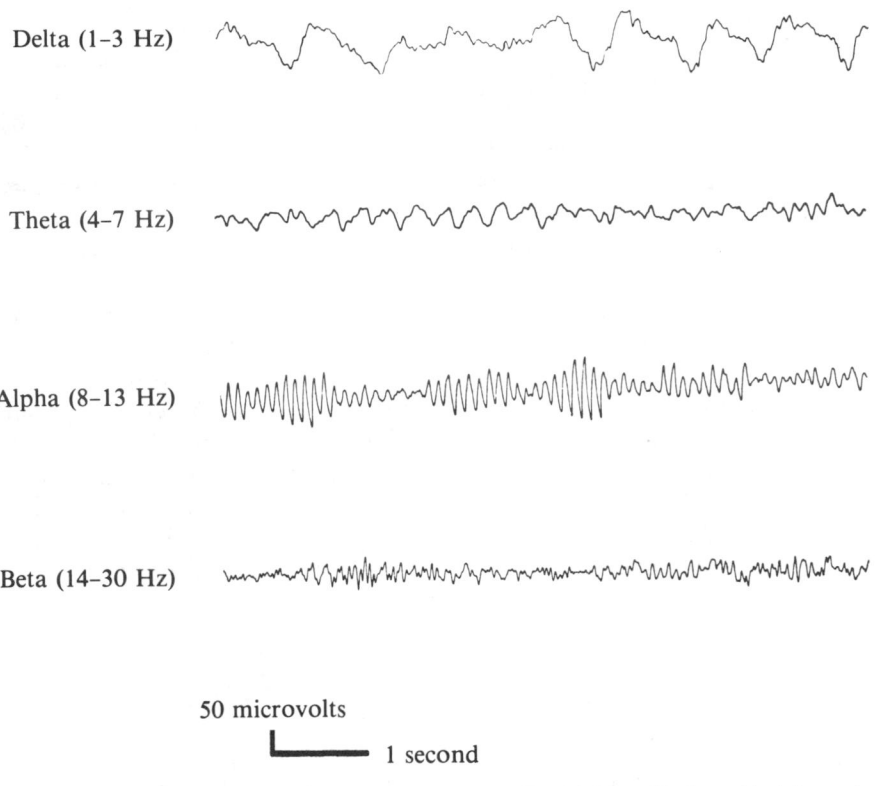

Delta (1-3 Hz)

Theta (4-7 Hz)

Alpha (8-13 Hz)

Beta (14-30 Hz)

50 microvolts

1 second

FIG. 2.10   Examples of EEG records containing primarily: (a) delta, (b) theta, (c) alpha, and (d) beta activity. From *EEG Handbook* (2nd ed., pp. 6.5-6.8) by A. R. Craib and M. Perry, 1975, Fullerton, CA: Beckman Instruments. Copyright 1975 by Beckman Instruments. Adapted by permission of TECA Corp.

Evoked Potentials. Thus far we have been discussing the data obtained when we simply hook someone up and record—the "spontaneous EEG." This EEG data is useful if one is studying whether the EEG differs between listening to jazz and classical music or whether there are connections between EEG and personality. But, when the researcher is interested in associations between EEG phenomena and specific external stimuli or experiential events, the spontaneous EEG is not the method of choice. The investigator must turn to "event related" or *evoked potential* methodology.

In this technique, a stimulus such as a flash of light, is presented, and, beginning with stimulus onset, the EEG is recorded for a brief period, such as 1000 milliseconds (one second). The effects of the light flash on the EEG would be the "visual evoked potential"; a sound would yield an auditory evoked potential. More complex stimuli, such as words, are often used. In many studies, several stimuli are presented and the major question concerns how their evoked potentials differ. Frequently the participant does not just sit passively and take in the stimuli, but must respond to them. In this way, it is possible to determine the EEG correlates of different types of perceptual and cognitive activity.

Each evoked potential will be imbedded in irrelevant spontaneous EEG activity, which in many cases is of considerably greater amplitude than the evoked potential itself. Somehow the two must be untangled. The basic solution was first suggested by Dawson (1950): present the evoking stimulus many times (in practice there are sometimes hundreds of presentations), and record the desired time sample of the EEG on each occasion. There will be spontaneous EEG in each time slice of EEG; however, being random with respect to the evoked potential, it will cancel out in the long run, leaving behind only the actual evoked potential.

The most common way to extract the evoked potential from the background EEG noise is to store the successive trials on a computer and then average them to derive the *average evoked potential*. An example of the smoothing and simplifying effects of this procedure is shown in Fig. 2.11.

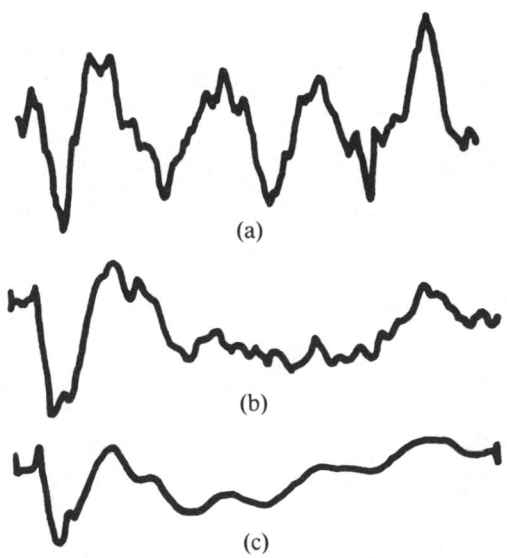

(a)

(b)

(c)

FIG. 2.11   Average evoked potentials: (a) a single EEG evoked potential, (b) the average evoked potential for 8 stimulus presentations, (c) the average evoked potential for 64 stimulus presentations. From *Biomedical Instrumentation and Measurements* (p. 247) by L. Cromwell, F. J. Weibell, E. A. Pfeiffer, and L. B. Usselman, 1973, Englewood Cliffs, NJ: Prentice-Hall. Copyright 1973 by Prentice-Hall. Adapted by permission.

It can be seen in Fig. 2.11 that an evoked potential is composed of a series of positive and negative going waves, varying somewhat in amplitude, and distinguished mainly by their delay, or "latency" with respect to the evoking stimulus. These components represent successive stages in processing of the stimulus, and reflect the contribution of different neural structures. In general, the earliest waves are generated by activity in sensory nerve fibers and circuits in the brainstem, which receive collaterals from every sensory input pathway. The next several components originate from participating structures in the middle of the brain and the appropriate cortical sensory projection regions. The late components of the evoked potential reflect parietal and frontal lobe processing, most likely involving perceptual organization, encoding for memory, decision making, and initiation of responses to the stimulus. As might be expected, the early components are more stable than the late components.

Evoked potential methods have many interesting uses. For example, the visual acuity development of a baby can be followed by presenting on a TV screen simple patterns, such as stripes or checkboards, of different gradations (e.g., Tyler, 1982). With progressively finer patterns the visual evoked potential eventually drops away, indicating the point at which the visual system begins to process the stimulus as a gray field, rather than as a pattern.

Evoked potentials may help clarify the psychophysiology of pain. Figure 2.12 shows the average evoked potentials to four intensities of electric shock stimulation after administration of aspirin as compared to a *placebo*, an inert substance presented as real (Buchsbaum, Davis, Coppola, & Naber, 1981). Notice that the major positive component increased with greater shock intensity, as did verbal ratings of pain; the evoked potentials were smaller following aspirin as compared to placebo, as was the self-report of pain.

The relationship between evoked potentials and cognition is an interesting problem. There has been particular interest in several components. The *P300* component is a positive wave with a latency from stimulus onset of about 250 to 350 milliseconds (Sutton, Braren, Zubin, & John, 1965), which appears to be associated with correct detection of stimuli for which there is some uncertainty. The *negative slow potential* is a slow negative drift of the entire EEG pattern that seems to reflect expectancy or preparation (see chapter 10).

Non-Electrical Measures of Brain Function.   A few methods have been developed to assess non-electrical aspects of brain function, especially local cerebral blood flow, local metabolism, and the magnetic fields created by the brain. None of these methods has been refined to the point that it is sufficiently free of hazard to the subject, inexpensive, and techni-

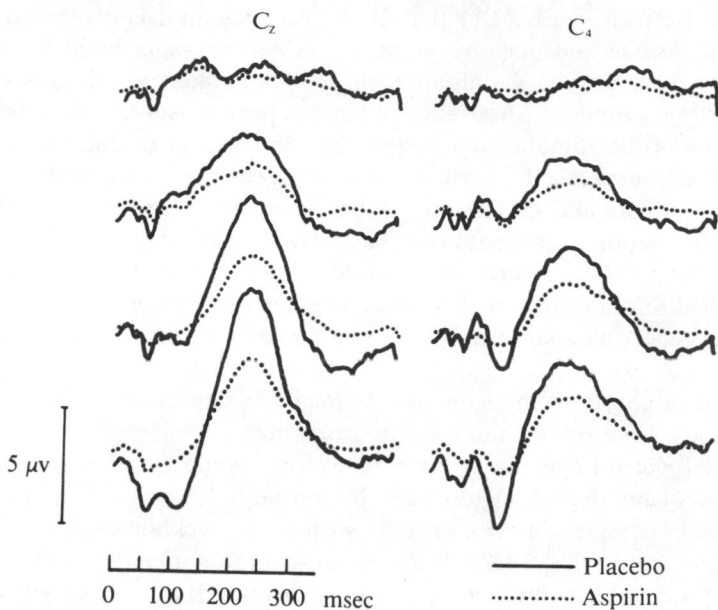

FIG. 2.12   Differences in the average evoked potentials to electric shock after taking aspirin as compared to a placebo. From "Opiate Pharmacology and Individual Differences. II. Somatosensory Evoked Potentials" by M. S. Buchsbaum et al., 1981, *Pain, 10*, 372. Copyright 1981 by Elsevier Biomedical Press. Reprinted by permission.

cally simple to be widely implemented in research. However, these methods offer great promise for understanding some of the complex properties of the whole working brain, due to recent advances in computing and applied mathematics. It is now possible to derive from these measures a functional image of the brain, with some techniques, in three dimensions. If time is added to the complex calculations, a moving picture can be created, displaying changing physiological activity in various parts of the brain over time.

One of the simplest methods involves having the subject inhale Xenon gas so that the prevalence of radioactive particles in different brain regions can be assessed using a bank of tiny radiation detectors. The prevalence of particles is proportional to local blood flow. The Xenon clearance technique has been applied to many questions of local cerebral blood flow, such as disturbances during migraine attacks, and possible altered cerebral circulation in psychopathology (Lassen, Ingvar, & Skinh, 1978).

Positron emission tomography (PET) is based on intravenous doses of a radioactive medium that contains positrons (Brownell, Budinger, Lauterbur, & McGeer, 1982). Each positron, when it is annihilated, shoots out two photons precisely 180 degrees from each other. Complex calculations are used to trace pairs of photons back to their common origin, enabling three-dimensional imaging of the brain. When the positrons are used to "label" glucose, PET results in an image of local brain metabolism, glucose being a major source of energy for the brain. *Nuclear magnetic resonance* (NMR) is the basis of another brain imaging technique that can be used to create a three-dimensional image of the brain. The concentration of hydrogen atoms within the head is determined by noting their effects on nearby magnetic fields. Figure 2.13 shows nine NMR images of a

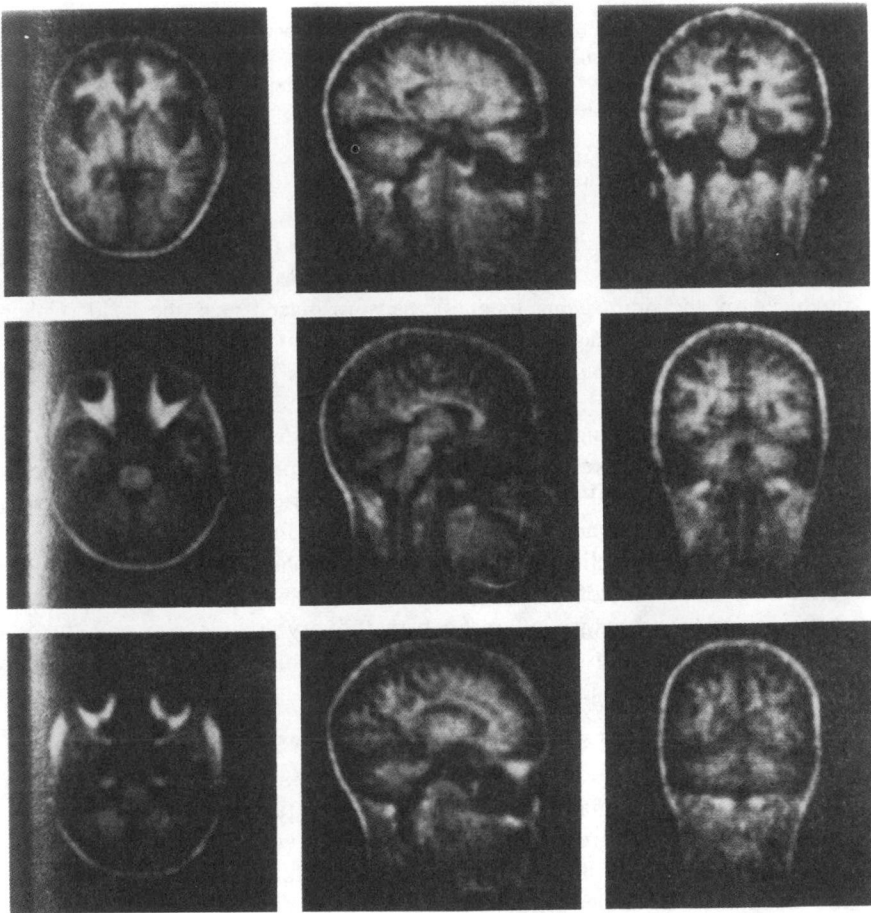

FIG. 2.13   NMR images of a human head from a single three-dimensional data collection. On the left are transverse images at three levels: through the center of the brain (top), at eye level (middle) and just below eye level (bottom). The three images in the center show a section at the midline (middle) and parallel sections about three centimeters to the left and right. The three images to the right show the head from the front at the brain's widest point (top) and at two regions farther to the rear. From "NMR Imaging in Medicine" by I. L. Pykett, 1982, *Scientific American, 246*(5), 79. Copyright 1982 by W. H. Freeman. Reprinted by permission.

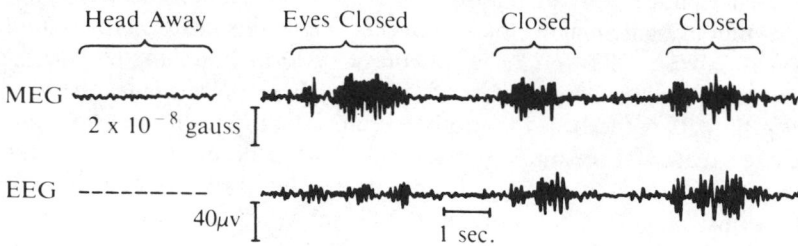

FIG. 2.14 A SQUID recording: The magnetoencephalogram (MEG). From "Magnetoencephalography: Detection of the brain's electrical activity with a superconducting magnetometer" by D. Cohen, 1972, *Science, 175,* 665. Copyright 1972 by the American Association for the Advancement of Science. Reprinted by permission.

human head reconstructed from a single three-dimensional NMR data collection.

Perhaps the most exciting approach is based on the superconducting quantum interference device (SQUID), which measures the weak magnetic field produced by the brain using magnetic sensors placed near the head (Cohen, 1972). Because this magnetic field is produced by the same brain currents that create EEG, a magnetoencephalogram (MEG) often resembles a concurrent EEG recording. This can be seen in Fig. 2.14, which shows one of the first MEG recordings; alpha blocking is evident in both the EEG and MEG when the eyes were opened. Because of properties of magnetic fields, the combination of MEG and EEG offers superior localization of current sources in the brain, and can contain different information than the EEG alone, thus complementing this older method (Cohen, in press).[1] The major présent disadvantages of the SQUID are that elaborate shielded rooms are needed to reduce background magnetism to very low levels, and that the magnetic detectors must be maintained at extremely low temperatures by immersing them in liquid helium.

THE SKELETAL MUSCLE SYSTEM

The muscles and the glands are the output apparatus driven by the CNS. The *skeletal muscles* are the action part of the voluntary movement system. This envelope of flesh, attached to the skeleton by tendons, enables humans and many lower animals to act on their environment, not just the other way around. Muscles are directly responsible for the most obvious functional difference between an oak tree and the child climbing it.

The psychophysiological approach to skeletal muscle function can be found in settings ranging from sharpening athletic performance to retrain-

---

[1] Footnote added in proof: Cohen, D. (in press). Magnetoencephalography (Neuromagnetism). In G. Adelman (Ed.), *Encyclopedia of neuroscience*. Boston: Birkhouser.

ing the simplest movements following a stroke. Skeletal muscle relaxation is the most common use of biofeedback. Nerve impulses whose natural destinations are various skeletal muscles are used to control artificial limbs, directing the actions of motors rather than muscles. Someday such nerve impulses may form the vital connection in ultra fast communication from humans to computers.

Neural Control of Skeletal Muscles

The executive neural control of voluntary movements arises in the motor cortex and adjacent, less specialized regions of the frontal lobes. From here, the neural pathways of the *pyramidal tract* descend to the spine without synapsing. *Alpha motor neurons* exit the spinal cord, their axons extending to the muscles they innervate. The interface between the nervous system and muscle tissue is the *neuromuscular junction*, where nerve impulses cause ACh to be released, which stimulates muscle contraction.

The simple path just described is complemented by many other neural structures, including alternate descending pathways that contribute elaborate involuntary and unconscious integration to skeletal muscle action. Structures in the middle of the brain, known collectively as the *basal ganglia*, coordinate "semivoluntary" movements such as twisting the body or running. The cerebellum (see Fig. 2.3) provides very fine integration, transforming what would otherwise be a series of twitches into a smooth movement. Additional coordination occurs at the spinal level where systems of reflexes create orderly patterns of muscular contraction and relaxation, for example, making sure that opposing leg muscles contract and relax together in walking. The large fiber alpha motor neurons are supplemented by about half as many smaller *gamma motor neurons* that innervate special motor fibers which are part of an involuntary and unconscious feedback system linked to the cerebellum (Guyton, 1981).

Skeletal Muscles

There are three types of muscle in the human body: (a) the *cardiac muscle* of the heart, (b) the *smooth muscle*, as surrounds the blood vessels, and (c) the *striate muscle*, which makes up the skeletal muscles and is named for its striped appearance. A skeletal muscle is composed of many *muscle fibers* held together by connective tissue. Individual muscle fibers are very narrow, only about 0.1 mm wide, yet they can be quite long, up to 300 mm in length. Secretion of ACh at the neuromuscular junction causes a wave of electrical activity to pass over the muscle fiber, stimulating it to contract by as much as 50% of its resting length.

The functional unit of muscle contraction is the *motor unit* (Fig. 2.15)—a motor neuron and the muscle fibers that it innervates. All muscle fibers in a motor unit contract simultaneously when stimulated by their governing motor neuron. Because nerve impulses are conducted down the axon on the order of 100 per second, the apparently smooth contraction of a muscle is actually composed of many quivering muscle fibers. At any given moment, the overall state of a skeletal muscle is determined by the number of motor units responding, and the rate of response of each unit.

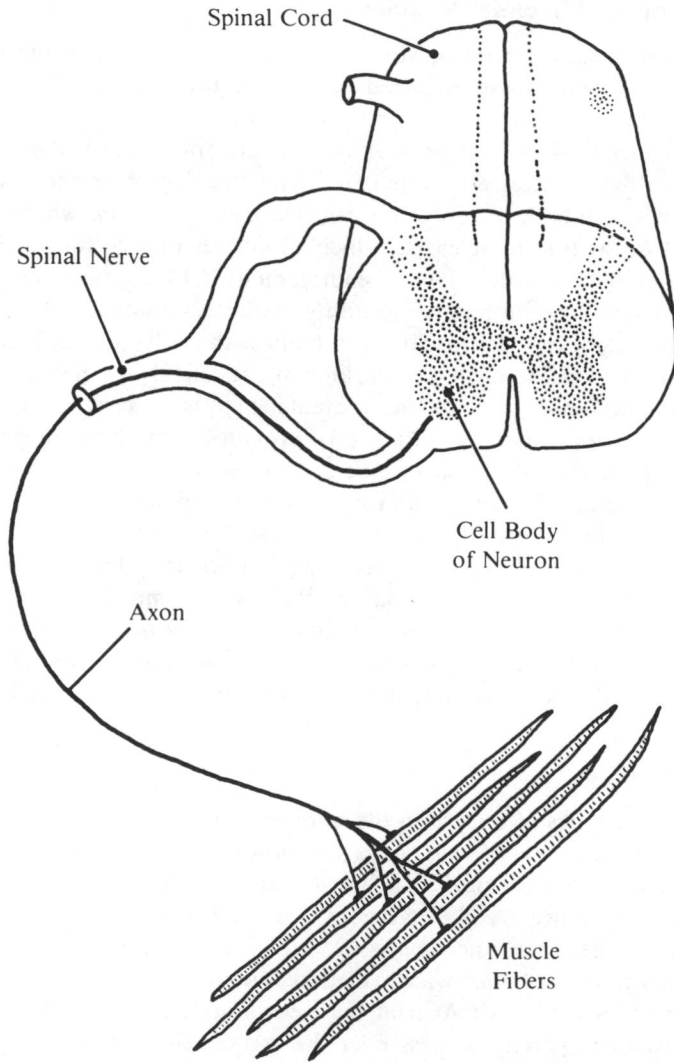

FIG. 2.15 A single motor unit. From *Muscles Alive* (p. 8) by J. V. Basmajian, 1967, Baltimore: Williams & Wilkins. Copyright 1967 by Williams & Wilkins. Adapted by permission.

One last consideration in muscle action is the number of muscle fibers controlled by each motor neuron. Large muscles that produce gross movements, such as those in the thigh, may have as many as 1000 muscle fibers driven by each motor neuron; however, the muscles controlling the eyes have only a few fibers per neuron, making possible a much more finely graded contraction of these muscles that enables precise positioning of the eyes.

Studying Skeletal Muscle Activity

The effects of skeletal muscle responses can often be observed directly, unlike the responses of the heart or brain. Even when visible movements result, researchers have had to develop precise methods of assessing them. One technique is the *goneometer*, a device that can be strapped over a joint, such as the elbow, to sense very small changes in the angle of the joint and indicate these in an electrical signal that is proportional to the joint angle. This instrument is useful in assessing the progress of patients with muscular impairment, and in biofeedback applications where accurate information concerning the extent of movement is essential. However, much of the skeletal muscle activity of interest in health psychophysiology is not visible to the naked eye, and must be detected by other means, primarily via electrical recordings of muscle activity known as the *electromyogram* (EMG).

The EMG reflects the electrical potentials that spread over muscle fibers when they are stimulated. If fine wire electrodes are inserted into the muscle, it is possible to record the activity of individual motor units, which appears on a polygraph record as a series of spikes, a few microvolts in amplitude and a few thousands of a second in duration. Some of the early research on voluntary control of single motor units is discussed in chapter 5.

In many applications, there is no interest in the electrical activity of single motor units, and the EMG is recorded non-invasively from standard or miniature disc electrodes on the surface of the skin (see Fig. 2.16). The frequency of the EMG ranges up to about 1000 Hz, with most of it falling between 10 Hz and 150 Hz (Stern, Ray, & Davis, 1980). A representative EMG recording is shown in Fig. 2.16, displaying the effects of muscular contraction and relaxation.

The EMG from surface electrodes always contains electrical activity from distant muscle fibers, the contribution of muscle fibers decreasing with the square of their distance from the recording site. In general, the more closely the recording electrodes are spaced, the more localization of the EMG signal. Recording electrodes placed directly over the "belly" of a large muscle will yield an EMG that reflects mainly the muscle fiber

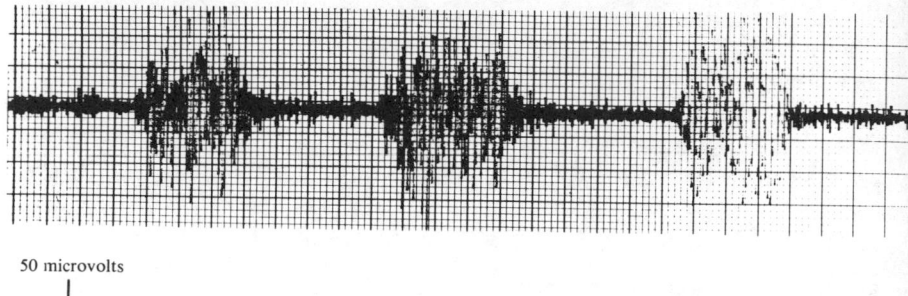

50 microvolts

1 second

FIG. 2.16   An electromyogram (EMG) recording from our laboratory showing skeletal muscle activity in the forearm when the fist was clenched periodically.

activity of that muscle. When electrodes are spread far apart the signal will reflect widespread muscle activity. For example, with electrodes placed on each wrist, the EMG includes activity from muscles throughout the upper body, and, when the person is thoroughly relaxed, the EKG is even evident in the record.

THE CARDIOVASCULAR SYSTEM

The cardiovascular system consists of the heart, blood vessels, and the blood they contain. Its function is to distribute oxygen and nutrients to bodily tissues and carry away wastes. The pump in this system, the heart, starts functioning after only four weeks of fetal development and, if all goes well, will execute 3 or 4 billion exquisitely timed contractions before its owner dies, usually from a malfunction somewhere in this same system.

The Heart

The heart is a large muscle surrounding four chambers (see Fig. 2.17). Oxygen-depleted blood returns to the heart via the *right atrium*, where it is forced through a valve into the *right ventricle*, then sent out to the lungs to pick up oxygen. Oxygen-rich blood is returned to the heart via the *left atrium*, and driven past a valve into the *left ventricle*, where it is finally pumped into the *aorta*, after which the blood is distributed throughout the body.

The heart has an intricate built-in electrical pacemaker system, as shown in Fig. 2.18. Each heartbeat is initiated by an electrical impulse generated at the *sinoatrial node* (S-A node), which elicits atrial contraction and spreads to the *atrioventricular node* (A-V node), where another impulse prompts contraction of the ventricles. This system is so self-sufficient that it will continue to cause a healthy heart, which has been completely disconnected from the nervous system, to beat rhythmically.

Normally, the ANS exercises neural control of the heart by means of SNS and PNS nerves that supply inputs to both the S-A and A-V nodes. SNS activity increases the firing rate of the S-A node, thereby increasing heart rate, while the PNS, via the *vagus nerve*, has the opposite effect. The

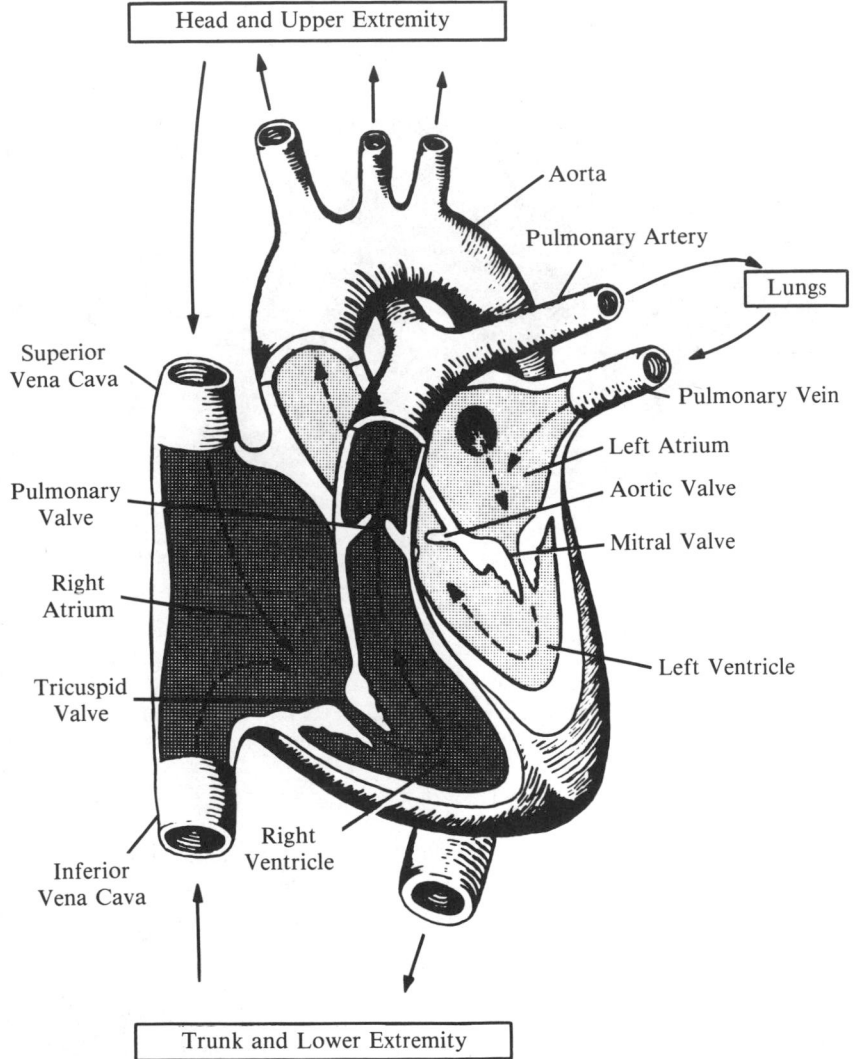

FIG. 2.17   The chambers and valves of the heart. From *Function of the Human Body* (4th ed., p. 94) by A. C. Guyton, 1974, Philadelphia: W. B. Saunders. Copyright 1974 by W. B. Saunders. Reprinted by permission.

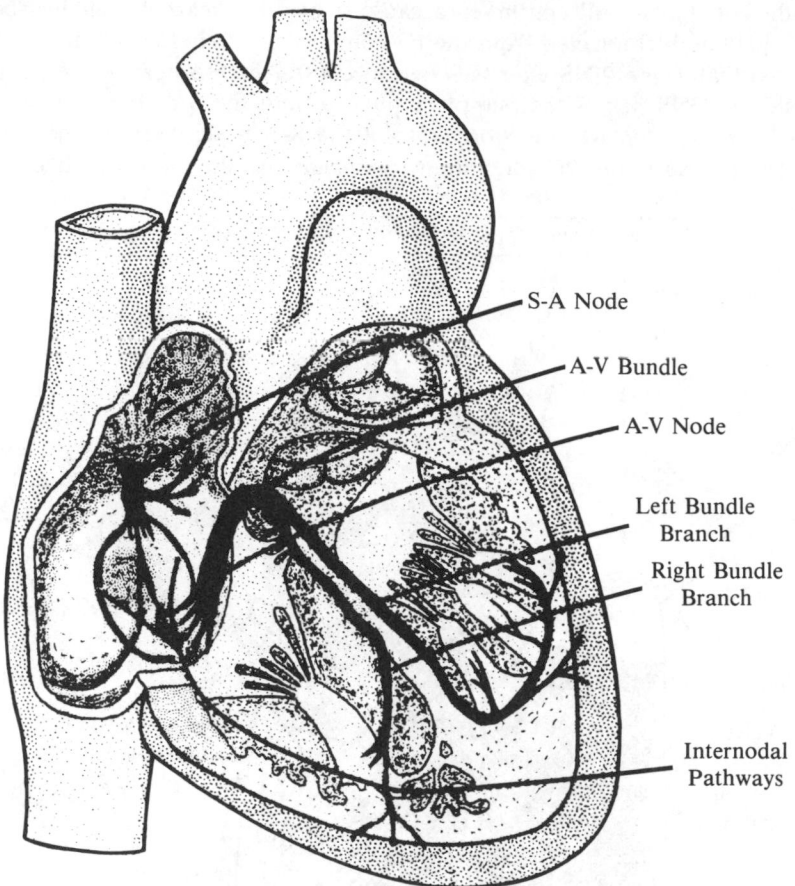

S-A Node

A-V Bundle

A-V Node

Left Bundle
Branch

Right Bundle
Branch

Internodal
Pathways

FIG. 2.18 The electrical pacemaker system of the heart. From *Function of the Human Body* (4th ed., p. 96) by A. C. Guyton, 1974, Philadelphia: W. B. Saunders. Copyright 1974 by W. B. Saunders. Reprinted by permission.

SNS also intensifies the force of contraction of the heart muscle, which increases the volume of blood circulated with each beat.

The Blood Vessels

The *arteries* transport blood away from the heart. They become progressively finer until they enter *capillary beds* of extremely fine vessels where the nutrient-waste exchange is made. Then the blood emerges into the *veins*, which carry the blood back to the heart.

In addition to the pumping action of the heart, the circulation of blood is controlled by responses of the vessels themselves. The SNS causes smooth muscles in arterial walls to constrict, reducing the diameter of the vessel, in a process known as *vasoconstriction*. The opposite response, *vasodilation*, is mainly due to decreased SNS action, since the PNS has little influence on vasomotor processes.

ANS neural control regulates the flow of blood to major areas of the body. There are also *autoregulation* mechanisms that automatically tune the flow of blood to localized regions according to the needs of those tissues. This action occurs in specific skeletal muscles when these muscles are exercised, and is seen in the shifting patterns of blood flow in different regions of the cerebral cortex as a function of localized neural activity.

The heart and brain are especially vulnerable to disruptions in the blood supply. A person will remain conscious less than 10 seconds when the flow of blood to the brain is interrupted. Longer periods of restricted cerebral blood flow, as in a *stroke*, may result in permanent damage to the brain tissue, and impairment of the functions subsumed by the affected brain area. The metabolic needs of the heart muscle itself are satisfied by blood supplied by the *coronary arteries* (Fig. 2.19). When one of the coronary vessels becomes blocked, as in *coronary heart disease*, the part of the heart muscle supplied by that vessel loses its ability to contract, and the person suffers a *myocardial infarction* or "heart attack."

Studying Cardiovascular Activity

The *electrocardiogram* (EKG, from the German spelling) is a recording of the electrical activity of the heart detected from the surface of the skin. There are standard placements for the recording electrodes, although the EKG can be detected from two electrodes placed anywhere on the skin, as long as they are fairly far apart. The EKG for several heartbeats is shown in Fig. 2.20.

The peaks and valleys of the EKG correspond to known events in the cardiac cycle. For example, the large upward deflection, the "R wave," reflects depolarization of the ventricles just before they contract. The EKG is a useful diagnostic tool in detecting *cardiac arrhythmias*, which are disturbances in the rhythmic beating of the heart. One of the most common arrhythmias is *premature ventricular contraction* (PVC), which is illustrated in the EKG shown in Fig. 2.21.

The simplest measure of cardiac activity is heart rate. This can be assessed manually by counting pulses at the wrist over a known time period, or extracted from the EKG by counting the number of R waves over time. Other important measures of cardiac performance are *stroke volume*, the amount of blood pumped into the aorta by each heartbeat, and *cardiac output*, the total amount of blood circulated by the heart per unit of time. Until recently, these could be measured accurately only by invasive procedures that required inserting sensors into blood vessels.

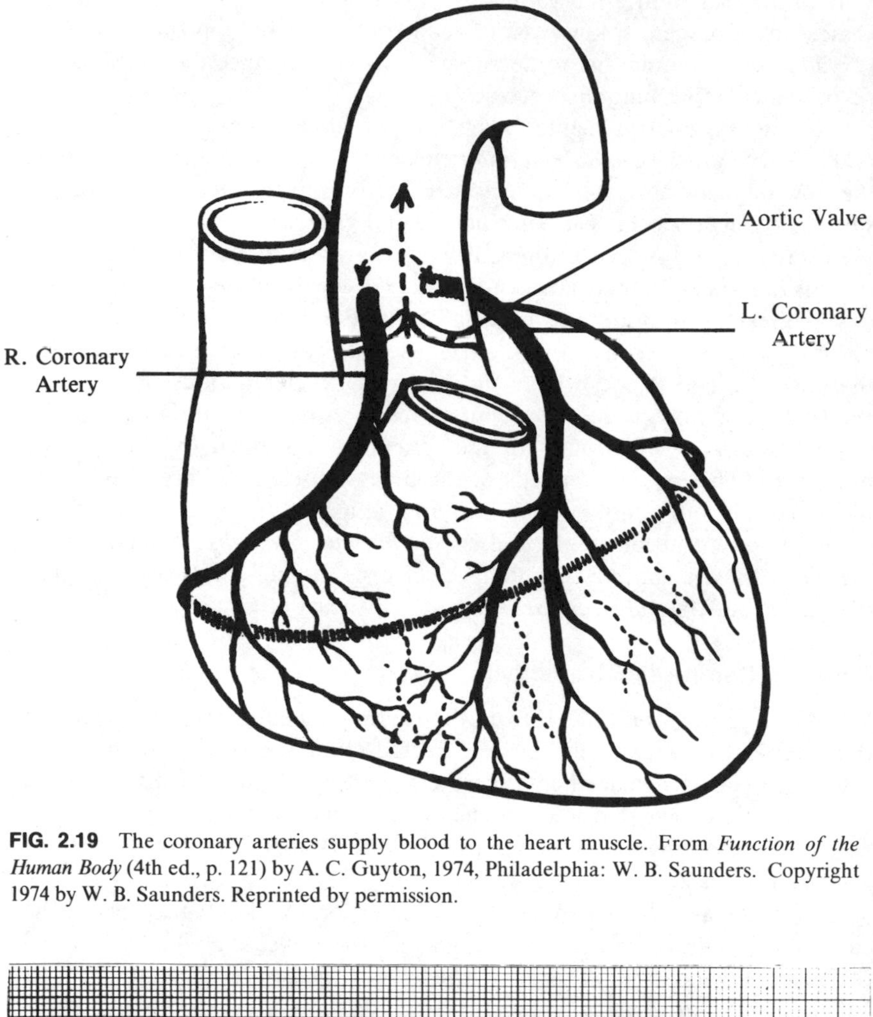

Aortic Valve

L. Coronary
Artery

R. Coronary
Artery

FIG. 2.19 The coronary arteries supply blood to the heart muscle. From *Function of the Human Body* (4th ed., p. 121) by A. C. Guyton, 1974, Philadelphia: W. B. Saunders. Copyright 1974 by W. B. Saunders. Reprinted by permission.

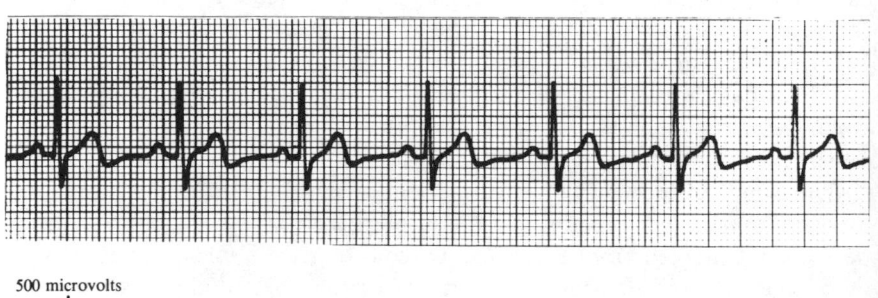

500 microvolts

1 second

FIG. 2.20 An electrocardiogram (EKG) recording of heart activity from our laboratory.

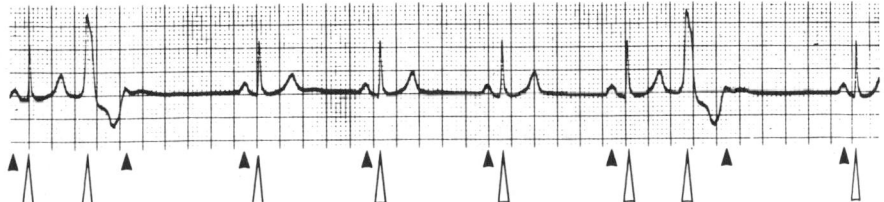

FIG. 2.21 Premature ventricular contractions (PVCs). Notice the normal regularly spaced small waves marked by the small dark triangles. On two occasions the R wave, marked by the long triangles, occurs prior to the small wave, constituting a PVC. From *The Cardiac Rhythms* (p. 220) by R. G. Phillips and M. K. Feeney, 1973, Philadelphia: W. B. Saunders. Copyright 1973 by W. B. Saunders. Reprinted by permission.

However, through *impedance cardiography*, stroke volume and cardiac output can now be measured as easily as obtaining an EKG. A very high frequency, low intensity electrical current is passed through the chest between stimulating electrodes (usually bands of disposable aluminum-covered tape) encircling the chest at the armpits and bottom of the rib cage. Recording electrodes, similarly placed, record changes in the impedance (resistance) of the whole chest across the cardiac cycle, the impedance falling as blood is ejected by the heart. The resulting record, and its relationship in time to the EKG is shown in Fig. 2.22. Notice that

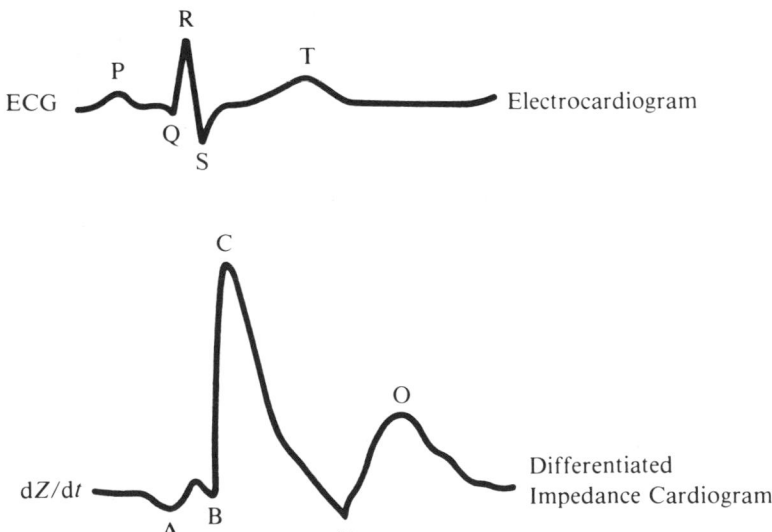

FIG. 2.22 An impedance cardiogram. From *Non-invasive Cardiovascular Monitoring by Electrical Impedance Technique* (p. 34) by S. N. Mohapatra, 1981, London: Pitman Medical. Copyright 1981 by Pitman Medical. Reprinted by permission.

the change in impedance, reflecting blood flow, lags a little behind the electrical events of the cardiac cycle. A serious disadvantage of this method is that measurements can only be taken between breaths, since respiration alters the volume, and hence the impedance, of the chest.

Blood pressure is determined jointly by: (a) the volume of blood a person has (blood volume), (b) the pressure exerted on the blood by the pumping action of the heart (cardiac output), and (c) the pressure the blood is subjected to by the blood vessels, through which the blood must move with each heartbeat (peripheral resistance). Peripheral resistance is determined by the degree of vasocontriction due to SNS neural stimulation, the levels of various circulating vasoconstricting and vasodilating substances, and by disease processes such as atherosclerosis (discussed in chapter 7). The unit of measurement for blood pressure is the height, in millimeters, of a column of mercury that the pressure of the blood can support (mmHg). Two pressures are often taken, the *systolic*, or peak pressure during ventricular contraction, and the *diastolic*, or resting pressure between heartbeats.

Blood pressure is usually measured in the clinical setting with a *sphygmomanometer* according to a procedure worked out in 1905 by a Russian physiologist, Korotkoff. A cuff is placed around the upper arm and inflated until it exerts enough pressure to prevent the blood from circulating, as indicated by the absence of "Korotkoff sounds" heard through a stethoscope placed over a large artery just below the cuff. When the cuff is slowly deflated, the first Korotkoff sound marks the pressure at which the blood is just able to overcome the pressure of the cuff, the systolic blood pressure. As the cuff is deflated further, a point will be reached when the cuff no longer interferes with circulation and the sounds disappear; this is the diastolic pressure.

There are many problems with the Korotkoff method (Dollery, 1985). Accurate determination of pressure requires some skill, and is somewhat subjective. Physicans often record levels only to the nearest 10 mmHg. One study found that systolic pressure increased an average of 26.7 mmHg and diastolic 14.9 mmHg in hospital patients when the physician arrived to take their blood pressure (Mancia et al., 1983). It is common to observe a 10 mmHg drop in blood pressure from the first office visit to the second office visit. Obviously, a diagnosis of *hypertension* (high blood pressure), or *hypotension* (low blood pressure) cannot be made from a single measurement taken by the Korotkoff method.

More advanced methods are often used in blood pressure research, especially for biofeedback, where continuous, accurate readings are desirable. One improved technique is the automated cuff method (Tursky, Shapiro, & Schwartz, 1972) in which a feedback arrangement is used to track systolic or diastolic pressure by automatically adjusting the cuff pressure based on the coincidence of pulses detected above and below the cuff. The cuff must be deflated periodically to avoid circulation problems. Each heartbeat causes a pressure wave that moves through the blood. The velocity of the wave is determined primarily by blood pressure. Based on this, *pulse wave velocity* methods have been developed that involve detecting small changes in the timing of pressure waves, or pulses, between several arterial locations or between a cardiac event such as contraction of the ventricles and arrival of the pulse at a peripheral artery. Pulse wave velocity is sometimes used as an indirect index of blood pressure, based on the previous reasoning and strong correlations between independent blood pressure and pulse wave velocity recordings (Gribbin, Steptoe, & Sleight, 1976).

Photoelectric *plethysmography* is a common method for measuring peripheral vasomotor activity. A light source may be placed on one side of an earlobe or a finger. A sensitive photocell on the other side measures how much light is passed through the tissue in between; the more blood flowing through the tissue, the less light is transmitted. For parts of the body that are too thick for this method, the amount of light reflected back can be used. *Blood volume* refers to the amount of blood circulating through the area, while *pulse volume* is the increase in blood volume that occurs with each heartbeat.

The blood heats the skin to some extent as it circulates through it. In fact, when such factors as temperature of the air, humidity, and sweating are constant, the surface temperature of the skin is proportional to the rate of blood flow just beneath it. Based on this, *skin temperature* is often used as an approximate index of peripheral vasomotor activity. Sensitive thermistors whose electrical properties are altered by temperature changes on the order of 1/100 degree, are typically taped or glued to the skin. This procedure is simple and inexpensive; however, it has some disadvantages. It is difficult to ensure an absolutely stable skin-thermistor contact, and to control other factors that might influence the skin temperature readings. Also, there is a troublesome delay between vasomotor activity and the resulting change in skin temperature.

THE RESPIRATORY SYSTEM

Anatomy And Physiology

The respiratory system includes the nose, mouth, the passages to and from the lungs, and the lungs themselves. The function of this system is to deliver oxygen to bodily tissues and carry away carbon dioxide. Once air enters the lungs it is drawn down finely branching passageways, the *bronchioles*, to the *alveoli*, which are tiny bags that inflate with each inspiration. Here, only a very thin membrane separates the air from blood in surrounding capillaries. Oxygen readily diffuses through the membrane from the air into the blood, whereas carbon dioxide passes in the opposite direction to be expelled with the next expiration. The purpose of breathing is to aereate the blood by forcing air into and out of the alveoli.

The mechanical aspect of breathing is accomplished by the diaphragm and a system of attached muscles. These are skeletal muscles, and are under some voluntary control, as shown by the acts of talking, singing, and laughing. Reflex control of these muscles is seen in the cough and sneeze reflexes, elicited by foreign particles in the throat and nose, respectively. The respiratory system is under an interesting combination of voluntary and involuntary control. We can hold our breath, but we do not have to remember to breathe.

CNS control of respiration is channeled through the *respiratory center* situated in the medulla oblongata and pons within the brain stem, where two assemblies of neurons have been identified that elicit inspiration and expiration when they are stimulated electrically. The respiratory center receives neural inputs from many brain structures, including the cerebral cortex, hypothalamus, and reticular formation. The lungs are innervated by both branches of the ANS, which have opposing effects. For example, SNS nerve impulses cause dilation of the bronchioles, PNS impulses, constriction. Neural control of respiration is itself regulated by the metabolic needs of the organism via a homeostatic feedback relationship involving blood carbon dioxide level. Elevation in blood carbon dioxide stimulates increased depth and rate of respiration, which brings the carbon dioxide level back into balance.

Studying Respiratory Activity

The most important quantifiable aspects of respiration are rate and volume. *Respiration rate* or breaths per minute, can be determined by direct observation, and volume measurement can be easily accomplished by checking the volume of air in a balloon that has been blown up. Usually, it is necessary to use less obtrusive procedures that are more accurate, but also more complex.

A small thermistor can be installed at the nostril to detect the alternating cool and warm air associated with breathing in and out. With proper calibration, this method can yield useful estimates of the depth of inspiration and expiration, as well as the duration and timing of respiratory events. More often, *tidal volume*, the volume of air in a breath, and *total ventilation*, the volume of air breathed in a minute, are estimated using *strain gauges* or a *spirometer*. Strain gauges measure the changing circumference of the chest and abdomen during breathing. Both chest and abdomenal components must be recorded because they can change independently. A spirometer is based on the balloon principle, and requires breathing into a device that makes direct volume measurements. More elaborate methods can be used to measure oxygen consumption, which, in turn, can be used to estimate *metabolic rate*, technically the rate of heat production by the organism.

Respiratory variables have not been extensively studied in health psychophysiology, although respiration is routinely recorded in the detection of deception, where the duration of inspiration is studied. Respiration is often recorded in research as a control against effects of respiration on other ANS variables, especially heartrate. *Sinus arrhythmia* is the reflexive change in heartrate seen across the respiratory cycle, with the heartrate accelerating during inspiration and slowing during expiration. Recently, interest has grown in respiratory psychophysiology with the development of self-regulation based interventions for respiratory problems such as asthma, *hyperventilation* (excessive breathing) especially when it is anxiety-related, and *sleep apnea* (the periodic cessation of breathing during sleep).

THE GASTROINTESTINAL SYSTEM

Anatomy And Physiology

The gastrointestinal system transports nutrients and fluids into the organism and transports wastes out; in between it accomplishes digestion and absorption of nutrients into the blood. The gastrointestinal tract is a long tube having valves that control the passage of substances though it, and includes the mouth, esophagus, stomach, intestines, and colon. Most of the gastrointestinal tract is covered with smooth muscle, the same type of muscle on the walls of blood vessels. Rhythmic contractions of these muscles move food along the tract.

Starting with saliva in the mouth, various digestive juices are secreted into the gastrointestinal tract where they are mixed with the contents, breaking down food into usable substances. Many digestive chemicals are secreted by glands in the walls of the tract, whereas others are provided by the liver and pancreas. The stomach begins digestion of protein by secreting hydrochloric acid and pepsin. The stomach wall, the *mucosa*, is made of protein and would be digested itself if it were not for the mucus it secretes that provides a protective covering. An *ulcer* is a hole in the mucosa resulting from a disruption in the digestion/protection balance.

The motility, secretions, and other responses of the gastrointestinal tract are controlled jointly by circulating hormones and ANS neural activity. Two of the most important hormones are *gastrin*, which stimulates release of digestive acids into the stomach, and *secretin*, which causes the pancreas to produce an acid-neutralizing fluid. As with many other ANS-innervated bodily functions, digestive processes are directed by the CNS mainly via the hypothalamus and medulla of the brainstem. Both SNS and PNS nerves exercise neural control at several stages (see Fig. 2.6 and Table 2.1). In general, the PNS stimulates digestive processes, for example stomach and intestinal motility and salivation, while the SNS inhibits such responses. As is the case for respiration, some responses of the digestive tract are under mixed voluntary and involuntary control. For example, although one can voluntarily initiate the swallowing response, this is possible only if there is something in the mouth to be swallowed, at least a few drops of saliva.

Studying Gastrointestinal Activity

Most of the gastrointestinal tract is inconveniently located for direct study, and, unlike the heart, does not give off strong electrical signals that can be readily linked to physiological events. Observation of human gastrointestinal activity is a difficult endeavor. Until this century, information about stomach secretions and contractions was due to individuals having a rare *gastric fistula*, which is a passageway all the way through the abdomen and into the stomach, introduced surgically, or due to an accident such as a gunshot wound. Through this window, the interested researcher has a firsthand view of the stomach in action and a means of taking gastric juice samples for chemical analysis. The first observed links between stomach activity and emotions can be found in Beaumont's classic 1833 monograph describing what he saw through the fistula of his cantankerous patient, Alexis St. Martin, who had suffered a gunshot wound to the stomach (Wolf, 1981).

One of the most thoroughly studied individuals was a man named Tom who, in 1895, had a gastric fistula created surgically after having swallowed scalding clam chowder, which caused severe damage to his esophagus (Wolf & Wolff, 1948). Daily observations in varied realistic circumstances were possible, because he was employed at the laboratory as an assistant. Tom was an especially interesting subject because some of his stomach lining had pushed up through the passageway to externally surround the fistula like a collar. The investigators could readily monitor gastric blood flow by checking the color of the external mucosa, which they reported showed distinct color variations ranging from "vivid cardinal red" to "pale orange-pink." His stomach lining, like his face, became flushed when he was angry and pale when he was fearful.

A staple laboratory method for many years was to have a dedicated volunteer, often a student, swallow a balloon attached to flexible tubing.

Once the subject had succeeded in keeping it down, the balloon was inflated and attached to pressure-sensitive equipment that resulted in a running record of stomach contractions as indicated by changes in the pressure inside the balloon. In 1911, Cannon used this method to confirm his suspicion that "hunger pangs" were linked to stomach contractions (Cannon & Washburn, 1912). Figure 2.23 shows his first recording, taken from the stomach of his student, Washburn. The top tracing is from the balloon, the middle indicates Washburn's subjective report of hunger pangs, the bottom is a recording of abdominal muscle activity taken to rule out its involvement. Notice the coincidence of hunger pangs with strong rhythmic contractions, approximately one per minute. The hunger pang is not sensed until the contraction is well underway, suggesting that the sensation is the result of the contraction and not the other way around.

"High tech" alternatives to swallowing balloons have been explored, including pressure-sensitive capsules that also contain miniature transmitters. An external receiver decodes the pressure signals from a swallowed capsule. It is not always easy to keep track of the location of the capsule or to retrieve the expensive devices.

The *electrogastrogram* (EGG) is a recording of gastrointestinal motility from the surface of the skin. As typically recorded from abdominal electrodes on the skin, the EGG reflects mostly smooth muscle activity from the lower portion of the stomach. In many EGG recordings there is a pronounced three per minute pattern of contractions thought to represent an

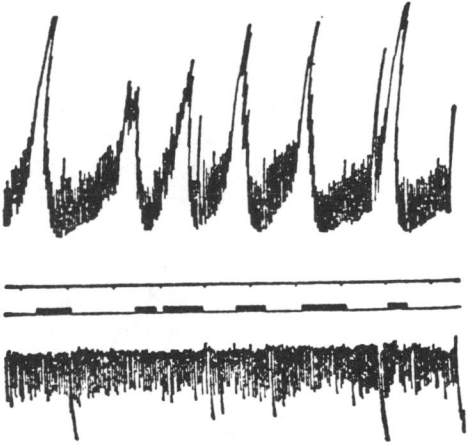

FIG. 2.23 Cannon's first recording linking stomach contractions and hunger pangs. Reproduced from *The Wisdom of the Body* by Walter B. Cannon, by permission of W.W. Norton & Co., Inc. Copyright 1932, renewed 1960 by Cornelia J. Cannon. Revised edition copyright 1939 by Walter B. Cannon, renewed 1966, 1967 by Cornelia J. Cannon.

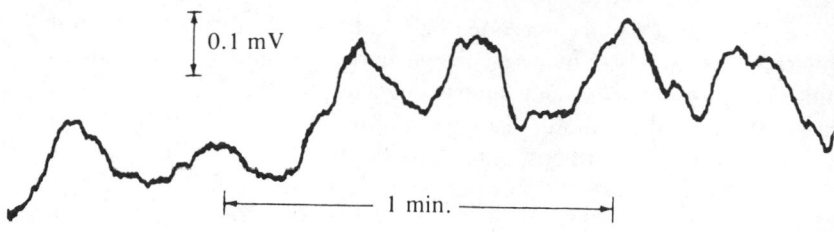

FIG. 2.24 An electrogastrogram (EGG) recording. From *Psychophysiological Recordings* (p. 165) by R. M. Stern, W. J. Ray, and C. M. Davis, 1980, New York: Oxford University Press. Copyright 1980 by Oxford University Press. Reprinted by permission.

intrinsic rhythm of the stomach, which is known to continue its rhythmic contractions even when the nerve supply has been totally disconnected (Stern, Ray, & Davis, 1980). A representative EGG recording is shown in Fig. 2.24.

THE IMMUNE SYSTEM

Anatomy And Physiology

The immune system defends the body against potentially harmful chemical toxins, cancer cells, and organisms such as bacteria and viruses. There are two types of protection—*innate immunity* and *acquired immunity*.

Innate immunity includes an assortment of general processes that do not depend on having experienced the foreign agent. These general processes are: (a) digestion in the stomach of any tiny organisms that happen to be swallowed, (b) resistance to invasion by the skin, (c) the presence in the blood of chemicals that attach to and destroy foreign particles, and, most importantly, (d) *phagocytosis* (Guyton, 1982). In phagocytosis, alien agents, particularly bacteria and viruses, are attacked and, in effect, eaten by cells that are specialized for that purpose. These cells are primarily *macrophages* and *leukocytes*. Macrophages are continuously present in many tissues throughout the body and are the first line of defense against a foreign invasion. Leukocytes, more commonly known as *white blood cells*, are the mobile attack units in this system. They are produced in the bone marrow and by the lymph glands, then transported by the blood to the body areas where they are needed.

Leukocytes and macrophages contribute to *inflammation*, a coordinated series of tissue changes that follows any kind of injury, including bacterial invasion. Inflammation begins with the immediate release of several substances, including *histamine*, which increases the flow of blood to the damaged tissue and causes fluids to leak into the area. The net result is a walling off of the affected area from surrounding tissue, which minimizes the spread of infectious agents. The macrophages present in the area immediately begin phagocytosis. Certain leukocytes migrate to the area where they also participate in phagocytosis. If the infection continues, production of leukocytes will increase enormously. For this reason, the level of leukocytes in the blood is often checked in testing for certain diseases.

Innate immunity is supplemented by acquired immunity, which is the ability to develop specific defenses against newly encountered foreign material. Each substance to which we develop acquired immunity contains its own unique chemical identifier, called an *antigen*. The first time the antigen is experienced, the lymph glands create specialized *lymphocytes* (types of white blood cells), which are then able to recognize, attack, and destroy anything that contains that antigen, should it be encountered again.

The fundamental principle of acquired immunity was noted as early as 400 B. C. by Thucydides when he perceived, after having observed a plague that struck Athens at about that time that "the same man was never attacked twice" (Strand, 1978, pp. 361-362). Unfortunately ancient health practitioners did not understand immunity well enough to manipulate it. By 1000 A. D. African tribes were employing a practical method of deliberate exposure to prevent smallpox, but it was not until the 1880s that Louis Pasteur and others began to introduce vaccines for a variety of diseases. In *vaccination*, acquired immunity is created by intentionally exposing the individual to a specific antigen in a safer form than it is found casually in nature.

There are two complementary mechanisms of acquired immunity, *cellular* and *humoral* (Guyton, 1982), both of which are based on cells originating in the bone marrow. Humoral immunity involves *B cells*. When an antigen is first encountered, the dormant B cells enter into a series of transformations and interactions with other cells that, within a few days or weeks, result in the appearance of new *antibodies* in the blood. An antibody recognizes and attaches to its specific target antigen. By covering the surface of the antigen-bearing particles, sometimes even binding them together in large clumps, the invading agents are inactivated and readied for phagocytosis. When antibodies combine with their antigen, this also automatically activates the *complement system*, a complex of enzymes that intefers with and weakens the foreign material through a variety of effects, such as rupturing the cell membrane of bacteria and encouraging the migration of phagocytes into the area.

Humoral immunity is supported by cellular immunity, which is based on the action of *T cell* lymphocytes. Although T cells originate in the bone marrow, cellular immunity depends on normal function of the *thymus gland* during fetal development and the first few months of life, where T cells undergo "preprocessing." The cells are then transported to the lymph glands where they await detection of antigens, at which time vast quantities of specially sensitized lymphocytes are created. Like antibodies, the sensitized lymphocytes recognize and combine with their antigen and either destroy it directly or facilitate other forms of attack, as by attracting and activating phagocytes. Over a lifetime the body probably creates thousands of types of specialized antibodies and sensitized lymphocytes, each one designed to protect the organism against a particular antigen-labelled invader.

An important recent development is the discovery of a subpopulation of lymph-type cells known as *natural killer cells* (Herberman & Ortaldo, 1981). These cells have a natural affinity for several types of antigens that does not depend upon previous exposure. Natural killer cells spontaneously attack a variety of tumor cells; their action is rapidly facilitated by the hormone, *interferon*. Natural killer cells may be important in maintaining natural resistance against tumors, and, as discussed in chapter 3, they seem to help mediate the effects of stress on immunity, including a possible link between stress and cancer.

Since the body is under continuous invasion by potentially harmful agents and is constantly producing cancerous cells, our health is critically dependent on our immunological status. It is no exaggeration to observe that an infectious disease or malignant tumor can only become established in the body when there has been an immunological failure. As discussed in the next chapter, immune function is linked to stress in ways that are just beginning to be worked out. The relationship between stress and immunity is one of the most important, but least understood topics in health psychophysiology. Other immune problems of special interest are: (a) *allergies* including asthma, which are side effects of immunity; (b) *autoimmune diseases*, the loss of immune tolerance for ones own tissues, and the related problem of tissue rejection in organ transplantation; and (c) *acquired immune deficiency syndrome* (AIDS), loss of acquired immunity which is seen primarily in homosexual males.

Studying Immune Function

Immunologists have developed many useful procedures for assessing very specific aspects of immune function; most of these procedures are far too technical to introduce here. In this text, we are interested in more global measures that might reasonably be interpreted as indices of the general level of immune function, sometimes known as *immunocompetence*. However, given the complexity of the immune system, any single measure needs to be taken with a grain of salt.

Immunocompetence may be inferred indirectly. Examples are the speed of recovery from an infectious disease, such as mononucleosis, or the degree of resistance to agents to which we are exposed continuously, such as the herpes simplex virus, or the normal bacteria that inhabit the mouth. Failure to reject a foreign skin graft is a sign of suppressed immunity. Changes over time in reactions to standard skin tests, as the tuberculin skin test, may indicate fluctuations in immune function; certain tests for allergy can be interpreted in the same way.

Direct measurement of immune function may be used to assess specific aspects of immunocompetence. The level of antibodies and lymphocytes in the blood can be determined, as well as their ability to bind with antigens, and to execute some of their other normal functions. The rate of phagocytosis can be measured.

THE ENDOCRINE SYSTEM

Anatomy And Physiology

The endocrine system is an interdependent system of glands that produces chemicals called *hormones* and deposits them directly into the blood stream. The hormones are then transported to various parts of the body where they influence the function of their "target organs." Hormones are "informational molecules" (Strand, 1978) carrying specific instructions to their target organs. Although hormones are circulated indiscriminately in the blood, their actions are selective, because only their target organs have the right chemical receptors to "understand" the hormone, as in a lock-and-key arrangement.

The action of hormones was first demonstrated by Berthold in 1849 when he transplanted the testicle of a rooster into a capon and observed the development of a partial crest. News of this experiment led to the "monkey gland" craze, during which monkey testicles were implanted in men who wished to enhance their sex life (Strand, 1978). It was eventually noted that monkey testicles have no specific effect on the sexual performance of the human male.

The endocrine system reminds us that even on the biological level, a human is a highly integrated whole organism. In humans, the nervous system has the more important role in controlling immediate interactions with the environment. The endocrine system, because its actions depend on circulating chemicals, responds more slowly, although in a more prolonged way, in some cases sustaining the effect initiated by the nervous system. Integration is ensured since the endocrine system is regulated by the nervous system through the hypothalamus. However, the hypothalamus is also regulated by the endocrine system, the hypothalamus detecting and responding to the levels of circulating hormones. The integrated action of the nervous and endocrine systems is seen particularly in stress, which is discussed more fully in chapter 3.

Following, we survey briefly the endocrine glands, the hormones they produce, and the effects of these hormones on their target tissues.

Thyroid Gland

The *thyroid gland* is shaped like an H, the upright lobes flanking the trachea. The major thyroid hormone is *thyroxine*, which increases general metabolism, as reflected in the rate that carbohydrates are turned into energy, and extends wakefulness. Iodine is essential for production of thyroid hormones. During fetal growth, iodine deficiencies can lead to *cretinism*, a form of incomplete brain development; in adults, lack of iodine leads to enlargement of the thyroid gland, known as *goiter*. These conditions have become rare since it was discovered that adding iodine to salt effectively prevents thyroid deficits.

Parathyroid Glands

The four tiny *parathyroid glands* are situated just behind the thyroid gland in the neck. They secrete *parathyroid hormone* that controls the calcium level in the blood and extracellular fluid by taking calcium from the bones when it is needed by the fluids. The resting polarization of nerve fibers and contractile force of the heart muscle are influenced by calcium levels.

Pancreas

The *pancreas* is a large gland located just behind the stomach that secretes into the small intestine a number of enzymes necessary for proper digestion. The pancreas also produces the hormone *insulin* that regulates glucose metabolism. Insulin increases the rate of glucose transfer into the cells, lowering the concentration of glucose in the blood (*blood sugar*) and extracellular fluid. *Hypoglycemia* results if the glucose level drops too far. Conversely, too little insulin allows glucose to build up in the blood, which is the situation in *diabetes*, a condition that results when the pancreas does not produce enough insulin.

Ovaries and Testes

The *ovaries* and *testes* are the female and male sex glands, respectively. Each specializes in producing its own sex hormones, although both female and male sex glands produce small quantities of the opposite sex hormones.

The testes synthesize primarily *testosterone*, or androgen. Testosterone from the embryonic testes is necessary for development of the male reproductive tract in the fetus. Later, testosterone is responsible for the typical pattern of male secondary sexual characteristics such as deepened voice.

Testosterone accelerates protein synthesis in skeletal muscles, thereby increasing muscle mass, and is required for the production of complete sperms.

The ovaries produce *progesterone* and *estrogen*. Estrogen actually refers to several very slightly different hormones with apparently identical functions in directing female sexual development. Estrogen stimulates growth of the female reproductive system, development of female secondary sexual characteristics such as fat in the breast, and helps regulate the monthly female sexual cycle. Progesterone contributes little to female sexual development, but participates in regulating the female sexual cycle and prepares breasts to secrete milk.

Adrenal Glands

There are two *adrenal glands*, one atop each kidney. The inner portion of each adrenal gland is the *adrenal medulla*, which is composed of modified nerve cells and is considered part of the SNS. In response to SNS neural stimulation, the medulla liberates large amounts of epinephrine and smaller amounts of norepinephrine directly into the blood leaving the adrenals. The circulating epinephrine and norepinephrine intensify and prolong SNS effects.

The outer layer of the adrenal glands is the *adrenal cortex*, which is divided into several layers, each layer containing specialized cells that produce different hormones. *Mineralocorticoids* are one class, the most important member being *aldosterone*. The mineralocorticoids are important regulators of fluid balance and enhance inflammation.

Glucocorticoids are the second class of hormones produced in the adrenal cortex; *cortisol* is currently thought to be the most important of these. The glucocorticoids tend to inhibit inflammation, and help regulate the metabolism of glucose, fatty acids, other carbohydrates, and proteins. An extremely important function of the glucocorticoids is their modulating effect on the immune system.

Pituitary Gland

The *pituitary gland*, only about the size of a jelly bean, lies inside a bony depression beneath the brain. Its *anterior* and *posterior* lobes function quite independently. The posterior pituitary is connected directly to the hypothalamus by a short stalk of neural tissue. *Antidiuretic hormone*, or "vasopressin," is an important hormone secreted by the posterior pituitary. This hormone acts to prevent bodily fluids from becoming too concentrated by influencing kidney function. Since antidiuretic hormone increases fluid volume, it elevates blood pressure somewhat.

The hypothalamus secretes five or six "releasing" and "inhibiting" hormones that influence the anterior pituitary, and are the basis of an elaborate series of feedback loops by which the CNS and endocrine system coordinate their actions. An especially important releasing factor is the *corticotropic releasing hormone* (CRH), which causes the anterior pituitary to secrete *adrenocorticotropic hormone* (ACTH). ACTH is the chemical messenger that stimulates the adrenal cortex to release its hormones and, as discussed in chapter 3, is an essential element in the organism's integrated stress response. Among its other important hormones, the anterior pituitary produces *somatotropin*, which is the pituitary growth hormone, and *thyrotropin*, through which it regulates the thyroid gland.

Prostaglandins

Even though they are not always classed as hormones, the chemical messengers *prostaglandins* deserve mention because of their important, diverse effects as one of the most potent of all biological molecules. They are found in tiny amounts in almost all tissues, except in semen, where they are found in great concentrations. Different prostaglandins stimulate vasoconstriction and vasodilation, influencing blood pressure. They may regulate secretion and transport of hormones by altering local blood flow. Prostaglandins influence gastric secretions and fat metabolism. They participate in inflammation, inhibit the action of norepinephrine in the SNS, and are released following all sorts of trauma, suggesting that they are important in stress and relaxation. Aspirin may act by blocking prostaglandin synthesis. Prostaglandins readily stimulate uterine contraction, and are used to induce labor. They have been implicated in *dysmennhorea*, the pre-menstrual syndrome that affects some females. The presumed common mode of action that underlies these diverse effects of prostaglandins is unknown.

Studying Endocrine Function

Pathological processes that attack the endocrine glands can tell us something about the normal function of these glands in the same way that localized brain damage can help reveal the normal function of particular brain Areas. For example, in *Addison's disease* the adrenal cortex is destroyed. The devastating effects of the loss of the mineralocorticoids and glucocorticoids secreted by the adrenal cortex are evident and hormone replacement therapy must be undertaken immediately.

The activity of particular hormones can be monitored by using their known effects as an index—changes in blood glucose as a reflection of insulin action, or elevation in blood pressure as an estimate of antidiuretic hormone action. Obviously all other variables must be kept reasonably constant. Radioactive tracers can be used to estimate the rate at which labelled hormones accumulate in particular target organs. However, the most commonly used procedure to make inferences about endocrine function in humans is to assay the blood concentration of the hormones of interest.

3 Stress

THE CONCEPT OF STRESS

The contemporary notion of stress as it relates to health, dates only to 1936 when it was introduced by Hans Selye in a brief report entitled "A Syndrome Produced by Diverse Nocuous Agents," in the British scientific periodical, *Nature* (Selye, 1936). At the time, Selye was a young endocrinology researcher at McGill University in Canada. As is often the case with scientific discoveries, he had launched his investigations with something different in mind. His original purpose was to search for a new sex hormone. He experimented by injecting extracts of ovarian and placental tissues into rats to look for effects that could not be due to any sex hormones that had already been identified. He was elated to find that his first set of injections yielded just such a novel effect—enlargement of the adrenal cortex. Further study revealed that the adrenal enlargement was accompanied by atrophy (shrinking) of all the lymphatic structures, a diminished supply of lymphocytes to combat infection, and deep, bleeding stomach ulcers. Here he was, Selye reflected, only 28 years old and on the brink of discovering a new sex hormone!

This dream did not last long. When he continued his research he found that extracts from any organ whatsoever would produce the new syndrome—he was obviously not studying the effects of any sex hormone. When Selye discovered that he could get the physiological effects by injecting diluted Formalin, a chemical preservative, he gave up.

As the disappointed scientist pondered his apparently failed experiments, he happened to recall the first real patients he had ever seen examined; the incident had occurred during one of his second-year medical school courses (Selye, 1956). A distinguished professor had presented and examined a series of patients, all of whom were in the early stages of infectious diseases. The professor was absorbed in showing how one arrives at specific diagnoses, and as the demonstration progressed he enumerated an array of extremely subtle signs and symptoms of particular infectious diseases; these were to occupy the full attention of the student diagnosticians. In fact, Selye could discern none of these. Quite the opposite, Selye was impressed with how alike the patients were, as seen in obvious symptoms such as looking and feeling sick, a coated tongue, general aches and pains, loss of appetite, and so on. The professor had no interest in any of these. They were nonspecific and hence of no use to the diagnostician. The idea quickly became lost in the day to day routine of studying for exams. Now, as he looked back on his earlier experience as a student, he made a crucial connection—maybe the "syndrome of just being sick" and the physiological changes he had been seeing in his rats were really the same thing. Selye (1936) would conclude in his article:

> Experiments on rats show that if the organism is severely damaged by acute non-specific nocuous agents such as exposure to cold, surgical injury . . . excessive muscular exercise, or intoxications with sublethal doses of diverse drugs . . . a typical syndrome appears, the symptoms of which are independent of the nature of the damaging agent . . . and represent rather a response to damage as such. (p. 32)

Some of the consequences were immediately apparent. The unique effects of specific diseases must be superimposed on their common effects as stressors. Furthermore, it was possible that the consequences of stress might be every bit as debilitating and harmful to health, or even more so, than the specific effects of a disease. Selye was later to propose that a person can die from the stress of being sick.

Stress is used in this text to refer to a set of psychophysiological changes that are a consequence of certain factors at work in both the environment and the organism; stress is a response, a state of the organism. Among the contributing factors of stress are particular stimulus situations or environmental circumstances that have stress-eliciting properties; these we will call stressors or stress situations.

Unless there is a global nuclear war or accident, most of the readers of this text will die of stress-related disorders. Even so, it is a gross oversimplification to suggest that stress is bad per se. Performance of tasks— from reaction time, to taking an exam, to running 100 meters—can be facilitated by the right amount of stress (see chapter 10). Certain situations that are stressful, like working in a hospital emergency room or running for public office, can lead to personal growth. Amusement parks are able to sell tickets for rides on their rollercoasters because stress can be fun. There are stressors imbedded in the inevitable demands of just living. A full life is not possible without stress, as Selye indicated in dedicating his book, *The Stress of Life*, in part to "those who are not afraid to enjoy the stress of a full life" (Selye, 1956). Selye, himself, died at age 75 of a stress-related disorder, heart disease, in 1982.

INITIATION OF STRESS

Although the concept of stress is a recent innovation, the experience of stress is nothing new to the human species. Our distant ancestors could reasonably expect, on any given day, to encounter many threats to life and limb. Physical survival was precarious; any large boulder was liable to conceal a hungry saber-toothed tiger, or probably worse, a fellow human being ready to fight over possession of food, shelter, or sexual partners.

In contemporary technological societies, day to day existence is much more secure for most of us. Our stressors are primarily psychological, rather than physical. Ironically, this may be dangerous, and even fatal in the long run, for we respond psychophysiologically to a final examination as if it were a saber-toothed tiger. The high incidence of stress-related disorders in technological societies can be blamed partly on chronic elicitation of our "fight-or-flight reflex" in the absence of any subsequent physical activity to help return the participating physiological systems to balance (e.g., Carruthers, 1969).

A study of New York City residents indicates the kinds of stressors that persons in contemporary societies encounter regularly (Dohrenwend, Krasnoff, Askenasy, & Dohrenwend, 1978). The participants were asked to respond to the question "What was the last major event in your life that, for better or for worse, interrupted or changed your usual activities?". The 100 events that were mentioned most frequently fell into the 11 categories shown in Table 3.1.

Life Change

Not only are many significant stressors inevitable, but important life events like those in Table 3.1 can conspire to pile up within a relatively brief period of time. When this occurs—say, loss of a job, being arrested, getting married, inheriting a great sum of money from a distant relative, within a period of about a year—there is considerable evidence that the individual is at increased risk of illness (see Sarason, Levine, & Sarason,

TABLE 3.1
Sources of Life Change
(Dohrenwend, Krasnoff, Askenasy, & Dohrenwend, 1978)

Source	Example
School	Started school or a training program
Work	Changed job for a better one
Love and marriage	Became engaged
Having children	Became pregnant
Family	New person moved into the household
Residence	Moved to better residence
Crime and legal matters	Assaulted
Finances	Took out a mortgage
Social activities	Increased church or synagogue, club, or other organizational activities
Health	Physical health improved
Miscellaneous	Entered the Armed Services

1982, for a review). The accumulated sum of these stressors has been termed the individual's amount of *life change* (Holmes & Rahe, 1967).

The Schedule of Recent Experiences developed by Holmes and Rahe (1967) was the first, and has been the most widely used, instrument to assess life change. It is a self-report scale of 43 events that were culled from the life history charts of about 5,000 hospital patients in Seattle, Washington. Other subjects then rated how much readjustment each of the items would require, with "Marriage" used as an arbitrary anchoring point of 50 life change units. Thus, different items ended up worth particular numbers of points—"Death of spouse" was worth the most points (100), while "Christmas" yielded only 12. A person's life change score is the sum of the points for those events that have been experienced recently, usually within the past six months or one year.

There are some difficulties with the Schedule of Recent Experiences. A few items, such as "Change in work hours or conditions" or "Change in sleep habits," could just as easily be symptoms of illness rather than causes of illness. Also, this scale has no procedure for taking into account different appraisals (see the following) of a given situation. These and other problems have been addressed in later life change assessment devices. For example, the Life Experiences Survey (Sarason, Johnson, & Siegel, 1978) allows individuals to weigh each item according to its impact and generates separate positive and negative life change scores.

Although there is some debate regarding the best way to measure life change, it is agreed that when stressful life events pile up, the individual is at increased risk of many health problems (Sarason et al., 1982). Among other things, there is increased risk of sudden cardiac death; myocardial infarction; pregnancy and birth complications; miscellaneous chronic illnesses; childhood leukemia; menstrual discomfort; accidents, including bone fractures; psychological disorders such as schizophrenia and depression; and a host of minor health problems. Contrary to the view of Holmes and Rahe (1967), who emphasized the importance of change per se, more recent evidence suggests that events having negative impact on the person are much more important than positive life change events in elevating susceptibility to various health problems (Johnson & Sarason, 1979).

Appraisal and Stress

It is easy enough for anyone to recall a situation that has been personally stressful, such as getting stuck in traffic and missing a plane, experiencing a life-threatening illness, or failing miserably at something that was important. But it is surprisingly difficult to arrive at a rule that successfully specifies what kinds of circumstances are and are not stressful. Following are some illustrations: (a) a family subjected to the noise of living beneath an airport approach path versus the crowd at a night spot with music so loud it makes ripples on top of their drinks, (b) the pain of a marathon runner versus the pain of a toothache, (c) a person facing life-threatening surgery versus a skydiver who jumps out of airplanes for enjoyment, and (d) one gymnast in a championship meet, trembling and pale, versus another who is smiling, obviously enjoying herself. Not only are the situations that can be stressful quite diverse, but the same event might be stressful for one individual and not for another. Identical circumstances might be stressful on one occasion, but not on the next for the same individual.

The root of the problem is that *the stressful qualities of events reside, not in the events themselves, but in our perception of them.* More specifically, the actual effects of potential stressors are mediated by our *appraisal* of the situation, as we ask ourselves, sometimes implicitly, "Am I okay, or am I in trouble?" (Lazarus, 1966). For example, in chapter 7, we shall meet the type A individual, from whose perspective a casual pingpong game is yet another battle in which there will be a winner and a loser.

The most graphic illustrations of the potent effects of appraisal on stress are the cases of people who literally frighten themselves to death because they believe that they have been doomed by a fatal curse, usually brought on by some transgression. In his classic paper, "Voodoo Death," the physiologist Walter Cannon (1942) told of a Maori tribeswoman in New Zealand who had eaten some fruit only to discover that it had been picked in a tabooed place of great significance to her chief. She expected the offended spirit of her chief to kill her, and died within 24 hours. Cannon argued that this and many similar reported cases of voodoo death are real, but they do not require supernatural explanations. Later research suggests that voodoo death may be a special case of the more general "instantaneous cardiac death" phenomenon caused by lethal disruptions of the cardiac rhythm, often due to intense emotions (Engel, 1976).

Personality and Stress

We have already discussed one somewhat individualized determinant of the impact of a potentially stressful life event, the appraisal process. In general, the response to stressors is partly determined by the person's typical style of thinking, behaving, and responding emotionally—by personality characteristics. Depending upon one's personality, such events as giving a speech, driving on a freeway, or attending one's daughter's wedding may, or may not, be perceived as stressful. In addition to appraisal, several personality constructs have been implicated in mediating the initiation of stress.

Sensation Seeking

Sensation seeking is the degree to which the individual has a desire or need to seek out stimulation. A person whose hobby is rock climbing would be higher in sensation seeking than a person whose hobby is rock collecting, all other things being equal.

There is some evidence that only low sensation seekers experience extreme discomfort during periods of elevated life change (Smith, Johnson, & Sarason, 1978). High sensation seekers can undergo considerable life change, including negative life events, without much discomfort. It is not known whether these high sensation seekers are also immune to heightened risk of stress-related disorders following accelerated life change.

Type A Personality

Type A individuals interact with their environment in a way that exaggerates the impact of common stressors; they, in effect, manufacture their own stress situations. The hallmarks of the type A personality are chronic feelings of time urgency, excessive competitiveness, and diffuse hostility toward other individuals who get in their way (Friedman & Rosenman, 1974). Because of the special relationship between type A characteristics and coronary heart disease, this personality dimension is discussed in detail in chapter 7.

The Hardy Personality

Kobasa (1979) studied a large sample of middle and upper level executives at a large public utility company who had been experiencing high levels of stressful life events. Some of the executives had become ill, while the others had not. Various demographic variables did not distinguish between the individuals who did, and did not, get sick. Kobasa found that the two groups were differentiated by a constellation of personality variables that have been collectively labelled *hardiness*. The persons who were less vulnerable to stress, were characterized by: (a) control—they felt in control of what occurred in their lives, rather than helpless; (b) commitment—they had a sense of purpose that caused them to become actively involved in events; and (c) challenge—they perceived change, including potentially stressful life events, as part of the normal course of living, and an opportunity for growth, rather than a burden to be endured. Later research, including longitudinal studies (Kobasa, Maddi, & Kahn, 1982), has shown that the hardy personality diminishes the potentially negative impact of stressful life events.

Hardiness is a rather broad personality construct, which probably subsumes other variables such as sensation seeking, and locus of control. Also, each of the personality characteristics introduced previously probably affects stress responding, at least in part, by influencing the appraisal process.

THE STRESS RESPONSE

Cannon (1930) referred to the immediate physiological reaction to a stressor as the "fight-or-flight reflex." In doing so, he drew attention to the adaptive consequences of such physiological adjustments as increased blood pressure, elevated heart rate, and release of epinephrine in dealing with a behavioral emergency situation. Resources are mobilized for intense physical activity—to do battle or to flee. W. R. Hess (see Gloor, 1954) viewed the same set of responses a little differently, and designated them the *ergotropic reflex*, meaning roughly "moving in the direction of work," in order to emphasize that these responses increase energy expenditure. He also proposed that an opposing *trophotropic reflex* acts in the interest of energy conservation, returning systems to balance from their emergency status, and carrying out restorative physiological activities. Recent interest in self-regulation approaches to psychophysiological relaxation has rekindled interest in the trophotropic reflex, which Benson and his colleagues (Benson, Beary, & Carol, 1974) have renamed simply the *relaxation response*. This is an important topic in chapters 5 and 6, when we consider self-regulation methods of dealing with stress. In the present chapter, we are concerned primarily with the ergotropic or fight-or-flight reflex—the immediate physiological adjustment to a stressor.

The stress response includes two major physiological systems or axes—the *sympathetic-adrenal* and the *pituitary-adrenal*. Their organization and effects are summarized in Fig. 3.1 and discussed next.

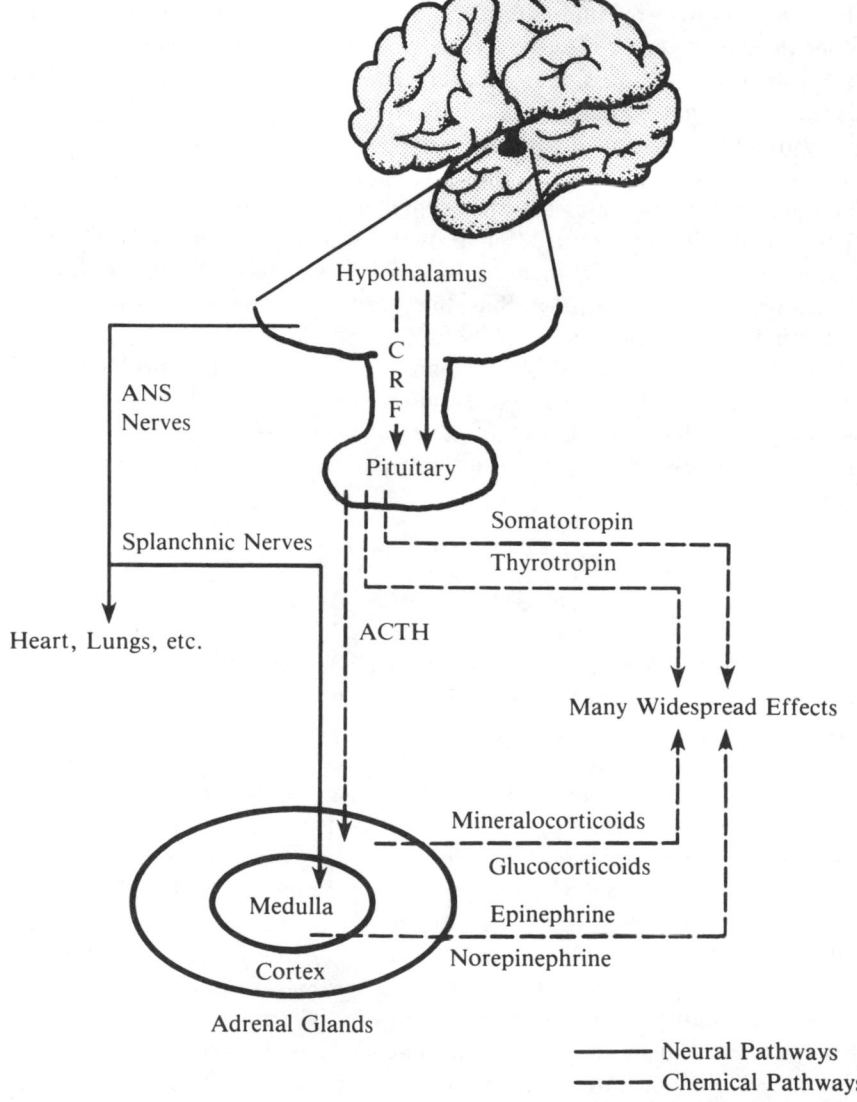

FIG. 3.1   Physiological mechanisms of the stress response. (Neural pathways constitute the sympathetic-adrenal axis; chemical pathways constitute the pituitary-adrenal axis.)

Sympathetic-Adrenal Axis

During stress there is "sympathetic activation"—a shift in autonomic nervous system (ANS) function toward greater sympathetic (SNS) relative to parasympathetic (PNS) action. To review (see chapter 2), sympathetic activation (e.g., speeding the heart rate) is initiated by the posterior areas of the hypothalamus; the anterior hypothalamus is capable of exerting the opposite effect (e.g., slowing the heart rate). These influences are transmitted directly to particular target organs via the various sympathetic and parasympathetic nerves (see Fig. 2.6). As a consequence, during stress a number of physiological functions regulated by the ANS are altered (see Table 2.1).

The most important aspects of sympathetic activation in stress are: (a) increased cardiac output and blood pressure; (b) inhibition of most digestive functions, including salivation (a dry mouth); (c) dilation of certain blood vessels and constriction of others, resulting in a redistribution of the blood supply so that less flows to the skin (cold hands and feet) and internal organs, except the heart and lungs, and more to the brain and skeletal muscles; (d) piloerection of body hairs (they stand up), and increased sweating; and (e) decreased lens accommodation for better distance viewing and enlargement of the pupillary opening.

In addition to the various SNS and PNS nerves that directly innervate their particular target organs, there is a second mechanism of sympathetic activation. This involves the *splanchnic nerves*, a set of SNS nerves supplying the adrenal medulla, the inner core of the adrenal gland. Nerve impulses in the splanchnic stimulate the adrenal medulla to secrete the hormones epinephrine (adrenaline) and norepinephrine (noradrenaline) into the blood stream, where they circulate throughout the body. Because these are the primary SNS neurotransmitters, the net effect is to intensify and prolong SNS activation whenever the adrenal medulla is stimulated via the splanchnics.

Cannon demonstrated the importance of this mechanism long ago in a clever experiment with a cat who was exposed to a barking dog for one minute, once in its normal state, and once when its adrenal medullas had been incapacitated (Cannon & Britton, 1927). Heart rate changes for both situations are shown in Fig. 3.2. When the adrenals were intact there was a large increase in heart rate which persisted long after the dog had been removed; in contrast, when the adrenals could not function, there was only a small and very brief heart rate response to the stressor. In general, SNS effects persist longer than PNS effects, mainly because of the mechanism just explained—there is no parallel mechanism for the PNS. Thus, it is physiologically easier to sustain the stress response than the relaxation response.

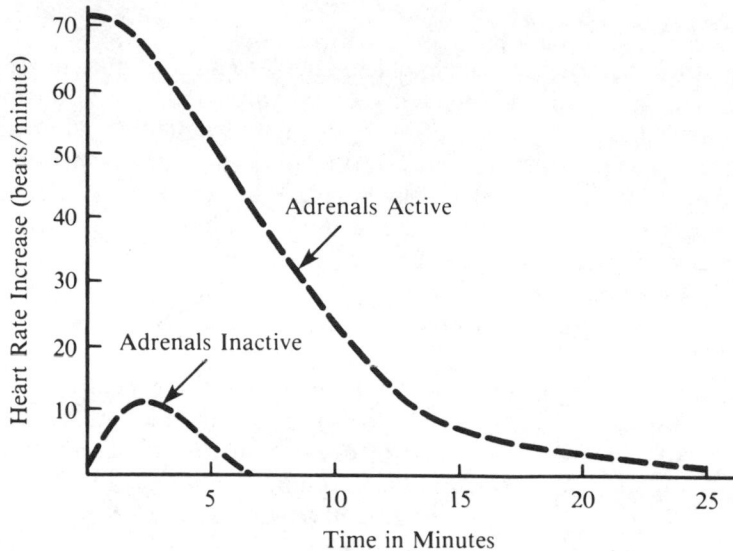

FIG. 3.2 Cannon's observations of the heart rate response of a cat, with and without functioning adrenal medullas, to a barking dog. Reprinted from *The Wisdom of the Body* by Walter B. Cannon, by permission of W.W. Norton & Co., Inc. Copyright 1932, renewed 1960 by Cornelia J. Cannon. Revised and enlarged edition copyright 1939 by Walter B. Cannon. Copyright renewed 1967.

Pituitary-Adrenal Axis

The hypothalamus controls the anterior pituitary via both neural pathways and chemical pathways, the latter in the form of small blood vessels into which the hypothalamus secretes several chemical releasing factors (see chapter 2). Each releasing factor causes the nearby pituitary to dispense a particular hormone into the blood stream where it circulates and eventually exerts a specific effect when the hormone reaches an endocrine gland that is sensitive to it.

The hypothalamus directs the pituitary to release several hormones in stress situations. One is somatotropin, the pituitary growth hormone, which, among other things, stimulates the growth of connective tissues, a useful effect in the event of damage to the organism during fighting or fleeing. Somatotropin also facilitates inflammation (another functional precaution should the organism suffer a wound with potential for infection), causes stored fats to become more readily available for metabolism into energy, and increases blood glucose. Too much somatotropin can result in diabetic conditions. Also, the anterior pituitary secretes thyrotropin, the thyroid stimulating hormone; in response, the thyroid glands produce thyroxine which increases metabolism, cardiac output, and blood pressure. Whereas these hormones are obviously important, the most critical hormone released by the pituitary in stress situations is adrenocorticotropic hormone (ACTH).

Acting as a chemical messenger, ACTH stimulates the outer layer of the adrenal glands—the adrenal cortex. The adrenal cortex then produces and releases corticosteroids. One class of these hormones is the mineralocorticoids, the major example being aldosterone. In addition to enhancing inflammation, the mineralocorticoids are important regulators of fluid balance due to their action on the kidneys. They cause more potassium to be lost in the urine, yet more sodium to be retained in the body. This creates a situation in which water builds up in the fluid outside the cells, due to osmosis. Extracellular fluid volume can increase as much as 20%. Eventually the kidneys may be damaged which further disturbs fluid balance, establishing a degenerating cyclic relationship. With increased fluid retention blood pressure is automatically elevated, because now there is a greater volume of blood that must circulate within a system of fixed capacity. This is obviously an undesirable situation if the person already has high blood pressure or impaired cardiac functioning.

Glucocorticoids are the second class of steroids produced in the adrenal cortex; cortisol is the most important of these. The glucocorticoids tend to decrease inflammation (hence cortisone is administered for severe allergic reactions such as asthma). The adaptive function of this inflammation suppression may lie in the fact that an extremely intense inflammation can be more harmful than the injury or disease that precipitated it; rheumatoid arthritis, is a good example of inflammation gone awry. The glucocorticoids have a second major set of functions insofar as they are centrally involved in regulating the metabolism of glucose, fatty acids, other carbohydrates, and proteins. Through a number of actions, release of cortisol by the adrenal cortex causes blood glucose concentrations to rise to levels as much as 50% above normal. Probably the most important role of the glucocorticoids in stress is their influence on the immune system, discussed later in this chapter.

Cholesterol and Stress

Cholesterol and Coronary Heart Disease

Both the sympathetico-adrenal and the pituitary-adrenal components of the stress response appear to contribute to the elevation of *cholesterol* in the blood during stress (see van Doornen & Orlebeke, 1982, for a review). Drugs blocking norepinephrine synapses inhibit the usual rise in cholesterol during stress, whereas the glucocorticoids have been implicated because of their role in fat mobilization. The importance of the stress-cholesterol connection is that *serum cholesterol*—the level of cholesterol found in the cell-free part of the blood, the serum—is a known risk factor in coronary heart disease (CHD), which is the leading cause of death in the United States. From pooling the results of eight independent studies, it has been estimated that individuals with levels of serum cholesterol within the upper 20% of the population have about 2.4 times the risk of CHD as those in the bottom 20% (Pooling Project Research Group, 1978).

In CHD, the coronary arteries, whose task it is to supply the heart muscle with oxygen-rich blood, have usually developed patches, or *plaques*, composed mostly of cholesterol. This process, *atherosclerosis*, restricts coronary blood flow and creates dangerous obstacles that can result in total plugging of the artery, like a fallen tree can eventually dam a stream as floating debris becomes enlodged in its branches. The extent of atherosclerosis found in the coronary arteries is positively related to serum cholesterol levels.

Given the association of serum cholesterol level and CHD, it is surprising to note that by weight about 0.3% of the human body is cholesterol (Guyton, 1982). Because of its patch-building properties, cholesterol is essential in maintaining the integrity of cell membranes and, when broken down chemically, it becomes one of the necessary building blocks in the formation of corticosteroids and sex hormones. Large amounts of cholesterol are found in foods that are high in animal fats, such as bacon and all dairy products, unless the fat has been somehow removed. However, 80% to 90% of the total cholesterol found in the body is actually manufactured inside the body, primarily by the liver. Furthermore, there is a feedback arrangement so that normally, as dietary cholesterol intake rises, manufacture of cholesterol in the liver is inhibited. As might be expected, given this homeostatic arrangement, several extensive studies have failed to obtain anything but a trivial relationship between diet and serum cholesterol when both variables have been assessed in large samples of adults in the United States (reviewed by Mann, 1977) and children (Weidman, Elveback, Nelson, Hodgson, & Ellefson, 1978).

Recent work in blood chemistry has clarified some details concerning the role of cholesterol in CHD. The cholesterol in serum is contained in small particles called lipoproteins, so called because they are mainly made up of fats and proteins. Cholesterol is concentrated primarily in *low density lipoprotein* particles, whereas high density lipoproteins contain much more protein and relatively little cholesterol (Guyton, 1982). Atherosclerosis and CHD are positively related to the level of low density lipoproteins, but negatively to the level of high density lipoproteins (e.g., Castelli, Abbott, & McNamara, 1983).

Effects of Stress on Serum Cholesterol

Effects of stress on serum cholesterol have been amply demonstrated. For example, numerous studies have reported elevations in serum cholesterol of about 10% to 20% in college and medical school students during final examination periods (e.g., Thomas & Murphy, 1958). One of the earliest investigations of stress and cholesterol involved tax accountants, whose job stress varied considerably from week to week and at different times of the year (Friedman, Rosenman, & Carrol, 1958). For 40 accountants in high responsibility positions, careful records were kept of diet, weight, exercise, work load, and any unusual stressors across six months. On a bi-weekly basis, the accountants rated their subjective stress level and had their blood sampled for serum cholesterol determinations. Among the interesting findings was that cholesterol in the blood peaked just before April 15, the federal income tax deadline. For 91% of the subjects, their highest serum cholesterol was recorded during their two-week period of highest subjective stress; similarly, 76% had their lowest cholesterol reading during their period of least experienced stress. Overall, cholesterol was 17% higher during the high stress periods as compared with the low stress periods. None of the other variables, such as diet, were systematically related to cholesterol. Fig. 3.3 shows the relationship between subjective stress and cholesterol level across time for one accountant. Notice the close correspondence between the top and bottom curves.

With regard to the question of diet, if the results of the study just presented are compared with investigations of the effects of dietary cholesterol, it can be concluded that a 70% increase in cholesterol intake

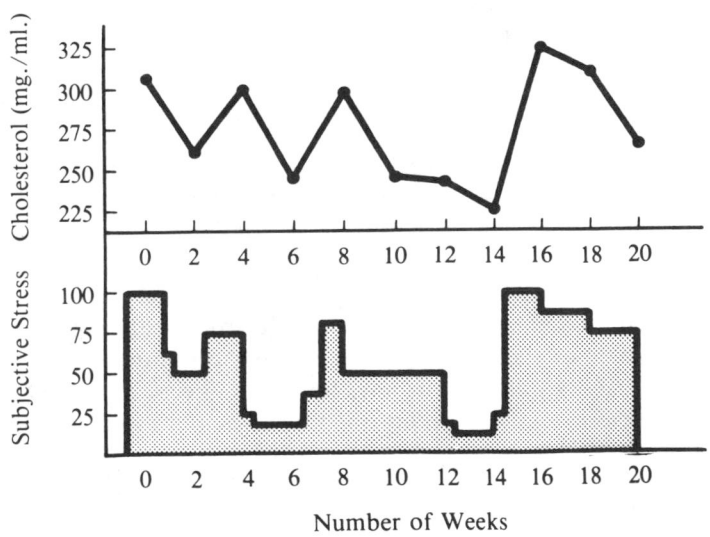

FIG. 3.3   Relationship between subjective stress and serum cholestrol level over time for an individual accountant. From "Changes in the Serum Cholesterol and Blood-Clotting Time in Men Subjected to Cyclic Variation in Occupational Stress" by M. Freidman et al., 1958, *Circulation, 17*, 858. Copyright 1958 by the American Heart Association. Adapted by permission.

would be required to match the fluctuations in serum cholesterol induced by stress (van Doornen & Orlebeke, 1982).

Individual Differences in Stress Responding

The concepts introduced by Cannon and Hess, discussed previously, are extremely valuable in understanding the integration, coordination, and adaptive functioning of the physiological response to emergencies. However, later research has revealed that, just as individuals differ psychologically in their response to stressors, they also differ physiologically.

Each of us tends to react across a range of stressful circumstances in a physiologically individualized way. This can be easily verified by asking a few friends how they personally recognize stress. Some will report that they get a queasy, unsettled feeling in their stomach (gastrointestinal responses); others may mention that their heart pounds or their hands get cold (cardiovascular responses); still others might comment primarily about tightness or pain in the muscles of their shoulders, neck, and forehead (skeletal muscle responses). Even though integration and coordination exists among response systems within the ANS, and between the CNS and endocrine system, there is ample room for physiological individualization. This phenomenon has gone under many labels, and will be called *individual response stereotypy* (Lacey & Lacey, 1958) here, meaning that a person responds to stressors in a physiologically stereotyped way—the response is individually unique, yet in a consistent manner. Each of us has our own stress signature.

Individual response stereotypy within the ANS has been examined experimentally. In one early investigation, Lacey and Lacey (1958) exposed subjects to four mild stressors: (a) mental arithmetic (multiplying a two-digit number by a one-digit number, then adding a one-digit number to the result, then on to the next problem); (b) a word fluency test; (c) a "cold pressor" test (submerging an arm in ice water); and (d) anticipation of the cold pressor test. Systolic blood pressure and diastolic blood pressure, palmar conductance (an electrodermal response), heart rate, variability in heart rate, and pulse pressure were recorded throughout. Fig. 3.4 shows the results for two subjects, expressed as their rank from highest to lowest among the 42 subjects for each physiological measure during each stressor.

These particular subjects demonstrate a high degree of stereotypy. Notice that Subject 32 is among the very highest responders for palmar conductance and pulse pressure to all of the tasks, but among the lowest for each task in heart rate variability. The marked ANS stereotypy shown in this figure is based on the absolute level of blood pressure, heart rate, and so forth, during the stressors. When just the change in response level

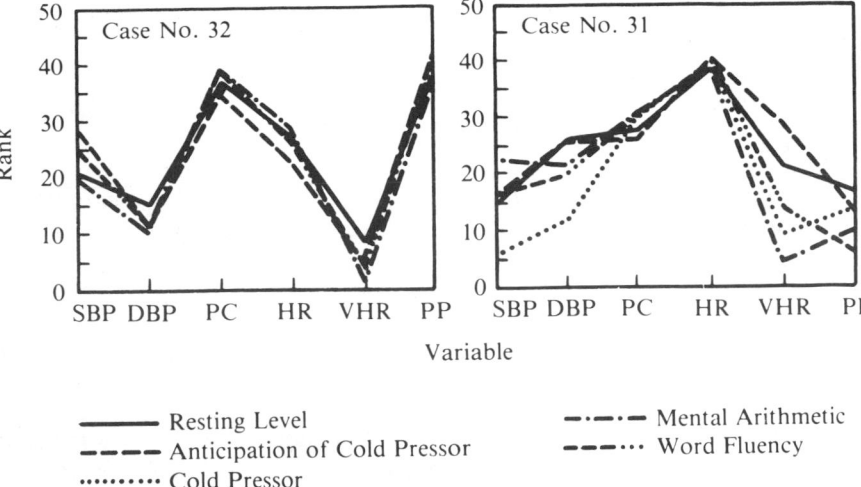

FIG. 3.4   Stress responses for two subjects showing individual response stereotypy. (SBP = systolic blood pressure; DBP = diastolic blood pressure; PC = palmar conductance; HR = heart rate; VHR = heart rate variability; PP = pulse pressure). From "Verification and Extension of the Principle of Autonomic Response Stereotypy" by J. I. Lacey and B. C. Lacey, 1958, *American Journal of Psychology, 71*, 60. Copyright 1958 by The University of Illinois Press. Adapted by permission.

from the onset of the stressor is used, the degree of response stereotypy is considerably lower (Lacey & Lacey, 1958). Some of their subjects did not show nearly as much stereotypy. This has been noted in other studies; Engel (1960) found statistically significant stereotypy in 8 of 20 normal subjects using similar methods. It appears that some individuals are more rigidly stereotyped in their stress responding than others.

Individual response stereotypy may be the key to explaining why a particular stress-related disorder develops in one individual and not another, when they appear to be in similarly stressful circumstances and use similar patterns of coping. Engel and Bickford (1961), using methods similar to those of Lacey and Lacey (1958), compared response stereotypy in hypertensive patients and normotensive individuals. The two groups were quite similar in many aspects of their physiological stress responding except for blood pressure. Blood pressure was the most reactive physiological response for 15 of the 20 hypertensives, whereas this was true for only 5 of the 20 normal subjects. Similarly, Moos and Engel (1962) found that hypertensives had greater blood pressure responses than did arthritic patients to mild stressors, but the arthritic patients had larger skeletal muscle responses near their symptomatic joints as compared to the hypertensives. It is possible that a specific physiological response that is hyperreactive to stressors is at increased risk of eventually developing into a stress-related disorder.

THEORIES OF STRESS AND ILLNESS

There have been many attempts to explain some of the connections between stress and illness. Four approaches to stress-related disorders are presented in this season. The theories introduced are sufficiently different in their emphasis that each may have some value in understanding the etiology of stress-related disorders.

General Adaptation Syndrome

The General Adaptation Syndrome (GAS) represents the organism's attempt to adapt physiologically to difficult circumstances. According to Selye (1936), the GAS progresses through three phases over time (see Fig. 3.5). The ordinate of Fig. 3.5 represents the ability of the organism to deal with stressors, including disease, on the physiological level. The lower the curve, the more susceptible the organism.

The first phase is the *alarm reaction*. This initial call to arms includes the hormonal and ANS adjustments that Cannon (1930) labelled the fight-or-flight reflex. Note that while the organism is physiologically occupied with the ongoing stressor, its resistance is decreased to any additional stressors that might be encountered. If the stress situation persists, the

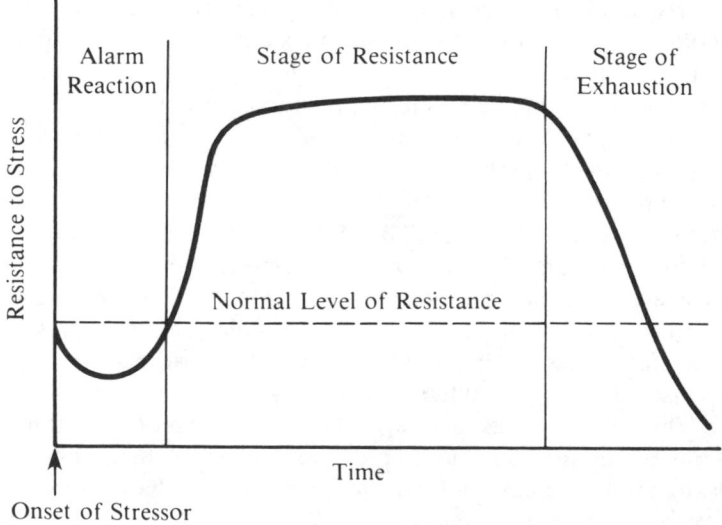

FIG. 3.5   Selye's general adaptation syndrome.

physiological responses of the alarm reaction will diminish, and the organism will pass into the *stage of resistance* or adaptation. The organism adapts to the sustained strain by creating a semblance of homeostasis in the continued presence of the stressor. Unfortunately, this requires some physiological acrobatics, some of which can be quite injurious; Selye sometimes called ulcers, essential hypertension, and other stress-related disorders, the diseases of adaptation for this reason.

During the stage of resistance, the ability of the organism to withstand stressful circumstances is heightened, but at a cost even beyond the diseases of adaptation. According to Selye, each of us has a finite supply of adaptive energy to expend on resistance to stress. If this is used up, resistance to stress gives out altogether and the organism enters the third and final phase—the *stage of exhaustion.* The pituitary and adrenal cortex lose their ability to secrete hormones and the organism is defenseless. Continued stress will lead to death.

Although the GAS is generally accepted as a plausible representation of the overall course of events during extended stress, the theory is not very specific, as Selye himself freely admitted. The remaining theories to be presented attempt to explain why a particular individual falls prey to a particular stress-related disorder.

Three-Factor Theory

Sternbach's (1966) Three-Factor theory can be expressed in the form of the simple and logical "If-Then" proposition shown in Table 3.2. All three factors must be present for a stress-related disorder to develop.

Preferred Stress Response

The first factor is the presence of individual response stereotypy, a concept that was introduced previously in this chapter. Persons with marked individual response stereotypy are said to have a *preferred stress*

TABLE 3.2
Sternbach's (1966) Three-Factor Theory

IF, an individual has:

1. A preferred stress response,

    AND

2. Frequent triggering of the stress response,

    AND

3. Homeostatic failure of the stress response,

    THEN The individual will experience a stress-related disorder.

---

response—"preferred" in the physiological sense, of course. Sternbach did not attempt to specify the origin of particular preferred stress responses; this is certainly an important research question. One possibility is some kind of hereditary predisposition or organ vulnerability. Others have speculated that learning may contribute.

It may seem highly implausible at first to suggest that one's preferred physiological response to stressors is in any way learned. However, consider Miller's (1969) argument and hypothetic example, based on the well-established phenomenon of reward learning in the ANS (see chapter 5):

> For example, supposed a child is terror-stricken at the thought of going to school in the morning because he is completely unprepared for an important examination. The strong fear elicits a variety of fluctuating autonomic symptoms, such as a queasy stomach at one time and pallor and faintness at another; at this point his mother, who is particularly concerned about cardiovascular symptoms, says, "You are sick and must stay home." The child feels a great relief from fear, and this reward should reinforce the cardiovascular responses producing pallor and faintness. If such experiences are repeated frequently enough, the child, theoretically, should learn to respond with that kind of symptom. Similarly, another child whose mother ignored the vasomotor responses but was particularly concerned by signs of gastric distress would learn the latter type of symptom. (p. 444)

If Miller's analysis is correct, it would provide an interesting non-genetic explanation as to why certain stress-related disorders tend to run in families. Perhaps parents who, themselves, suffer from particular symptoms are especially sensitive to the same symptoms in their children and inadvertently reward these symptoms.

Miller and Dworkin (1977) have gone on to suggest that individuals who cannot deal with stress situations psychologically may learn to minimize their impact through ANS learning. Although this may ameliorate stress in the short run, it may eventually lead to chronic disorders, such as high blood pressure, by disrupting the function of natural automatic regulatory mechanisms.

An important recent finding is that ANS response stereotypy increases with age (Garwood, Engel, & Capriotti, 1982). For men aged 30 to 80, the older the subjects, the more consistent were their physiological responses to a variety of stressors. The most distinct increase in ANS stereotypy was between the decades of age 40 to 49 and age 50 to 59. Assuming that a stereotyped or preferred response to stressors contributes to the etiology of stress-related disorders, these results may help explain the increased incidence of such health problems in older persons. This finding is quite compatible with the learning explanation of response stereotypy, although there are certainly plausible alternative explanations. Another interesting result was an age-related shift in which response systems were the most reactive. With increasing age, respiration and systolic blood pressure became more reactive, while heart rate and electodermal responding became less reactive.

Frequent Triggering

The second of the three necessary elements in the Three-Factor Theory is *frequent triggering* of the stress response. An environment that is particularly rich in potential stressors would contribute to frequent triggering—for example, a harried executive with great job responsibility, an unhappy marriage, and financial problems, who is living in a large metropolitan area requiring a long daily commute. Research linking life change and illness, discussed previously in this chapter, in a general way supports the contribution of frequent triggering to the stress-illness relationship. Triggering would depend on personality variables including the appraisal process. One important prediction of the theory, which has not been adequately tested, is that individuals without marked response stereotypy should be able to live in stressful environments, even with risk factors such as low hardiness, and not develop stress-related disorders.

Homeostatic Failure

Homeostatic failure completes Sternbach's Three-Factor triad of necessary elements. According to the theory, as long as an over-reactive physiological system is equipped with adequate homeostatic restraints, even when it is made to respond frequently, it will still return to baseline and there will be no stress-related disorder. However, a system with inadequate restraints will suffer homeostatic failure and remain elevated, or in a chronic fight-or-flight mode. At this point the misbehaving system becomes disordered, as in the chronically elevated blood pressure of essential hypertension.

The concept of homeostatic failure apparently originated in an old psychophysiological study comparing patients having severe chronic anxiety to normals drawn from the hospital staff (Malmo, Shagass, & Davis, 1950). As the subjects reclined quietly on a hospital bed, every so often a brief, but intense, 80db tone was delivered to them through earphones; the electromyogram (EMG) was measured from their forearm. As might be expected, both groups showed an abrupt EMG startle response to the tone. The response was even similar in magnitude for the two subject groups. However, for the normals, EMG returned quickly to the prestimulus baseline level; in contrast, the anxious individuals displayed further augmentation of EMG afterward and a very slow return to the baseline level.

Autonomic Balance

Eppinger and Hess (1910/1917) were the first to see, in the antagonistic effects of SNS and PNS influences on ANS functions, a basic principle that might underlie certain autonomic disorders. If normal function requires SNS/PNS balance, then a shift toward either SNS or PNS dominance would result in autonomic dysfunction.

A modern variation on this idea was introduced by Marion Wenger (1941) who proposed that individuals differ, one from another, in their characteristic SNS/PNS balance. In a randomly selected population there should exist a continuum ranging from individuals with marked SNS dominance (e.g., with cold, moist hands) to those who show extreme PNS dominance (e.g., with warm, dry hands). Most persons would fall somewhere in between. Wenger devised a standard method for assessing where a person fell along this continuum by taking the following measures of ANS responding: (a) dermographic persistence—the length of time a red mark persists on the forearm after the skin has been firmly stroked with a thin pencil-like object; (b) salivary output; (c) heart rate; (d) respiration rate; (e) electrodermal responding from the palm; (f) and forearm; and (g) pulse pressure—the difference between systolic and diastolic blood pressure. These measures were then weighted according to a complex formula and then combined to form an *autonomic balance* score. A score of 70 indicated an evenly balanced ANS, whereas scores above 70 reflected PNS dominance, and below 70, SNS dominance. Autonomic balance has been shown to be a relatively stable characteristic of the individual across time.

During World War II a total of 2112 aviation cadets were given Wenger's autonomic balance test battery as part of a program to develop predictors of success in flight school (see Wenger & Cullen, 1972, for a review). Twenty years later as many of the original subjects as could be located were sent a questionnaire that included questions about their health, including whether they had developed an assortment of ANS-related health problems. Table 3.3 shows the disorders that were reported, the number of respondents who indicated each of these health problems, and the mean autonomic balance score from 20 years earlier for each disorder group. Although the data are not perfectly orderly, there is a distinct relationship between the variables. The lowest autonomic balance scores are for subsequent health problems that we would associate with excess SNS activity, such as high blood pressure; the largest scores are for individuals who developed disorders characterized by too much PNS activity, such as low blood pressure. Thus, autonomic imbalance seemed to predispose certain subjects to particular types of health problems many years later.

TABLE 3.3
Original Autonomic Balance Scores of Men
Who Later Developed Various Disorders

Disorder	Number of Men	Mean Autonomic Balance Score
High blood pressure	23	64.74
Persistent anxiety	33	66.47
Apprehension or fear	49	65.80
Excessive sweating	52	67.30
Heart trouble	21	67.66
Hay fever	52	68.27
Stomach pains	63	68.53
Allergies	78	68.55
Migraine	15	68.99
Arthritis	28	69.74
Asthma	16	70.06
Peptic Ulcer	40	70.38
Low blood pressure	12	73.54
No disorders reported	111	68.22

Note. From "Studies of Autonomic Balance: A summary" by M. A. Wenger, 1966, *Psychophysiology, 2,* p. 184. Copyright 1966 by the Society for Psychophysiological Research. Adapted by permission.

Other results, and conceptual problems associated with them, complicate matters considerably (see Wenger & Cullen, 1972, for a discussion). Only about one-third of adults tested have a consistent SNS or PNS type pattern across the seven tests in the battery; the rest have a mixed pattern combining opposite responses such as rapid heart rate (SNS dominance) and high salivary output (PNS dominance).

Psychodynamic Approaches

Psychoanalytic Theory

It has been proposed that various psychophysiological disorders are caused by underlying psychodynamic conflicts. Perhaps the most influential of these approaches has been Alexander's (1950) psychoanalytic theory. According to Alexander, each psychophysiological disorder results from a different type of conflict. For example, individuals with ulcers are supposed to have suffered, as infants or children, from frustration of their dependency needs. This leads to repressed anger, which fuels a lifelong struggle to satisfy dependency needs through overcompensation, as seen in excessive striving for achievement. The underlying psychological tension creates stress, which leads to ulcers. Although psychological conflicts do seem to be common correlates of psychophysiological disorders, there has not been much success in tracing different disorders back to different types of early conflicts (Wittkower & Dudek, 1973).

Specific Attitude Hypothesis

Graham (1972) has developed a different psychodynamic approach to stress-related disorders. According to Graham, individuals have characteristic attitudes about salient events in their lives; we each have an attitudinal style toward the world that colors our emotional life. Many of these attitudes have unique patterns of physiological activity associated with them. These changes can lead to dysfunction in the respective physiological response systems. Therefore, according to this specific attitude hypothesis, individuals with different attitudes will be predisposed to different stress-related disorders. Altogether, 18 attitude by illness relationships were proposed by Graham (1972), a few of which are:

1. Essential hypertension: felt threatened with harm and had to be ready for anything.
2. Low backache: wanted to run away.
3. Raynaud's disease: wanted to take hostile gross motor action.
4. Hyperthyroidism: felt he might lose somebody or something he loved and took care of, and wanted to prevent loss of the loved person or object.
5. Urticaria (hives): felt he was taking a beating and was helpless to do anything about it. (p. 857)

Graham and his colleagues have marshalled some empirical support for the specific attitude hypothesis (summarized by Graham, 1972). One of their methods was to examine hospital admission interview records for evidence of specific attitudes and then look at the illnesses shown in the records. Several studies with suitable control for potential rater bias and expectations have obtained above chance correspondence between attitudes and predicted disorders. One of the most interesting ideas has been to hypnotize normal subjects, induce through suggestions the attitudes held to characterize a particular disorder, and then see if the predicted physiological changes occur. Graham, Stern, and Winokur (1958) suggested to hypnotized subjects the attitudes for hives and for Raynaud's disease (see chapter 8). These particular attitudes were chosen because hives is associated with increased peripheral blood flow, which was

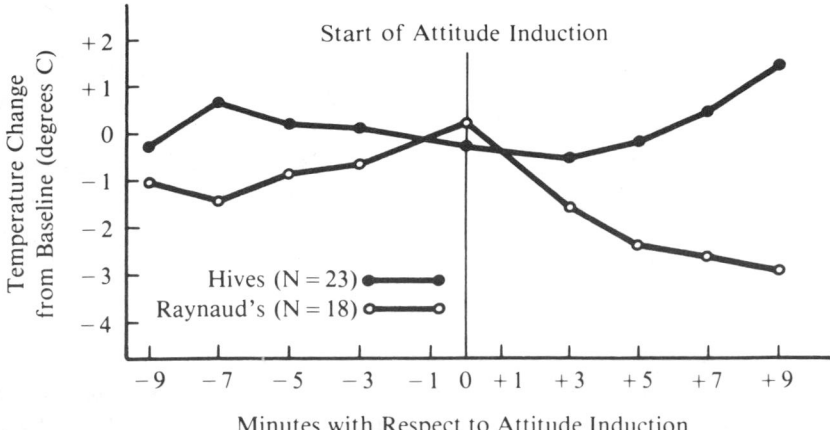

FIG. 3.6 Skin temperature changes in hypnotized subjects during suggested attitudes hypothesized to be associated with hives and Raynaud's disease. Reprinted by permission of Elsevier Science Publishing Co., Inc. from Experimental Investigation of the Specificity of Attitude Hypothesis in Psychosomatic Disease, by D. T. Graham et al. *Psychosomatic Medicine, 20,* 451. Copyright 1958 by The American Psychosomatic Society, Inc.

expected to be reflected in skin warming, whereas Raynaud's is accompanied by restricted peripheral circulation, hence skin cooling. The two attitudes were suggested in different 10-minute periods for the same subjects, with a brief break in between. The effects of the attitude inductions on skin temperature are shown in Fig. 3.6. The results supported the predictions.

STRESS AND IMMUNITY

The impact of stress is not confined to a single uniquely sensitive portion of the anatomy, nor is the route from stress to illness to be understood from a single set of psychophysiological concepts. In addition to the dysfunctions involving the ANS responses that participate directly in the stress response, there are other, less direct impairments as a consequence of stress. The most important, and currently least understood, link between stress and illness may be indirect, via the effects of stress on immunity. The function of the immune system is summarized in chapter 2.

Effects of Stress on the Immune System

Several converging lines of evidence indicate that high concentrations of corticosteroids disrupt normal immune system function in humans (Bassen, 1977). For example, there are cyclic changes across time in production of the major human glucocorticoid, cortisol. Early in the morning, when cortisol levels are typically highest, concentrations of lymphocytes in the blood are at their lowest. Experimental administration of a dose of corticosteroids results in an abrupt decrease in circulating lymphocytes followed by a gradual return to normal levels within 24 hours. Skin test reactions to an assortment of antigens are depressed for a period of about 24 hours after administration of corticosteroids. These and other studies indicate that it is mainly cellular immunity that is impaired by stress via corticosteroid release, although some impairment of humoral immunity has been noted, perhaps because T cells help regulate the function of B cells that are essential in the formation of antibodies.

Natural killer cell activity (see chapter 2) may be an important mediator of immunosuppression by stress in humans. In one investigation, blood samples were taken from volunteer first-year medical students during a low stress period in the middle of the term, and on the first day of their final examinations (Kiecolt-Glaser, Garner, Speicher, Penn, Holliday, & Glaser, 1984). The vigor with which natural killer cells in the blood samples attacked selected target cells was determined by a complex assay procedure. Life change scores were obtained, as well as scores on a scale of loneliness. The results are shown in Fig. 3.7. Killer cell activity

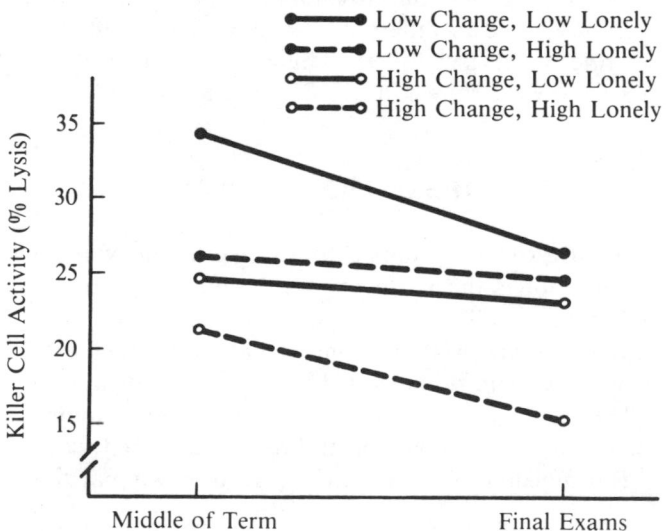

FIG. 3.7 Differences in natural killer cell activity between a low stress period and final exams in medical school students differing in life change and loneliness. Reprinted by permission of Elsevier Science Publishing Co., Inc. from Psychosocial Modifiers of Immunocompetence in Medical Students, by J. K. Kiecolt-Glaser et al. *Psychosomatic Medicine, 46,* 10. Copyright 1984 by the American Psychosomatic Society, Inc.

was suppressed significantly during final exams; students with high life change within the past year had significantly lower killer cell activity as did the most lonely students. As can be seen in Fig. 3.7, the effects were additive—the lowest natural killer cell activity was seen in the lonely, high life change students during finals.

Related studies have reported depressed natural killer cell and T-cell activity in high loneliness psychiatric patients as compared to patients who were less lonely (Kiecolt-Glaser et al., 1984). Among healthy undergraduates, those who had experienced high life change, but with few psychological symptoms, had higher natural killer cell activity as compared to students with high levels of both life change and psychological symptoms (Locke, Kraus, Leserman, Hurst, Heisel, & Williams, 1984). This suggests a positive relationship between successful coping and immune function. In this study, there was a negative relationship between killer cell activity and subjective symptoms such as anxiety and depression. Perhaps it is subjective distress, whether or not it is stress-related, that triggers immunosuppression.

Given the physiological data just summarized, it is not surprising that stress appears to increase the incidence and severity of certain infections (reviewed by Rogers, Dubey, & Reich, 1979). Many animal studies have shown increased susceptibility to various types of infections such as poliomyelitus virus, herpes simplex virus, and infection by tapeworms, following experimental stressors—physical crowding, painful electric shocks, high intensity sounds, or exposure to predators (even without any physical contact). Several studies with humans have found that the incidence of respiratory infections and strep throat are higher after stressful life events. Similarly, recovery from influenza and mononucleosis is slower when accompanied by heightened stress.

Stress and Cancer

A possible relationship between cancer and stress, mediated by the immune system, is the most important and controversial issue involving stress and immunology. According to the *immune surveillance theory* of cancer, cancer cells, which are always present in the body, do not normally proliferate and develop into tumors because they are detected and destroyed by the immune system. When the immune system is suppressed, the cancerous cells elude the immunosurveillance network and begin to grow unchecked, by which time it is too late for the immune system to defend against them. According to certain variations of the immune surveillance theory, stress is one of the factors that can suppress immunosurveillance. Various theories ascribe the immunological failure to different parts of the immune system, or even to the endocrine system via hormonal effects on cell division (Nandi, 1978). Because natural killer cells spontaneously attack cancer cells (Herberman & Ortaldo, 1981), and, as we have just seen, the activity of natural killer cells is suppressed by stress, it is a good possibility that these cells play an important role in immune surveillance against cancer and its possible suppression by stress. Regardless of the specific physiological mechanism, many theories, in one way or another, implicate psychosocial factors, including stress, in the etiology of cancer (Barofsky, 1981).

Research with animals (reviewed by Riley, 1981a) indicates that a variety of stressors can indeed lower the resistance of animals to the growth of cancer cells. Stress consistently accelerates the growth of tumors and shortens the life span of animals with experimental tumors. The effect appears to be due to enhanced corticosteroid production resulting in impaired cellular immunity.

Although the animal research is not without conflicting findings and methodological problems (reviewed by Riley, 1981b), difficulties are compounded in attempts to explore possible connections between stress and cancer in humans, because we are obviously limited to studying the association between naturally-occurring stressors and cancers. Two of the most serious and limiting methodological problems are: (a) establishing that the presumed cause (stress) preceded the onset of the cancer and not the other way around; and (b) in retrospective studies with patients who have already contracted cancer, making sure that their self-reports about earlier events, including stressful life events, are not influenced by their knowledge of their illness.

Increased incidence of cancer following catastrophic life events has been reported in some studies but not in others (see Morrison & Paffenbarger, 1981, for a review). One important negative finding resulted from an investigation in which United States mortality statistics were examined for the 20 leading causes of death. For persons who had been widowed, deaths from every cause were elevated, but the elevation in risk of cancer was relatively small as compared to the other causes of death (Kraus & Lilienfeld, 1959). Because of conflicting findings and the methodological limitations mentioned previously it is too early to make firm judgments about the role of stress in the onset of cancer in humans, even though the evidence from animal studies is highly suggestive.

If stress contributes to cancer in humans, then relaxation training may be a useful preventative measure, and/or may be beneficial for patients who already have cancer. Several self-regulation approaches based on meditation are discussed in chapter 6. Preliminary attempts to assess the effects of relaxation on immune function in normals are reviewed in chapter 10.

COPING DURING STRESS

Stress is seldom endured passively. We endeavor to deal with events—to fix the flat tire or study for the examination. If nothing else, we might search for the silver lining in a miserable set of circumstances. All of these are examples of *coping*, which includes all attempts, whether behavioral or cognitive, to deal with environmental and internal demands, including conflicts among these demands (Lazarus, 1981).

How we cope during stress is guided by our appraisal of the situation. One critical function of appraisal is the initial push it provides in the direction of either: (a) problem-focused coping—dealing directly with the problem that is producing the stress, or (b) emotion-focused coping—dealing with any associated emotional distress (Folkman & Lazarus, 1980). This process implies an appraisal of oneself in relation to the situation, and that this self-assessment, as well as the overall stress appraisal, will be influenced by many characteristics of the individual, such as presence of relevant problem solving skills, habitual defense mechanism, and other personality factors.

Problem-focused coping attempts to alter the stress situation—to solve the problem that is producing the stress. Studying for a difficult examination, or having a suspicious breast lump examined are examples of problem-focused coping. Emotion-focused coping is oriented toward dealing with oneself rather than environmental circumstances. Rather than studying for a big exam, the student might eat enormous quantities of ice cream, go on a clothes buying spree, or get drunk. Emotion-focused coping is not necessarily maladaptive or ineffective. For example, emotional coping is a critical task during a serious illness, and the outcome influences the recovery process. In the great majority of situations, most of us engage in both kinds of coping. Over a one-year period a large sample of middle-aged adults reported using both problem- and emotion-focused coping in 98% of 1,332 stressful experiences (Folkman & Lazarus, 1980).

The concepts of appraisal and coping are useful in analyzing such diverse situations as the potentially stressful qualities of the classroom for children, the work setting for adults, and the circumstances in which patients are given health care. Extended presentations of these problems can be found elsewhere (e.g., Cohen & Lazarus, 1979; Lazarus, 1966). The present discussion will be limited to two aspects of coping and stress that are particularly important and relevant: (a) the controllability of stressful events, and (b) the problem of coping with the stress associated with serious illness.

Controllability of Stressful Events

The controllability of stressful events is an extremely important determinant of the impact of these stressors. Specifically, uncontrollable aversive events have particularly debilitating effects (Seligman, 1975). Most of the research in this area has been done with lower animals, for ethical reasons, although related studies with humans have obtained parallel results. Pervin (1963), for example, found that college students preferred predictable over unpredictable painful electric shock, and preferred to administer the shocks to themselves, rather than having the experimenter deliver the shocks.

One of the most important animal studies required rats to experience painful shocks to their tail in two situations (Weiss, 1972). The avoidance rats had access to a lever which, if it was pressed in time, enabled them to avoid getting shocked, and, even if they pressed it after the shock had commenced, at least allowed them to terminate the shock. These rats had some control over the situation. The yoked rats had access to an identical lever, but it was not functional; they received shocks whenever the avoidance rats did. The yoked rats experienced the same shocks as the avoidance rats, but they had no control. A third group of rats were locked into the same apparatus for identical time periods because even being handled and confined in a small enclosure is somewhat stressful for a rat. The effect of these three experiences on the formation of stomach ulcers is shown at the left in Fig. 3.8. Having some control over the situation reduced the severity of the stress reponse as measured by the development of gastric ulcers.

Interestingly, the results were just the opposite if the avoidance rats were required to cope with a more difficult set of circumstances (see the right section of Fig. 3.8). Here, the set-up was as before, but now a lever-press, in addition to avoiding a rather lengthy shock, also *delivered* a brief immediate shock to the animal. Forced to confront this conflict repeatedly, the avoidance rats developed severe ulcer conditions, even though, like the original avoidance rats, they had some control over the situation.

Joseph Brady (1958) reported a similar phenomenon in his famous study of "executive" monkeys. The arrangement was similar to Weiss's (1972), in that the executive monkeys had access to a lever that could be used for shock avoidance, whereas the yoked control monkeys experienced the same shocks as the executive monkeys. The executive monkeys suffered the most ulcers. Brady believed that these results illustrated the

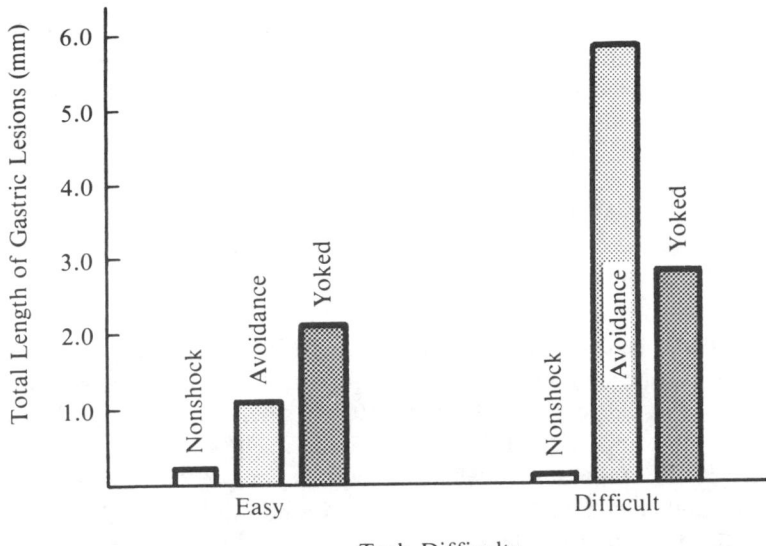

FIG. 3.8 Stomach ulcers in rats following difficult versus easy tasks in Nonshock, Avoidance, and Yoked conditions. From "Psychological Factors in Stress and Disease" by J. M. Weiss, 1972, *Scientific American, 226*, 108, 112. Copyright 1972 by W. H. Freeman and Company. Adapted by permission.

stressful effects of great responsibility, where responsibility is defined as having to respond in difficult circumstances, which seems reasonable enough. Later research indicated that the executive monkey phenomenon depended on a particular temporal arrangement of working days and time off, however, the important point is that it is another example of a situation whose potential controllability only makes matters worse. The problem for Brady's executive monkeys was that they had no warning signal to tell them when it was time to respond. A shock was scheduled every 17 seconds, but was cancelled if the monkey pressed the lever during that time period. Although they could avoid shock altogether, they had to keep track of time continuously to do so. The pressure never let up.

Several phenomena in this area appear to be consistent with an interesting idea known as the *safety-signal hypothesis* (Seligman & Binik, 1977). Typically, unpredictable aversive events are more debilitating than predictable ones—the physiological evidence of stress is greater, and both lower animals and humans usually prefer signalled over unsignalled aversive events, if given a choice (reviewed by Abbott, Schoen & Badia, 1984). According to the safety-signal hypothesis, this is because, when aversive events are signalled, the organism can predict when they will not occur;

any time that the warning signal is absent is, by definition, a safe period. The organism can relax.

How would the safety-signal hypothesis apply to the question of controllability? In some circumstances, due to the demands of the situation and the organism's capabilities, the organism is able to create safe periods by virtue of its own responses. The avoidance rats in Weiss's (1972) first experiment would be an example. In these situations, controllability should reduce stressfulness. However, controllability will not defuse the potential stressfulness of aversive events when responding does not create safe periods because either: (a) the situation is too difficult for the aversive events to be controlled adequately, as in Weiss's (1972) second experiment; or (b) the situation is such that the organism must respond continuously, as was the case in Brady's (1958) experiment. In the latter circumstances, it appears that the act of coping itself is stressful.

There are important behavioral effects of uncontrollable aversive events. Overmier and Seligman (1967) found that dogs who had been exposed to uncontrollable shocks did not make escape or avoidance responses to shock later, when they had the opportunity to do so; instead these dogs tended to just lie down in the experimental apparatus and endure the shocks, even when all they had to do to escape the situation was jump over a small barrier. This is the *learned helplessness* phenomenon, which has been demonstrated since in many species, including humans (Seligman, 1975). Learned helplessness results when either aversive events are intrinsically uncontrollable or when the individual lacks the capacity to execute the necessary problem-focused coping responses. Learned helplessness is often accompanied by depression, and it has been proposed that this may explain why extended stress sometimes leads to depression in humans (Abramson, Seligman, & Teasdale, 1978).

In summary, if the organism can control stressful events via effective coping responses that are not themselves excessively demanding, then the act of control buffers the organism against the potentially stressful qualities of the situation. The potential for control does not automatically defuse stress. The act of coping can be stressful. Brady's monkeys and humans who, from day to day, feel that they have no respite from their perceived responsibilities are in such a dilemma. Behavioral studies suggest that a steady diet of stressful experiences, with which one cannot cope, leads to giving up, helpless behavior in the face of future stressors, and possibly depression. If the safety-signal hypothesis is correct, it is important for individuals in chronically high-stress circumstances to have regular safe periods, perhaps daily periods of psychophysiological relaxation.

Coping With Illness

Becoming ill and being treated can be highly stressful. The daily routine of the person is drastically rearranged, new and possibly very serious threats to the physical and psychological well-being of the patient are introduced, and the future is uncertain. Coping with the emotional distress caused by these and other stressors is a critical aspect of recovery. Individuals differ in their psychological responses to illness and treatment, and these responses can differentially facilitate or interfere with recovery.

Practitioners generally recognize that psychological factors in the patient can maintain illness in the face of treatment that should be effective. However, there is very little detailed practical knowledge about how to minimize the negative effects of coping on illness, and possibly recruit the coping process as a positive force in healing. Useful working procedures are limited to general practices such as conducting surgery first thing in the morning for anxious patients thereby shortening the period of pre-surgical distress. Many complex issues remain. For example, consider screening programs that identify individuals who are at increased risk of early CHD. Giving the person this knowledge, in itself, is a potential stressor, and could possibly accelerate the course of the disorder if the patient does not cope effectively with this threatening information (Horowitz et al., 1983).

The meaning of a significant threat to health can vary considerably from patient to patient (Lipowski, 1970). Different patients can view the same health problem as a challenge to be met, a form of punishment, as an opportunity for personal growth, an event signifying irreparable loss or damage to themselves, or even as a welcome chance to escape from pressing responsibilities. The impact of these various interpretations of illness on recovery has not been assessed systematically, although it seems likely that alternate interpretations would result in different approaches to emotional coping. For example, the patient who greets an illness with relief may obtain secondary gains from being sick that may sustain the illness, but at the same time the patient may not experience much anxiety in connection with physical symptoms.

Byrne (1964) and others have maintained that there are two fundamentally different ways of psychologically coping with threat. One defense, *repression,* is characterized by denying the importance of the threat and trying not to think about it. The opposite, *sensitization,* involves obtaining as much information as possible about the situation, attempting to minimize uncertainty and eliminate ambiguity; however, in doing so the individual probably displays considerable anxiety. Lipowski (1970) has applied similar concepts to the health setting. One patient may engage in *minimization*, in which symptoms are ignored or rationalized, the seriousness of the illness is minimized, and the person tries to carry on as if nothing were the matter. Another patient may employ *vigilant focusing*, that is, trying to find out as much as possible about etiology and prognosis, and attending closely to symptoms.

There is no simple relationship between these and other coping methods and illness. Whereas denial can have disastrous consequences, such as when it delays cancer diagnosis and treatment, it is true that denial reduces the subjective distress of disease and possible death. Vigilant focusing may result in better compliance to treatment and more active participation by the patient in the healing process, but there is some evidence that patients who most actively seek out information about their impending surgery experience the highest incidence of post-operative complications (reviewed by Cohen & Lazarus, 1979). The kinds of stressors facing the patient vary at different stages of illness and treatment, demanding different coping strategies (Moos, 1982).

4 Pain

The "Anzio Effect" refers to striking observations made by Henry Beecher as he treated battlefield casualties at the Anzio Beachhead during World War II (Beecher, 1956). Most of the seriously wounded soldiers whom he examined experienced little or no pain as revealed through systematic questioning; only 32% of the men requested medication to relieve pain. They appeared to be thinking clearly and showed no signs of shock. Later, Beecher conducted a comparative survey using a sample of male surgery patients, carefully selected to match the soldiers in terms of severity and location of tissue damage. Most of them complained of great pain, and 83% requested medication. Beecher believed that the explanation could be found in the very different meanings of these two kinds of bodily injury. The civilians experienced their surgery as a depressing, threatening, even catastrophic event. In contrast, the wounded soldiers had escaped with their lives from an extremely dangerous battlefield. They experienced relief and thankfulness for their wounds. It was as if, since their wounds were a good thing, they did not hurt.

The Anzio Effect illustrates dramatically the weak and highly flexible connection between tissue damage and pain. This can also be seen in certain fascinating cultural practices. The Basques of the Pyrenees are said to have followed a custom in which a pregnant woman would work until the moment of childbirth. Following delivery, she was expected to return immediately to her duties. In the meantime, the father remained in bed to gather his strength from the ordeal (Kroeber, 1948). *Bagad*, or "hook-swinging," may still be practiced in remote areas of India. Once a year, an honored villager is suspended from a long post by hooks put through the skin of his lower back (Kosambi, 1967). He is then carried around the village and swung a specified number of times to bless the fields and all

99

babies born since the last celebration. An observing anthropologist reported that the " . . . celebrant was in a state of exultation and showed no trace of pain" (Kosambi, 1967, p. 111).

A related phenomenon is the powerful effect of placebo on pain. Approximately 35% of patients obtain satisfactory relief from severe post-operative pain when they are given a neutral agent they believe will help them (Beecher, 1959). Similarly, hypnotic analgesia exploits the loose relationship between body tissue injury and the experience of pain. Hypnosis is now used extensively to help manage pain, especially in surgery, childbirth, and dentistry. Hypnotic analgesia and placebo are of great significance in the psychophysiology of pain.

Unfortunately, psychological forces contribute just as actively to the manufacture of pain as to the mitigation of it. In fact, the most vexing clinical problem with pain is that it is so frequently experienced long after the initiating organic problem has healed. This is regularly the case with back pain. In the United States each year about 1.25 million persons experience back injuries, and about 65,000 individuals suffer permanent partial or complete disability due primarily to continuing pain (Beals & Hickman, 1972). However, in most cases of chronic back pain there is no lingering neurological or other physical damage; the hundreds of thousands of low back surgeries performed yearly yield meager lasting pain relief. Models incorporating psychological factors have been proposed to account for chronic low back pain (reviewed by Turk & Flor, 1984).

Until recently there was little agreement on where the pain phenomena just described might best fit into the "puzzle of pain" (Melzack, 1973). Instead, an uneasy dichotomy was maintained between "real" physical or organic pain and "imaginary" psychogenic or functional pain. This awkward opposition had unfortunate consequences, both for those from whom effective treatments, such as hypnosis, were withheld (because their pain was "real"), and for those who, following a diagnosis of psychogenic pain, were treated as "mental cases", since their pain was "only in their head." The psycho/physiological bisection of pain has given way to the more reasonable view that every instance of pain is an intrinsically psychophysiological event.

PSYCHOPHYSIOLOGICAL BASIS OF PAIN

Anatomical Structures

The detection and processing of noxious stimuli are not completely understood. *Free nerve endings*—undifferentiated bush-like dendritic processes—are thought to be the primary detectors, and are typically considered to be pain receptors. They are distributed throughout the skin and deep within the body. A serious difficulty with the pain receptor concept is that pain does not result from a single kind of physical stimulus in the way that vision is the result of light falling on the rods and cones. If there are specialized pain receptors, what are they specialized to detect?

Guyton (1982) has summarized the current neurophysiological understanding of pain. Sensory fibers are classed according to anatomical features and designated by an English alphabetical character with a Greek letter subscript in the case of subclassifications. Information about noxious stimulation is carried into the spinal cord primarily by two types of neurons with different speeds of neural conduction. Small, myelinated *A-delta fibers* conduct nerve impulses rapidly, on the order of 6 to 30 meters per second. These fibers seem to transmit pricking-type pain that is subject to rapid adaptation, for example the initial sharp pain of an incision or needle penetration. Slow burning/aching pain qualities are conducted by small, unmyelinated *C fibers* with a slower neural conduction rate of only 0.5 to 2 meters per second. This type of pain not only fails to adapt, but increases in intensity with time, a pain phenomenon known as *temporal summation*. This helps explain the intolerable quality of extended pain. The major pain conducting fibers enter the spinal cord from the rear, passing into the *dorsal roots*, the A-delta and C fibers terminating in different spinal layers. At this point, within the *substantia gelatinosa*, there is a network of short inter-connecting neurons in the pathways, after which long fibers originate that cross to the front of the cord, and run up to the brain via the *spinothalamic pathway*.

Many of the ascending fibers terminate at synapses in the brainstem, including throughout the reticular activating system, which accounts for the arousing and alerting effects of pain, and interference with sleep. Other spinothalamic fibers terminate within the thalamus, a brain structure that participates in processing many types of sensory information. In the case of the pricking pain system, there are projections from the thalamus to the somatosensory area of the cerebral cortex, which is responsible more for the localization of pain than for the simple detection of it. The somatosensory cortex does not seem to participate in burning/aching pain, which may explain why this type of pain is poorly localized.

Modulation of Pain

The great 17th century French mathematician and philosopher, René Descartes, proposed an explanation of reflexive behavior that includes a theory of pain that is a useful point of departure (see Fig. 4.1). A noxious stimulus (the flames) excites pain pathways that conduct messages to the brain where the actual pain experience is created. The brain sends back messages causing withdrawal of the burned foot. Descartes believed that peripheral sensory information about noxious stimulation is communi-

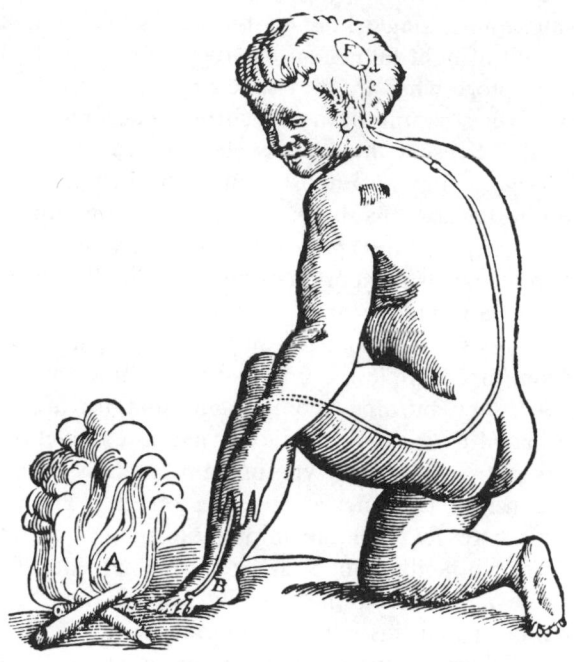

FIG. 4.1 Descartes' 17th century theory of pain perception. From *Treatise of Man* (p. 35) by R. Descartes (T. S. Hall, Trans.), 1972, Cambridge, MA: Harvard University Press. (Original work published 1665)

cated directly and faithfully to the brain. It is now understood that pain is processed in a much more complicated way so that incoming potential pain information is subject to alteration or *modulation*, beginning at the spinal level.

Two major developments have led to the appreciation of psychophysiological pain modulation and its implications for pain control: (a) the *gate-control theory* of pain (Melzack & Wall, 1965); and (b) the discovery of natural pain modulating substances, the endorphins, in the human brain.

Gate-Control Theory

According to the gate-control theory:

> . . . a neural mechanism in the dorsal horns of the spinal cord acts like a gate which can increase or decrease the flow of nerve impulses from peripheral fibres to the central nervous system. Somatic input is therefore subjected to the modulating influence of the gate before it evokes pain percep-

tion and response. The degree to which the gate increases or decreases sensory transmission is determined by the relative activity in large-diameter (A-beta) and small diameter (A-delta and C) fibres and by descending influences from the brain. When the amount of information that passes through the gate exceeds a critical level, it activates the neural areas responsible for pain experience and response. (Melzack, 1973, p. 153)

This model of pain is shown schematically in Fig. 4.2.

At the level of the spine, large (L) and small (S) diameter neural fibers project both to transmission cells (T) that relay pain messages to the brain, and to cells in the *substantia gelatinosa* which exert an inhibitory influence on the transmission cells when stimulated by large-diameter fibers. "Central control" indicates the influence of descending messages from the brain, which can also inhibit the transmission cells, and block pain. This mechanism explains pain modulation by psychological factors such as expectations and attitudes, and diminution of pain by placebo. The "action system" refers to the actual experience of pain, and pain responses.

The opposing fiber feature of the theory suggests that peripheral stimulation that selectively activates large sensory fibers should block pain. This prediction has kindled interest in electrical nerve stimulation as a method to control clinical pain. The gate-control theory has also been used to explain *phantom limb pain* in amputees. Most amputees experi-

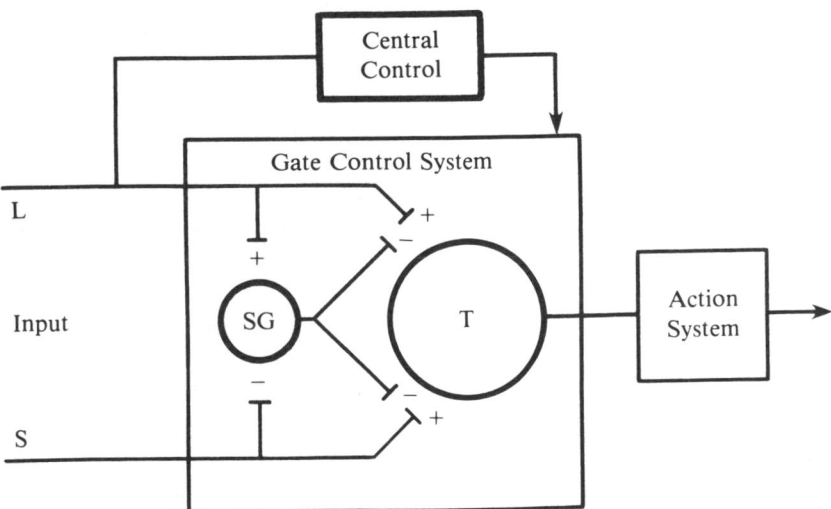

FIG. 4.2 The gate-control theory of pain. From "Pain Mechanisms: A New Theory" by R. Melzack and P. Wall, 1965, *Science, 150*, 975. Copyright 1965 by the American Association for the Advancement of Science. Reprinted by permission.

ence their absent limb as if it were still present, with the full range of sensations, even including movement. Gradually, the phantom limb seems to recede into the stump. Unfortunately, about 5% to 10% of amputees experience intractable pain in their phantom limb that may intensify rather than diminish with time (Melzack, 1973). According to the gate-control theory, this pain is caused by loss of inhibitory input from large diameter fibers in the amputated limb, coupled with the tendency of small diameter fibers to regrow into the stump.

The gate-control theory cannot be considered a detailed account of pain modulation, but the basic features of the theory—a spinal pain modulator influenced by both peripheral stimulation and a descending path from the brain—are well-supported by evidence. As a general framework, the theory represents a highly successful integration of important psychological and neurological aspects of pain.

Chemistry of Pain Modulation

The analgesic properties of opiates have been known for centuries. The *narcotic analgesics*—particularly morphine, codeine, and the synthetic opiate trade-named Demerol—are the most potent pharmacological pain killers in common use, yet their mechanism of action was unknown until the 1970s.

The chemical action of opiates was known to be extremely specific. Drugs with only slightly different chemical structure have no analgesic properties. Therefore, it was proposed in the 1960s that there must be specific opiate receptors in the human brain that cause some neurons to respond only to opiate-like chemicals. In 1973, several research groups at different universities announced, at about the same time, that they had found the suspected opiate-sensitive neurons (e.g., Pert & Snyder, 1973). They were located throughout the brain but were densely concentrated in a few regions, especially the brainstem. Now that the opiate receptors were known to exist, the search was on for naturally-occurring chemicals within the brain to which these neurons were responsive. The existence of such substances seemed inevitable—otherwise the opiate receptors would be locks without keys, an unlikely evolutionary circumstance.

Within two years, a family of opiate-like brain-produced chemicals had been identified (Barchas, Akil, Elliott, Holman, & Watson, 1978), which were eventually named the "endogenous morphines," or endorphins, for short (Hughes et al., 1975). Different types of endorphins are chemically distinguishable, including the *enkephalins*, meaning, literally, "in the head." It is believed that narcotic analgesics such as morphine inhibit pain because they resemble the brain's own endorphins sufficiently to mimic their action. Several lines of evidence support the idea that endorphins and endorphin-modulated neural circuits participate in pain inhibition, as summarized by Akil and Watson (1980): (a) administration of endorphins produces analgesia; (b) some chronic pain patients show decreased levels of endorphins in their cerebrospinal fluid; (c) electrical stimulation that causes analgesia also causes release of endorphins; and (d) naloxone, which chemically blocks opiates by occupying their receptor sites, interferes with many types of analgesia. Consistent with the gate-control theory, one consistent locus of action for endorphins is the substantia gelatinosa, indicating that the spinal gate is an endorphin-modulated circuit (Basbaum, 1980).

Endorphins do not typically function as neurotransmitters; that is, they are not released into the synaptic cleft as chemical messages from one neuron to another. Rather, because of their slow build-up and breakdown (among other reasons) they are thought to be neuromodulators—substances whose release in the area of the synapse produces rather extended facilitation or inhibition of the normal activity of that synapse (see chapter 2). Some endorphins probably circulate widely, functioning as hormones to influence distant parts of the body.

It is generally agreed that there are additional pain inhibitory mechanisms beyond the known endorphin circuits of the brainstem and spinal cord. One of the first neurotransmitters identified, Substance P, appears to be an important neurotransmitter in spinal pain pathways (Jessell, 1982). In addition, some forms of analgesia still operate when endorphins have been chemically blocked, indicating that there must be non-opiate pain modulation systems. In the brain, serotonin synapses participate in pain control, and must interact with endorphin circuits, because morphine analgesia depends on serotonin (Besson, 1980).

The physiological basis of non-drug analgesia will be taken up at the end of the chapter, following a survey of some important non-pharmacological alternatives in pain control—placebo, behavior therapy, acupuncture, electrical nerve stimulation, hypnosis, and multidisiplinary pain centers.

CONTROL OF CLINICAL PAIN

Placebo

Placebo as Treatment

In the early 19th century Trousseau is said to have advised his medical colleagues to "treat as many patients as possible with the new drugs while they have the power to heal." This practical wisdom suggests that the curative effects of chemical agents is not limited to their specific pharmacological properties. One might hope so, given the bizarre (to the contemporary observer) substances that have been administered over the years—such things as unicorn horns, crocodile sperm, lizard blood, fly dung, powdered mummy, and eunuch fat (Shapiro, 1960). Among the procedures that have been standard practice at one time or another are "purging, puking, cutting, cupping, blistering, bleeding, freezing, heating, sweating, and shocking" (Shapiro, 1960, p. 112). That healing practices and the healers themselves have been highly respected and honored throughout medical history is a ringing testimonial to the power of placebo.

Placebo has been defined as "the psychological, physiological, or psychophysiological effect of any medication or procedure given with therapeutic intent, which is independent of or minimally related to the pharmacological effect of the medication or to the specific effects of the procedure, and which operates through a psychological mechanism" (Shapiro, 1960, p. 109). The term is derived from the Latin verb "to please" and means, literally "I shall please."

Any treatment is delivered with a message, either explicitly stated by the practitioner or implicitly suggested—that it *will heal*. Placebo effects are not limited to transparently bizarre treatment methods, nor to health conditions with evident and well-known psychological involvement. For example, in the 1950s it became extremely popular to tie off, or ligate, the internal mammary arteries for patients having angina pain connected with heart disease. It was believed that the coronary circulation was thereby enhanced by forcing more blood through other arteries supplying the heart muscle. The procedure fell into disfavor following an experiment that could not be conducted today because of greater restrictions imposed by research ethics screening committees (Cobb, Thomas, Dillard, Merendino, & Bruce, 1959). Patients with angina pain were anesthetized, and the surgery proceeded until the artery in question was exposed. At this point, the surgeon opened an envelope that indicated whether to go ahead and tie off the artery or to simply close the incision. Afterwards, neither the patients nor the investigators following the postsurgical results were aware as to whether the real surgical procedure had been performed. The majority of the patients rated themselves at least 40% improved. They were able to exercise longer without chest pain and took less medication for heart pain. However, the patients who had received the sham operation improved just as much as the patients who had received the real procedure. In neither group was the EKG during exercise improved. Some of the patients improved remarkably. One patient who had not been working because of his heart disease returned to work and reported himself 100% improved after 6 months and 75% improved after 1 year. This patient had received the sham operation. This study indicated that the benefits of internal mammary artery ligation did not require tying off the arteries.

The post-surgical reduction in angina pain was apparently due to non-specific placebo effects.

Research on the possible physiological actions of placebo has been limited, in part by the tendency to take as a given that placebo has no physiological basis. For example, 60% of hospital physicians surveyed admitted having administered placebo in an effort to discover whether a patient was really in pain (Goodwin, Goodwin, & Vogel, 1979). If the patient responded favorably to the placebo, then the pain was not real, presumably because "real pain" can be controlled only by "real treatment," such as an analgesic drug. Implicit in this practice is the belief or assumption that placebo has no physiological basis, and can be expected only to produce an effect such as a boost in spirits or change in attitude concerning the health condition in question. The physiology of placebo has been explored mostly with placebo analgesia, where the major question has been whether placebo control of pain is mediated by the action of endorphins. The evidence, which suggests that this is apparently the case, is discussed at the end of the chapter.

Given the pervasiveness of placebo, it is more realistic to think about the relative contribution of specific and placebo components to the overall efficacy of a treatment. One would imagine that placebo makes only a modest contribution in the orthopedic repair of a broken arm, but plays a powerful role, relative to any specific mechanisms, when a practitioner attempts to clear an infection by casting out demons. Most interventions lie somewhere in between. The Placebo-Active Therapeutic Index provides a framework for considering both the overall efficacy of a treatment, and the balance of the placebo/specific elements (Stroebel & Glueck, 1973). Of two treatments that are equally efficacious, one might act primarily through a specific mechanism, the other via placebo. The most stable, lasting effects seem to be obtained when the strength of the two components is balanced. The ideal situation is when a treatment with strong, specific effects is accepted by the patient with "expectant faith" (Frank, 1982) in a positive outcome.

Detecting Placebo Effects

When I was a child there was a stubborn wart on the back of my hand. Then my father administered his cure for warts. This involved rubbing a penny on the wart and then throwing the coin into the cornfield beside the house—the idea was to "lose" the wart. It vanished! How are we to understand my father's cure for warts? We cannot, from such an anecdotal case report. What would have happened if the penny had been rubbed elsewhere on my skin, then thrown into the cornfield? Or rubbed on the wart, and thrown into a wheatfield? Or had not been thrown anywhere at all? What if my father had stolen into my bedroom while I was sound asleep and secretly applied his cure for warts, and I had never found out about it? Or if he had rubbed the wart but convinced me that pennies act like wart fertilizer? What if there had been no treatment? Maybe the wart happened to be all set to cure itself. These are not questions that children ask fathers (nor many patients, their practitioners!), but they are the thorny questions that we must raise if we are to arrive at sensible conclusions about the efficacy and modes of action of particular treatment methods.

Every intervention is presented as something other than placebo. How can it be determined if a particular treatment really has any specific effects beyond its action as placebo? One approach is to see if symptomatic improvement is accompanied by the specific physiological (or psychological, in the case of psychotherapy) change that is proposed to be the mechanism of action. If not, then we must suspect placebo (or conceivably an undetected specific mechanism). A second approach is to experimentally compare the effects of the treatment with the effects of placebo alone, by secretly withholding the active ingredient in a placebo condition. To the extent that real treatment is superior, it must have specific effects beyond its action as placebo. This procedure is most straightforward in evaluating the effects of pharmacological agents, where a capsule can be filled with powdered sugar rather than vitamin C, or a syringe with saline and not morphine. In this way inert substances, often called placebos, can be delivered in a manner that is indistinguishable from the real thing by either the patients or the practitioners. This arrangement is called a *double-blind* procedure—both the patient and the therapist are in the dark about what is going on.

The strengths of this method are apparent, but the double-blind has some limitations. For one thing, it is extremely difficult or impossible to administer fake versions of some interventions in a successful double-blind manner. For example, electrical nerve stimulation is perceptible, so that the practitioner is probably well aware from the individual's comments as to whether real stimulation is being delivered. In biofeedback, a fake feedback signal is sometimes employed that bears no relationship to any physiological activity in the patient—but it is not difficult for subjects to discover whether or not the feedback is accurate. A second difficulty is that, mainly for ethical reasons, fake treatments are seldom administered in the presence of full-blown expectations that the treatments are genuine. Rather, the persons involved are aware that the treatment could be real or fake, but do not know which is actually the case. For many reasons, this probably systematically works against treatment success for both the actual and the placebo treatments. These problems are so severe with some modes of therapy that they probably cannot be fairly evaluated under double-blind conditions. It has been argued that we should not expect treatment success with biofeedback in a double-blind arrangement, not because biofeedback is strictly placebo, but because the specific treatment effects of biofeedback depend on positive expectations and attitudes in both the therapist and the patient (Surwit & Keefe, 1983). This remains a controversial issue (e.g., Kewman & Roberts, 1983).

In general, it appears wise to withhold judgment on whether a remarkable new treatment has useful specific efficacy until the dust has settled, for, as Trousseau knew, some of these treatments have a way of losing their power to heal, and giving way to the next wonderful treatment.

Behavior Therapy

We are familiar with the experience of pain; there are also important behavioral aspects of pain. Recognition of this has led to behavioral strategies for evaluating and treating chronic pain. *Pain behaviors* are overt responses that, at least initially, are elicited by pain or are otherwise closely associated with it. A person in pain may show certain behavioral signs of pain—verbal complaints, outcries, facial grimaces, or unnatural postures suggestive of a person in pain. Another class of pain behaviors is the seeking of relief from pain by taking medication, pursuing other forms of treatment, or just sleeping. Ordinary physical activity is avoided.

Pain behaviors are adaptive at first; they are functional ways of adjusting to pain. Unfortunately, as with all overt responses, pain behaviors have environmental consequences, some of which are highly rewarding. One reward is the unemployment compensation benefits for a worker disabled due to chronic pain. Other reward contingencies are less tangible. These include the attention and sympathy of friends and family, and avoidance of unpleasant responsibilities—who could expect a person with a bad back to take out the garbage on a cold, rainy evening? If, in good health, the individual had not possessed a very successful repertoire of responses for dealing with life, he or she might even find a much more satisfying and comfortable existence in the role of a chronically sick person. Having been rewarded in these ways for months or years, pain behaviors can acquire a separate existence that is no longer dependent on pain. As with any behaviors that are rewarded over a long period of time they become extremely resistant to modification. These behaviors are no longer adaptive and are serious obstacles to successful treatment unless they are addressed adequately. For these reasons, programs incorporating some of the techniques of behavioral analysis and behavior therapy have proven useful with chronic pain patients.

Fordyce (1976) has developed a behaviorally oriented chronic pain treatment plan that has been adopted widely. There are three major goals of intervention: (a) to identify and eliminate rewards that are strengthening and supporting pain behaviors; (b) to increase the level of physical activity, and (c) to withdraw the patient from pain medication.

Patients are considered good candidates for the program if: (a) specific pain behaviors and promising rewards for use in treatment can be identified; (b) there are reasonable posttreatment outcomes that may be anticipated; and (c) the spouse and family appear to be supportive of treatment and behavior change (Fordyce, 1976). At the outset, a thorough behavioral analysis of pain is conducted that includes detailed daily pain logs supplemented by relevant information from family, employers, and health care personnel. The role of reward contingencies in maintaining the patient's pain is explained, but in a way that makes it clear that there is no question about the reality of the patient's suffering. With the patient and his or her family, a detailed plan is worked out for altering existing pain contingencies. It is commonly necessary to help the patient acquire more effective "well behaviors" to sustain long-term improvement. Increased quotas of physical activity are gradually phased in and the patient becomes accustomed to "working to quota" in place of "working to pain tolerance"—in this way cessation of unpleasant activities can no longer serve as a reward for pain.

Medication taking is an especially troublesome factor in chronic pain. Patients may suffer from disruptive side effects, such as sedation, that limit their activities and impair their cognitive performance. Some are physiologically addicted or psychologically dependent on their medication. When medication is taken "as needed" the potential exists for this highly rewarding event to maintain pain in the long run, since medication taking is contingent on having pain. A surprising number of patients cease to complain of pain once they have been withdrawn from medication (and detoxified, if necessary). The essential first step in this procedure is to shift the patient from "as needed" medication to a fixed, time-based schedule of medication.

Acupuncture

In contemporary acupuncture, thin needles are inserted beneath the skin and then physically manipulated, heated (moxibustion), or stimulated electrically (electroacupuncture). The traditional Chinese explanation of acupuncture, as with all of classical Chinese medicine, is based on the Yin-Yang energy model of Taoism. Health is a function of the distribution of a life force called *Chi* among concentric spheres of energy within the individual. The life forces flow through 14 pathways or conduits called *meridians* that radiate throughout the body. Good health depends on a harmonious balance of energies conducted through the meridians; illness and pain are symptomatic of disharmony. Acupuncture needles are

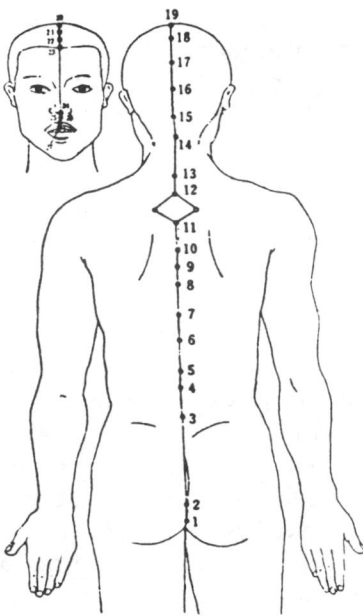

FIG. 4.3   The meridian of the governing vessel and its 27 acupuncture points. From *The Complete Guide to Acupuncture* (p. 266) by M. Toguchi, 1974, New York: Frederick Fell, Publishers. Copyright 1974 by Frederick Fell. Reprinted by permission.

inserted at different prescribed points along the meridians, depending on the diagnosis, which bring the life forces back into harmony and restore good health. One of the meridians, the "Meridian of the Governing Vessel," is shown in Fig. 4.3 along with its 27 acupuncture points.

The classical Chinese medical theory provides a perspective on human physiology and health that is completely different from the more familiar Western scientific model. Most Western physicians would argue that our health is nothing more than the health of our various organs. However, the traditional Chinese physician is concerned with the functioning of particular organs only insofar as they happen to be connected to energy spheres and meridians. The classical Chinese system is adamantly holistic. Because it is not based on the anatomical concepts of Western science, the meridian system looks peculiar when the prescribed acupuncture sites are expressed in familiar anatomical terms. For example, needling at point 13 of the Governing meridian is recommended for the common cold, at point 8 for high blood pressure, and at point 11 for low blood pressure (Toguchi, 1974).

There are some anomalies concerning neural activity and "where it hurts" that have been familiar to Western practitioners for many years.

Phantom limb pain has already been mentioned. *Referred pain* occurs when there is poor correspondence between the subjective locus of pain and the tissue distress initiating that pain. This is particularly common in the case of tissue damage to internal organs, for which pain localization is imprecise to begin with. The pain accompanying a heart attack is often referred to the shoulder, neck, or arm. The most plausible theory (Head, 1893) of referred pain explains the phenomenon by the convergence at the spinal level of sensory information from two parts of the body, as from the heart and the neck. The neuron or neurons, thus stimulated, relay information to the brain, where, in the case of a heart attack, it is often misinterpreted as having originated from the more familiar source of pain—the neck, rather than the heart. *Trigger zones* are related phenomena—areas of the body where there are neural complexes that, when stimulated by touch or mild pressure, give rise to intense pain. In many cases, the pain is referred to other bodily locations.

Although some acupuncturists adhere to the classical Chinese theory and rigorously insert the needles at prescribed meridian points, others, even in China, do not. The evidence is mixed on the need to follow the meridian points. Sham acupuncture—needling at locations other than the prescribed meridian points—seems to control clinical pain in about 50% of patients, whereas real acupuncture is effective for about 70% of patients (Lewith & Machin, 1983); however, there have been too few carefully-controlled, double-blind studies to determine if the small advantage of proper needle placement may be due to failure to present sham acupuncture convincingly. There are several studies of chronic pain which indicate that needling at pain trigger points or near the subjective location of the pain (tender area needling), is as beneficial as meridian point acupuncture (Chapman, Chen, & Bonica, 1977). It should also be noted that, using accepted scientific standards, there is little evidence in support of the hypothesized energy spheres or meridians. It has recently been proposed that the meridians are a third route for fluid transport, in addition to the blood vessels and lymph ducts, and that the life force that flows in them is made of sodium ions (Takase, 1983).

In the absence of evidence to the contrary, many Western scientists have adopted the conservative position that acupuncture analgesia is a form of counterirritation or *hyperstimulation analgesia*. According to this view, the needling, which is often accompanied by sensations of aching or pressure, stimulates large diameter afferent neurons, whose impulses block extended pain at the spinal level via an endorphin circuit. The extent of pain relief with acupuncture is correlated with the degree of increase in circulating endorphins in the blood (Kiser, Khatami, Gatchel, Huang, Bhatia, & Altshuler, 1983).

Electrical Nerve Stimulation

Hyperstimulation analgesia is seen most clearly in the electrical stimulation of afferent nerves, because large-diameter fibers are known to have a lower threshold of excitation to electrical current than small-diameter fibers. Some large diameter fibers are so responsive that they can be activated by currents that are perceived more as tingling or buzzing sensations, than as pain. Stimulating needle electrodes may be used to penetrate the skin and get closer to the neural target—a pain trigger point, an afferent pathway, or the subjective locus of the pain. Occasionally, the electrodes are permanently implanted; an example is *dorsal column stimulation*, where the stimulating apparatus is installed in or on the dorsal portion of the spinal cord. However, by far the most popular method uses non-invasive surface electrodes and a simple patient-operated stimulator, a procedure known as *transcutaneous electrical nerve stimulation*(TENS).

In TENS the person wears a small battery-powered unit resembling a transistor radio or a paging device that is connected to several stimulating electrodes, which adhere to the skin. Current intensity and frequency are usually adjustable; trains of square waves on the order of 10 to 100 Hz are often employed. Usage ranges from a few minutes per day to nearly continuous stimulation for some patients. Patients for whom TENS is helpful can obtain hours of pain relief from 5 or 10 minutes of stimulation. The most serious side effect of concern is occasional skin irritation.

Hypnosis

In 1846 an English physician, James Esdaile, described surgeries that had been performed in India using hypnosis (see chapter 6) as the only method of pain control (Esdaile, 1977). His report had special significance because surgery at that time was conducted with no anesthesia whatsoever, and entailed a mortality rate of approximately 50%—some of which must have been stress-related due to excruciating pain. His work had little immediate impact on the practice of medicine because of opposition from the medical establishment and the introduction of chemical anesthesia in surgery later that year. However, subsequent research, including studies of experimentally produced pain in normal volunteers and clinical pain in patients, have made it clear that hypnotic suggestions can diminish pain sufficiently to be of clinical use.

Experimental Studies

The advantage of laboratory studies is that the response of subjects to a known controlled painful stimulus can be observed. Experimental pain is often administered by having the subject immerse one arm in ice water

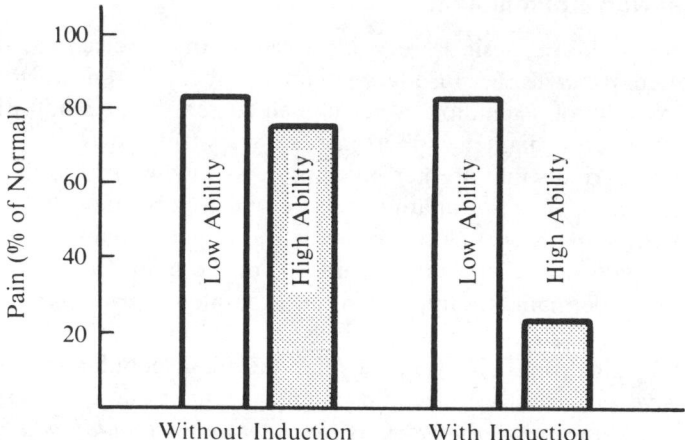

FIG. 4.4   Pain reported by volunteers high or low in hypnotic ability, with or without hypnotic induction, all with suggested analgesia. From *Divided Consciousness* (p. 192) by E. R. Hilgard, 1977, New York: Wiley. Copyright 1977 by John Wiley & Sons. Adapted by permission.

which typically results in intense pain within about 30 seconds. In one important investigation, Hilgard (1977) used the items shown in Table 6.1 to select subjects who were high or low in hypnotic ability. These subjects rated pain from ice water immersion in the absence of any suggestions in order to establish baseline pain tolerance. They also rated the same stimulation in two other situations: after suggested analgesia preceded by hypnotic induction, and after suggested analgesia without prior induction. The results are shown in Fig. 4.4.

Notice that, even without hypnotic induction, suggested analgesia resulted in an approximate 20% reduction in rated pain. The magnitude of this effect did not depend on hypnotic ability; however, the large (about 80%) diminution in pain after hypnotic induction was obtained only for high hypnotic ability subjects. Hilgard argues that the mild analgesia obtained for everyone without hypnosis, and for the low ability subjects during the hypnotic state, has nothing to do with hypnosis, and instead represents the effects of placebo. Only the profound analgesia seen in the high ability subjects following induction is true hypnotic analgesia. As discussed again at the end of this chapter, it appears that hypnotic and placebo analgesia are physiologically different phenomena.

There are several important limitations of laboratory pain research: (a) normal volunteers are considerably less motivated than pain patients, (b) laboratory pain is of short and known duration, and (c) laboratory pain originates from an external stimulus, while clinical pain ordinarily does not. Following, clinical research is briefly reviewed for three selected applications of hypnosis: dentistry, cancer, and major surgery.

Control of Clinical Pain

Dentistry. Some individuals are allergic to the local chemical anesthetic agents that are commonly used in dentistry. The numbness associated with local chemical anesthesia is extremely unpleasant to others, and phobic reactions to hypodermic needles are not unusual. In dental surgery, as in any surgical setting, chemical general anesthesia involves some risk to the patient. For these reasons, hypnotic suggestion is an attractive alternative or adjunct to the chemical agents in dentistry.

In one case study (Gheorghiu & Orleanu, 1982) a patient who was allergic to chemical anesthetic agents faced dental implant surgery in which it would be necessary to surgically create a trench in his jaw three or four centimeters long by about two centimeters deep in which to seat a permanent dental bridge. The area of the gums to be removed was richly supplied by branches of the trigeminal nerve which is highly sensitive to nociceptive stimulation. Because the patient was experienced in hypnosis and high in hypnotic ability, the operation was undertaken using only hypnotic analgesia. Following induction, suggestions were offered that the patient was in a pleasant, relaxing setting, and that a friend was telling him about how he, the friend, had undergone a dental implant under hypnosis. During the 25-minute operation there were no physical signs of pain, such as squeezing the practitioner's hand, which the patient held throughout. After the procedure the patient reported having felt that "some frightening things were happening, and I learned of all this, but I would not have learned if somebody else had not told me they were actually happening . . . I was—separated from myself" (Gheorghiu & Orleanu, 1982, pp. 69-70).

As regards the general dental patient population, accumulated evidence indicates that only a minority of highly hypnotically talented individuals will achieve sufficient depth of hypnosis for hypnotic suggestions to create adequate analgesia, but that many additional patients can benefit from the uses of hypnosis as an adjunct to chemical anesthesia (Wadden & Anderton, 1982). One notable exception to this conclusion is the work of Joseph Barber and his colleagues with "rapid induction analgesia"—so called because only 10 or 20 minutes elapse from greeting the patient to the beginning of the dental treatment. In one investigation (Barber, 1977), 100 patients in 10 dental offices were studied over a period of three months. All but two of the patients said that they had had no experience with hypnosis. The induction emphasized comfort and relaxation throughout, provided posthypnotic suggestions intended to elicit analgesia later during the actual dental treatment, and suggested amnesia for the events during the trance. The most distinctive feature of the induction was the continual subtle reassurance that the patient was in control. All communications from the hypnotist were extremely permissive—the phrases "it doesn't matter" and "I don't know" were used repeatedly in their low-key minimizing sense. Following the induction and suggestions, the patients were aroused and only after they were fully alert was the dental treatment begun. Reportedly, 99 of the 100 patients given rapid induction analgesia completed their dental treatments comfortably and without the need for chemical anesthesia. The procedure is unusual, first, insofar as the analgesia is linked to a posthypnotic suggestion so that the patient is not explicitly hypnotized during the dental work, and second, because the success rate is so high that the effect must not depend on hypnotic ability. Barber speculates that the permissive induction enables low hypnotic ability patients, who would feel threatened by, and resist, other induction techniques, to enter trance.

Cancer. Cancer is often accompanied by intractable pain. Narcotic analgesics are commonly administered in attempts to control the pain. Unfortunately, these rapidly lead to drug tolerance (progressively greater doses must be given to achieve the same analgesic effect) and to profound physiological dependence. Demerol, especially, is frequently encountered in cases of "physician-induced addiction of patients" (Julien, 1981, p. 111). Some patients and their families object to the clouding of consciousness and confusion that is a side-effect of these drugs. Surgery, such as interruption of spinal pain pathways, is sometimes useful, but can have serious complications, and is undesirable if the life expectancy of the patient is short.

The value of hypnosis in controlling cancer pain is demonstrated in a series of studies with hospitalized cancer patients (Cangello, 1961, 1962). In one investigation, hypnosis was used with 81 hospitalized cancer patients, selected on the basis of adequate mental ability, suggestibility, and willingness to cooperate (Cangello, 1962). Depending on the individual patient, direct or indirect induction procedures (see chapter 6) were used. For the indirect induction, the word hypnosis was not used and the procedure was presented as a form of relaxation. When they were judged to be in trance, all of the patients were given the posthypnotic suggestion that "No reaction, no matter how severe so far as your illness is concerned, need hurt, upset you or bother you in any way" (Cangello, 1962, p. 220). Subsequent reinforcement sessions were given to the patients "when necessary," usually during daily ward rounds. All of the hypnosis sessions were conducted in multi-bed wards, indicating that hypnosis can be used in the ordinary hospital environment. The results were expressed in global ratings by nurses and other health care personnel based on the mood, activities, appetite, and general attitude of the patient. The out-come was rated "excellent" for 41%, "good" for 27.5%, "fair" for 19%, and "poor" for 12.5%. In this study there was no systematic assessment of relief from pain.

In a second study, drug usage was monitored as an objective index of pain distress (Cangello, 1961). There were 22 cancer patients studied, all of whom were being maintained on narcotic analgesics administered every four hours. Hypnotic induction, posthypnotic suggestions, and follow-up sessions were delivered as before. Of the 22 patients, 8 decreased their drug intake by 75% to 100%; 4 of these patients withdrew from medica-tion altogether. Another 5 patients decreased their dosages from 50% to 74%, while the remaining 9 patients showed little or no change. Hypnotic analgesia would seem to be quite useful with cancer patients, especially when one considers the low incidence of complications with hypnosis as compared to narcotic analgesics. Hypnosis can be reasonably cost effective. It can be administered wherever the patient is situated and, in the second study reported here, an average of only 2.7 contact hours per patient was required. Hypnosis has also been used in a much more inten-sive and individualized way with cancer patients (Sacerdote, 1970).

Surgery.   The first surgery on record may have been performed under hypnoanesthesia, as reported in Genesis 2-21: "And the Lord God caused a deep sleep to fall on Adam, and he slept, and He took one of his ribs and closed the flesh instead thereof." Despite such an auspicious introduc-tion to surgical practice, hypnosis has not often been used since as the sole agent to control pain in surgery. The effects of hypnosis are less predict-able, and, for some individuals, weaker than the effects of chemical anesthesia. It typically takes longer to administer hypnoanesthesia, and trained hypnotists are not readily available in most surgical facilities. It has been shown, however, that hypnosis can be a useful standard adjunct to chemical agents, where it helps to control presurgical anxiety, an important factor in the success of surgery (Williams & Jones, 1968), to deepen the analgesia initiated chemically, and to facilitate postoperative recovery (Hilgard & Hilgard, 1975).

Some of the disadvantages and dangers associated with chemical anesthesia have already been discussed in connection with dentistry. The extremely high cost of malpractice insurance for anesthesiologists reminds us that the patient is always at some risk when general anesthesia is pro-duced by drugs. If inhalation is the route of administration, there are possible postoperative complications, so that a significant aspect of recovery is the clearing from the respiratory system of the chemicals that have been used; the necessary coughing can be extremely painful immedi-ately following major abdominal surgery. In childbirth, the health of the baby is endangered by chemical anesthesia because the mother and baby share a common blood supply. The widespread use of chemical anesthesia in deliveries has become a cause for some concern, and it has been argued strongly that hypnosis should be the anesthetic of choice for childbirth (Werner, Schauble, & Knudson, 1982). For many years in the Soviet Union expectant mothers were tested for hypnotic ability, and 60% of all deliveries were performed under hypnoanesthesia alone (Werner et al., 1982).

In some circumstances the risks of chemical anesthesia are so grave that it cannot be used. One such case was a woman who weighed 287 pounds, had swollen face and limbs, severe headaches and frequent vomiting; her blood pressure was 230/160 in spite of medication given her to control it (Winkelstein & Levinson, 1959). She was two weeks overdue for childbirth and it would be necessary to deliver the child by caesarean section, a major abdominal surgical procedure. Various forms of chemical anesthesia had been ruled out because of substantial risks to the patient or to the baby. She was hypnotized without difficulty and given suggestions of complete anesthesia, which continued during the operation. After a successful delivery, very small amounts of nitrous oxide were administered in the course of repairing the abdominal and uterine incisions.

When hypnosis is used with real patients who are undergoing real surgery, their safety and comfort must take precedence over scientific methodology. As in other research areas, the realism of the clinic typically lacks the controls of the laboratory. During most of the surgeries involving hypnosis, at least one chemical agent that could conceivably alter pain perception is administered at some point. This makes it difficult to know whether control of pain is actually linked to the hypnoanesthesia. However, there are scattered reports of cases in which absolutely no medication was administered. The earliest, of course, was the extensive use of hypnosis by James Esdaile, mentioned previously.

One case of surgery under hypnoanesthesia using no medication is especially interesting because the author, Victor Rausch, was also the patient (Rausch, 1980). At the time of his surgery, Rausch had had 16 years of experience with hypnosis as a dental surgeon, teacher, and researcher. When he was advised that his gall bladder needed to be removed, he elected to have the operation under self-hypnosis (see chapter 6), and, according to his case report, was given no medication whatsoever in connection with the surgery. Understandably, he did not undertake this adventure as a skeptic, but as a believer with a "burning curiosity and desire to experience firsthand the mental changes that would have to occur within myself if the procedure was to be successful" (Rausch, 1980, p. 124). The night before the operation he relaxed deeply, visualized himself on an imaginary movie screen, and went through the entire operative procedure, ending with a positive outcome. Feeling success and elation, he drifted off to sleep and awoke in the morning in a dreamlike state with no apprehension. He entered the operating room with no premedication and climbed onto the table, reporting that he was aware of tension in the others in the room (none of whom had had any experience with hypnosis), but felt very calm and quite detached himself. A particular piece of music, as performed by a specific artist, which Rausch could imagine very clearly, was used as an attentional focus, with the image cued, as planned, to the opening of his abdomen. The chart of the "backup" anesthesiologist, as well as interpretive notes added later, is shown in Fig. 4.5.

Following an elevation in systolic blood pressure and pulse rate at the time of the initial incision, these responses returned to near normal, although Rausch sweated profusely throughout the 75-minute operation. He reports, "Consciously I felt completely detached and subjectively felt absolute amazement at what was happening. It was as though I were an observer rather than the patient" (Rausch, 1980, p. 127). He recalls controlling the surgical pain by mentally directing an unusual force that flowed throughout his body to the location of the surgery to cancel sensations arising there. He walked back to his room afterward, where he alternated between sleep and dreamlike wakefulness for 16 hours, at which time he abruptly "snapped" back together. Recovery was uneventful.

Dissociation and Pain

The leading contemporary explanation of hypnotic analgesia is Hilgard's (1973a) *neodissociation theory*—"*neo*dissociation" because it resurrects and elaborates a 19th century theory of hypnosis. We have just seen several examples of dissociation in hypnotic analgesia, as indicated by self-reports of feeling "completely detached" and "separated from myself." (It may be useful at this point to look at the discussion of dissociation as a key feature of hypnosis in chapter 6). Such descriptions, implying a splitting and walling off of segments of consciousness, suggest that during hypnotic analgesia the pain may still be present at some level that is inaccessible to the ordinary conscious part of the person. Hilgard has called this submerged and ordinarily unexpressive part of a person, metaphorically, the *hidden observer*.

Hilgard's conception of hypnotic analgesia is shown schematically in Fig. 4.6. The normal pain situation is shown on the left. Hypnosis and suggestions of analgesia cause restructuring by creating amnesia-like barriers around that portion of the person where the pain still exists. Thus, if you were hypnotized and subjected to a pin prick, pain would result, more or less as usual, but this pain would be isolated and known only to the hidden observer; the familiar everyday "you" would feel no pain.

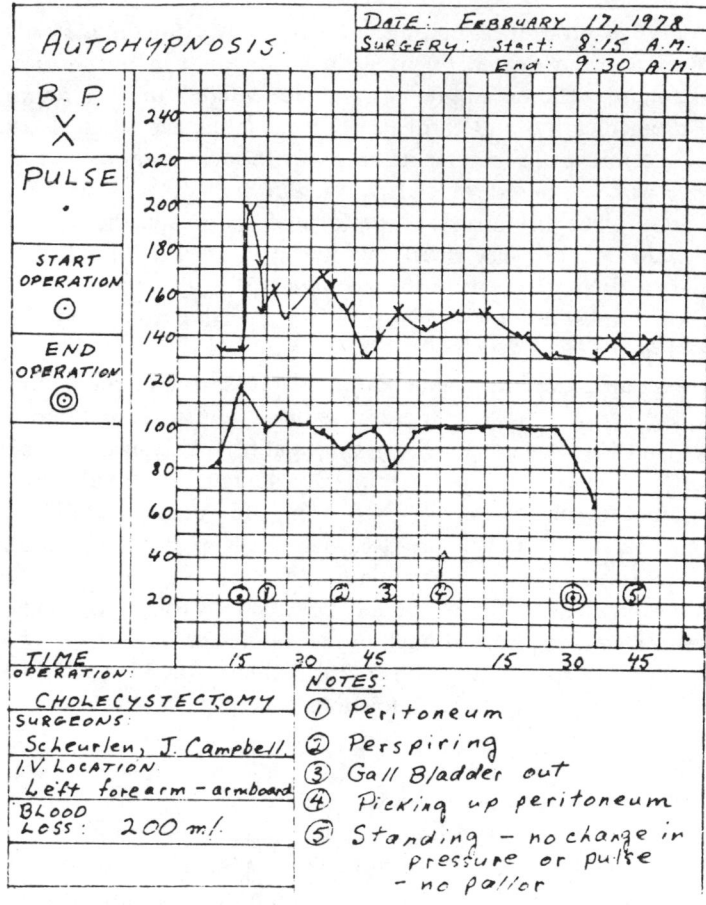

INTERPRETATION OF CHART

— Start of operation. 8:15 A.M.

— Blood pressure—135

— Pulse rate 82 beats per minute.

When the initiation incision was made my blood pressure spiked to 190 immediately and my pulse rate rose to 115. Going through the peritoneum.

— approximately six minutes into the operation.

Both the blood pressure and pulse dropped to a more normal level. At this point I was perspiring profusely, yet the blood pressure and pulse rate remained fairly steady. After approximately 50 minutes the gall bladder was out. Blood pressure and pulse steady. Picking up the peritoneum. Blood pressure and pulse rate steady. Operation finished. 9:30 A.M. Blood pressure steady. Pulse rate dropped to 65 beats per minute. Standing.

— No change in pressure or pulse.

— No pallor.

— Walked to room.

FIG. 4.5 Gall bladder removal under self-hypnotic analgesia: Chart of the backup anesthesiologist with interpretive notes by the patient. From "Cholecystectomy with Self-Hypnosis" by V. Rausch, 1980, *The American Journal of Clinical Hypnosis, 22,* 126. Copyright 1980 by the American Society of Clinical Hypnosis. Reprinted by permission.

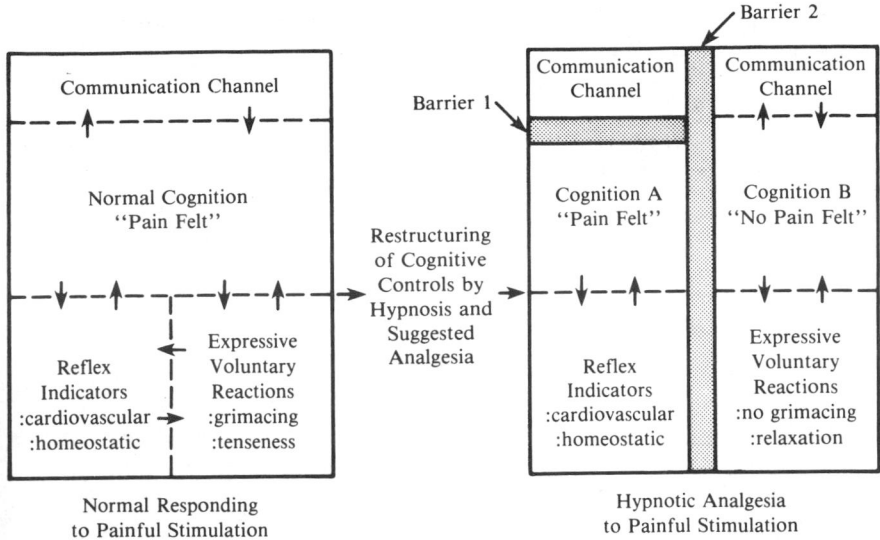

FIG. 4.6   Hilgard's conception of hypnotic analgesia: The role of dissociation. From "A Neo-dissociation Interpretation of Pain Reduction in Hypnosis" by E. R. Hilgard, 1977, *Psychological Review, 80,* 399. Copyright 1977 by the American Psychological Association. Adapted by permission.

How can we establish contact with, and thereby show the existence of, the proposed secret, hidden observer, when the person under hypnosis is not even in communication with this part of her or his self? In fact, the neodissociation theory was partly prompted by a classroom conversation with a hidden observer (Hilgard, 1977). Hilgard was demonstrating suggested deafness during hypnosis, and had shown that his experienced, high hypnotic ability subject was unresponsive even to a gunshot. A student argued that there might be some part of the person who could still hear during suggested deafness. Hilgard immediately tested this possibility (although he considered it unlikely) by explaining to the hypnotizee that he was now speaking to a submerged area of the person who could still hear, and that this subdivision of the person could now indicate as much by raising one finger. To Hilgard's astonishment, up went the finger! In subsequent formal experiments, the hidden observer has been allowed to communicate through "automatic writing" or automatic keypressing, where one arm is concealed from the participant's view under a box. The general conclusion from these studies is that at the level of the hidden observer, pain is present at roughly the same intensity as outside the hypnotic state (Hilgard, 1977).

Dissociation and the hidden observer in no way undermine the reality nor the utility of hypnotic analgesia. There is no reason to doubt the honesty of self-reports of successful pain control; the validity of these reports is supported by the absence of any overt signs of pain, and by the evident amazement of the person if presented with evidence of a report of pain using the hidden observer method.

Dissociation or divided consciousness leads us into several intriguing areas including multiple personality, amnesia, repression, and the psychophysiological consequences of hemispheric deconnection surgery. Unfortunately, a full discussion would stray far from the topic of this text.

Multidisciplinary Pain Centers

The 4-week inpatient pain program at Miller-Dwan Hospital in Duluth, Minnesota is a representative multidisciplinary center. The treatment provided includes: physical therapy and exercise; psychophysiological relaxation training to help control the stress of extended pain; behaviorally-oriented medication reduction; active involvement of family and "significant others"; careful self-monitoring by patients; establishment of individual contracts spelling out long-term goals; and group therapy sessions in which pain behaviors are analyzed, alternative behaviors encouraged, and emotional support is provided. After treatment there are bimonthly follow-up group meetings.

One particularly valuable assessment of this program is available, which includes pre-treatment data for comparison purposes and a 12-month follow-up period (Cinciripini & Floreen, 1982). The first 121 patients entering the program were studied, 62% of whom were female. Admission required having intractable pain for at least one year (average was 8 years) that had originated from identifiable physical alteration of body tissue—surgery, injury, a disease such as arthritis, or a structural anomaly like congenital curvature of the spine. About 90% had pain in the head/neck region or the lower back. Before treatment, 91% had experienced significant time off (average was 3.0 years) from work or their customary daily activities; 41% were receiving compensation payments. The entering patients had heavy medication usage (average was 3.0 prescriptions per patient); 66% were taking analgesics and 39% minor tranquilizers (Librium or Valium). During the inpatient phase, observers periodically rated the frequency of pain talk ("My back hurts"), nonverbal pain behavior (limping, grimacing, etc.), nonpain complaints (e.g., about the food), pro-health talk (statements referring to well-being or improvement), and assertive behavior.

At discharge, each of the above behaviors had changed in the desired direction, several of them dramatically. There was about six times less pain talk, four times more pro-health talk, and three times less nonverbal pain behaviors. At discharge 92% were free from medication as compared to only 2.4% at admission. Measures of physical activity showed substantial improvement at discharge. Self-ratings of pain had decreased from 4.63 to 2.24 on a scale of 0 to 10. After 12 months, self-rated pain had decreased further to 1.17. Only 7.2% of the patients were unemployed and not looking for work, and only 20% were receiving any form of disability compensation payment. They exercised, did physical therapy routines, and practiced relaxation training several times per week. In the one year following discharge, 61% had had no pain related visits to physicians and at the end of the year 85% were still taking no prescription drugs.

Multidisciplinary pain centers offer: (a) multiple treatment modalities; (b) potential insights from the interaction of professionals from different disciplines; and (c) sophisticated, in depth assessment of the biological, psychological, and social dimensions of a chronic pain problem. Beyond this, pain centers differ somewhat in their orientation; some include methods such as hypnosis, biofeedback, or acupuncture in the regimen, some specialize in outpatient, rather than inpatient treatment, and some prescribe medication selectively as part of the overall treatment plan. Despite these differences, therapeutically useful effects have been reported consistently for the multidisciplinary approach to chronic pain (reviewed by Aronoff, Evans, & Enders, 1983). Pain centers exist in every major metropolitan area of the United States. Given the resistance of chronic pain to traditional medical treatment (drugs, progressing to surgery) pain centers are a welcome innovation and one of the most fruitful applications of the psychophysiological approach to health. Treatment at a pain center is expensive in the short-run compared with simple drug treatment, however the potential long-run savings are enormous. The hospital cost alone for the approximately 200,000 persons who had low back pain surgery in 1974 was $1 billion (Pheasant, 1977).

ENDORPHINS AND PAIN CONTROL

Some of the methods just reviewed may control pain in the same way that the narcotic analgesics do—by activating endorphin systems. The major research method used has been *naloxone blockade*. Naloxone, by occupying the receptor sites on opiate-modulated neurons, prevents any drug or procedure that ordinarily activates these neural circuits from doing so. For this reason, naloxone is used in hospital emergency rooms to treat heroin overdoses. Should the analgesic effects of a procedure diminish or vanish altogether in the presence of naloxone, we would suspect that the blocked analgesia, when left to itself, acts via an endorphin mechanism.

Naloxone blockade studies need to be carefully conducted and cautiously interpreted. In particular it must be shown that an analgesic effect is actually present when naloxone is introduced, and that naloxone specifically interferes with that effect, rather than simply intensifying the perception of pain (Grevert, Albert, & Goldstein, 1983). Also, supportive evidence beyond successful naloxone blockade is useful to conclusively implicate an endorphin mechanism because the neural effects of naloxone are not limited strictly to blocking opiate-sensitive neurons (Sawynok, Pinsky, & LaBella, 1979). Therefore, it is helpful to know: (a) whether endorphins are actually released during the analgesia, and (b) whether the time courses of analgesia and endorphin change are reasonably similar. Even though there is at least one report of successful naloxone blockade for every pain control method under consideration here, because of the methodological considerations just mentioned, conclusions about possible endorphin mediation remain somewhat speculative.

It appears that placebo is capable of activating pain modulating endorphin systems. There are several reports of reversal of placebo analgesia by naloxone (e.g., Levine, Gordon, & Fields, 1978), including one study that has incorporated the methodological refinements mentioned previously (Grevert et al., 1983).

Placebo analgesia may depend on a simple form of learning—*classical conditioning*—whereby a stimulus acquires the ability to evoke a response from having been paired or associated with another stimulus that can already evoke the response. It is an example of classical conditioning when a dog salivates at the sight of a can of its favorite dog food. The role of classical conditioning in placebo is seen quite clearly in veterinary medicine where a placebo analgesic is sometimes intentionally created by systematically and repeatedly administering together the (future) placebo and an effective pharmacological analgesic (Pesut & Kowalczyk, 1983). Later, the placebo can be used alone in circumstances where the drug would be undesirable because of known side-effects. For human patients the association is more often symbolic, as when the physican comments, while writing out a prescription for chemically inert tablets, "Here is something that will help your pain." A very salient piece of the puzzle is that opiate-related neurochemical responses are readily classically conditionable, a phenomenon that is illustrated dramatically when a heroin user injects tap water to obtain a classically conditioned heroin "rush." More directly to the point, endorphin release itself has been classically conditioned in the lab (Hayes, Bennett, Newlon, & Mayer, 1978). For these reasons it appears likely that placebo analgesia acts via classically conditioned release of endorphins.

At present, the situation with the neurochemistry of hyperstimulation analgesia is rather muddled. Although the earliest reports with naloxone blockade were positive (e.g., Mayer, Price, & Rafii, 1977), more recent studies, some with sophisticated methodology, have not always supported these findings (e.g., Chapman, Bendetti, Colpitts, & Gerlach, 1983). With acupuncture, the location of the needling, relative to the subjective location of the pain, may help explain some of the conflicting findings (Watkins & Mayer, 1982). In the case of electrical nerve stimulation, the frequency of the stimulation may make a difference—endorphin mediation appears more likely for low frequency trains of pulses (Sjolund & Erikkson, 1980). Given that placebo is able to release endorphins, failure to take into account the possibly varying placebo properties of different methods of delivering acupuncture and nerve stimulation may also help explain some of the difficulties in this research area.

Evidence is weakest for endorphin modulation in hypnotic analgesia. This may seem curious, since effective placebos seem to liberate endorphins, and both hypnotic and placebo analgesia operate through suggestion. However, it appears that placebo and hypnosis are only superficially similar, as shown by Hilgard's (1977) experiment discussed earlier in this chapter. The reader will recall that it was possible to distinguish between placebo-related and hypnosis-related pain reduction following a hypnotic induction procedure. Furthermore, hypnotic analgesia appears to be based on dissociation, whereas placebo analgesia is not. Most investigations have found that naloxone does not prevent hypnotic analgesia (e.g., Barber & Mayer, 1977). In addition, the time courses of hypnotic analgesia and endorphin changes do not correspond well. While hypnotic analgesia can be initiated promptly and terminated abruptly, endorphin levels change only gradually. Dissociation from pain is not commonly noted with acupuncture, electrical nerve stimulation, placebo, or naroctic analgesics. Interestingly, the pharmacological agent, nitrous oxide, used mostly in dentistry, has properties very like hypnosis—it creates analgesia quickly, and is accompanied by a distinct feeling of dissociation from whatever may be going on in one's mouth. As with hypnotic pain control, nitrous oxide analgesia is not reversed by naloxone (Levine, Gordon, & Fields, 1982).

The physiological basis of pain control by hypnosis and nitrous oxide has not been discovered. Nonetheless these forms of analgesia are among the reasons to believe that there are multiple pain inhibitory systems in the human nervous system. Perhaps as the anatomical basis and neurochemistry of these other systems becomes better understood, new methods of clinical pain control will be developed.

5 Biofeedback and Progressive Relaxation

Not too long ago it seemed that vast areas of human psychophysiological function were inacessible to voluntary control. While one might acquire sufficient skeletal muscle skill to master a musical instrument, one could not dream of "playing the internal organs" (Lang, 1970). However, the borders of the involuntary realm are being pushed back by research that is revealing the ability of humans to control their bodies and minds in ways that were previously unthinkable. It is apparent that there are extensive control systems that normally lie dormant, but may be cultivated into action using the self-regulation techniques introduced in the next two chapters. We explore the ability of human beings to heal themselves, maintain good health, and perhaps take their minds to places that used to be known only to the Eastern mystics. Five major self-regulation techniques are discussed: biofeedback, progressive relaxation, hypnosis, autogenic training, and meditation.

Self-regulation is most definitely a psychophysiological endeavor. After successful relaxation training, we might notice that we *feel* more calm or *experience* less anxiety; we would be talking about the mind. We might also discover that our blood pressure has gone down and that our skeletal muscles have become less tense; here, we would be talking about the body. There is little basis at present for claiming that one or the other perspective is somehow more fundamental or illuminating. Nonetheless, it is possible, and convenient, to group self-regulation techniques according to the relative importance of physiological considerations (body) as compared to cognitive factors (mind) in the reasoning behind them. This chapter introduces the two major techniques whose origins are most clearly physiological—biofeedback and progressive relaxation. The next chapter deals with three methods that are more cognitively-oriented—hypnosis, autogenic training and meditation.

BIOFEEDBACK

The Biofeedback Principle

Each of the following examples incorporates the essence of the biofeedback principle: (a) a physical therapy patient attempts to manipulate an oscilloscope display reflecting the amount of skeletal muscle activity in her partially paralyzed forearm; (b) each time the blood vessels in one ear, but not the other, dilate, a rat receives a highly rewarding, electrical discharge through a stimulating electrode implanted in a specific brain area—the rat would eagerly press a lever to experience this reward; (c) a reward of 5 cents is tallied on a counter each time that a blood pressure reading is lower than the preceding one; (d) a research subject attempts to increase the pitch of a tone controlled by the skin temperature of her index finger; (e) whenever muscle activity in the forehead drops below a preset criterion level, a headache sufferer hears a brief recording of waves lapping a beach; and (f) an epileptic child pretends he is piloting a light as it moves across a display board, each advancing step of the light is generated by a burst of brainwave activity thought to suppress seizures.

What is it that these situations share? For one thing, each involves an involuntary response. Few individuals can raise or lower blood pressure on command, except perhaps by running up a flight of stairs, but that would be cheating. Even though the skeletal muscles are usually under adequate voluntary control, this may not be true after a stroke. Therefore, one characteristic of biofeedback is that an involuntary bodily response is measured in some way, usually by a sophisticated electronic gadget.

Second, in each example the involuntary response is made to have some external consequence: changes in muscle activity alter the oscilloscope display, finger-warming makes the tone go higher, a drop in blood pressure produces a nickel, and so on. These physiological responses normally do not *do anything* to the external environment. Not only are they controlled automatically, they operate outside of awareness. This is just as well, because continuous status reports from the internal organs would be distracting to the point of madness. However, this absence of feedback may be the reason that many bodily responses are normally beyond voluntary control (Brener, 1974)—learning to control them voluntarily would be like learning to drive a car while blindfolded. Therefore, a second characteristic of biofeedback is that the measured response is made to have an external consequence, which is viewed as either a source of informational feedback or as a reward.

Third, there must be appropriate motivating conditions. This may be in the form of instructions to a patient to "turn on the soothing waves by relaxing your muscles," supported by the motivating knowledge that muscle relaxation may lessen head pain. Because instructions have little inspirational value for a rat, the external consequence must be in the form of an effective reward linked to, or contingent on, the target response defined by the experimenter. Contingent rewards, without instructions, can also be used to modify involuntary responses in humans. This particular biofeedback phenomenon is somewhat counterintuitive, so some evidence will be introduced.

In one of the first studies of heart rate biofeedback (Levene, Engel, & Pearsen, 1968), five normal female college students were recruited to participate in a learning experiment, but were never told that heart rate control was being studied. Since cardiac recording electrodes are not placed over the heart, the recording procedure did not give the researchers away. The participants were told only to lie in bed as quietly as possible and to breath normally so as not to "foul up our measurements." They were supposed to keep a light on and a clock running by making unspecified "correct responses," and were paid wages of 1/4 penny for each second of time accumulated on the clock. Two other lights indicated that the correct response was either heart rate speeding or slowing, but the participants knew only that a different response was correct when the cue light changed. Training went on for 6 to 12 2-hour sessions, depending on how quickly the individual learned. By the end of training the cue lights changed at 1-minute intervals, requiring the person to alternately speed and slow the heart rate at 1-minute intervals.

Representative heart rate recordings from the end of training are shown for each participant in Fig. 5.1. As can be seen, some of the participants were more adept at this task than others, but each showed a clear pattern of appropriate changes in heart rate. Only one participant (#3) guessed that heart rate was the response controlling the reward light and the clock.

To summarize, three important features of biofeedback are: (a) measuring an involuntary response, (b) providing an external consequence of that response, and (c) arranging appropriate motivating conditions.

As previously explained, the external stimulus is often viewed as information or feedback to the subject. In this case the intended effect of this arrangement is called "voluntary control" or "self-regulation" of the physiological response. Some researchers prefer to view the external stimulus as a reward (or in technical language, as "reinforcement") and describe the effects of biofeedback training as *instrumental* or *operant conditioning* of the response in question. In most biofeedback situations there is no

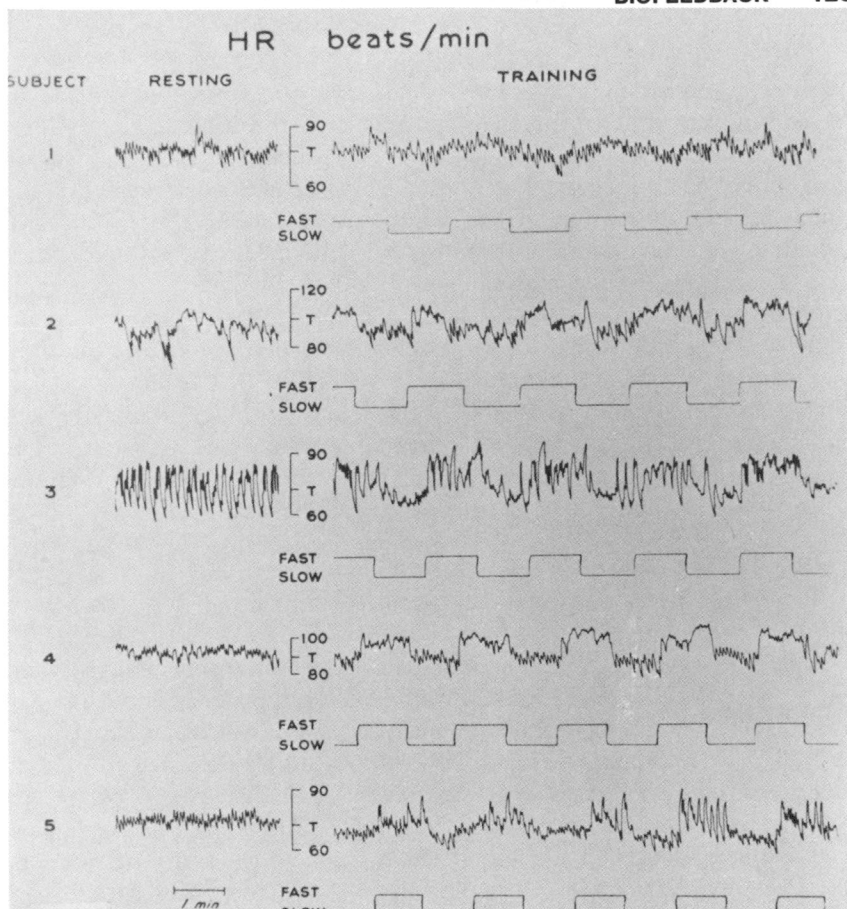

FIG. 5.1 Representative cardiotachometer records from each subject at rest and during alternating fast and slow heart biofeedback training, showing heart rate fluctuation around the trigger level (T). Reprinted by permission of Elsevier Science Publishing Co., Inc. from Differential Operant Conditioning of Heart Rate, by H. I. Levene et al. *Psychosomatic Medicine, 30,* 840. Copyright 1968 by the American Psychosomatic Society, Inc.

way to determine whether the external stimulus functions as information or as reinforcement.

Distinctive Features of Biofeedback

Biofeedback differs from the other self-regulation techniques in several ways, specifically, in the use of physiological monitoring instruments, and in some of the peculiar physiological effects of biofeedback training.

Instrumentation

The responses studied in biofeedback are not noticeable outside the organism; therefore sensitive instruments must be used to detect them, often via surface recordings from electrodes attached to the skin. This has had several consequences. The impressive wires and electrodes have contributed to the mysterious, yet scientific, aura surrounding biofeedback. In addition, since physiological responses must be measured in biofeedback, it is a relatively simple matter to record data for analysis and thereby evaluate the physiological effects of the biofeedback training. Finally, since the technique is tied to instrumentation, when away from the training setting, a patient cannot directly practice the exact procedure employed in the clinic. It is always necessary in clinical biofeedback to ensure that the voluntary control trained in the clinic transfers to the natural setting without biofeedback. Many clinical biofeedback failures can be traced to insufficient attention to this critical matter.

Feedback-Specific Effects

Biofeedback has the potential to create "unnatural acts" (Schwartz, 1976).

The reader will recall the situation in which rewarding brain stimulation was contingent on differential vasomotor responses between the ears of the rat—parallel responses in the two ears were not rewarded (DiCara & Miller, 1968). Similarly, in our lab, human subjects learned to produce skin temperature differences between the left and right cheeks of the face when a feedback tone reflected the left/right temperature difference (Bennett & Suter, 1980). Other researchers have trained children to create temperature differentials between two fingers of one hand when the feedback signal reflected the temperature differential (Lynch, Hama, Kohn, & Miller, 1976). If the feedback signal indicates the difference between corresponding points over the left and right hemispheres, in the amount of EEG alpha activity, some persons are able to create EEG differences between the two sides of the brain (e.g., Ray, Frediani, & Harman, 1977).

The experiments just reviewed show that very specific feedback contingencies can create remarkably discrete physiological changes. In biofeedback training the physiological change is sometimes limited to the response in the feedback loop, even when this is not required. It is as if there were a greedy, but lazy, genie tucked away inside us who wishes to turn on the feedback tone with the least possible "psychophysiological effort." An example of this feedback-specific tendency involves two psychophysiological activities that are normally correlated: EEG alpha and the electrical resistance of the skin. Ordinarily, when alpha becomes more prevalent in the EEG, there is also an increase in skin resistance. However, in our lab these responses changed independently of one another when biofeedback was based on either one alone (Suter, 1977); the feedback situation uncoupled their natural relationship.

Feedback specificity could be a problem if the aim of training is generalized psychophysiological relaxation. A patient might finish biofeedback relaxation training with a limp forehead in an otherwise tense body. Biofeedback clinicians circulate a tale about a dentist working with Bruxism (teeth-grinding, especially nocturnally) who confined biofeedback muscle relaxation training exclusively to the masseter muscle on one side of the face. Feedback-specific muscle relaxation is supposed to have unhinged the unfortunate person's jaw.

There are several ways to encourage a more generalized biofeedback response in clinical practice. These include: (a) feeding back EMG from multiple sites simultaneously (Shirley, Burish, & Rowe, 1982); (b) changing a single EMG feedback locus from muscle to muscle within a session (Manning, 1978); (c) using a non-feedback self-regulation technique such as autogenic phrases to augment biofeedback training—the only one of these suggestions commonly used in clinical practice; and (d) creating a joint contingency based on simultaneous changes in several psychophysiological responses.

The last approach is nicely illustrated in an experiment exploring the joint control of heart rate and systolic blood pressure (Schwartz, 1972). Different participants were assigned to one of four conditions in which a feedback tone and light were contingent on: (a) simultaneous increases in both responses, (b) decreases in both, or (c) concurrent changes in opposite directions. Participants were told that the researchers wanted to see if the participants could learn to control involuntary body processes, but were not told what processes were being studied. The results are shown in Fig. 5.2. The most distinct changes in both heart rate and blood pressure were seen when the correct response was a change in the same direction for both heart rate and blood pressure. Self-reports of relaxation were greatest when both heart rate and blood pressure were trained to go down. Thus, an individual achieves a greater feeling of relaxation when two response systems rather than one are under the "relaxation contingency" of the feedback loop. A group of researchers in West Germany have carried this approach further with an "average pattern" biofeedback arrangement, in which the averaged status of as many as 10 psychophysiological responses determine a feedback signal on a video screen (Wildgruber, Lutzenberger, Elbert, & Birbaumer, 1977).

Feedback specificity can work to our advantage in therapeutic situations in which a highly discrete physiological response is desirable. For example EMG biofeedback has been used to train stringed instrument players to reduce excess muscle tension in the extensor muscles of the fingering arm without undesirable generalization of the relaxation to the

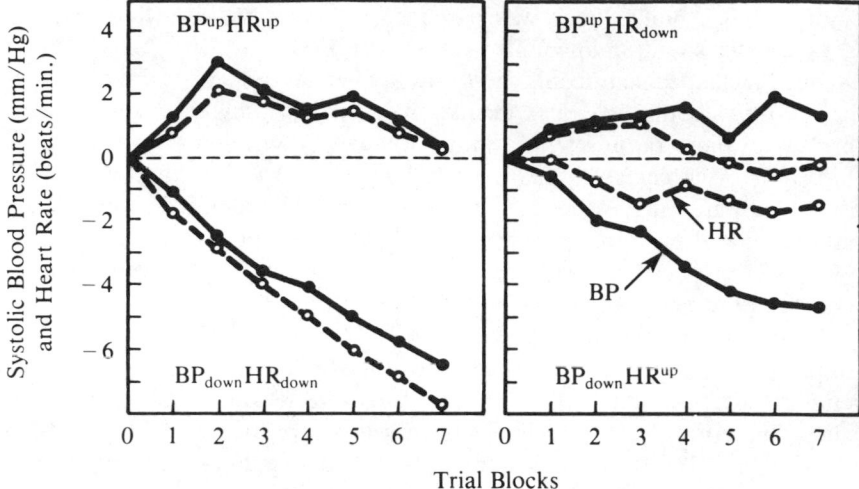

FIG. 5.2 Median systolic blood pressure (BP) and heart rate (HR) during four joint feedback contingencies. From "Voluntary Control of Human Cardiovascular Integration and Differentiation through Feedback and Reward" by G. E. Schwartz, 1972, *Science, 175*, 92. Copyright 1972 by the American Association for the Advancement of Science. Adapted by permission.

flexors of the same arm (Morasky, Reynolds, & Clarke, 1981). Another research group used an infra-red optometer to feed back information about the thickness of the lens in the eye (Trachtman, Giambalvo, & Feldman, 1981). There were clinically significant improvements in the acuity of their nearsighted subjects.

Origins of Biofeedback

In the early 1960s, researchers studying neuromuscular rehabilitation, brain function, and simple learning processes all began to report similar phenomena when they allowed physiological responses to interact with the environment.

Autonomic Responses

The widely held view among learning theorists from the 1930s until the 1960s was that autonomic responses are not subject to instrumental conditioning procedures (Konorski & Miller, 1937); that is, a hungry rat could not learn to alter its heart rate for food reward. B. F. Skinner, the most prominent learning theorist, was originally quite open-minded on the possibility, musing that perhaps a child could be "conditioned to cry 'real tears' because tears have been followed by positive reinforcement" (Skinner, 1937, p. 279). However, in response to intense criticism, his position hardened so that Skinner (1953) later wrote:

Glands and smooth muscles do not naturally produce the kinds of consequences involved in operant reinforcement, and when we arrange such
consequences experimentally, operant conditioning does not take place. We
may reinforce a man with food whenever he 'turns red,' but we cannot in
this way condition him to blush 'voluntarily.' The behavior of blushing like
that of blanching or secreting tears, saliva, sweat, and so on cannot be
brought directly under the control of operant reinforcement. (p. 114)

However, Skinner was not dogmatically closed to the possibility, and
personally encouraged Herbert Kimmel in his pioneering work. Further,
Skinner was very insightful about the implications of biofeedback effects,
if they could be created somehow. Skinner (1953) wrote about this possibility, "If some technique could be worked out to achieve this result, it
would be possible to train a child to control his emotions as readily as he
controls the position of his hands" (p. 114). Nonetheless it became the
prevailing view that autonomic responses could not be modified by
reward or punishment, that is, by their consequences, even though the
possibility had never been subjected to a thorough empirical test. According to a major learning textbook published in 1961 "Although autonomically mediated reactions such as GSR and vasoconstriction are readily
conditioned classically, they seem to be impossible to condition by instrumental methods" (Kimble, 1961, p. 100). When evidence to the contrary
began to surface in the early 1960s it was received cautiously, but with
great interest.

In 1961, Lisina, in the Soviet Union, reported successful instrumental
conditioning of finger vasodilation responses using the termination of
painful electric shock as reinforcement, supplemented by the visual feedback of allowing the subjects to view their photoplethysmograph recordings (Razran, 1961). Fowler and Kimmel (1962) used the onset of a dim
light in an otherwise dark room to positively reinforce spontaneously-
occurring electrodermal responses—the small, brief, fluctuations that
continuously punctuate skin resistance recordings. There were more electrodermal responses when the light presentations were contingent on their
occurrence, as compared to the control situation in which the lights were
presented randomly without respect to responding. Also in the early
1960s, other workers began to explore instrumental conditioning of heart
rate (Shearn, 1962). Evidence accumulated, with an empirical literature of
22 studies by 1967 and 95 studies of autonomic biofeedback by 1974.

EEG Alpha

At the same time the previous scientists were first reporting the effects
of autonomic-environmental interactions, others were discovering ways to
expose the electrophysiological activity of the brain itself to external contingencies, and reporting similar phenomena. The independent develop-

ment of EEG alpha biofeedback procedures by Joe Kamiya, Barbara Brown, and Thomas Mulholland illustrates the unpredictability of basic scientific research.

In 1958, during psychophysiological sleep research at the University of Chicago, Kamiya became fascinated with the prominent, slowly waxing and waning, alpha rhythm that dominated his pre-sleep EEG chart recordings. Might there be some discernable change in consciousness associated with this striking electrophysiological phenomenon? His first step was to see whether people could learn to distinguish between the presence and absence of alpha in their occipital EEG. The subjects guessed, whenever they were signalled, whether they were in "State A" or "State B," and were told whether each guess was correct. Across several hours of this EEG "discrimination training," accuracy typically rose from about 50% at the beginning to about 75% to 80% at the end. When questioned, many participants were unable to explain how they were able to perform the EEG discrimination task with such accuracy. The critical discovery, reported at a psychology convention in 1962, was that once the participants had learned to discriminate between the EEG states, they could produce the states on command (Kamiya, 1969).

Soon afterward, now at the Langley Porter Neuropsychiatric Institute in San Francisco, Kamiya devised a more efficient way to train control of EEG alpha. He constructed a circuit so that a tone signalled the occurrence of alpha above a set criterion level. From the subjects' perspective they were learning to control the tone. As a "scientist of private experience" Kamiya was interested not only in determining if his subjects could control the alpha rhythm, but also in their experiences during the low alpha state and high alpha state. There was some agreement in their subjective reports that low occipital alpha was associated with active attention to visual imagery. High alpha was described as generally pleasant, quite relaxing, and frequently accompanied by suspension of critical thinking. Interestingly, at about the same time there was a report that alpha increases dramatically in the same cortical locations during Zen meditation (Kasamatsu & Hirai, 1969). Perhaps meditation and alpha biofeedback were two paths to the same psychophysiological destination?

The biofeedback principle emerged, again in serendipitous circumstances, during investigations of imagery and color vision led by Brown at the Sepulveda Veteran's Administration Hospital near Los Angeles in the middle 1960s. Her plan was to create an experimental situation whereby different colors of illumination would be linked to different EEG frequencies—alpha turning on one color, beta another, and so on, enabling "a palette of colors to be activated into vivid colored pictures by somehow internally, feeling or mentally directing the energy of the brain waves" (Brown, 1974, p. 29). A prototype circuit was developed in which alpha caused the onset of soft blue illumination. Quite unexpectedly, while testing this device, Brown found that her subjects began to amuse themselves, turning on the light by manipulating their EEG alpha rhythm. Brown said that she was struck immediately by the potential of this discovery, and she redirected her efforts in order to study this new phenomenon. Subsequent studies in her lab (e.g., Brown, 1970) noted experiential correlates of EEG alpha enhancement very much like those reported by Kamiya.

Mulholland arrived at alpha biofeedback from the perspective of control systems while conducting basic brain research at the Massachusetts Institute of Technology. As discussed in chapter 2, a visual stimulus, such as a flash of light, causes cortical desynchronization or alpha blocking as EEG alpha is replaced by faster, less regular, beta activity, especially in the occipital region. Alpha blocking diminishes, or habituates, with repeated stimulation, even when the light presentations are spread out in time, which indicates a very simple kind of learning. Mulholland wondered what would happen if a feedback loop were created so that whenever EEG alpha rose above criterion, a flash would occur to cause alpha blocking; when alpha gradually reappeared there would be another flash that would block alpha again, and so on (Mulholland & Runnals, 1962). This has the main ingredients of alpha biofeedback, but it may not be obvious because the light is intended to control the EEG pattern, not vice versa. It soon occurred to Mulholland and his colleagues that this experimental set-up could just as well be viewed the other way around, if the light were made less intense and the participant were given proper instructions. This critical change in perspective (Runnals & Mulholland, 1965) completed the third independent discovery of EEG alpha biofeedback procedures.

Skeletal Muscle Responses

Although the skeletal muscles are the voluntary musculature, there are some limitations on our control of them. Voluntary control is severely curtailed following a stroke or in the spastic movements that accompany cerebral palsy. Even when there is no neurological impairment, we are reminded of our imperfect skeletal muscle control when we careen down a ski slope, attempt to coax music from a flute, or try to juggle three oranges. Many individuals are unable to effectively lower the residual level of tension in their skeletal muscles at rest; that is, they cannot relax. Finally, one ordinarily cannot isolate and individually control single motor units (SMUs). Recall from chapter 2 that an SMU is made up of one motor neuron and the muscle fibers that it innervates. Thus, to control an SMU is to voluntarily manipulate the electrical activity of a single cell of the body. Remarkably, several early studies indicated that this feat is not difficult, given sufficient feedback.

Virginia Harrison and her colleagues were the first to conduct SMU biofeedback studies. They used implanted needle electrodes to detect the EMG activity of SMUs in the tibialis anterior muscle, which is located along the shin and responsible for flexing the foot (Harrison & Mortenson, 1962). A speaker provided audio feedback, and an oscilloscope and a chart recording provided visual feedback of SMU activity. Typically, subjects were able to immediately isolate and control SMUs, with some subjects gaining individual control of as many as six SMUs. Control was impossible without feedback. A sample of the performance of one of the subjects is shown in Fig. 5.3. This subject demonstrates precise SMU control by counting from one to nine. John Basmajian (1963) replicated and extended these findings using the abductor pollicis brevis, a muscle located at the base of the thumb and controlling some of its movements. His subjects learned "how to maintain very slight contractions, which were apparent to themselves only through the response of the apparatus" (p. 440). As training progressed, most subjects were able to execute complex rhythms with SMUs, literally playing individual body cells as musical instruments.

The work with SMUs is another illustration of the feedback-specific potential of biofeedback. It is interesting to speculate about possible human-machine interfaces that might be driven by SMU firing. Imagine a

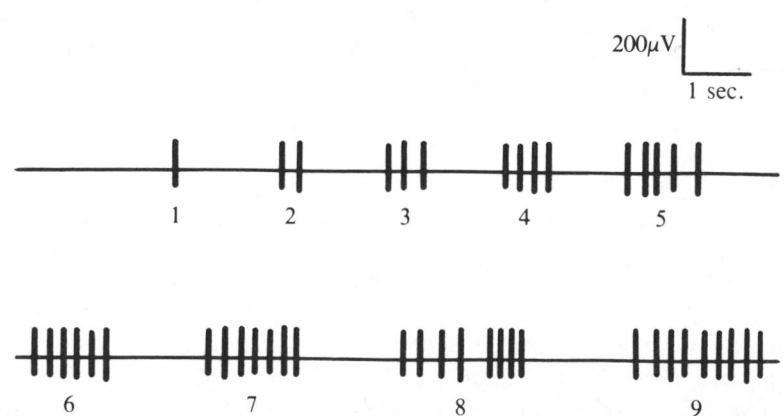

FIG. 5.3 Electromyogram demonstrating voluntary control of SMU activity following biofeedback training—subject produces successively longer "counts" (1-9) using SMU contraction. From "Identification and Voluntary Control of Single Motor Unit Activity in the Tibialis Anterior Muscle" by V. F. Harrison and O. A. Mortenson, 1962, *Anatomical Record, 144*, 115. Copyright 1962 by Alan R. Liss, Inc. Reprinted by permission.

typewriter or piano whose operation is not limited by the slow and clumsy movements of our fingers, driven by a collection of SMUs, each of which can fire at up to about 50 impulses per second. Electro-mechanical artificial limbs have already been developed whose movements are controlled fairly precisely by motor nerve firing (Mann, 1973).

Perhaps the earliest instance of EMG biofeedback in therapy occurred in the late 1950s at Indiana University. As Stern and Ray (1977) tell the story, physical therapists were having difficulty getting children, whose muscles had weakened because of polio, to do their exercises. This was understandable because when the children attempted to tense their muscles, nothing seemed to happen. Someone thought to amplify the EMG from the muscles being trained so that an increase in tension lit up a clown's face. In this new feedback situation, the children were said to be quite happy to exercise. Apparently, this work was never reported formally by the original investigators.

The first systematic use of EMG biofeedback for neuromuscular reeducation was reported by Marinacci and Horande (1960). Partial motor control was restored to several patients with different disorders. In one hemiplegic patient, 20% function was restored in previously nonfunctioning muscles of the upper arm within one hour of training. In another study, Andrews (1964) discussed more thoroughly the results of EMG training with patients whose movement impairments had existed for one to fourteen years. All were static on traditional physical therapy at the onset of biofeedback treatment. Of the 20 hemiplegic patients, 17 learned to exert some SMU control within the first *five minutes* of visual and auditory biofeedback training.

Surprisingly, following the work of Marinacci and Horande, nearly a decade was to elapse before Budzynski and Stoyva (1969) suggested extending EMG biofeedback methods, using surface electrodes, to the problem of skeletal muscle relaxation in tense individuals. They described an initial study in which normal volunteers were assigned to either: (a) a biofeedback group, in which the pitch of a tone varied directly with EMG levels of the frontalis muscle located in the forehead, (b) a constant tone group, in which a constant low tone sounded without respect to EMG level; or (c) a silent group, in which the subject heard nothing. All groups were instructed to relax as deeply as possible, especially the forehead, while the biofeedback subjects were instructed about the relationship between their EMG and the tone. The major results are shown in Fig. 5.4. Although the biofeedback group started with higher EMG, by Session 5 they were significantly below the other groups. Expressed as percentages, the biofeedback group decreased EMG by 50%, the silent group by 24%, while the constant tone group *increased* by 28%. The authors suggested that the new method might accelerate and deepen the relaxation process

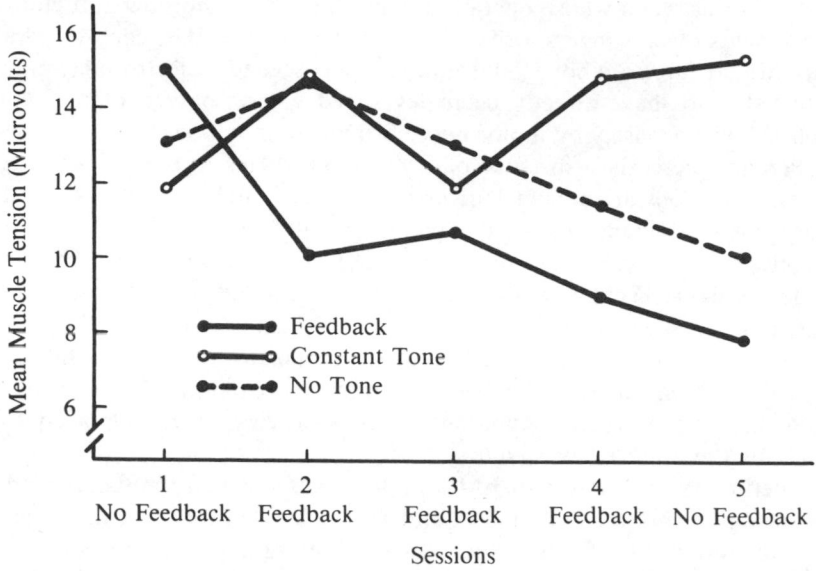

FIG. 5.4 Skeletal muscle tension over sessions for normal individuals receiving either auditory biofeedback, a constant tone, or no tone at all. From "An instrument for Producing Deep Muscle Relaxation by Means of Analog Information Feedback" by T. M. Budzynski and J. M. Stoyva, 1969, *Journal of Applied Behavior Analysis, 2*, 233. Copyright 1969 by the Journal of Applied Behavior Analysis. Adapted by permission.

in situations where progressive relaxation or autogenic training were the traditional approaches.

Applications of Biofeedback

Many uses of biofeedback, progressive relaxation, hypnosis, autogenic training, and meditation are reviewed in the chapters on specific health problems. Therefore, applications of the self-regulation procedures are considered in overview in chapters 5 and 6.

ANS Feedback

The idea of correcting common and serious cardiovascular conditions such as essential hypertension or cardiac arrhythmias by training a person to voluntarily regulate the misbehaving response system has been one of the more intriguing possible uses of biofeedback. Major research efforts along these lines have been funded by the National Heart Institute and the National Institute of Mental Health. After nearly 20 years of rather intense research efforts, these treatments remain very much experimental; they have not replaced drugs as the treatment of choice. Promising developments in the treatment of essential hypertension are reviewed in chapter 7.

Biofeedback, especially of vasomotor responses, is used rather widely with migraine, and appears to be consistently efficacious, but the mechanism underlying the treatment effect is still being debated. Biofeedback has also been explored with a variety of less common problems with autonomic nervous system manifestations. These problems include: (a) asthma (Kotses & Glaus, 1981), (b) sexual dysfunctions (Hatch, 1981), (c) Raynaud's Disease—vasospasms of the fingers and/or toes (Freedman, Lynn, Ianni, & Hale, 1981), and (d) gastrointestinal disorders such as ulcers, fecal incontinence, and involuntary regurgitation (Schuster, 1974). Some of these treatments are discussed in more detail in chapter 8.

EMG Feedback

The most consistently useful applications of biofeedback to date are in physical therapy or neuromuscular reeducation. The major physiological objectives are to establish functional neuromuscular pathways by: (a) exercising motor units that are functional at the onset of treatment, but produce little evidence of their action without enhanced feedback; and (b) encouraging return to function of motor units that are not functional at the outset. The behavioral objective is to achieve better control of muscles in ways that are of significance to the patient. A non-ambulatory patient may wish to be able to walk with the aid of a brace, while a person with a paralyzed arm might wish to be able to grasp objects. The behavioral and physiological objectives are accomplished by providing to the patient a feedback signal reflecting contraction of muscle fibers, and giving the patient the opportunity to practice controlling the signal in a supportive atmosphere. In addition to paralysis, EMG biofeedback has been used with some success in decreasing the spastic movements associated with cerebral palsy (Finley, Niman, Standley, & Wansley, 1977), facilitating the control of artificial limbs (Mann, 1973), and in training suppression of the involuntary movements of the mouth and tongue seen in tardive dyskinesia, a serious side effect of prolonged use of certain anti-psychotic drugs such as chlorpromazine (Sherman, 1979).

Of all the applications of biofeedback, the most common is EMG feedback to encourage relaxation. This training is usually undertaken for muscle contraction headache or anxiety, and as with treatment of migraine, consistent success is reported, but the mechanism of action is not clear. Also, non-feedback self-regulation methods are successful in these situations. The pattern of evidence requires us to ask whether the machines are necessary. Biofeedback machines are expensive, operation of the devices, and working effectively with the underlying bioelectrical recording principles requires special knowledge. Some skill and attention to detail are needed to install electrodes properly, and special pains must be taken to get treatment effects to generalize from the clinic to the everyday setting where external feedback is absent. The other self-regulation-based relaxation procedures do not present these difficulties. Therefore, where equivalent treatment effects are expected, a non-feedback method such as progressive relaxation would seem to be the treatment of choice. But, to be able to make wise choices among self-regulation treatments we must know much more about self-regulation than we presently do. For example, might one self-regulation method be the treatment of choice for one individual and a different method be optimum for another? If EMG biofeedback and progressive relaxation were each successful with 70% of patients with muscle contraction headache, perhaps, by pairing the right treatment with the right patient, the effectiveness of both treatments could be increased to 90%. The machines may not be necessary in some situations, but we do not yet know how to identify those situations. In the meantime, it may be useful to explore staged self-regulation treatment. For example, Blanchard et al. (1982) have demonstrated such an approach with headache, beginning with progressive relaxation for all patients, followed by EMG biofeedback for those patients who were not helped by the first stage training.

EEG Feedback

The most thoroughly researched application of EEG biofeedback is in training self-regulation of seizure activity in epileptics using EEG feedback of the "sensorimotor rhythm" or some other relatively high frequency pattern (Sterman, 1981), which is discussed in some detail in chapter 9. Several other potential uses of EEG biofeedback are presented in chapter 10. These involve attempts to enhance attention by learned suppression of slow waves in the EEG, and research investigating the role of two special EEG characteristics—the 40 Hz pattern and slow potentials—in cognitive peformance.

Certain cognitive tasks may be performed better when the two sides of the brain are engaged in different EEG patterns, which would be indicative of differential cortical involvement in the task. For example, it would seem that the left hemisphere areas specialized for language processing ought to be especially active during reading, as compared to the corresponding locations in the right hemisphere. Differences in the EEG between corresponding left and right hemisphere sites are known as *EEG asymmetries*. We have trained individuals, using biofeedback, to create EEG asymmetries by self-regulation of the relative prevalence of alpha waves in the EEG of the left and right hemispheres (Suter, Griffin, Smallhouse, & Whitlach, 1981). Suppression of alpha in one side of the brain relative to the other is thought to correspond to cortical activation within the hemisphere showing decreased alpha. We have reported, for a single individual, better performance remembering the spatial location of briefly-presented dots when the subject was suppressing right-hemisphere EEG alpha in relation to the left, as compared to when the subject was doing the opposite (Suter et al., 1981). This is noteworthy, given the importance of the right hemisphere in organizing visuospatial information. Perhaps someday individuals will routinely enhance their cognitive performance by training themselves, using biofeedback, to enter and maintain the appropriate "mind-brain mode" for the task at hand.

The best known application of EEG biofeedback is as a potential means of altering consciousness. How has this endeavor fared in the 20 years since the discovery of alpha biofeedback? Subsequent research has qualified some of the more enthusiastic early endorsements of alpha biofeedback as the new Yoga of the West. The very concept of "alpha state," suggesting a single, unitary, whole-brain neuropsychological phenomenon, is inconsistent with the way the brain is constructed and the way it works. The idea requires the brain to be homogenous in structure and uniform in function throughout—rather like a potato. But the brain is not made like a potato. Most areas of the cerebral cortex are functionally specialized, so that the neuropsychological significance (including experiential correlates) of an EEG phenomenon such as EEG alpha depends on the function of the cortical area producing it. For example, visual and kinesthetic imagery can be distinguished electrophysiologically by localized alpha blocking in the occipital and sensorimotor areas, respectively, of the cerebral cortex, the cortical areas specialized for these perceptual modalities (Davidson & Schwartz, 1977).

Also, it is incorrect to assume that whenever a localized increase in alpha is observed in EEG alpha biofeedback, the whole brain has "gone into an alpha state." Although there is some generalization to other cortical areas, the EEG control accomplished by using alpha biofeedback tends to be greatest at the cortical location that is in the feedback loop (Eberlin & Mulholland, 1976), another example of feedback specificity. Therefore, EEG alpha biofeedback studies using different electrode placements are probably dealing with rather different neuropsychological states.

Empirical studies of subjective experiences during biofeedback training for alpha enhancement have led to further qualifications. First, there is some continuing support (e.g., Tyson & Audette, 1979) for the early reports of pleasant, relaxed, mind-wandering experiences during heightened occipital alpha, but marked variability between the experiences of different individuals has been noted (Travis, Kondo, & Knott, 1975). Personality characteristics of the individual may play an important role (Tyson & Audette, 1979).

Several other factors in addition to the actual alpha biofeedback training, seem to help determine the conscious correlates of enhanced alpha. These include: (a) expectations of the participant about what he/she might experience (Plotkin, 1977); (b) the extent to which the participant is led to believe he/she is actually producing the intended EEG pattern (Plotkin, 1977); (c) sensory deprivation effects due to the biofeedback training environment (Plotkin, 1978); and (d) the status of other physiological responses, such as EMG, during the biofeedback task (Marshall & Bentler, 1976).

There are many methodological problems in this area. Perhaps the most serious is the duration of biofeedback training. With the exception of Kamiya's Langley Porter group, there has not been much interest in the experiential correlates of extended alpha-enhancement biofeedback. We seem to know less today about the "alpha experience" than we thought we knew 20 years ago.

Enhancing Clinical Efficacy

Biofeedback research has moved far beyond merely demonstrating the phenomenon, yet there are a number of research areas in which our understanding of biofeedback effects is quite limited. The clinical efficacy of biofeedback would be greatly enhanced if we knew more about some of the following.

Understanding feedback-specific effects would help clarify the mechanisms of biofeedback and might even make it more clear what it is to do something "voluntarily." Research in this area may eventually lead to a *psychophysiological* understanding of what is commonly called "the will." On a more immediately practical level, further research should assist practitioners in cultivating feedback-specific effects when they are desirable, and in discouraging them when they are unwanted.

In any biofeedback experiment, some participants are more adept than others in the self-regulation task; similarly, in the clinical biofeedback setting, some patients benefit more than others from any particular biofeedback treatment. We need to know how the "biofeedback athlete" differs from other individuals, and to know when biofeedback is, and is not, the treatment of choice on a person by person basis. Research is under way examining variables that are mainly: (a) psychological, such as personality differences (e.g., Ray, 1974); physiological, such as the "lability" (tendency to fluctuate) of the response system (Guglielmi, Roberts, Tellegen, & Zimmerman, 1981); or (c) psychophysiological, such as the accuracy with which the individual can perceive internal bodily sensations (e.g., Katkin, Morell, Goldband, Bernstein, & Wise, 1982).

Certain, as yet poorly understood, characteristics of the person operating the equipment and collecting data or administering the therapy seem to make a difference in how large the biofeedback effects will be, or whether there will be any effect at all. Edwin Taub (1977) has called this the "person factor," and reported that skin temperature self-regulation was much more readily demonstrated with a warm, friendly, nurturant experimenter than when this same person interacted with the participants in a cold, detached fashion. Perhaps related to this effect is research showing that the expectations of the experimenter about biofeedback seem to help determine the results that are actually obtained (Segreto-Bures & Kotses, 1982). Understanding these effects better would not only help untangle some of the conflicting findings in the biofeedback literature, but help practitioners who use biofeedback to enhance their therapeutic effectiveness.

A well-known psychological principle, the Yerkes-Dodson law, says that for any given task, there is an optimum level of motivation, such that either too little or too much motivation will result in less than peak performance. Recent findings suggest that this principle holds for biofeedback (Bregman & McAllister, 1982). Related to this is an observation about biofeedback that has been offered repeatedly in various forms, namely that a "passive attitude" (Green, Green, & Walters, 1970) facilitates, or is even necessary for, self-regulation in biofeedback. The idea is "allowing" oneself to relax versus "making" oneself relax. There seems to be no research on this important possibility. The question of passive versus active involvement in the context of self-regulation is discussed further in chapter 6.

Theories of Biofeedback

When we ponder how biofeedback works, we are brought face to face with the weakest link in our understanding of ourselves—the mind-body problem. How these aspects of a human being interact remains a mystery, as was emphasized in chapter 1. It is one thing to simply note the psychophysiological effects of biofeedback yet quite another to explain these effects in any fundamental sense.

The title of a film about biofeedback, *Mind over Body* (Sabbagh, 1973), and the title of a popular book surveying biofeedback, *New Mind, New Body* (Brown, 1974), convey the essence of one view of biofeedback—that the mind can learn to control a great many involuntary bodily functions, if only given the proper opportunity. Biofeedback creates that opportunity. This idea is so compelling that it is taken as a comfortable assumption among many workers in the field, especially practitioners. But how is it that the insubstantial mind can exert causation on a physical organ, for example, to alter the beating of the heart? As discussed in chapter 1, how does the mind "will" the body to do anything?

Interestingly, we sometimes find ourselves looking at biofeedback the other way around. The skeletal muscles (body) relax, causing the person to experience (mind) less anxiety. Similarly, the person learns to intensify the EEG alpha rhythm (body) which results in a pleasant, free-floating, state of consciousness (mind). The mind-body problem is not diminished when we reverse our perspective. How does the body influence the mind?

Several theoretical approaches seem to avoid the mind-body problem altogether. For example, biofeedback can be analyzed in cybernetic system terms (e.g., Anliker, 1977), so that the person and the biofeedback situation are seen as a feedback control system in which a servomechanism (a thermostat is an example) exerts "error control." Alternatively, biofeedback effects have been cast as instances of operant conditioning (e.g., Black, Cott, & Pavloski, 1977), as was discussed earlier in connection with the first studies of autonomic biofeedback. A physiological response, such as an increase in EEG alpha, is rewarded, causing it to be strengthened and made increasingly probable. Neither the cybernetic nor the operant conditioning formulations make any particular mind-body assumptions.

Still differently, one might try to explain biofeedback in terms of the development of new functional neural pathways from presently unknown areas of the brain that are responsible for volitional control of the body, to organs that are not normally under such control, such as the heart. However, one would then wonder about the role of the mind in volition—and we find ourselves back at the mind-body problem.

With regard to the question of volition, it is possible that some biofeedback effects might not be mediated consciously at all—what could that rat possibly be thinking about to dilate the blood vessels in one ear? There is some evidence for this possibility in humans (e.g., London & Schwartz, 1980), including the observation that biofeedback participants are frequently able to control the response in question but are utterly unable to explain how they do it. The reader will appreciate this difficulty by attempting to explain how he/she accomplishes *any* simple voluntary act, such as turning the pages of this book.

No theory of biofeedback, as yet, has attempted to explain why biofeedback effects are sometimes curiously elusive. For example, across a series of four studies conducted in our laboratory, skin temperature self-regulation by children ranged from quite impressive to none (Suter, Fredericson, & Portuesi, 1983; Suter & Loughry-Machado, 1981). Since there were no important changes in the biofeedback setup from one study to the next, there must have been other, unknown, but very powerful, variables influencing the ability of these children to warm and cool their hands. Results such as these suggest that an acceptable theory of biofeedback, as well as explaining how the feedback arrangement facilitates self-regulation, must successfully predict when feedback will, and will not lead to self-regulation, probably by taking into account attitudinal, interpersonal, and cognitive factors (Suter et. al, 1983).

It will be a long time before biofeedback effects are adequately explained. In the meantime, we can ponder whether, in EEG biofeedback, the EEG pattern changes consciousness, consciousness changes the EEG pattern, or whether these are even sensible questions.

PROGRESSIVE RELAXATION

Jacobson and the Rationale

Edmund Jacobson was trained as both a researcher in physiology (Ph.D. from Harvard, 1910) and as a practicing physician (M.D. from University of Chicago, 1915). Combining these two perspectives, he provided some of the first careful measurements of physiological responses to stress, and a cogent analysis of the integrated functioning of the mind and body. Although his progressive relaxation self-regulation method was developed very early in his career, elaboration of the idea was his life's work. If the man himself is any reflection of his methods, then we would do well to study them closely for, in 1978, at the age of 91, Jacobson was still bustling happily between his private practices in Chicago and New York.

Jacobson uses "tension" and "relaxation" in reference to opposite states of the skeletal muscles; his usage will be adopted for the remainder of this chapter. Muscle tension occurs most obviously when skeletal muscles are made to contract in order to move particular parts of the body. Muscle tension is also necessary to maintain posture. However, Jacobson was especially concerned with tension in muscles that are not directly involved in any particular task. For example, while you are reading this book you may be jiggling one foot or clenching your teeth. Any tension in muscles that are not supporting the book or maintaining your posture is wasted. "Tense people spend too much energy," he once said (Jacobson, 1978, p. 13). Contraction of any of our 1,030 skeletal muscles literally uses up energy. The result can be unnecessary fatigue, exhaustion, or a number of stress-related disorders. Tension in the wrong muscles at the wrong time can disrupt execution of the task at hand. It may be merely distracting when you are attempting to read and comprehend, but it may render the smooth execution of a basketball free throw impossible.

Even when we lie down to rest, our muscles do not rest, Jacobson observed. An immobile muscle usually retains some non-functional residual tension. Because of this, when we attempt to rest, we may end up wasting still more energy and do not feel refreshed. Beyond this, chronic tension was seen as a contributing factor to a host of stress-related disorders—"It precedes some diseases as the whole or part of the cause, either predisposing or exciting" (Jacobson, 1929, p. 16). Contemporary investigators have tended to view heightened muscle tension as symptomatic of other problems rather than causing them, but his major points about wasting muscle energy and the mind-body interaction this implied, are well taken. Also, Jacobson proposed that muscle tension and anxiety are closely linked, and that muscle relaxation will lead to a reduction in anxiety. Although current researchers are not so convinced that muscle tension causes anxiety, there is some agreement that muscle tension and anxiety are correlated and that deep muscle relaxation is ordinarily accompanied by a reduction in anxiety.

Clearly one cannot relax simply by finding a quiet comfortable spot and remaining motionless. Relaxation must be learned and practiced like any other skeletal muscle skill. A deceptively simple idea is one of the keys to relaxation—just as tensing a muscle is an act of "doing," relaxing it is an act of "not doing" (Jacobson, 1978, p. 170); to relax is to refrain from producing tension.

To learn to relax, one must develop what Jacobson called muscle sense, or sensitivity to the amount of tension in the various skeletal muscles. Once this sense has been sharpened, the presence of muscle tension can function as a cue for relaxation—telling the tense individual that it is time to relax. The purpose of progressive relaxation is to train the muscle sense sufficiently to enable one to learn to relax. With progressive relaxation training the person gradually moves toward a state in which relaxation is more or less automatically maintained. It is as if a skeletal muscle tension thermostat is reset at a lower level. This psychophysiological resetting phenomenon shows up frequently as a consequence of self-regulation procedures. For example, after SMR EEG biofeedback training, seizure patients have less slow seizure-type EEG activity, *even while they are asleep* (Sterman, Macdonald, & Stone, 1974); the targeted psychophysiological state is being maintained automatically.

Progressive Relaxation Procedures

Most therapists today use brief, highly condensed versions of progressive relaxation. Progressive relaxation was not originally seen as a speedy procedure. Jacobson warned that it would require weeks, months, or in the case of slow-learners, even years to escape the chronic tension state. Regular daily practice at home, for periods of about one hour, once or twice a day, was emphasized.

At the first session the patient receives an explanation of the rationale of progressive relaxation. Then a comfortable position is adopted. It is easiest to begin learning to relax lying down with the head on a thin pillow to prevent it from bending back and pulling on the neck ligaments. Any tight-fitting clothes should be loosened or removed. In general, distracting skin contact between parts of the body is to be avoided, thus the legs should not be crossed but situated several inches apart; similarly, the arms should rest comfortably a few inches away from the sides. The patient is allowed to gradually "wind down" for three or four minutes at the beginning, very gradually closing the eyes. Then the first exercise is conducted, in which the individual bends his or her left hand back gradually at the wrist; the therapist might provide some resistance against the hand to make the sensation of tenseness more distinct.

The idea of the first exercise is to observe the faint sensation of tenseness in the forearm, originating from the muscle group executing this movement. It is essential that one does not confuse the more distinct feeling of "strain" from the wrist with muscle tension. The bending is increased steadily for several minutes. Then the contraction is ended and the left hand is allowed to fall of its own weight. When this happens the tenseness is replaced by relaxation. The only purpose of the contraction exercises is to show the person what *not* to do when relaxing. This exercise is repeated several times, and at this point the person is approximately midway through the first session. The remaining half hour of the session is devoted to continuous relaxation while attending to the sensations of tenseness or relaxation in different parts of the body without intentionally tensing any skeletal muscles.

Muscle groups are relaxed in a fixed order beginning with the larger muscle groups because it is easier to recognize and eliminate tension in these muscles. It is also easiest for the therapist to detect residual tension in large muscles, for a limb that is truly relaxed offers no resistance to movement by the therapist and is flaccid. As new muscle groups are added, all of the old groups are simultaneously relaxed with the newest muscle group.

As long as relaxation is commencing smoothly, a new muscle group is added in each session with the tension-relaxation exercise repeated three times. Every third session or so a session is devoted entirely to relaxation, with no contraction exercises at the beginning. The rest of the skeletal muscles are gradually phased in—the other arm, then the legs one at a time, the muscles of the trunk, and finally muscles in the neck and the face. The full program would run 50 or 60 sessions for a reasonably adept pupil.

Before training, rest was accompanied by signs of residual tension such as slight movements of the limbs, occasional swallowing, small jerky deflections of the eyeballs under the closed lids, partial winks, frowns, creases in the forehead, breathing irregularities, sighs, tremors, and perhaps slightly elevated blood pressure and heart rate. The mind was still active, and if worry or anxiety were present at the beginning of rest they would persist. After training, these signs should be gone, with the person able to lie motionless, no trace of tension anywhere, experiencing a pleasant feeling of relaxation and diminished mental activity, including calming of the emotions.

A person who has reached this stage may go on to practice relaxing unused muscles during everyday activities, a psychophysiological state Jacobson called, *differential relaxation*. Graceful dancing or successful tennis depends as much on the proper pattern of relaxation among hundreds of unused muscles as on coordinated contractions of the skeletal muscles actually producing the movements. This can be seen clearly in the awkward movements of a beginning dancer, symptomatic of simultaneous contractions of opposing muscle groups. Jacobson found that "general relaxation" once trained, could be extended to unused muscles during various activities such as reading, writing, talking, driving a car, or even walking.

Systematic Desensitization

As mentioned previously, much briefer versions of progressive relaxation than were originally envisioned by Jacobson are usually used nowadays. This modification is due mainly to Joseph Wolpe who borrowed and condensed progressive relaxation for use as the first step in his *systematic desensitization* procedure. This therapy technique was developed in the course of a series of experiments with cats in which they were first placed in enclosed boxes and then shocked to make them fearful of those places; then they were tested with various experimental procedures designed to eliminate these fears. Wolpe's approach was to create phobias in cats and then try to cure them. He eventually became quite successful with his cat patients, and arrived at a simple, elegant principle that has been used to treat tens of thousands of human patients with very real phobias—such things as fear of heights, elevators, snakes, taking exams, and the like. Wolpe (1958) summarized the principle as follows:

> If a response antagonistic to anxiety can be made to occur in the presence of anxiety-evoking stimuli, so that it is accompanied by a complete or partial suppression of the anxiety responses, the bond between those stimuli and the anxiety responses will be weakened. (p. 71)

For systematic desensitization, relaxation is used as the response anta-gonistic to anxiety. One cannot relax and feel anxious at the same time.

Wolpe reports that with his version of progressive relaxation patients are often able to achieve deep muscle relaxation within seven sessions. After an explanation of the relationship between relaxation and anxiety, the person grips the arm of the chair and notices the sensation of tension. Then the person is to alternately push and pull against the force of the therapist who holds the person's wrist. After maintaining the tension in the bicep for perhaps 30 seconds, the person is asked to relax that muscle completely and to continue relaxing all of the arm muscles on both sides for about 15 minutes. The second session is devoted to smoothing out tension in the muscles of the forehead; the other muscles of the face begin to be phased in later in the session, or in subsequent sessions, depending on how quickly the person is learning to relax. The patient then learns to relax the neck, shoulders, back, abdomen, and legs, in that order. The therapist may use attention to respiration as a relaxation device, particu-larly to the relaxation of the muscles of inspiration occurring each time a person exhales. Other suggestions and even hypnosis and drugs might be used to facilitate muscle relaxation.

Wolpe's goal in administering this accelerated progressive relaxation training is somewhat more modest than Jacobson's. All that he wishes is that his patients attain a sufficiently relaxed state to proceed successfully with the actual desensitization of the phobia. Desensitization requires that the patient and therapist construct a hierarchy of anxiety stimuli, com-posed of a list of situations having to do with the phobia. For example, if the person were undergoing treatment for fear of heights the hierarchy might range from wearing high-heeled shoes (very mildly anxiety-provoking), to shopping on the third floor of a department store (moderately frightening), to standing on a narrow ledge atop a tall build-ing (quite terrifying). Additional situations would occupy intermediate points in the hierarchy. Once the hierarchy has been established, the desensitization commences with the patient relaxing, then with the aid of suggestions from the therapist, imagining as vividly as possible the scene occupying the lowest rung in the hierarchy. As the individual relaxes and imagines, say, wearing high-heeled shoes, this scene, which used to be anxiety-provoking, gradually becomes associated with relaxation. Should any anxiety whatsoever creep in, the person is to stop imagining the scene and return to relaxation. When it is possible to imagine the scene vividly for extended periods without experiencing any sign of anxiety, it is time to move up to the next step in the hierarchy. This procedure is repeated until situations at the very top can be imagined without anxiety, at which point the person is cured. When executed perfectly, the therapy program enables the patient to banish a phobia without experiencing any anxiety during the entire course of treatment.

Applications of Progressive Relaxation

In addition to the brief variation developed by Wolpe, there are many other versions. In a review of progressive relaxation research published in the 1970s, it was necessary to use 22 categories to organize the progressive relaxation methods reported (Hillenberg & Collins, 1982). The techniques differ primarily in the muscle groups that are used, in what order they are trained, how much time is spent with each muscle group, whether other relaxation methods such as autogenic training or hypnosis are combined with progressive relaxation, and the extent to which a therapist has an active role in the training procedure. In its various manifestations, progressive relaxation is the most widely used self-regulation relaxation method in the United States, with autogenic training preferred in Europe. Progressive relaxation is simple, easily explained to the patient, lacks the occult connotations that worry some patients about meditation, and does not require expensive equipment as does biofeedback.

Despite the many procedural variations, the weight of the evidence indicates that even the brief versions of progressive relaxation produce muscle relaxation, and frequently change autonomic responses in the direction of generalized psychophysiological relaxation. There is some indication that a full 16-muscle group sequence is superior to the use of only a few muscle groups in the relaxation routine (Russell, Sipich, & Knipe, 1976), and that more extended training leads to greater relaxation as compared to briefer programs of training (Borkovec & Sides, 1979). Clinical research suggests that progressive relaxation is useful in treating a variety of stress-related disorders, but, as with biofeedback, the mechanism of action is not always clear. Progressive relaxation appears to be a useful component of self-regulation programs to control essential hypertension (Glascow, Gaarder, & Engel, 1982), as discussed in chapter 7.

One of the more interesting uses of progressive relaxation is with patients who are extremely anxious in the dental chair. In one study (Miller, Murphy, & Miller, 1978), a dentist recruited some of his patients to participate in an experiment, but they were not just any patients—they were from among the top 1% of his patients in dental anxiety, according to his judgment. At the beginning of an initial dental session in which dental work was actually to be conducted, each person rated his or her anxiety in the situation and a baseline EMG reading from the frontalis muscles was taken. Then there were 10 training sessions over the next 4 weeks, with each patient randomly assigned to one of three treatments: (a) biofeedback training for frontalis muscle EMG reduction, (b) progressive relaxation training, or (c) "self-relaxation" in which the person was left to relax as best he or she could for the 10 sessions. A second dental appointment followed training, where EMG measurements and self-reports of anxiety were obtained as before. The results are shown in Fig. 5.5. Frontalis EMG decreased significantly across the 10 sessions of training for the biofeedback and progressive relaxation groups, but not for the self-relaxation group. Similarly, EMG dropped from the first to the second dental sessions for the first two groups but not for the other group. Finally, reported dental anxiety was reduced after training for both the biofeedback and progressive relaxation groups, but not for the patients left to practice relaxing on their own. Both progressive relaxation and EMG biofeedback were beneficial to acutely anxious persons in situations that were, for them, extremely stressful.

A final important use of progressive relaxation is in reducing the stress of chemotherapy in cancer patients by helping them to relax. About 25% of cancer patients experience nausea and vomiting in anticipation of chemotherapy. Morrow and Morrell (1982) randomly assigned 60 cancer

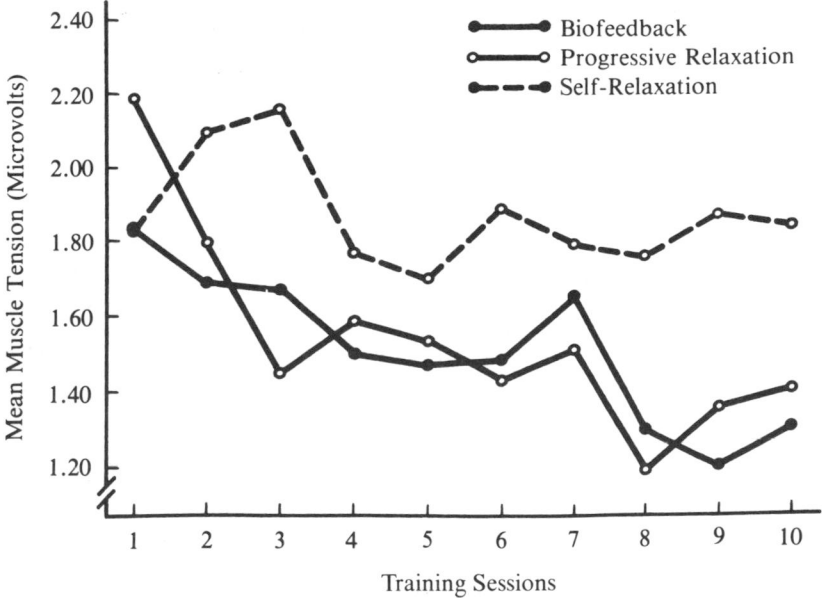

FIG. 5.5 Skeletal muscle tension over sessions for highly anxious dental patients receiving either EMG biofeedback, progressive relaxation training, or self-relaxation. From "Comparison of Electromyographic Feedback and Progressive Relaxation Training in Treating Circumscribed Anxiety Stress Reactions" by M. P. Miller et al., 1978, *Journal of Consulting and Clinical Psychology, 46,* 1293. Copyright 1978 by the American Psychological Association. Adapted by permission.

patients with anticipatory nausea and vomiting to either: (a) a two-session systematic desensitization treatment, (b) two sessions of supportive counseling, or (c) no treatment. In follow-up chemotherapy sessions, both nausea and vomiting were reduced only for the patients trained with systematic desensitization. While anticipatory nausea remained for 95% of the untreated and 80% of the counseled patients, only 50% of the desensitized patients still reported nausea. Of the latter individuals, 8 out of 10 had shorter duration nausea than prior to treatment. Only 33% of the desensitized patients still vomited in anticipation of chemotherapy, as opposed to 82% and 100% of the untreated and counseled patients, respectively. Morrow and his colleagues are exploring cost-effective methods of making systematic desensitization widely available to cancer patients using group training methods and audio tapes of standard relaxation instructions.

6 Hypnosis, Autogenic Training, and Meditation

HYPNOSIS

Mesmer and the Discovery of Hypnosis

In the year 1766, scientists were experimenting with electrical charges, and primitive storage batteries. They were conducting spectacular drawing room demonstrations with great flashing bolts of electricity. Newton's Law of Gravity was well established. Coulomb would soon show that the law held for electrical and magnetic attraction and repulsion. Children learned in school that the Earth itself was a magnet. Scientists, and even educated lay persons, were changing the way they thought of the universe, now that it seemed to be filled with invisible, yet powerful, mysterious, yet lawful, forces.

Given the spirit of that period, the doctoral dissertation that Anton Mesmer presented in 1766 for his medical degree at the University of Vienna was not so fantastic: "The Influence of the Planets in the Cure of Diseases." His basic premise was that the heavenly bodies influence living creatures through a force or fluid that he called "animal magnetism" to distinguish it from ordinary magnetism. Experiments, in which he touched and stroked his patients' afflicted parts with magnetized steel instruments, seemed to indicate that an infusion of animal magnetism could cure a variety of complaints. When he discovered that he could obtain the therapeutic effects without the implements, like a good scientist he revised his theory, concluding that animal magnetism must be present in unusual quantities within his own body.

The Medical Faculty of Vienna had taken a dim view of Mesmer's activities from the beginning. "Solid doctors bled their patients and sweated, purged, cupped, and dosed them in the good old-fashioned way" (Winkler & Bromberg, 1939, p. 41). Following an investigation, they rejected animal magnetism and discounted the apparently successful cures as mere figments of the patients' imagination. Forced to leave Vienna, Mesmer settled in Paris where he set up medical practice, and was shortly in such demand that he introduced a device that made possible group therapy—his famous "baquet," meaning "tub." A huge round container was filled with water and iron filings. Numerous metal rods protruded for patients to grasp (Fig. 6.1). A group of patients could encircle the baquet, hands joined, their bodies connected to the device with cords. Meanwhile

FIG. 6.1 Mesmer's magnetic bacquet. From a 1784 print housed at the Bibliotheque Nationale, Paris. Reprinted by permission.

Mesmer, often dressed as a magician in a flowing silk robe, passed among them, staring, touching, and gesturing in sessions that went on for hours. There were rumors of sexual goings-on between Mesmer and his mainly female patients. The French government launched an investigation by a commission of both physicians and scientists, including Benjamin Franklin, who summed up their opinion when he wrote of animal magnetism, "What could not be smelt, felt nor seen was not there" (Winkler & Bromberg, 1939, p. 53). Like the earlier group, this commission denounced animal magnetism, Mesmer, and his cures. Mesmer retired in disgrace to Switzerland where he died in 1815.

Most contemporary students of hypnosis are convinced that Mesmer was mistaken when he concluded that the strange phenomena he observed in his patients were caused by a force that he emitted. Hypnotic induction is not an art practiced by only the specially-endowed. Some therapists have a new patient hypnotize them first, before inducing trance in the patient, so as to dispel anxiety. Nearly anyone can learn to achieve hypnotic induction in others with a little practice. Persons who are extremely high in hypnotic ability enter trance spontaneously during everyday activities. In general, it seems that individuals can hypnotize themselves about as easily as they can be hypnotized (Johnson, 1979).

For the above reasons, the current consensus is that the forces responsible for hypnotic induction and hypnotic state phenomena reside within the subject, and are activated by the hypnotist-subject interaction. It is better to use "hypnotic talent" or "hypnotic ability" to describe the ease with which an individual enters the hypnotic state, rather than the older term, "hypnotic susceptibility," which rather misleadingly, suggests something such as "lack of willpower."

Hindsight reveals that Mesmer was misguided, but so were the investigatory commissions when, having *correctly* inferred that the therapeutic effects of hypnosis depended on powers originating within the patients, they went on to *reject* Mesmer's cures, for that reason—throwing out the baby with the bacquet water. In doing so they were guilty of seriously underestimating the ability of individuals to cure themselves.

Hypnotic Induction

Hypnotic induction refers to the process whereby the subject achieves the hypnotic state as well as any procedures used to encourage this transition. There is no single way to accomplish induction, nor even a recognizable key ingredient of the varied induction methods. At one extreme, induction procedures may be wholly *direct* and conscious, where the hypnotist proceeds overtly and explicitly, with the subject's awareness, to attempt induction. At the other extreme, some methods are entirely *indirect* and nonconscious, so that the hypnotist facilitates the shift toward the hypnotic state much more subtly, without the awareness or explicit participation of the subject.

The varied induction techniques seem to incorporate many of the following elements: (a) narrowing of attention, (b) the feeling of fatigue, (c) the perception of being controlled by the hypnotist, (d) relaxation, and (e) cognitive confusion or clarification.

Direct Induction

The following is a condensation of a direct hypnotic induction procedure described in full by Barber (1969, pp. 251-254). A metronome emitting a rhythmic "tock" and a simultaneously blinking light at which the subject is supposed to gaze are provided as aids. The function of the metronome is to provide an attentional focus, and to fatigue the eyes. This encourages the subject to perceive eye closing as an involuntary event initiated by the hypnotist—"My God, he *is* controlling my eyes!" Related methods use a dim light bulb, any convenient shiny object, or even the "phosphenes" in the visual system—those dots, specks, lines and patterns that can be observed by introspection when your eyes are closed and the lids are illuminated (Hunchak, 1980). It is not necessary to ask the subject to attend to a specific object; for example, certain kinds of poetry that invite rapt attention seem to be trance-inducing (Snyder & Shor, 1983). In many circumstances the voice of the hypnotist provides adequate attentional focusing.

Initial instructions request the cooperation of the subject:

> Your ability to be hypnotized depends entirely on your willingness to cooperate . . . if you pay close attention to what I say, and follow what I tell you, you can easily learn to fall into a hypnotic sleep. . . . Hypnosis is nothing fearful or mysterious. . . . Your cooperation, your interest is what I ask for. . . . Nothing will be done that will in any way cause you the least embarrassment . . .

Suggestions to relax follow:

> Relax completely. . . . Relax the muscles of your legs. Relax the muscles of your arms. . . . Relax completely. . . . Your legs feel heavy and limp. . . . Your arms are heavy, heavy . . . sleepy, sleepy. You are concentrating on the sound of my voice. Your lids are heavy . . . pushing down . . . your eyes are blinking . . . closing.

Once the eyes have closed, the state is deepened:

> Just keep your thoughts on what I am saying . . . you will have no trouble hearing me . . . I shall now begin to count. At each count you will feel your-

self going down, down, down, into a deep, comfortable . . . sleep. A sleep in which you will be able to do all sorts of things I ask you to do.

Instructions and exercises intended to further deepen the hypnotic state continue for perhaps five minutes at the end of which the subject is instructed to remain with eyes closed until told to open them at the end of the experiment. The full induction procedure takes about 10 minutes.

Suggestions to relax and instructions calling attention to the sensations of warmth and heaviness in the extremities that accompany psychophysiological relaxation appear to facilitate hypnotic induction, but they are not essential. An outstanding counter-example is the case of a soldier who, during WWII, tried to kill a military physician who was also a skilled hypnotist. It seems that the physician, through a clerical error, had reassigned the soldier to active duty rather than providing for a medical discharge as had been promised. A violent struggle ensued; at one point the soldier ended up with his face near an ink bottle, the physician holding him from behind. On the spur of the moment the physician shouted, "Look at that ink bottle and keep looking at it!" (Spiegel & Spiegel, 1978, p. 24). Within a few seconds the patient relaxed and slumped to the floor. Accidental hypnotic induction by fright may happen frequently in family situations, schools, and court rooms that are both stressful and authoritarian.

In the standard induction procedure, the hypnotist talks about going to sleep, but this is only for ease of communication. The hypnotized person is not asleep, nor even necessarily less alert than is usual. The sleep metaphor is helpful because most of us regard sleep and its borderline stages as alterations in consciousness that are non-threatening. Also, there is a kind of "letting go" that accompanies presleep drowsiness and sleep onset. Furthermore, we consider anything that we might do during sleep as quite beyond our control. For these reasons, presenting hypnotic induction as a sleep-encouraging procedure facilitates responsiveness to suggestions during the hypnotic state.

None of the elements of the standard procedure described previously seem to be absolutely essential for entering the hypnotic state. The statement, "Please sit in that chair and go into hypnosis," can be used to induce trance in persons with very high hypnotic ability (Moss, 1965).

Indirect Induction

Direct hypnotic induction procedures were used almost exclusively until the 1940s, at which time more "permissive," indirect approaches were introduced, mainly through the work of Milton H. Erickson. Indirect induction is useful in the clinical setting where the person to be hypnotized may feel anxious and defensive. Erickson's approach to hypnosis was informal, leisurely, and always carefully attuned to the requirements of the particular patient. Erickson would often spend an hour or so moving gradually toward trance, and saw no special reason to produce trance quickly, because, in his opinion, the eventual depth of trance was not related to the speed with which it was achieved (Erickson, 1952).

His "My friend John" method demonstrates one way in which he adjusted to resistant patients (Erickson, 1964). Supposedly as part of a lengthy explanation of hypnosis, he would demonstrate, so thoroughly and carefully, the induction procedure that he uses on his imaginary friend, John, that the resistant patient, who has not been directly challenged by the hypnotist, follows John's example and enters into the hypnotic state.

It is possible to avoid authoritarian directives altogether. A good example of this is a case study of a previously unhypnotizable cancer patient with no apparent hypnotic ability (Barber, 1980). The induction begins with an extremely low key request from the therapist, "I just wonder if you've ever noticed that *without even looking*, you know where your right arm is?" The patient has indeed noticed this, to which the therapist responds, "That's right." The conversation continues along these lines for a series of questions with the patient answering in the affirmative and the therapist responding with "That's right." Then the therapist casually says, "And so I just wonder if, as I lift your left arm . . . ." He lifts the arm about 18 inches from the patient's lap. " . . . and *just leave it right there*." The patient's arm is left hanging in midair, indicating that the patient has responded successfully to the subtle suggestion that her arm is *supposed to be* suspended in front of her. With the arm in that position, the therapist says, "I'm going to press down on your hand, and if I encounter a kind of resistance to my pressure . . . that's all right." This resistance is explained as the kind of upward force that she has no doubt noticed in a piece of wood that, when pressed down in the water, just bounces right back up to the surface, "*right where it belongs*." The patient was hypnotized and the subsequent therapy for chronic pain was successful.

Effects of Hypnotic Induction

Assessing Hypnotic Ability

The Stanford Hypnotic Susceptibility Scale is one of the more popular methods for assessing hypnotic ability. The items from one form of the scale, shown in Table 6.1, illustrate some of the behavioral characteristics of the hypnotic state (Hilgard, Weitzenhoffer, Landes, & Moore, 1961). Each of these items taps a behavior that would be highly unusual in ordinary circumstances. For example, the instructions for "finger lock" are to place the palms together and interlock the fingers, after which the suggestion is made that the subject cannot separate the hands. Then the

TABLE 6.1
Items in the Stanford Hypnotic Susceptibility Scale (Form A)

Item	Passing Criterion	Percent Passing
Postural sway	Falls without forcing	69
Eye closure	Closes eyes without forcing	58
Hand lowering	Lowers at least 6 inches within 10 seconds	81
Immobilization	Arm rises less than 1 inch within 10 seconds	14
Finger lock	Incomplete separation of finger within 10 seconds	32
Arm rigidity	Less than 2 inches of arm bending within 10 seconds	32
Hands moving together	Hands move together as close as 6 inches	70
Verbal inhibition	Name unspoken for 10 seconds	23
Hallucination (fly)	Any movement, grimacing, acknowledgement of effect	35
Eye catalepsy	Eyes remain closed at end of 10 seconds	30
Posthypnotic suggestion	Any partial movement response at signal	49
Amnesia test	Recall of 3 or fewer of the above items	32

Note. From *Hypnotic Susceptibility* by Ernest R. Hilgard, copyright 1965 by Harcourt Brace Jovanovich, Inc. Reproduced by permission of the publisher.

request is made, "Try to open your hands. Go ahead and try." If the fingers have not been completely separated within 10 seconds, the subject passes this item. Verbal inhibition is tested by asking subjects their names, after having suggested to them that they cannot provide their names. The "posthypnotic" test uses a suggestion made during the hypnotic state that when a certain cue word is spoken after arousal from the trance, the individual will get up and move to a different chair. All of the criteria for passing, and the percentage of a large number of Stanford college students who actually passed each item are shown in Table 6.1. As would be imagined, some of these items are more difficult than others; only 23% could not give their names, but 70% moved their outstretched arms together when told that an invisible force was pushing them together.

As expected, the persons tested showed differing degrees of hypnotic ability. This was examined by adding up the number of items passed by each person to yield that person's score (which could range from 0 to 12) and then checking to see how many persons got each of the possible scores. This information is shown in Fig. 6.2.

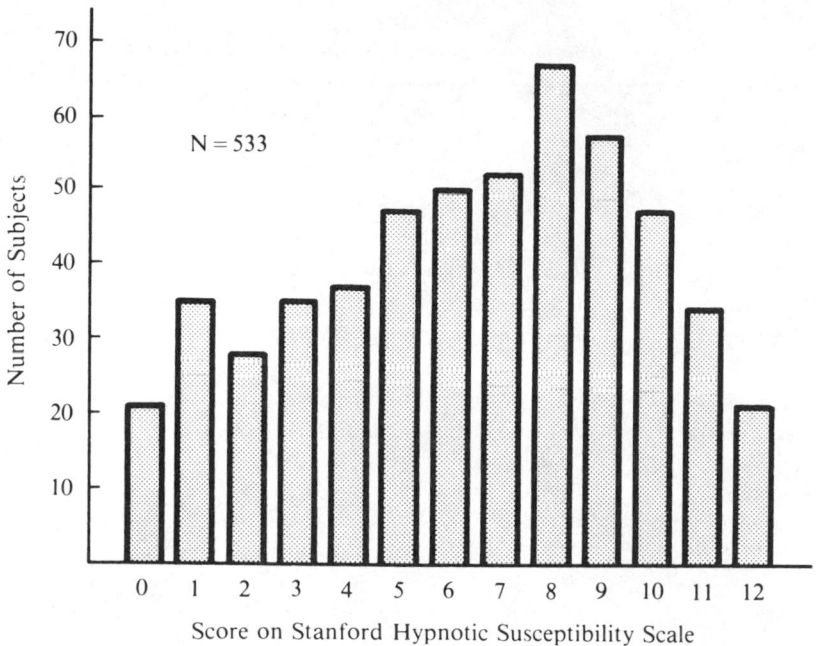

FIG. 6.2 Distribution of scores for Stanford students on the Stanford Hypnotic Susceptibility Scale. From *Hypnotic Susceptibility* (p. 215) by E. R. Hilgard, 1965, New York: Harcourt, Brace & World. Copyright 1965 by Harcourt, Brace & World. Adapted by permission.

It is apparent that there is a wide range of hypnotic abilities. A few of the students passed all of the items, a few passed none of the items, whereas the great majority fell somewhere in the middle. Incidentally, other research has shown that such hypnotic ability scores are about as stable over time as scores on intelligence tests (Hilgard, 1965). Because the induction procedure made no special provisions for alleviating anxiety, overcoming resistance, or producing great depth of hypnosis, nearly all of the persons at the bottom end of the scale would pass more items under more favorable circumstances. Yet, a few individuals passed all of the items after a rather mild induction procedure. Individuals with extremely high hypnotic ability may spontaneously move in and out of trances during routine everyday activities. Such people may have trouble staying out of hypnotic trances!

Heightened Suggestibility

The hypnotic state phenomena just introduced are indicative of *heightened suggestibility*. For example, in response to suggestions that one's hands are stuck together or that one's eyes cannot be opened, the hypnotized subject behaves accordingly. Similarly, suggestions to forget are followed by inability to recall the banished item, that is, by amnesia. Amnesia can be demonstrated either during the hypnotic state, or, with the proper suggestions, some or all of the events within the trance will not be recalled afterward.

In general, a *posthypnotic suggestion* is an instruction given during the trance that is to be carried out later, usually when elicited by a particular posthypnotic cue. The subject might be told that he will run his hand through his beard whenever he hears the word "Thursday." In the therapy setting, posthypnotic suggestions are often accompanied by suggested posthypnotic amnesia for having been administered the suggestion.

Hallucinations

The hypnotic phenomena discussed thus far are merely exaggerations of ordinary behaviors. Most of us are fairly cooperative, and often comply with another person's request without much reflection. We certainly forget things without the aid of hypnosis. Other trance effects depart more dramatically from the ordinary, and seem to involve a marked alteration in how the hypnotized person perceives reality. Simple or very elaborate reorganizations of perceived reality are possible. Both *positive hallucinations*—a perception that has no basis in physical reality— and *negative hallucinations*—failure to perceive something that is really there— can be created through suggestions.

A deeply hypnotized subject is able to hallucinate an imaginary person and to carry on a conversation with that person. Interestingly, the subject often spontaneously reports that the hallucinated person is translucent, so that the entire chair in which the imaginary person is seated is visible behind the body. The subject treats the hallucinated image as a real person, yet, at the same time, is well aware that a real person is not translucent. The tendency to accept such logical inconsistencies—*trance logic*—is one of the characteristics of deep hypnosis (Orne, 1959). Another example would be interacting with a hallucinated person, while being aware of that actual person seated in another part of the room. The reader may have experienced this peculiarly tolerant kind of reasoning during dreams that are structured so that the "dreaming-you" follows the actions of the "actor-in-the-dream-you" from the perspective of an outside observer, as if you were watching yourself in a movie. This would be seriously disturbing during ordinary consciousness, because there is supposed to be only one "you." The implied doubling of self is readily accepted while dreaming.

Posthypnotic hallucinations can be created using such posthypnotic suggestions as "See a bird when the door closes," "Hear music when you move your legs," and "Do not hear voices of anybody but me" (Spiegel & Spiegel, 1978, p. 78).

Hallucinations can be used therapeutically. Erickson, in a psychotherapy case, asked a patient with identity confusion to hallucinate a number of crystal balls, and then to further hallucinate in each ball a different important life experience (Erickson, 1952). The patient could then compare the experiences and draw relationships among them, in order to create a sense of continuity from one experience to the next. *Hypnotic analgesia* (see chapter 4) is the loss of sensibility to pain as a result of hypnotic suggestions, and may be viewed as an example of negative hallucination. As such, it is by far the most important therapeutic use of hallucination. The analgesia may be extended beyond the trance using a posthypnotic suggestion, usually linked to a cue that will instigate the analgesia. For example, in dentistry, the sound of the dental drill can be used as the cue.

Dissociation

Ernest Hilgard has argued convincingly that the experience of hypnosis and many hypnotic behaviors such as hypnotic analgesia can be explained by *dissociation*—a splitting or dividing of consciousness and behavioral control mechanisms (Hilgard, 1977). Dissociation occurs when the "stream of consciousness flows in more than one channel at a time" (Hilgard, 1973b, p. 213), or the behavioral control mechanisms become divided and the person carries out several very different activities simultaneously. According to Hilgard, we commonly experience dissociation in everyday activities without our paying much attention to it. Studying Spanish from an audio cassette while driving the freeway to work demonstrates dissociation; some accomplished musicians can carry on a conversation while they play. In hypnosis the divided areas seem to become even more distinctly separated from one another—the boundary between them is no longer permeable to attention. A walled off part of the person responds to suggestions, functioning quite autonomously from the rest of the person, from whose perspective the behavior is utterly involuntary. This second part of the person is amazed to find that he cannot open his eyes no matter how hard he tries. Dissociation occurs in perception as well as in behavior, as in hypnotic analgesia. If questioned carefully, a patient often admits that the pain is still there, but that it is as if it belongs to another person, and can be observed with detachment so that it does not "hurt" (see chapter 4 for a discussion of dissociation in hypnotic analgesia).

Hypnotic State Versus Role-Playing

Several researchers have argued that there is not enough evidence to support the idea of a hypnotic state (e.g., Barber, 1969; Sarbin & Coe, 1972). They cite the difficulty in specifying unique physiological correlates of hypnosis, and suggest that various hypnotic phenomena can be explained by role-playing. Role-playing certainly occurs in some individuals following hypnotic induction, as they modify their customary behavior in peculiar ways to conform to what they perceive to be the demands of this unusual situation. However, not all effects of hypnotic induction can be explained in this way. Among the most notable exceptions are: (a) suggested amnesia, because the material to be forgotten is subjectively inaccessible to recall; (b) hypnotic analgesia, because individuals role-playing the hypnotic state cannot tolerate as much pain as hypnotized subjects; and (c) trance logic, because individuals pretending to be hypnotized do not spontaneously adopt this highly unusual way of thinking. Therefore, it seems reasonable to conclude, as have Hilgard (e.g., 1977) and many others, that hypnotic induction can lead to an altered psychophysiological condition or "state."

Self-Hypnosis

In self-hypnosis the person serves simultaneously as hypnotic agent and subject. In the following discussion, ordinary hypnosis is termed *hetero-hypnosis*—literally "hypnosis-by-another"—in order to distinguish it from self-hypnosis.

Self-Hypnotic Induction

There are as many approaches to self-hypnotic induction as there are to hetero-hypnosis. The method to be described has been used for many years by Paul Sacerdote in the clinical setting, and begins with a hetero-hypnotic induction procedure (Sacerdote, 1981).

Induction begins with reversed hand levitation. While the subject's elbow rests comfortably on the arm of the chair, the therapist grasps the wrist and raises the subject's forearm to the vertical position, then gradually achieves passive immobility of the limb (catalepsy) by delicately increasing and decreasing support of the wrist as needed, all the while noting the degree of muscle tension in the arm. Meanwhile, in a monotonous voice, Sacerdote explains that a skill is being learned that will enable the subject to activate his or her capacity to acquire other new skills; the learning process is something like learning to ride a bike, where an instructor might help out at first but is no longer needed once the learning process is underway. When the hand is being supported on its own, the therapist almost imperceptibly presses down on it, gradually causing it to move to the horizontal position, explaining that the lowering of the arm symbolizes entry into a deeper and deeper state of relaxation. At some point during the initial catalepsy, or the forearm lowering, the person is likely to show signs of trance, such as fixation or closing of the eyes. This entire induction can be performed without any verbal communication whatsoever, with the arm catalepsy and deepening of the trance implied merely by the actions of the therapist and, presumably, by the expectation of the subject. Once medium depth of trance is noted, suggestions are introduced to the effect that whenever reversed hand levitation occurs it will promptly initiate the same trance or an even deeper one. The subject is counted out of trance, from ten to one.

After a discussion of the trance experience, the therapist lifts the subject's wrist once again, reassures the subject that the therapist will be present for any assistance that might be required, and encourages the person to initiate the hypnotic state by lowering his or her arm from the vertical to the horizontal position. This time, the subject, not the therapist, lifts the trance by counting backward at the end. Finally, the last step is for the subject to enter, deepen, and terminate the trance on his or her own. Home practice begins whenever the subject seems to be sufficiently skilled.

Effects of Self-Hypnotic Induction

Studies in which the subjects hypnotize themselves and then self-administer items like those shown in Table 6.1 have indicated that naive individuals hypnotize themselves about as easily as they can be hypnotized using a standard hetero-hypnotic induction procedure (Johnson, 1979). Furthermore, the general behavioral effects are similar—a self-hypnotized person is about as likely to produce an involuntary finger lock in response to that self-suggestion, as a hetero-hypnotized subject is to respond appropriately to the same suggestion delivered by the hypnotist (Johnson, 1979).

Erica Fromm and her colleagues at the University of Chicago have carried out an extensive investigation of the experiential aspects of self-hypnotic trance (Fromm, Brown, Hurt, Oberlander, Boxer, & Pfeifer, 1981). One theme in the results was the similarity of the trances resulting from hetero- and self-induction. In particular, the states were equally "absorbing," that is, the subjects became equally caught up in their experiences and their ordinary orientation toward reality was equally diminished in both. There were several distinct differences between the states. In self-hypnosis there was more fluctuation in the depth of trance, attention was more free-floating and more inwardly focused, and there was more frequent and more vivid imagery. Self-hypnosis and daydreaming share this absorption with self-generated imagery and may involve the same process (Singer & Pope, 1981).

The self-directed quality of self-hypnosis can be seen in this narrative recorded in the personal journal of one of the subjects:

> I did my hypnosis on the bus coming back to Hyde Park along Lake Shore Drive (She was, of course, not supposed to practice SH in any place other

than the designated study.) It was very interesting. The people and the inside of the bus were like an illustration. Each person became somebody to me. I felt apart from the scene just watching. I watched the bus driver who seemed like a character in a short story. When I got off the bus I walked very slowly. And time slowed down with me. I suggested that my legs be very heavy and difficult to move. They became so. Then I suggested they be light, and I floated home. It was very pleasant. I believe I've walked around in trances before without realizing it. The world becomes a new place. Never dull. (p. 233)

Physiological Correlates of the Hypnotic State

For about 100 years, researchers have been looking for a physiological index of hypnosis. But, even though the hypnotic state is highly distinctive from the subject's experiential perspective, it remains "physiologically invisible" (Engstrom, 1976). No physiological sign has been discovered that indicates trance in the same way that, for example, rapid eye movements signify dreaming. Physiological signs of relaxation usually accompany induction (Benson, Arns, & Hoffman, 1981), but whatever physiological changes occur following hypnotic induction appear to be determined by the kinds of suggestions that are introduced during the trance.

Suggestions to feel comfortable and relaxed are accompanied by decreased SNS and skeletal muscle activity and heightened EEG alpha; instructions that arouse anxiety or excitement have the opposite physiological effects. Hypnosis is sometimes used in an attempt to facilitate psychophysiological relaxation in treating stress and stress-related disorders, but current evidence indicates that hypnotic induction does not add anything to whatever relaxation procedures are used, including simple suggestions to relax (Wadden & Anderton, 1982).

Absence of an identifiable physiological consequence of hypnotic induction has not deterred attempts to explain hypnosis in neuropsychological terms. According to these theories, the hypnotic state reflects a basic reorganization in brain function. Because hypnosis clearly involves alterations in attention and perception, several theories have suggested that the underlying neural mechanisms of hypnosis must be the brainstem reticular activating system (RAS) and/or the thalamus, two brain areas directly implicated in attention (Sarbin & Slagle, 1980). Other explanations have appealed to the anatomical separation of the left and right cerebral hemispheres and their specialization to perform different functions. Perhaps, in hypnosis the normal relationship between the hemispheres is altered. It is intriguing that commissurotomized patients, who lack direct communication between the two hemispheres, experience the same kind of dissociation phenomena that can be demonstrated in intact normal subjects during the hypnotic state. Perhaps the corpus callosum is the anatomical locus of dissociation (Galin, 1974). It has also been noted that certain characteristics of the hypnotic state, such as trance logic, could be explained neurologically by the right hemisphere having somehow gained ascendancy over the normally dominant and analytical left hemisphere (Carter, Elkins, & Kraft, 1982).

Other investigators have wondered whether the varying degrees of hypnotic ability seen in different individuals might be associated with an underlying physiological difference. Here, too, there has been some interest in hemispheric specialization. Several studies have found that the selective involvement of the left hemisphere in language tasks and the right in visuospatial tasks is more distinct in high hypnotic ability subjects (MacLeod-Morgan & Lack, 1982). There is limited evidence that these individuals have more right hemisphere cortical activity outside the hypnotic state than is seen in low hypnotic ability subjects (Bakan, 1969).

Other research has examined hypnotizability as a function of the prevalence of the alpha rhythm in the EEG without regard to cerebral hemisphere. Persons with more EEG alpha may be more highly hypnotizable; the fact that both EEG alpha and hypnotizability decline from childhood to adulthood is consistent with this (Engstrom, 1976), as is the report that training individuals to increase the production of EEG alpha via biofeedback enhances hypnotic ability (Engstrom, 1976).

Applications of Hypnosis

Hypnosis is probably the most commonly used of the self-regulation procedures. A 1982 survey of American Psychological Association members indicated that, of those who engaged in psychotherapy or counseling, 35% used hypnosis at least once a month (Kraft & Rodalfa, 1982). Substantial numbers of physicians, especially psychiatrists, as well as dentists and other health care professionals, also use this treatment modality. For example, a report indicated that about 50% of the patients referred to the pain clinic of the Walter Reed Army Hospital received some form of hypnosis (Wain, 1980).

Hypnosis has been used in many ways with a great many disorders. For example, hypnosis has been employed in at least 16 ways just in the treatment of cigarette smoking (Katz, 1980). It is no more possible to arrive at a global generalization about the utility of hypnosis than it would be to do so for surgery as a treatment. A major use of hypnosis, to control pain, was explored in chapter 4. Another common use—to help break bad habits—is discussed here, as well as some special applications of self-hypnosis.

Self-Initiated Disorders

Conditions such as alcoholism, cigarette smoking, and obesity from overeating are related to actions that are considered part of a person's voluntary behavior. For this reason such bad habits have been called the "self-initiated disorders" (Wadden & Anderton, 1982). Hypnosis is a popular treatment modality in programs designed to help obese people lose weight, alcoholics control their drinking, and smokers "kick the habit."

Once hypnotic induction has been attained, there are many interventions that are possible. These include straightforward suggestions to change the behavior in question, rehearsal in imagination of desirable new behaviors that are incompatible with the bad habit, and aversive conditioning, such as establishing a posthypnotic suggestion that the sight of ice cream will arouse nausea and vomiting. Other approaches are more cognitive, such as a popular single-session intervention in which, following hypnotic induction, the therapist attempts to get the patient to accept the ideas that smoking poisons the body, and that the patient very dearly needs his or her body (Spiegel, 1970). Some therapists may be interested in the role the bad habit might play in the personality dynamics of the patient and use hypnosis to help gain insight into this.

There have been a number of recent reviews of research in this area (Holroyd, 1980; Katz, 1980; Wadden & Anderton, 1982; Wadden & Penrod, 1981). From these reviews it is apparent that there is a large gap between clinical practice and empirical research in connection with hypnosis and self-initiated disorders. There are many positive cases, along with a number of comparisons, in which a group whose treatment includes hypnosis shows greater change on a dependent variable, such as weight loss, as compared to an untreated waiting list control group. Clearly, hypnotherapy programs are often successful; it has yet to be established that hypnosis is among the active ingredients of these programs. The techniques mentioned in the previous paragraph are often used to treat self-initiated disorders without hypnosis and are not thought to depend on hypnosis for their effects.

Special Uses of Self-Hypnosis

Self-hypnosis appears to be an effective means to control pain, as shown, for example, by the compelling surgical case study presented in chapter 4, and studies with chronic pain using the self-hypnosis methods of Sacerdote (1981). Self-hypnosis may be an especially valuable therapeutic tool with children, who are known to be superior to adults in hypnotic ability, peaking at from 9 to 14 years of age (Morgan & Hilgard, 1973). Self-hypnosis is widely used in hypnotherapy programs for controlling self-initiated disorders, but there is no basis for claiming overall differences in efficacy as compared to hetero-hypnosis.

There is an assortment of applications at the upper end of the illness-wellness continuum for which self-hypnosis has been preferred over hetero-hypnosis. The reader is probably familiar with stories of baseball players who break out of their hitting slump after having learned self-hypnosis, or golfers who use the technique to control anxiety during putting. Individuals in sales learn self-hypnosis in order to implant self-suggestions of successful selling. Self-hypnosis has been advocated in pursuit of transcendence, in the same way that the Eastern meditative methods are more commonly used (Havens, 1982). None of these uses of hypnosis to enhance wellness has been researched thoroughly.

It is possible to speculate about some of the advantages and disadvantages that might be peculiar to self-hypnosis. Self-hypnosis enables the patient to function autonomously, avoiding dependency on the therapist. Self-hypnosis reduces the number of time-consuming and expensive office visits and makes possible home practice. Like the other self-regulation techniques, self-hypnosis may have rather general therapeutic effects linked to enhancement of the self-image.

There are also several potential difficulties with self-hypnosis. One simple, but serious problem is that there is no vigilant therapist present to prevent the person from falling asleep. Conversely, the person must exercise enough critical thinking to maintain the trance, a task that may periodically draw the subject out of trance. Should anxiety-provoking material surface during trance, without assistance, the subject may suffer psychological damage, or at a minimum have an extremely unpleasant experience. Some guidance is recommended, at least initially, in self-hypnosis.

AUTOGENIC TRAINING

Autogenic training was developed in the 1920s by the late German neurologist and psychiatrist, Johannes Heinrich Schultz, who had been influenced by earlier research in clinical hypnosis. Regular practice with self-hypnosis seemed to have a general recuperative and healthful effect. His own hypnosis research convinced him that when individuals relax deeply, they consistently experience feelings of heaviness and warmth, mainly in the limbs. These sensations can be noted during the process of falling asleep. Hypnosis results in feelings of heaviness and warmth, but perhaps, Schultz speculated, it might also work the other way around. Maybe patients could enter a healthful hypnotic-like state by imagining heaviness and warmth in their bodies. His research along these lines led directly to the methods of autogenic training.

In European countries, the U.S.S.R., and Japan, autogenic training has been a familiar treatment method in psychotherapy and for psychophysiological disorders for many years. Although Schultz's book, *Das Autogene Training* (Schultz, 1932), had been available in German since 1932, practically nothing about autogenic training was published in English until 1959, when it was finally translated into English (as the book was in press for its tenth German edition). By 1963 about 1,000 articles and books about autogenic training had accumulated, but only about 1% of them were in English (Luthe, 1963).

Another German-born psychiatrist, Wolfgang Luthe, is almost single-handedly responsible for bringing autogenic methods to the attention of English-speaking practitioners and researchers. Luthe, who first studied, then collaborated, with Schultz, was responsible for the 1959 English translation of Schultz's book and authored, with Schultz, a six volume collection on autogenic therapy published in English between 1969 and 1973 (Luthe, 1970a, 1970b, 1973; Luthe & Schultz, 1970a, 1970b; Schultz & Luthe, 1969).

Rationale

In autogenic training the orientation is not so much to *try to control* psychophysiological activity, as to help "natural systems use their inherent potentials of self-regulatory adjustment more fully" (Luthe, 1979, p. 167). Autogenic training is the opposite of manipulative treatments such as surgery or drugs that are imposed from outside the organism. Autogenic training is presented as a method of allowing "homeostatic self-regulatory brain mechanisms" (Luthe, 1979, p. 167) to carry out their natural healing and recuperative functions. In theory, autogenic training encourages the executive/conscious control centers in the cerebral cortex to stop interfering with the regulatory mechanisms in the lower parts of the brain, which are quite capable of taking excellent care of the body if left to themselves. Nature knows best! If autogenic training indeed frees up automatic regulatory centers in the brain, this would explain how such a general procedure could have therapeutic effects for a wide variety of disorders.

Consistent with this element of "letting go," an essential ingredient of autogenic training is passive concentration, a concept that shows up in one form or another with every self-regulation method. Recall that it was mentioned that a "passive attitude" may facilitate self-regulation through biofeedback, and that Jacobson stressed that relaxation is an act of "not doing." The hypnotic state appears to involve a certain passive detachment, certainly when dissociation occurs; as discussed later in this chapter, some types of meditation involve this almost paradoxical kind of attending. Usually, when we speak of concentrating or attending, we mean "actively concentrating," so that there is goal-directed interest, as in "paying attention" to your driving when behind the wheel. In passive concentration there is a casual attitude and indifference to the outcome; there is no goal-directed interest, nor even effort of any kind. It is like allowing oneself to relax versus making oneself to relax. It is necessary to maintain passive concentration or passive attention at all times during autogenic training to encourage, at least in theory, the cerebral cortex to relinquish its maladaptive control of lower regulatory processes.

Autogenic Procedures

Autogenic training is the first in a sequence of three treatment techniques that comprise autogenic therapy. Frequently, autogenic training is used by itself without moving on to either of the subsequent techniques— autogenic modification and autogenic meditation. The latter two procedures can only be undertaken once the individual can reliably enter and sustain the autogenic state. Regardless of the eventual goals of therapy, it always begins with thorough autogenic training.

Autogenic Training Procedures

Autogenic training may be carried out in a relaxed horizontal or sitting posture. There are six physiologically-oriented standard exercises, each based on a standard formula (see Table 6.2). The procedure is deceptively simple because the only activity is repeating the formula over and over to oneself. However, it is necessary to maintain passive concentration on the formula and on the part of the body indicated by the formula and to sustain a film-like mental representation of the formula through verbal, visual or acoustic imagery (Luthe, 1963). The formulas are to be practiced

TABLE 6.2
The Six Autogenic Training Standard Exercises

Exercise	Physiological Focus	Standard Formula
1	Heaviness in the extremities	"My right arm is heavy"
2	Warmth in the extremities	"My right arm is warm"
3	Calm and regular cardiac	"Heartbeat calm and regular"
4	Calm and regular respiration	"It breathes me"
5	Warmth in the upper abdomen	"My solar plexus is warm"
6	Coolness of the forehead	"My forehead is cool"

in the order shown in Table 6.2, and each is to be mastered before moving on to the next.

First Standard Exercise. Muscular relaxation is first in the autogenic sequence because it is the quickest, the most reliable, and among the most easily perceived of the physiological changes associated with psychophysiological relaxation. "Heaviness" is a shorthand way of describing subjective changes during muscular relaxation that include a feeling of almost flattening out if reclining, or drooping if sitting up, of sinking into the supporting surface, and of a pronounced disinclination to move the limbs. The dominant arm is used as the original focus because we are thoroughly in touch mentally with this extremity due to its important role in our everyday activities. Once the dominant arm consistently feels heavy during passive concentration on the first formula, the formula is shifted to the other arm, and eventually to the legs. The first standard exercise often concludes with the formula "My arms and legs are heavy." The first standard exercise generally requires from two to eight weeks of daily practice.

Every practice session begins with the formula "I am at peace." At first the exercises should be carried out for brief periods, on the order of 30 seconds. As the trainee becomes more skilled in the attitude of passive concentration, producing the formulas in a continuous flow and maintaining attentional contact with the proper part of his or her body, the periods may be lengthened to several minutes and eventually to 30 minutes or longer. Each period of autogenic training is terminated distinctly with the same three steps: (a) flexing the arms vigorously, (b) breathing deeply, and (c) opening the eyes—"Arms firm, breath deeply, open eyes."

Second Standard Exercise. The sensation of warmth in the extremities is due to vasodilation of peripheral blood vessels in response to decreased SNS activity as a component of psychophysiological relaxation. The flow of blood increases and the surrounding skin and muscle becomes warmer. It is also common to experience tingling in the affected area whenever there is pronounced vasodilation. Most trainees experience warmth in some part of the body during the first standard exercise (Schultz & Luthe, 1969). For some individuals, the second standard exercise is accompanied by excessive perspiration, due to continuing high SNS activity in pathways supplying the sweat glands. In this case, the formula "My right arm is dry" can be added. As with the heaviness formula, the warmth formula is applied to each limb in succession, and eventually to all of them together: "My arms and legs are warm."

Third Standard Exercise. During psychophysiological relaxation the heart beats more slowly and less vigorously, so that a lesser volume of blood is circulated with each beat. Note that the patient does *not* use a specific self-suggestion such as "My heart is beating slowly"—rather, in keeping with the emphasis on the "natural" self-regulatory mechanisms, the more general formula, "Heart beat calm and regular" is used. This exercise is intended to reinforce the cardiovascular regulation that has already begun during the first two standard exercises. It is more difficult to focus attention on heart activity than on sensations of either heaviness or warmth in the extremities; as an aid in establishing contact with the appropriate part of the body, the heart, the third standard formula may be practiced at first with one hand over the heart.

Fourth Standard Exercise. Regulating respiratory activity through autogenic training creates a special problem because breathing can be controlled voluntarily to some extent; however, any voluntary interference, such as intentionally slowing down one's respiratory pattern, will defeat the autogenic training. Therefore, the formula, "It breathes me" is particularly apt, even though the language construction is a bit strange in English, the phrase having been translated literally from the original German. Many trainees find this exercise to be particularly pleasant, as they finally achieve true passive concentration, with one person commenting, "It was as if my whole body were breathing" (Schultz & Luthe, 1969, p. 95).

Fifth Standard Exercise. The gastrointestinal system becomes more active during psychophysiological relaxation that is sometimes accompanied by an agreeable feeling of warmth in the upper abdomen. Sometimes the trainee is uncomfortable with the unfamiliar term, "solar plexus," even after a brief neuroanatomy lesson, and so the formula "My stomach is warm" may be substituted, because the solar plexus is located on the back of the stomach.

Sixth Standard Exercise. The final standard exercise directs the attention of the trainee back to his or her head. It is desirable for the cranial region to be cooler than the rest of the body, indicating that the brain is receiving a smaller share of the circulating blood. This state is one of the components of psychophysiological relaxation. Vasodilation of the cranial arteries, associated with warmth of the forehead, is to be avoided because this is an important physiological ingredient of vascular headache.

The entire six-step sequence is usually completed within four to ten months. By this time the trainee is able to enter the autogenic state in a matter of 20 or 30 seconds by self-administering several repetitions of each standard formula in order. The first two formulas are usually collapsed to "My arms and legs are heavy and warm."

Autogenic Modification Procedures

It may be that after a few months of otherwise successful autogenic training, there is a specific therapeutic change that has not yet occurred. For example, chronic constipation might persist, or the patient continues to be troubled by sleep-onset insomnia. In such cases a specific physiologically-related formula, "My lower abdomen is warm," or psychologically-oriented formula, "It sleeps me," would be added at the conclusion of the standard exercises.

Autogenic Meditation Procedures

Autogenic therapy was developed, not only as treatment for psychophysiological disorders but as an adjunct to psychotherapy. Schultz noted that the autogenic state encouraged unconscious material to bubble to the surface, probably because of the mental passivity of the trainee and the deep psychophysiological relaxation. As a psychiatrist, Schultz believed that any mental activity during the autogenic state, including imagery that might "spontaneously" appear, could be illuminating in understanding the psychodynamics of a troubled patient. The meditative exercises are designed to strengthen imagery during the autogenic state, and normally begin after 6 to 12 months of autogenic training.

Trainees practice a series of seven progressively more elaborate visualization exercises beginning with allowing a single uniform color to fill the visual field, and ending with "multichromatic cinerama" in which situations are imagined and the trainee becomes an active participant rather than an outside observer. These scenes should be so real that the border between fantasy and reality becomes blurred, and the individual cannot always distinguish imagination from reality. In the psychotherapeutic setting, the final stage is used to search for "answers from the unconscious."

Effects of Autogenic Training

Experiential Effects

Accumulated evidence indicates that most, but not all, autogenic trainees experience the sensations suggested in the formulas. About 60% of 200 participants reported a distinct feeling of heaviness in one or more extremities during their first session with the heaviness standard exercise (Schultz & Luthe, 1969). This effect was strong in only 4% of the subjects, and 21% of the participants never experienced heaviness during the first standard exercise. Schultz and Luthe (1969) have presented other data indicating that about 11% of trainees did not report any feelings of heaviness, but at the same time evidenced other physiological changes suggesting that the autogenic training was effective.

Most trainees experience warmth in their extremities, even during the first standard exercise, that is, prior to self-suggestions of warmth (Schultz & Luthe, 1969). Among participants who had been trained for more than three weeks, 29 of 35 felt warmth in their hands during passive concentration on the second standard formula; for all but two of these participants, the sensation of warmth was accompanied by an actual increase in blood flow in the fingers. Of the six who did not experience warmth, five, nonetheless, showed an increase in peripheral blood flow. Among a group of high school girls who practiced autogenic training over 4.5 months, those who experienced warmth in their hands showed significantly greater blood flow in their fingers as compared to those who did not feel their hands getting warm (Tebecis, Ohno, Matsubara, Sugano, Takeya, Ikemi, & Takasaki, 1976/77). Luthe has argued that the autogenic formulas function "merely as a technical key" (Luthe, 1973, p. 176) to producing functional changes in the brain, and he emphasizes that the sensations suggested by the formulas are not necessary for successful autogenic training.

Physiological Effects

Hand warming and muscle relaxation are obviously not uniquely associated with passive concentration on autogenic formulas. In fact, the physiological effects that are supposed to be encouraged by autogenic training would be expected to some extent whenever one sits quietly in a comfortable posture. This means that physiological changes observed during autogenic training are not necessarily due to the autogenic training. However, there is some evidence that the elements of autogenic training do contribute to physiological changes in the direction of relaxation.

In one investigation the physiological effects of two contrasting formulas were compared across six sessions of training (Blizard, Cowings, & Miller, 1975). Participants alternated between active concentration on cool and light extremities, and passive concentration on warm and heavy extremities. Although the two formulas and attention styles did not have different effects on EEG alpha, there were differences in heart and respiration rate, primarily elevations in both, associated with the active cool and light formula. There were no differential effects of the cool and warm formulas on skin temperature. These rather limited physiological effects are typical of those obtained when autogenic formulas are condensed, or used in succession within individual sessions, and where the training period is brief.

Other evidence shows more impressive physiological changes when autogenic training is carried out as advocated by Schultz and Luthe and for extended periods. Fig. 6.3 shows the skin temperature and blood volume of the arms during active concentration on warmth for an individual who had practiced autogenic training for about two years (Harano,

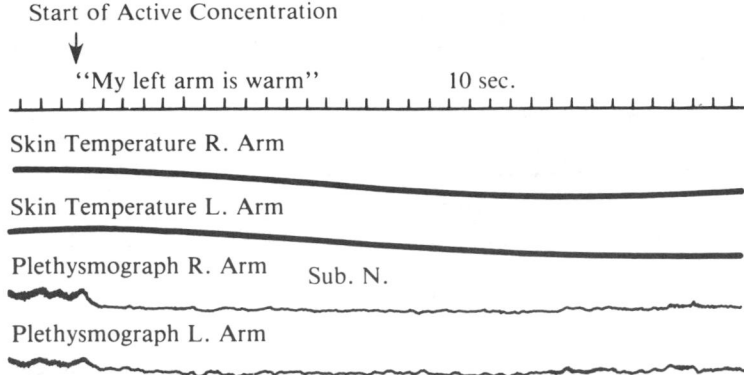

FIG. 6.3 Effects of *active* concentration on blood volume (plethysmogram) and skin temperature for an individual skilled in autogenic training. From "A Study of Plethysmography and Skin Temperature during Active Concentration and Autogenic Exercise" (p. 56) by K. Harano, et al., 1965, in W. Luthe (Ed.), *Autogenic Training: International Edition*, New York: Grune & Stratton. Copyright 1965 by Grune & Stratton. Adapted by permission.

Ogawa, & Naruse, 1965). Notice that active concentration was accompanied by a decrease in the skin temperature and blood volume of the arms, indicating vasoconstriction. Passive concentration (see Fig. 6.4) led to the desired opposite effects, associated with decreased SNS activity.

Heart rate deceleration has been noted many times during autogenic training, including during the first standard exercise. Luthe (1970b) observed the effects of autogenic training on the heart rates of 15 "neurotic" patients with unspecified complaints, but who had no cardiac disorders. Fig. 6.5 displays their heart rates before autogenic training and after four weeks of training with the heaviness formula. The data before training were collected while the patients reclined in the horizontal training posture and rested with eyes closed for three 3-minute periods with 5-minute intervals between each. In the subsequent autogenic training session, the 3-minute periods contained passive concentration on heaviness. Heart rate was lower during the autogenic training session and, within that session, heart rate was lower during passive concentration as compared to the intervals between the autogenic exercises.

Physiological changes in the stomach wall during the fifth standard exercise could be observed in a patient who had been equipped with an external tube leading into the stomach because of an earlier operation to remove cancerous tissue from the esophagous (Ikemi, Nakagawa, Kimura, Dobeta, Ono, & Sugita, 1965). The necessary physiological recording devices to measure blood flow and motility (digestive contractions) of the stomach wall were inserted through the tube and installed appropriately in the stomach of the trainee. Fig. 6.6 shows stomach wall blood flow and

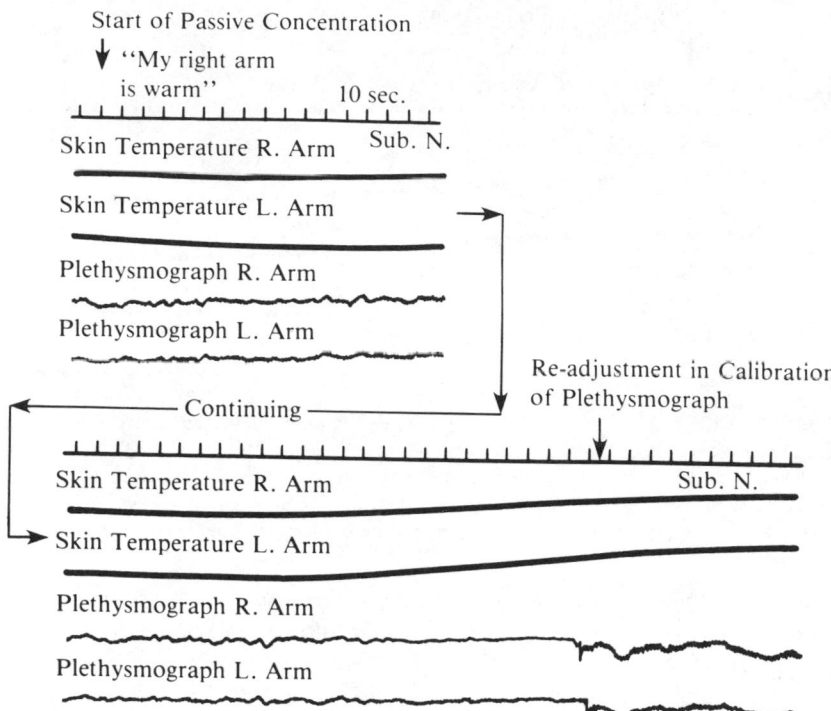

FIG. 6.4 Effects of *passive* concentration on blood volume (plethysmogram) and skin temperature for the same individual observed in Fig. 6.3. From "A Study of Plethysmography and Skin Temperature during Active Concentration and Autogenic Exercise" (p. 57) by K. Harano, et al., 1965, in W. Luthe (Ed.), *Autogenic Training: International Edition*, New York: Grune & Stratton. Copyright 1965 by Grune & Stratton. Adapted by permission.

motility during autogenic training, including passive concentration on the formula "My solar plexus is warm." Motility increased when the autogenic exercises began, and still larger contractions were evident during the fifth standard formula. Large parallel fluctuations in the blood flow of the stomach wall accompanied increased motility.

Applications of Autogenic Training

Autogenic training has been applied to a variety of psychophysiological disorders such as ulcers, constipation, anorexia nervosa, obesity, miscellaneous cardiac conditons, high and low blood pressure, hemorrhoids, several types of headache, asthma, thyroid dysfunction, sexual dysfunctions, epilepsy, and many more. These applications have been systematically reviewed by Luthe and Schultz in volumes II (*Medical Applications*)

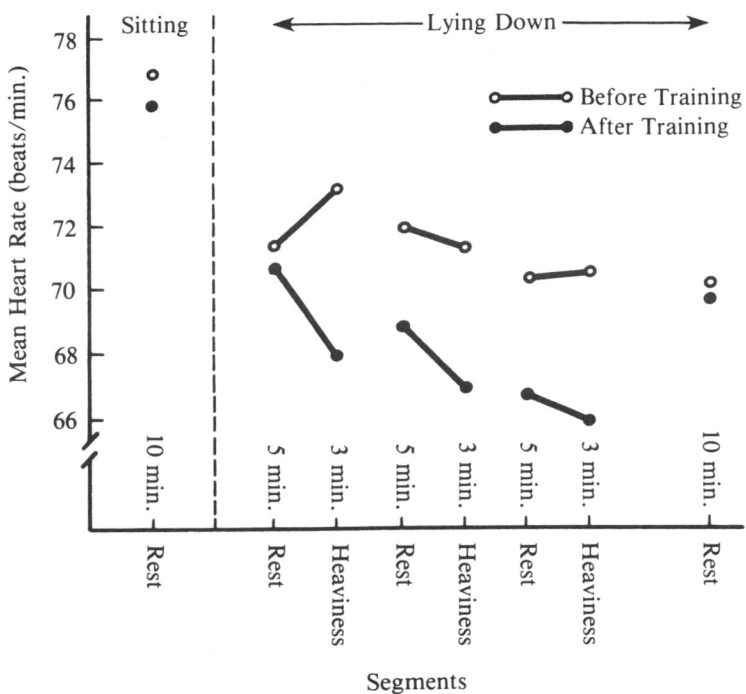

FIG. 6.5 Changes in heart rate during passive concentration on heaviness as shown during alternating periods of autogenic training and rest, before and after four weeks of training. From *Autogenic Therapy: Research and Theory* (p. 59) by W. Luthe, 1970, New York: Grune & Stratton. Copyright 1970 by Grune & Stratton. Adapted by permission.

and III (*Applications in Psychotherapy*) of *Autogenic Therapy* (Luthe & Schultz, 1970a, b). The evidence presented represents mainly an accumulation of successful cases rather than comparisons with other treatments or with untreated control groups. However, the overall picture is consistent with Schultz's original observation that autogenic training appears to have a normalizing effect on a number of physiological processes. Several physiological effects are of particular note: (a) reduction in serum cholesterol levels with autogenic training (Luthe, 1965b), which indicates that autogenic training may be useful in reducing the risk of coronary heart disease, and (b) reduction in iodine metabolism that may represent normalization of thyroid function (Luthe, 1965a), a physiological process intricately linked to homeostatic mechanisms and stress.

As discussed in chapter 7, essential hypertension deserves special attention as a psychophysiological disorder because of its high incidence and close association with the leading cause of death in our society, coronary heart disease. Fig. 6.7 shows blood pressure levels for a group of 26

TEMPERATURE

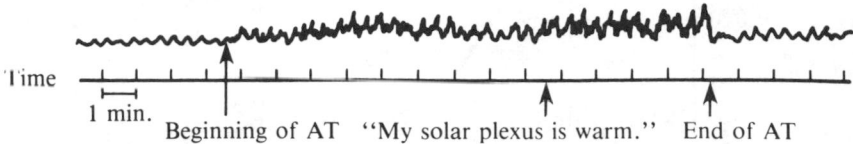

		34.9 °C		35.5 °C
Finger	33.1 °C			
Abdominal Wall	34.5 °C	35.4 °C		35.9 °C
Stomach	37.1 °C	37.1 °C		37.1 °C

GASTRIC MOTILITY

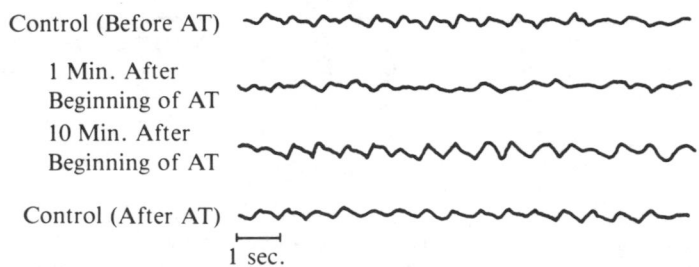

Time

1 min.

Beginning of AT   "My solar plexus is warm."   End of AT

BLOOD FLOW OF STOMACH WALL

Control (Before AT)

1 Min. After
Beginning of AT

10 Min. After
Beginning of AT

Control (After AT)

1 sec.

FIG. 6.6   Changes in blood flow and gastric motility during passive concentration in a patient with a gastric fistula. From "Bloodflow Change by Autogenic Training–Including Observations in a Case of Gastric Fistula" (p. 67) by V. Ikemi et al., 1965, in W. Luthe (Ed.), *Autogenic Training: International Edition*, New York: Grune & Stratton. Copyright 1965 by Grune & Stratton. Reprinted by permission.

hypertensive patients over four months of treatment with autogenic training (Klumbies, 1983). The greatest reductions in blood pressure occurred within the first month of treatment, and the greatest changes were seen in systolic blood pressure readings. Although there was considerable variation from subject to subject in the magnitude of the treatment effects, the decreases in blood pressure were great enough to be of clinical significance for many subjects.

Although autogenic methods, in the form developed by Schultz and Luthe, are used frequently in many countries, this is not true in the United States, where progressive relaxation has been preferred. As with progressive relaxation, various condensed versions of autogenic training are employed, sometimes with only the warmth and heaviness formulas or variations of them combined, or with all of the formulas administered in

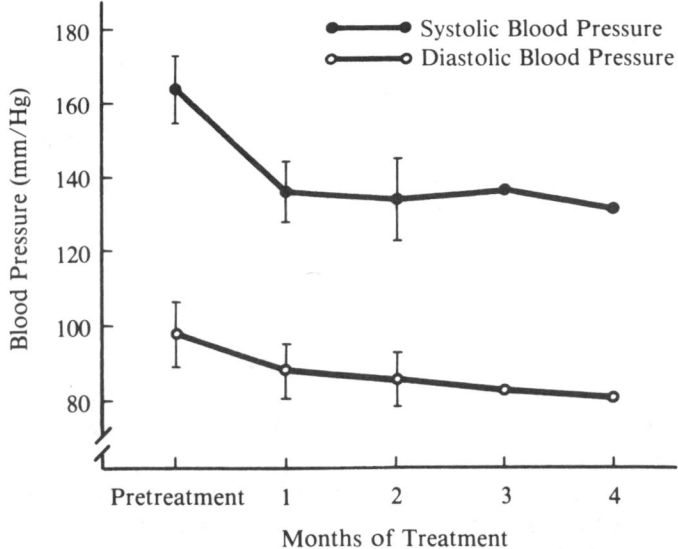

FIG. 6.7 Effects of autogenic training on systolic and diastolic blood pressure for 26 hypertensive patients (Vertical bars indicate standard deviations. From *Psychotherapie in der Inneren und Allgemeinmedizin* (vol. 4, p. 342) by G. Klumbies, 1983, Leipzig: Hirzel-Verlag. Copyright 1983 by S. Hirzel. Adapted by permission.

every session. Another departure is that many clinicians do not begin treatment with the very brief training periods advocated by Luthe. Finally, autogenic phrases are often combined with other self-regulation methods to yield a kind of "relaxation stew." A popular format has the patient begin training with a few minutes of progressive relaxation, then move on to EMG or skin temperature biofeedback, supported by parallel autogenic formulas.

One of the more interesting hybrid applications of autogenic training can be found in the United States space program, where autogenic training combined with biofeedback is being tested as a means to control the Space Adaptation Syndrome (SAS). The reported incidence of SAS has been on the order of 50% in the United States and Soviet manned space programs. Across the first nine United States Space Shuttle missions, the reported incidence was 48% among the 29 crewmembers (Homick, Reschke, & Vanderploeg, 1984). The most common symptoms of SAS are lethargy, headache, loss of appetite, nausea, vomiting, and a general feeling of "malaise." Researchers and visitors to space agree that SAS is closely related to the motion sickness commonly experienced in normal Earth gravity.

The impact of SAS on task performance in space is a sensitive issue, and little information is available in the open scientific literature;

although SAS has reportedly not influenced mission objectives during the Space Shuttle program (Homick et al., 1984), it is difficult to see how persons could function at their best while feeling, as several Spacelab 1 crewmembers described it, "kind of grim," "really sick," and "really sorry" (Oman, Lichtenberg, & Money, 1984). The Space Shuttle medical policy has been to require premedication of anyone with no space flight experience or with a positive history of SAS (Homick et al., 1984); pharmacological management has not been successful.

The use of "autogenic feedback training" (AFT) (e.g., Cowings, Billingham, & Toscano, 1977), is based on the marked changes in autonomically mediated responses, including heart and respiration rate, pulse volume, and electrodermal responding, that typically accompany motion sickness (Suter & Naifeh, 1984). Perhaps if individuals can learn to minimize these changes in situations that ordinarily provoke motion sickness or SAS, they will not get sick.

In AFT, the trainee passively concentrates on autogenic formulas while a broad "menu" of physiological responses, including the autonomic responses just mentioned, are fed back. The aim is to maintain the physiological response pattern at levels that are characteristic of resting conditions. A series of studies (e.g., Cowings et al., 1977) have shown that AFT provides resistance to ordinary terrestrial motion sickness.

On an experimental basis, selected shuttle crewmembers are now being pre-trained before missions and are provided with small wrist-mounted biofeedback units for practice sessions in space (Toscano, 1984). These units are able to provide numerical feedback for heart and respiration rate, pulse volume, and electrodermal responding from sensors attached to special underwear.

MEDITATION

"I am not my body . . . I am not my organs . . . I am not my senses . . . I am not this thought . . ." (Dass, 1979, p. 213). I stop my thoughts.

According to the Eastern mystical tradition these are the important stages in a journey of inward discovery and development whose destination is the true *YOU* and spiritual enlightenment. There is no higher goal or purpose in life, nothing of greater importance, than to become enlightened. Meditation is the pathway to enlightenment.

Meditation does not signify a single procedure such as autogenic training, or progressive relaxation, but a family of techniques about as closely related as, say, the activites described collectively as athletics. What the meditative disciplines share is their use of mental exercises to facilitate control of the mind with an aim toward some particular beneficial effect.

In the context of the Eastern religions, such as Buddhism and Hinduism, where the methods originated, the goals are spiritual, whereas a patient with essential hypertension may meditate simply to lower his or her blood pressure.

If I am not my body and I am not my thoughts, it follows that I am not a psychophysiological being. Although I think, I am not those thoughts; I am that which thinks those thoughts. According to this Eastern mystical model of the person, both mind and body are superficial manifestations of a deeper reality, the real *YOU* that, according to some Eastern religions, is part of a cosmic thread running throughout the universe and linking everything together. To discover yourself is to know the universe.

Deautomatization

Deikman (1966) has reflected, in terms that will be familiar to Western readers, on the path to enlightenment, as prescribed and practiced by Eastern meditative disciplines. According to Deikman, this requires an "undoing of the usual ways of perceiving and thinking" that he calls *deautomatization*. In particular, the meditator must learn to deautomatize (undo) the survival-oriented processes that organize and interpret perceptual input during ordinary consciousness. This is the goal of mental practice in which attention is exercised, so that it can be reinvested in perception, rather than cognition. Thus, the student shifts from the typical active intellectual style to a receptive perceptual mode. In many formal disciplines, the contemplative aspect of the path is supported by renunciation of wordly and psychological goals—for example taking up a life of poverty, chastity, and isolation. The intent is to free the student further from distractions that may interfere with the direct, nonanalytic apprehension of perception.

The Meditative Disciplines

Although there are many types of meditation, there is a scientific literature for only three: Zazen, Yoga, and Transcendental Meditation (TM).

Zazen

Buddhism was founded by Siddhartha Gautama (the Buddha) in India during the 6th century B.C., spread throughout Southeast Asia, China, Korea, and Japan, and has attracted increasing numbers of adherents in Western countries within the last several decades. Zen meditation—*Zazen*—is an important ingredient of Zen Buddhism.

It is through the practice of Zazen that the student achieves the transcendent state called *satori*, whereby reality itself is apprehended, as distinct from ideas about reality. Along the way the student must learn to get rid of all thoughts (which are by definition irrelevant) to view the world with single-mindedness or "bare attention," a concept that Buddha himself is said to have explained this way: "In what is seen there must be just the seen; in what is heard there must be just the heard; in what is sensed (as smell, taste, or touch) there must be just what is sensed; in what is thought there must be just the thought" (Kapleau, 1965, p. 10). The mind does not ordinarily operate this way; the function of Zazen is to empty the mind, to strip it of all extraneous thoughts, preconceptions, expectations, opinions, and so on, thus enabling the student of meditation " . . . to enter into a full rapport with life" (Kapleau, 1965, p 11)

Walsh (1984), a psychologist and student of meditation, has described his own mental reorganization as follows:

> The more sensitive my meditation became, the more I was forced to recognize that what I had formerly believed to be my rational mind preoccupied with cognition, planning, problem solving, etc., actually comprised a frantic torrent of forceful, demanding, loud, and often unrelated thoughts and fantasies which filled an unbelievable proportion of consciousness even during purposive behavior. The incredible proportion of consciousness which this fantasy world occupied, my powerlessness to remove it for more than a few seconds, and my former state of mindlessness or ignorance of its existence, staggered me. (pp. 39-40)

Zazen is rather standardized with practice carried out under the close supervision of a Zen master whom the student is to emulate in every way. Meditation is typically conducted in the cross-legged lotus or half-lotus postures with the eyes open but fixated on a point such as the end of the nose. Advanced students may practice mobile Zazen while they go about their everyday activities.

Beginners first practice attention to the breathing process, initially counting inhalations and exhalations as an aid to concentration, then, having gained some control of attention, follow the breathing process passively but with total attention. The skeptical reader who feels that this is a trivially simple task should attempt total attention to breathing for a few minutes. It is remarkable how many things other than breathing clutter the mind.

Attention to breathing enhances mental discipline in general and begins to orient the meditator to the present, the "here and now." Once extraneous thoughts about the past and future are eliminated, the meditator can become absorbed in the present moment. This is not done in an awkward self-conscious way, rather, it is more like becoming *lost in* the present, something that happens to most of us on occasion when we become so wrapped up in whatever we are doing that we are no longer aware of our surroundings, and time passes without notice. Eventually the student is able to sustain this here and now orientation in daily activities, which may have practical as well as spiritual benefits.

When the student is ready, as determined by the Zen master, *koan* exercises commence. During these exercises, questions, statements, and bits of dialogue are contemplated during Zazen. Although the answers to the koans are supposed to be of the most profound significance, they are beyond logic, and the student has no clue as to what is expected. The aims are confusion of reality and frustration of meaning. A well-known koan asks "What is the sound of one hand clapping?" (Becker, 1961, p. 45). The student is, in effect, "edged toward a mental precipice and told to leap; but logic is no aid in the leap" (Becker, 1961, p. 46). The leap is necessary in order to continue the journey inward.

Even after many years of devoted practice, few meditators glimpse transcendence. Those who do are considered to have entered a state of being that is beyond physical life and death.

Yoga

Hinduism has been an important part of life in India for more than 3,000 years. Today, there are nearly one-half billion followers of this religion and way of life, concentrated mainly in India and smaller neighboring countries. Yoga, a set of self-development principles and practical exercises, has been an essential feature of Hinduism for over 2,000 years. There is much more diversity among practitioners of Yoga than of Zen Buddhism, and the many Yoga sects differ in the aspects of Yoga that are emphasized. Hatha Yoga, for example, stresses physical postures and exercises. Its practitioners are the stereotypical meditators who sit on beds of nails and allow themselves to be locked for hours in small airtight boxes. Other sects are more spiritually oriented, and their meditative practices are more clearly mental in nature.

Different *gurus*, the Yogic spiritual guides and teachers, may advocate different paths, but regardless of which meditative discipline a devotee follows, the ultimate goal is *samadhi*, a transcendental state in which union is achieved with the "Universal Self." Common to many of the Yogic exercises is *dharana*, the focusing of attention or concentration of the mind on a definite object (Spiegelberg, 1962). Often the object of attention is a repetitious, monotonous stimulus or behavior. Tiny finger cymbals might be tapped together rapidly and rhythmically or the person may repeat a *mantra* over and over during meditation. A mantra is a phrase or simple sound, usually of some spiritual significance, that is either spoken aloud or to oneself repeatedly and rhythmically to provide a focus of attention during meditation. A familiar example of a mantra is the one made famous by the "beat" poet, Allen Ginsberg, beginning in the 1950s—"Om," spoken aloud.

Transcendental Meditation

TM is a streamlined Westernized version of mantram Yoga developed by the Maharishi Mahesh Yogi and introduced in the United States by him in the 1960s. The Maharishi gained prominence when the Beatles travelled to India to study with him, and, for a few years, was a regular guest on United States and British television talk shows. Hundreds of thousands of Americans have paid about $100 to learn TM from certified instructors who recruit students via posters on university campuses across the United States. The TM procedure is straightforward and demands no fundamental alteration in life-style. As a result, TM is less strange and threatening to Westerners than other meditative disciplines. For the same reasons, TM is less spiritual in orientation and does not have many adherents in India. The popularization of TM has been a boon to psychophysiological researchers who have access to thousands of potential subjects near university campuses, all of whom have been trained identically, and often have no philosophical objection to participating in scientific research.

At the beginning of training, each student is given a brief individualized secret mantra in the form of a Sanskrit phrase. The student meditates twice daily for 20 minutes each time, silently repeating the mantra and using it as an attentional focus.

Herbert Benson, a cardiologist at Harvard University, and his colleagues have developed what they call a "noncultic" meditation technique using TM as a model (Benson, Beary, & Carol, 1974). The active ingredients are those that Benson believes underlie the psychophysiological effects of TM, namely: (a) a reasonably quiet environment free from distractions, (b) a comfortable posture, (c) a passive attitude toward the outcome, and (d) repetition of a monotonous attentional focus, in the noncultic technique the word "one" repeated silently in synchronization with breathing. Benson's noncultic meditation has been used as treatment for a variety of psychophysiological disorders.

Effects of Meditation

Experiential Effects

The meditative disciplines are the only self-regulation techniques where there is always an explicit intent to alter consciousness.

The changes in consciousness achieved through meditation are often referred to as mystical experiences (Deikman, 1966). Mystical experiences may result from a psychological manipulation, such as a set of mental exercises, a physiological alteration, such as fasting or ingesting a psychedelic drug, or can be precipitated primarily by environmental circumstances, as in a conversion experience at a religious rally. Regardless of their origin, mystical experiences seem to share several qualities that distinguish them from ordinary conscious experience.

There are formidable problems in discussing alterations in consciousness. The English language is not well-equipped to describe the landscape of the mind. Worse still, one of the defining features of mystical experiences is their resistance to verbal description. Perhaps this is because, as Charles Tart (1972) has argued, mystical states must be comprehended in their own right, not in terms of how they differ from ordinary consciousness; yet the describer and the reader must have some common basis for understanding. Even given these constraints, there is some agreement on the experiential qualities of mystical states. The following characteristics are adopted from Arnold Ludwig (1966) and Arthur Deikman (1966).

Ineffibility. One cannot communicate the essence of the experience to anyone who has not undergone a similar experience. Although meditators might provide lengthy written accounts of their experiences, they feel that mere words cannot convey the true significance of them.

Realness. There is a sense of "Truth"—that the person has become privileged to reality in a way that is not possible during ordinary consciousness. These Truths are not easily communicated, and may vanish in the transition to ordinary consciousness; they may even appear ridiculous to an outside observer. Ludwig (1966) has related an experience he had when, at the height of an LSD trip undertaken for experimental purposes, he entered a restroom:

> Standing by the urinal, I noticed a sign above it which read "Please Flush After Using!" As I weighed these words in my mind, I suddenly realized their profound meaning. Thrilled by this startling revelation, I rushed back to my colleague to share this universal truth with him. Unfortunately, being a mere mortal, he could not appreciate the world-shaking import of my communication and responded by laughing! (p. 229)

Cognitive Changes. The ordinarily sharp perceptual distinction between imagination and reality becomes blurred and, as in the trance logic of hypnosis, incongruities are readily accepted. Events that are usually perceived as existing within a cause-effect relationship may now be viewed as simply correlated in time. There may be a feeling of loss of control, which may be pleasant or unpleasant, depending on personality characteristics.

Perceptual Changes. There is a sense of heightened acuteness of perception, imagery may be intensified, and the person might experience hallucinations. The body image may undergo marked alteration in dimensions or size. The sense of body may vanish altogether in an "out of body" experience, or the person may seem to physically merge with the rest of the universe. Time perception may be altered so that an instant seems to last forever. There are frequently interesting descriptions of what Deikman (1966) has called "trans-sensate phenomena"—intense, vivid perceptions that are not, remarkably, among the ordinary sensory modalities such as vision, audition, and so on.

Unity. The person feels as one with the rest of the universe and/or with a superior entity. This is the essential feature of the experience of *transcendence*, regardless of the religious or cultural context in which it occurs. Not every meditation technique leads to all of the phenomena just mentioned. Even within a given discipline, the experiential effects of meditation are dependent on the amount of practice and skill of the meditator.

Physiological Effects

Bagchi and Wenger (1957) provided some of the earliest systematic physiological recordings from meditators when they studied 45 Yogis during a 5-month, 4,000-mile tour of India. A variety of physiological responses were observed during meditation using a battery-powered 8-channel polygraph in locations ranging from university physiology laboratories to a Himalayan mountain cave. There were some differences among various Yogis studied, but the results generally indicated autonomic changes in the direction of relaxation and lowered metabolism. In particular, skin resistance tended to increase and heart rate to decrease, both indicative of lowered SNS activity. Respiration rate slowed, often to 50% of the control level, and breathing became extremely shallow. The EEG records did not seem to differ markedly from waking, at least the investigators did not observe changes characteristic of sleep, such as delta activity.

One of the Yogis, who was studied in his cave, appeared to become totally withdrawn and unresponsive to the external environment, even as the investigators installed the recording electrodes. When questioned later, he indicated that he was not aware of his surroundings nor of environmental stimuli during his meditation period. The EEG recordings supported his experiential self-report. Recall from chapter 2 that the EEG shows desynchronization or alpha blocking in response to external stimulation. This effect can be interpreted to indicate that a stimulus has "gotten in." This Yogis' EEG showed no alpha blocking to external stimuli.

More systematic observations of Yogis who practice a technique during which they claim to be oblivious to all stimuli, have yielded similar results

(Anand, Chhina, & Singh, 1961). When four advanced Yogis were meditating, intense stimulation, including loud banging and touching them with a hot glass tube, had no effect on their EEG. When they were not meditating, the same stimulation was initially accompanied by alpha blocking, which then habituated or diminished with repeated stimulation, reflecting decreased attention to the stimuli.

In distinct contrast, a study of Zen masters (Kasamatsu & Hirai, 1966) found no habituation of alpha blocking to clicks during meditation, in comparison to control subjects sitting quietly, who showed the expected habituation of attention in their EEG responses. The subjective reports of the Zen masters supported the EEG data—the clicks were perceived more clearly during meditation as compared to non-meditation. A more recent study in the United States compared Zen, Yoga, and TM meditators and control subjects in an attempt to replicate the above findings (Becker & Shapiro, 1981). In this study, there was no difference between the groups in the EEG response to the clicks. The latter study was more carefully controlled than the first two investigations, but the meditators studied appear to have been less advanced than those in the first two studies.

Some Yogis claim that they can stop their heart. Careful psychophysiological studies have shown that this is not the case (Wenger, Bagchi, & Anand, 1961). Apparently what happens is that they execute a Valsalva maneuver, which involves holding the breath while strongly contracting the muscles of the abdomen and diaphram. This chokes off the blood pumped by the heart, as well as the heart sounds and the pulse, both of which may disappear. However, the EKG indicates that the heart continues to beat, although there is one recorded case in which the heart went into atrial flutter for about 20 seconds (Green, 1973). In this condition the heart beats as fast as it can, about 300 beats per minute, but it does not pump any blood because it is beating too fast to fill and empty its chambers.

One particularly interesting Yogic practice has been studied only recently (Benson, Lehmann, Malhotra, Goldman, Hopkins, & Epstein, 1982). The devotees of g Tum-mo Yoga engage in competitions in which they sit all night wrapped in sheets that have been dipped in ice water. As each sheet becomes dry it is replaced by a new cold, wet one. The Yoga who dries the most sheets by daybreak is declared the winner. A number of physiological responses before, during, and after g Tum-mo Yoga are shown in Fig. 6.8 for a single representative subject. Notice the marked increase in skin temperature of the fingers and toes, in the absence of any other marked physiological changes. This, in combination with the steady heart rate, suggests that rather than producing a generalized increase in metabolism, the Yogis seem to dry the sheets via selective peripheral vasodilation.

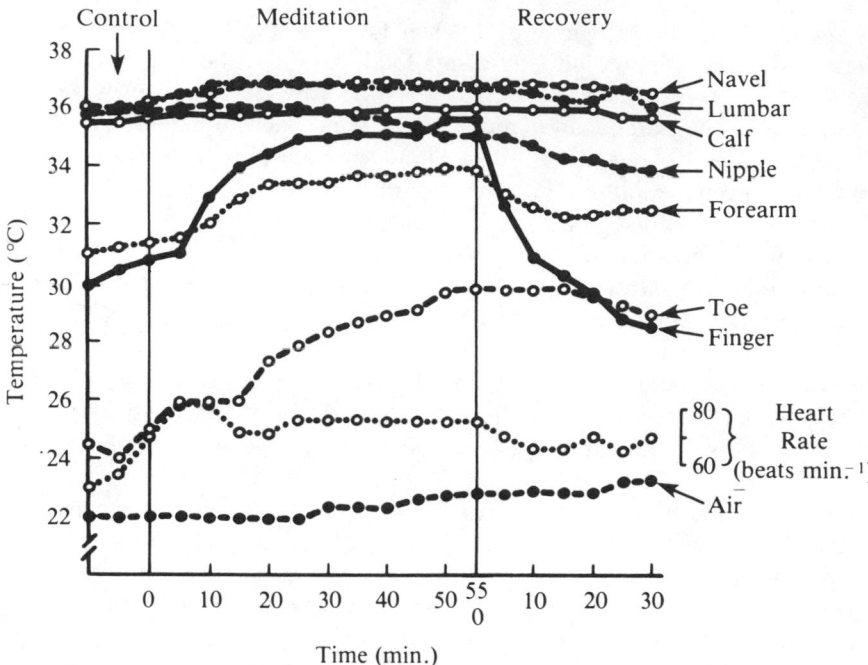

FIG. 6.8 Skin temperature, heart rate, and air temperature over time during g Tum-mo yoga. From "Body Temperature Changes during the Practice of g Tum-mo Yoga" by H. Benson et al. Reprinted by permission from *Nature, 295,* 235. Copyright 1982, Macmillan Journals Limited.

Because of the ready availability of subjects, considerably more is known about the physiological effects of TM than the other meditative techniques. Scientific interest dates to Keith Wallace's 1970 doctoral dissertation in psychology at UCLA—"Physiological Effects of Transcendental Meditation" (Wallace, 1970). Physiological responses during TM and quiet rest were compared for a group of 15 college-aged practitioners. In general, TM was accompanied by: (a) decreased autonomic arousal, as evidenced by elevated skin resistance; (b) lowered metabolism, as shown by decreased oxygen consumption and carbon dioxide elimination; and (c) a greater preponderance of slow waves, typically alpha activity, in the EEG. These changes prompted Wallace to describe TM as a "wakeful, hypometabolic state," a unique psychophysiological state to be distinguished from other states that have been associated with relaxation. Later studies have generally replicated Wallace's physiological results, but they have suggested important qualifications to his interpretation. Studies comparing physiological changes during TM and other self-regulation relaxation procedures have typically found no difference (Shapiro, 1982). For this reason, the proposed physiological uniqueness of TM is not generally accepted.

Herbert Benson, a colleague of Wallace's, has suggested that TM and other self-regulation relaxation procedures can elicit what he has called the *relaxation response*, a diffuse integrated psychophysiological response roughly the opposite of the response to stress (see chapter 3). His noncultic meditation procedure appears to encourage the relaxation response just as effectively as does TM (Beary & Benson, 1974).

Some advanced meditators who spend a great deal of time in meditation say that they have no need for sleep. However, physiological correlates of sleep are often observed during meditation, especially during TM (Pagano, Rose, Stivers, & Warrenburg, 1976). This may not be true for all forms of passive meditation. Practitioners of Ananda Marga, a mantram Yogic meditation related to TM, showed very little evidence of sleep in their EEGs, in contrast to control subjects who had been instructed to remain "wakefully relaxed" while sitting quietly for the same time period (Elson, Hauri, & Cunis, 1977). It may seem ridiculous to question honest self-reports about whether an individual has been sleeping, but it is well-known among psychophysiological researchers that a person can show the EEG signs of sleep onset, become unresponsive to environmental stimuli, yet vigorously deny having fallen asleep.

Robert Ornstein (1972) has suggested that, during passive meditation, one's attentional style or way of viewing the world shifts from the typical verbal and analytical orientation to a more intuitive and holistic perspective. If this were true, then during meditation we would expect relatively greater activity in the right cerebral hemisphere. Ornstein went on to propose that extended practice of meditation could result in a more or less permanent shift along these lines, so that an experienced meditator becomes a more "right-hemisphere oriented" type of person. The evidence is mixed on these interesting hypotheses (see Pagano & Warrenburg, 1983, for a review). One study has indeed found selective cortical activation of the right hemisphere during meditation, but two studies of TM have been able to find no such lateral shift in EEG activity. Meditators do seem to be superior to non-meditators in simple cognitive tasks for which the right hemisphere has shown some specialization, such as remembering a series of tones, a finding that would be expected if the meditators were more right-hemisphere oriented. Interestingly, there is evidence indicating that people who take up meditation tend more toward a non-verbal, holistic approach to apprehending the world around them to begin with. Untangling the possible pre-existing differences between meditators and non-meditators from the causal effects of practicing meditation will require further research.

Applications of Meditation

The most significant question about the consequences of meditation must be whether Zazen and the various Yogic meditative practices *really* lead to satori and samadhi, the proposed mystical states whereby the individual discovers the true nature of things. Unfortunately, this question probably cannot be answered from a Western scientific perspective, the guiding methodology of this book. However, it is striking that in India, Japan, and other Asian countries, many individuals spend a significant portion of their waking hours immersed in meditation. Are there more immediate personal rewards, in addition to the offered, eventual spiritual benefits, that help sustain this impressive devotion to the practice of meditation? We can only speculate with respect to Zazen and Yoga, but there is considerable evidence available about the effects of TM on personality variables, the relatively enduring characteristics of the person. It is necessary to use caution in interpreting research here because persons who become interested in, undertake, and stick with meditation probably differ in many ways, in advance, from other individuals. Even given this caution, sufficient evidence has accumulated to conclude that regular practice of TM results in: (a) a decrease in self-reported anxiety and stress responding, and (b) a more positive perception of oneself, a heightened feeling of well-being, and a stronger sense of self-actualization (Pagano & Warrenburg, 1983).

Various forms of meditation have been used as self-regulation approaches to treating psychophysiological disorders, particularly those that are stress-related, such as hypertension, and those that have an important cognitive element such as insomnia or alcoholism where the addicted individual has difficulty not thinking about the substance. In meditation we see that the mind can be a wonderful servant, however conditions such as alcoholism and insomnia remind us that the untrained mind can be a terrible master. In these cases meditation training has the potential for enabling self-regulation of the contents of consciousness. As with most empirical questions about meditation, good evidence is limited primarily to TM and its noncultic relatives. Several reviews of meditation, defined in this way, are available (e.g., Murray, 1982), including one requested by the American Psychiatric Association in order to assess the clinical effectiveness of meditation (Shapiro, 1982). The general conclusion must be that meditation is as effective as other self-regulation techniques, such as progressive relaxation with a variety of psychophysiological disorders, but not more so.

Representative of research in this area is an investigation comparing the effects of meditation and progressive relaxation training on sleep onset insomnia (Woolfolk, Carr-Kaffashan, McNulty, & Lehrer, 1976). Persons who regularly have difficulty getting to sleep usually experience unwanted "ruminative" thoughts that intrude while they are trying to go to sleep. Volunteers who reported an average sleep onset of 30 minutes or more, with an average duration of the problem of 14.1 years, were assigned randomly to either an untreated control condition, or to four training sessions of abbreviated progressive relaxation or meditation. Meditation was a noncultive method involving passive attention to breathing, repetition of a mantra ("in" and "out" with breathing), and eventually an attentional focus on a specific visual image. The data of major interest were the time to go to sleep and the rated difficulty of falling asleep, both rated by the patients each morning on awakening. The results are shown in Table 6.3. For both of the treated groups the time to go to sleep was cut in half, with the improvement maintained and even strengthened somewhat at the six-month follow-up. The subjective difficulty in getting to sleep followed the same pattern. The control subjects showed no improvement. The authors discounted attention-placebo as a potential explanation of the treatment effects, citing other studies indicating the resistance of insomnia to treatment by placebos.

The present lack of evidence showing meditation to be superior to other self-regulation methods in treating disorders with cognitive components, such as alcoholism and insomnia, should not be taken to mean that meditative exercises do not strengthen mental control. Rather, the evidence suggests that the other self-regulation procedures also facilitate control of attention and the contents of consciousness.

TABLE 6.3
Effects of Meditation and Progressive Relaxation
on Two Measures of Insomnia

	Pretest	Posttest	Follow-up
	Sleep onset latency (minutes)		
Meditation	74.08	34.19	24.51
Progressive Relaxation	65.01	29.20	26.73
Control	67.21	66.61	—
	Rated difficulty of falling asleep[a]		
Meditation	5.92	2.91	2.94
Progressive relaxation	6.35	3.48	3.28
Control	5.38	5.79	—

Note. From "Meditation Training as a Treatment for Insomnia" by R. L. Woolfolk, L. Carr-Kaffashan, T. F. McNulty, and P. Lehrer, 1976, Behavior Therapy, 7, p. 362. Copyright 1976 by the Association for Advancement of Behavior Therapy. Reprinted by permission of the publisher and the author.
[a] 10 = "extraordinarily difficult"

Meditation has been advocated in cancer treatment, as a means of influencing the immune system to retard or halt the growth of cancerous cells. The program devised by O. Carl Simonton and his colleagues is outlined in their self-help book, *Getting Well Again* (Simonton, Matthews-Simonton, & Creighton, 1978). This book begins, "Everyone participates in his or her health or illness at all times" (p. 3). Their patients learn to feel personally responsible for their psychophysiological state and regularly practice relaxation and a meditation technique in which they are to vividly imagine healthy cells attacking and destroying the cancerous cells in their bodies.

Proponents maintain that patients who practice this form of therapy live longer than would be otherwise expected, but there seems to have been no controlled studies of this cancer treatment program despite widespread publicity. Meares (1982/83) has reported cancer remission in several case studies using a different form of meditation. His patients practice a form of "dim visualization" that employs no verbalizations whatsoever. The aim is to pursue extreme "simplicity and stillness" of the mind, as distinct from vivid meditation focusing on visualization of the healing process. Controlled studies in this area would be extremely valuable.

7 Essential Hypertension and Coronary Heart Disease

The functioning of the cardiovascular system is very much a psychophysiological endeavor. A pump circulates fluid through some tubing to deliver essential supplies to various parts of the body and to carry away waste products. Remarkably, different components of this plumbing arrangement are able to blush in embarrassment, pound with excitement, and make their owner get "cold feet" just before a difficult examination. These are familiar and normal aspects of cardiovascular psychophysiology. "Voodoo death" (see chapter 3) is obviously a pathological example. Most deaths are due to failure of the cardiovascular system. In this chapter we survey two important cardiovascular disorders from the psychophysiological perspective—essential hypertension and coronary heart disease.

ESSENTIAL HYPERTENSION

Incidence and Characteristics

About 25 million persons in the United States, or 22% of the adult population, suffer from high blood pressure or arterial hypertension (Rowland & Roberts, 1982). In approximately 10% of these cases, high blood pressure can be traced to identifiable underlying diseases. For the remaining 90%, the etiology is unknown and their condition is termed *primary* or *essential hypertension.*

Essential hypertension is usually asymptomatic or silent, with no significant discomfort, especially in its earliest stages. As a consequence,

193

only about 50% of all hypertensives are detected prior to a catastrophic health event such as a stroke or heart attack. Of the individuals who have been detected, only about half are under treatment at any given time. A major reason is that anti-hypertensive drugs have unpleasant side effects for many individuals; this, compounded with the absence of discomfort from the illness itself, makes it understandably difficult for the patient to face a daily drug regimen that will probably remain in effect for the rest of his or her life. This is tragic, because the prognosis for untreated hypertension is very poor.

There appears to be no natural break between normal and abnormal blood pressure readings (Dollery, 1985), so that any cutoff used to define hypertension is somewhat arbitrary. The World Health Organization standard of at least 160 mmHg for systolic pressure and/or at least 90 mmHg for diastolic pressure is representative and reasonably well accepted (World Health Organization, 1962). Blood pressures of 140 to 160 systolic and/or 90 to 95 diastolic are often considered to represent borderline hypertension.

Phyiology and Etiology

Physiology

Although there is no agreement about the possible health consequences of blood pressures in the lower ranges, it is evident that moderate to severe chronic elevation in blood pressure is a grave and pervasive health problem. Hypertension subjects blood vessels to sustained heightened pressure, causing them to break down, which results in damage to vital organs. As a consequence, hypertension is one of the most powerful known risk factors in the development of atherosclerosis, coronary heart disease, congestive heart failure, kidney failure, stroke, and heart attacks, the latter alone accounting for over half of the deaths that can be traced back to hypertension (Dollery, 1985). In the 40 to 49 age range, the risk of stroke is about 10 times higher for persons with diastolic pressure above 104 mmHg as compared to those below 85 mmHg (Dollery, 1985). This is about as potent a risk factor for stroke as is smoking a pack or two of cigarettes per day for lung cancer in the same age group (Hammond, 1966).

As discussed in chapter 2, blood pressure is a function of blood volume, cardiac output, and peripheral resistance. An increase in any of these three factors will elevate blood pressure, at least momentarily, until some sort of compensating adjustment is made. Chronic high blood pressure results more from heightened blood volume and peripheral resistance than from cardiac hyperactivity.

The kidneys are thought to be involved in most cases of essential hypertension (Guyton, 1982) because of their role in regulating body fluids. The kidneys normally respond to a major increase in blood pressure by accelerating the excretion of fluid in the urine, which decreases blood volume, and hence blood pressure. Conversely, when blood pressure declines significantly, the kidneys normally step up production of renin, an enzyme that stimulates a biochemical chain of events leading to the manufacture of angiotensin II. Angiotensin II inhibits excretion of salt and water by the kidneys (thereby increasing blood volume and blood pressure) and stimulates the adrenal cortex to release aldosterone, a hormone that also causes the kidneys to retain salt and water. Also, angiotensin II enters the circulatory system where it acts as a potent vasoconstrictor. In essential hypertension, it appears that one or more of these mechanisms becomes more or less permanently reset to an inappropriately high level. There are several different physiological routes to essential hypertension; in particular, subgroups of hypertensives with abnormally high and low levels of renin in the blood have been identified (Dollery, 1985).

The risk of hypertension is mediated, in part, by hereditary factors. Evidence of this (summarized by Dollery, 1985) includes higher blood pressure correlations between: (a) monozygotic twins as compared to dizygotic twins, (b) genetically related family members as compared to spouses, and (c) parents and their natural children as compared to parents and their adopted children. A child has greater risk of hypertension if one parent is hypertensive, and still greater risk if both parents are hypertensive. Weiner (1977) has estimated that perhaps 30% of the difference in hypertension risk between persons is genetically determined.

A newly-discovered vasorelaxing hormone, *auriculin*, which is produced in the heart, may play an important role in the hereditary risk of hypertension. Cloning studies with rats have revealed a specific genetic mechanism that influences auriculin production, and, hence, blood pressure levels (Yamanaka et al., 1984).

Near the turn of the century two French physicians, Ambard and Beaujard, proposed that hypertension is caused by excessive sodium in the form of sodium chloride (salt), in the diet. Since then several compelling lines of evidence have supported the supposed link between salt in the diet and hypertension. Rats can be made hypertensive by requiring them to consume large quantities of sodium (reviewed by Tobian, 1979); if their kidney function is experimentally impaired beforehand, compromising their ability to excrete sodium, they develop even more rapid and severe hypertension. Conversely, a very low sodium diet in rats prevents hypertension, even when kidney function is disturbed. Rats can be inbred to produce strains that are highly sensitive or highly resistant to sodium hypertension. There are a few isolated, non-technological cultures, such as the Yanomamo Indians of South America, whose dietary intake of sodium is near zero; in these cultures, blood pressure does not rise progressively with age, and hypertension is extremely rare or entirely absent (reviewed by Page, 1979). Finally, blood pressure reductions have been noted in hypertensive patients being maintained on a strict diet of rice and fruit, which severely curtails sodium intake (Kempner, 1948).

From the evidence just presented, too much salt in the diet would seem like an excellent single-cause explanation of essential hypertension; unfortunately, the picture is more complicated. Within a given culture, there is little or no relationship between salt consumption and blood pressure (Dollery, 1985). In one of the most systematic investigations along these lines, 3,123 randomly selected households in Connecticut were surveyed (Holden, Ostfeld, Freeman, Hellenbrand, & D'Atri, 1983). Residents had their blood pressures taken several times and completed a detailed dietary questionnaire on salt consumption, assessing the extent to which they salted food at the table, and ate high sodium foods at home, such as canned soups, canned vegetables, or cold cuts. The average systolic blood pressures of those who fell in the top and bottom 10% of the sample in terms of salt consumption were 123.4 mmHg and 121.2 mmHg, respectively; the corresponding diastolic pressures were 77.4 mmHg and 76.8 mmHg. These are trivial differences.

Even stronger evidence against the sodium hypothesis emerged from an extensive analysis of a nationwide United States health and nutrition data base (McCarron, Morris, Henry, & Stanton, 1984). The relationship between blood pressure and 17 nutrients was observed among 10,372 adults, none of whom were aware of being hypertensive or were on special diets. Higher intake of sodium was associated with *lower* systolic blood pressure and lower risk of hypertension. The strongest nutrient correlation with hypertension was lower calcium intake.

Proponents of the sodium-hypertension hypothesis have countered by reminding us of the absence of hypertension in non-salt cultures, and argue that salt consumption in the United States is so extraordinarily high that even persons with relatively low salt intake, such as those in the bottom 10% of the population, still consume excessive amounts of salt with respect to risk of essential hypertension (Scribner, 1983). But, if practically all of us habitually consume far too much salt, then why are only 20% of us hypertensive?

Psychophysiology

The Sodium-Stress Hypothesis. Perhaps one can safely consume large amounts of sodium as long as the kidneys remove the excess. Along these lines, Anderson (1981) has proposed that the efficiency of sodium elimination by the kidneys is highly sensitive to stress. Specifically, potassium levels may rise during certain types of stress situations which then triggers aldosterone production, which, in turn, results in sodium retention by the kidneys, increasing blood volume and consequently blood pressure. One implication is that in a low stress environment, the kidneys may function well enough in most individuals to eliminate the excessive sodium of a high salt diet. However, when both stress and excessive salt intake are present, some of these same individuals would run the risk of hypertension.

Many experimental studies have provided direct evidence of stress-induced sodium retention in lower animals (reviewed by Anderson, 1984). While this provocative psychophysiological analysis of hypertension has not been tested extensively in humans, it has received some experimental support. One investigation involved 40 college students, who were classified as high or low risk candidates for hypertension on the basis of whether or not they had at least one hypertensive parent, or were borderline hypertensive themselves (Light, Koepke, Obrist, & Willis, 1983). The students were studied under either stressed or unstressed conditions. The unstressed subjects simply read or rested in a quiet room; the stressed subjects engaged in competitive reaction time tasks. Heart rate was measured and sodium excretion was assessed periodically from urine samples. Sodium excretion decreased markedly in the stressed condition for the 50% of the high risk individuals who responded to stress with the greatest heart rate increases. Because heart rate acceleration during stress seems to be sympathetically-controlled, these findings suggest that, in some predisposed individuals, SNS hyperactivity to chronic stress may result in sodium retention, which contributes to the development of hypertension.

Stress and Hypertension. Much of the evidence linking hypertension to stress is correlational (see reviews by Gutmann & Benson, 1971; Weiner, 1977). In general, hypertension and the health problems to which it predisposes, such as coronary heart disease, are much more prevalent in technologically advanced nations. Within countries, the risk of hypertension is greater in the stressful urban environment as compared to the more relaxed rural setting (e.g., Berkson, Stamler, Lindberg, Miller, Mathias, Lasky, & Hall, 1960). In some United States cities, the average blood pressure varies considerably from neighborhood to neighborhood. In Detroit, blood pressure was found to be especially high among blacks living in an area with high unemployment, low education, high crime rates, and widespread poverty (Harburg, Erfurt, Hauenstein, Chape, Schull, & Schork, 1973). In Massachusetts, the highest hypertension-related mortality rates were in the neighborhoods whose residents had the lowest educational background and occupational status; this social stress pattern was not related to race (Jenkins, Tuthill, Tannenbaum, & Kirby, 1979). Stressful living conditions and higher blood pressure even seem to be associated within prison populations. D'Atri (1975) discovered the same pattern in the two prisons he studied—male inmates living in single occupancy cells had lower blood pressures as compared to prisoners housed in more crowded, and dangerous, conditions. Because some jobs seem to be more stressful than others, we would expect to find higher rates of hypertension in certain occupational groups. Consistent with this, a sample of male air traffic controllers had 5.6 times more new cases of hypertension within a 2-year period compared with a group of men in other aviation industry occupational groups (Cobb & Rose, 1973).

If stress contributes to hypertension, then one would expect blood pressure to rise in stress situations. This is well illustrated in a study during which the participants were subjected to realistic stressors, in an experimental arrangement that would not be ethically acceptable today (Schachter, 1957). The participant, wired up to an assortment of electronic gadgets, experienced a series of apparently accidental electric shocks that ominously increased in intensity, while technicians dashed about apprehensively shouting such things as "Something has gone wrong; I have to check the machine . . . Look out! A short circuit! . . . My God, that's dangerous! Don't move . . ." (pp. 18-19). This brief scenario led to average increases in systolic pressure of 25 mmHg and in diastolic of 14 mmHg. There were similar blood pressure responses to situations in which the participants experienced anger and pain. Both normal and hypertensive subjects participated in the experiment, with hypertensives making blood pressure responses about twice that of normotensives.

Several other studies were presented in chapter 3 indicating that the blood pressure of hypertensives is overreactive to stressors (Engel & Bickford, 1961; Moos & Engel, 1962). As explained in chapter 3, Sternbach (1966) has warned that a physiologically "preferred response to stress" predisposes one to develop a disorder in that response system. The necessary longitudinal observations to determine whether blood pressure hyperreactivity exists in persons before they become hypertensive have not been reported. An even more fundamental piece of the puzzle is missing—whether repeated elicitation of blood pressure responses can result in chronic high blood pressure, due to something like Sternbach's (1966) homeostatic failure. Studies using lower animals point in this direction (e.g., Forsyth, 1969).

Personality and Hypertension. There have been several attempts to link hypertension and personality, the most influential of which has been Alexander's (1939) repressed hostility hypothesis. From Alexander's psychoanalytic perspective (see chapter 3), there is a characteristic hypertensive personality marked by a severe, largely unconscious, conflict between opposing passive, dependent and aggressive, hostile impulses. Lacking the psychological wherewithall to openly express their hostility or comfortably accept their passivity, hypertensives suffer "a kind of emotional paralysis" (Alexander, 1939, p. 175), leading to chronically inhibited aggression or repressed hostility. These repressed emotions result in chronic high blood pressure, just as a brief burst of overtly expressed anger causes a momentary elevation in blood pressure. This inner turmoil is not evident to others because it is covered up by excessive self-control and outward friendliness.

There is some empirical support for Alexander's thinking (reviewed by Goldstein, 1981; Weiner, 1977). The major results of an interesting series of laboratory studies (e.g., Hokanson & Burgess, 1962) can be interpreted within Alexander's hostility-hypertension framework. Hokanson experimentally induced anger by having an accomplice provoke his subjects by harassing and insulting them while they tried to solve problems. This resulted in an abrupt increase in blood pressure. But blood pressure returned promptly to normal for those subjects who were able to express their anger toward the provocateur by delivering (fake) electric shocks to them in a supposed learning experiment. However, other subjects, who had no such opportunity to express their anger, showed continued elevation in blood pressure.

Treatment

Sodium Restriction

In small segments of the population, consumption of normal amounts of sodium (by United States standards) has important clinical consequences. There is a subset of hypertensives who consistently benefit from moderate dietary sodium restrictions (MacGregor et al., 1982). Some individuals with kidney disease must minimize sodium intake to survive. Other persons who are highly sensitive to sodium can be identified by following their blood pressure response to a high dose of sodium; they benefit from removal of sodium from their diet (Brackett, 1983). Nonetheless, evidence presented above indicates that dietary salt is not an important factor in blood pressure regulation for the majority of Americans. There appears to be no justification for widespread dietary salt restriction nor for routinely advising hypertensives to limit their sodium intake (Holden et al., 1983; McCarron et al., 1984).

Pharmacological Stepped Care

Among physicians in the United States the overwhelming treatment of choice for essential hypertension is the pharmacological "stepped care" approach (Brackett, 1983). Three types of anti-hypertensive drugs are introduced, if needed, in successive steps, each one in gradually increasing doses. In Step I, a diuretic is prescribed to reduce blood volume by enhancing sodium and water elimination by the kidneys. If large doses of diuretics do not result in satisfactory blood pressure control, or if effective doses cannot be tolerated because of side effects (possible gastrointestinal irritation, weakness, drowsiness, diarrhea, nausea, muscle cramps, and male impotence), the patient is moved to Step II with the addition of an SNS blocking agent, such as reserpine. Lethargy, tiredness, and even serious depression are relatively common side effects due to depletion of catecholamines in the CNS. If the Step II combination is not successful, a vasodilator is added as Step III. All of the side effects mentioned previously are possible with vasodilators, plus secondary salt and water retention, and tachycardia induced by the peripheral vasodilation. If the first three types of agents do not adequately control blood pressure, various drugs may be added or substituted as Step IV last ditch measures.

The utility of pharmacological treatment of hypertension has been evaluated in several major studies. As part of the nationwide Hypertension Detection and Follow-Up Program initiated in 14 United States cities in 1972, 10,940 persons with diastolic blood pressure above 90 mmHg were studied for five years after initial door-to-door screening (Forum on Hypertension in Minority Populations, 1982). Half of the patients received pharmacological stepped-care with an aggressive support program to strengthen compliance, while the remainder were simply "referred to their physician" (although many of them must not have had a physician). There was a 17% greater reduction in total mortality in the stepped-care group as compared to the other patients. Of the stepped-care patients, 52% reached their goal blood pressure within the first year of treatment and 65% by the fifth year.

Several studies have reported a lack of success in pharmacological treatment of mildly elevated blood pressure (Smith, 1977). This is an extremely serious problem, because millions of persons fall into this category, and these borderline hypertensives suffer about 100% greater overall mortality as compared to individuals with lower blood pressure (Julius, 1977). Debate continues on the merits of subjecting them to the considerable cost, inconvenience, and possible hazards and unpleasantness of a lifetime of medication.

Success rates as high as 80% have been mentioned for the stepped-care approach (Brackett, 1983); these figures are grossly misleading because they seem to indicate that hypertension is currently being treated effectively. The asymptomatic nature of the disorder coupled with the noxious side effects of anti-hypertensive medications result in a dropout rate from pharmacological treatment as high as 74% (Caldwell, Cobb, Dowling, & Jough, 1970). The National Center for Health Statistics (1975) has noted that about 85% of all diagnosed hypertensives are either being treated inadequately or not at all. On a more positive note, the rate of detection and treatment of hypertension has been improving since about 1960 (Rowland & Roberts, 1982; Stamler, 1981). Psychologists could make an important contribution to the nation's health by devising an effective and cost efficient way of increasing compliance to treatment among hypertensives (e.g., Meyers, Thackwray, Johnson, & Schlesser, 1983).

Self-Regulation

There are many candidates who could benefit from nonpharmacological alternative or complementary methods of blood pressure control. They include many of the millions of patients with mildly elevated blood pressure, those whose condition has been resistant to antihypertensive drug treatment, persons who suffer especially noxious drug side effects, and at least some of the patients who are unwilling or unable to follow a daily drug regimen for the rest of their lives. Research has concentrated on two self-regulation procedures—blood pressure biofeedback and relaxation training.

Large blood pressure changes are evident very quickly when instrumental conditioning procedures are applied to rats that have been curarized to prevent them from "cheating" (e.g. DiCara & Miller, 1968). In normal humans, blood pressure biofeedback effects are not so large and emerge more slowly, but voluntary changes on the order of a few mmHg are consistently observed (reviewed by Elder, Geoffray, & McAfee, 1981). Perhaps humans are autonomic slow learners, or perhaps, by paralyzing the skeletal muscles, curare makes autonomic learning easier by eliminating irrelevant physiological "noise." Whatever the explanation of the apparent species difference, it is clear that in both humans and lower animals blood pressure can be modified using biofeedback procedures. Yet, the accumulated research on controlling hypertension with blood pressure biofeedback has been disappointing—at least relative to the great expectations under which the first trials were launched in the early 1970s (reviewed by Seer, 1979). Statistically significant reductions in the blood pressure of hypertensives are obtained regularly, but few studies have reported therapeutic changes in blood pressure that are comparable to the effects of anti-hypertensive medications; statistical significance does not equal clinical significance (Blanchard & Young, 1973).

The entire spectrum of psychophysiological relaxation methods—autogenic training, meditation, progressive relaxation, hypnosis, and biofeedback-assisted relaxation—have been explored with hypertensive patients. The effects of two mixed self-regulation approaches to essential hypertension have been tested rather thoroughly, both with encouraging outcomes.

One method, developed by Chandra Patel and her associates, combines several modalities of biofeedback, autogenic phrases, and some features of yogic meditation (Patel, 1977). Electrodermal, EMG, and EEG biofeedback are employed in an apparently unstructured, individualized fashion that has not been described in detail. During biofeedback training, the trainee attends to breathing and repeats autogenic phrases such as "My arms are heavy." Patients are urged to practice at home twice daily without feedback in addition to the 30-minute formal training sessions that are conducted two or three times per week over three months.

In one investigation, Patel (1975) randomly assigned, to a treated group or to a control group, 40 hypertensives, most of whom were receiving, and continued to receive, medication. Control patients attended the same number of sessions as the treated patients, but simply rested quietly on a couch. There was no change in blood pressure throughout the study for the controls. In contrast, the treated patients lowered their systolic blood pressure from an average of 159 mmHg to 139 mmHg across training, and their diastolic from 100 mmHg to 86 mmHg. These are clinically useful reductions in blood pressure, and significantly, these gains persisted across a 12-month follow-up period during which the trainees were encouraged to continue home practice. For 12 of the treated patients, medication levels were reduced by an average of 42%. When the control hypertensives were shifted over to the treatment condition, somewhat smaller, but still clinically significant, therapeutic effects were obtained.

Patel believes that it is therapeutically significant that treated subjects were able to extend their blood pressure control to exercise and stress situations. Treated and control hypertensives were tested during brief periods of physical exercise and cold pressor stress, immersing the left arm in ice water for 80 seconds, at the beginning of the study and after the training period. The blood pressure responses to the cold pressor stress are shown in Fig. 7.1. The arrows indicate that the treated subjects made smaller blood pressure responses to stress during the second test, that is, after they had been trained, while the control subjects actually made somewhat larger responses the second time. The major findings were that the treated subjects made smaller systolic and diastolic responses to the stressor, and recovered from it more quickly, as compared to the controls.

Another mixed self-regulation approach to essential hypertension, using strictly home practice, has been devised and tested by Bernard Engel and his colleagues at the Gerontology Research Center, Baltimore City Hospital (Engel, Gaarder, & Glascow, 1981; Engel, Glascow, & Gaarder, 1983; Glascow, Gaarder, & Engel, 1982). Their self-regulation components are: (a) systolic blood pressure biofeedback using a special procedure developed for home use; (b) an abbreviated form of progressive relaxation; and (c) a meditation technique they have not described in any detail.

Only borderline hypertensives were studied, about half of whom were taking diuretics and continued to do so until medication was withdrawn for some of them late in the study. Of 127 who started off, 90 patients completed the six-month treatment period. This is a substantial dropout rate, but those who withdrew did not seem to be different in any important

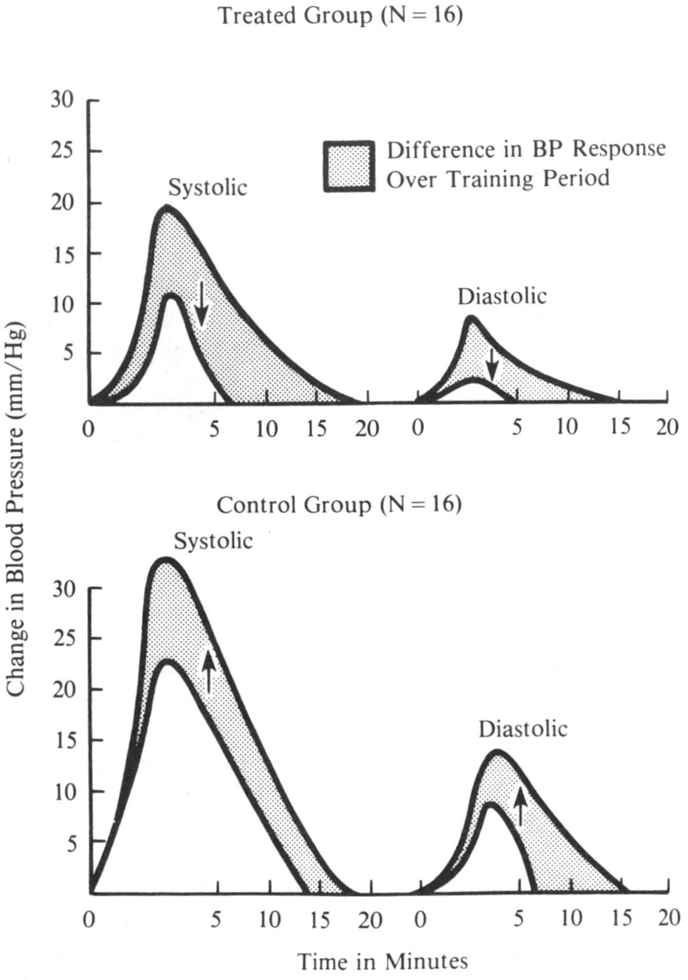

FIG. 7.1   Effects of self-regulation training on blood pressure responses to cold water stress in treated and control hypertensives. (Shaded area represents a reduction in blood pressure over the training period for the treated group, and an increase in blood pressure over the training period for the control group) From "Biofeedback-Aided Relaxation in the Management of Hypertension" by C. H. Patel, 1977, *Biofeedback and Self-Regulation, 2,* 32. Copyright 1977 by Plenum Publishing Corporation. Adapted by permission.

way from those who continued; the overwhelming reason given for leaving the study was that it took too much time.

Prior to treatment, all of the patients took their blood pressure at home at three different times daily, taking three consecutive readings each time for enhanced reliability, for one month. This resulted in an appropriately conservative blood pressure baseline insofar as it is known that blood pressure is artificially elevated the first few times it is measured. Patients were then randomly assigned to either a control group, in which they continued to self-monitor blood pressure, or to active treatment. Half of the actively treated patients started off with biofeedback, the others with relaxation training. Biofeedback was practiced at home, several times per day. Beginning in the second month they were instructed to try to identify any subjective feelings that were associated with blood pressure reductions. Beginning in the third month they practiced using certain environmental cues as signals to begin brief blood pressure reduction sessions in the natural environment without the cuff "as frequently as possible each day." Relaxation training involved combined progressive relaxation and meditation, practiced for about 10 minutes several times per day; otherwise, the details were the same as for biofeedback training. After three months of training, half of the patients in each treatment group were switched to the other self-regulation method, while the remainder continued with their original treatment method through the second, final, three months of therapy. Thus, in addition to the control group, one group received biofeedback throughout, one received relaxation training throughout, one experienced biofeedback then relaxation, and the final group relaxation then biofeedback. Patients were monitored carefully throughout to encourage compliance with their home practice schedule, and all were seen once a month at an outpatient facility.

Blood pressure gradually declined across the six-month treatment period for all groups, including the control group that simply engaged in intensive self-monitoring of blood pressure. The reductions in blood pressure were greater for the actively-treated as compared to the control subjects; those who practiced, in sequence, both forms of self-regulation were significantly superior to those who experienced only one of the techniques for the entire training period. The most effective combination was biofeedback followed by relaxation training, which led to blood pressure reductions across training of about 10 to 15 mmHg in systolic and 6 to 8 mmHg in diastolic, both at home and at the clinic. These therapeutic gains were generally maintained satisfactorily over a six-month posttreatment follow-up period. Diuretics were withdrawn successfully from 13 of the patients taking medication—they were able to sustain adequately reduced blood pressure for at least nine months after they had discontinued medication.

Based on these results, the authors advocate a staged nonpharmacological approach to essential hypertension which, coupled with behavioral changes such as weight loss and exercise, they believe "could significantly reduce the need for anti-hypertensive pharmacotherapy" (Glascow et al., 1982, p. 170). The first stage should be simply self-monitoring, because intensive daily self-monitoring resulted in clinically useful decreases in blood pressure for some of their patients. The next stage, if needed, is three months of blood pressure biofeedback home practice, followed by three months of relaxation if needed.

CORONARY HEART DISEASE

Incidence and Characteristics

In the 20th century there has been a virtual epidemic of coronary artery or coronary heart disease (CHD) in the Western industrialized nations. Using statistics corrected to take into account that people in the 1950s were living longer and the risk of CHD increases with age, by the mid-1950s a person in the United States had about twice the risk of dying of CHD as compared to the beginning of the century (Levy, 1982). Then, CHD mortality began to decline. Since 1950 the rate of all cardiovascular deaths, adjusted for age, has decreased by 41.5% (Levy, 1985). Neither the initial rise nor the subsequent fall in CHD is well understood. It may be noteworthy that since the 1950s, detection and treatment of hypertension have been improving, and during this same time period American dietary habits and lifestyles have been changing, including fewer people smoking cigarettes, and, in general, greater public awareness of the importance of maintaining good health (Levy, 1982). Nonetheless, CHD remains a health problem of awesome dimensions. For example, in 1979 CHD cost an estimated $80 billion in the United States for treatment and lost productivity (Levy, 1985). Even as the epidemic wanes, CHD continues to be the leading cause of death in the technologically advanced countries; in 1983 there were 766,000 deaths from heart disease in the United States (National Center for Health Statistics, 1984).

In CHD there is an insufficient supply of oxygen-rich blood to the heart muscle due to gradual narrowing or sudden blocking of the coronary arteries, frequently both. This can be the result of an obstructing clot (an embolism) or more commonly, atherosclerosis—formation on the inside arterial wall of patches or "plaques" composed of smooth muscle cells, connective tissue, but mainly of cholesterol. Without an adequate supply of blood, the affected section of heart muscle cannot function properly, at least temporarily. Sudden, severe, and extended restriction of the coronary circulation results in irreversible damage (infarction) to the heart muscle (the myocardium), an event known as a *myocardial infarction* or heart attack. Less traumatic oxygen deficiencies in heart muscle are signalled by *angina pectoris*, an intense pain in the left chest area sometimes extending into the arm and side of the neck.

Angina attacks typically occur in individuals with preexisting atherosclerosis when, during heightened cardiac output brought on by physical exercise or a stress situation, the heart muscle suddenly needs more oxygen than the coronary arteries can provide. Death from CHD is usually due to uncontrolled fluttering (*fibrillation*) of the ventricles which greatly diminishes or totally eliminates the pumping action of the heart. The most common single fatal consequence of CHD is *sudden cardiac death*, in which there is abrupt and complete cessation of cardiac functioning and death within a matter of seconds or minutes. In the United States, sudden cardiac death is the leading cause of death in men between ages 20 and 60 (Willerson, 1982b).

Physiology and Etiology

Traditional Risk Factors

Several variables are widely accepted as established risk factors for CHD: (a) age, with CHD increasing with age, perhaps due to accumulated exposure to the other risk factors; (b) gender, with more CHD in males; (c) diabetes, with more atherosclerosis among diabetics; (d) exercise, with absence of physical activity contributing to CHD; (e) cigarette smoking, with smokers at greater risk, although the causation—which could involve either carbon monoxide or nicotine, or both—has not been worked out; (f) serum cholesterol, which is positively related to atherosclerosis and CHD (see chapter 3); and (g) hypertension, with CHD associated with higher blood pressures, in part because hypertension accelerates atherosclerosis, much as overinflation weakens a tire and invites patches. Being overweight does not, in itself, increase the risk of CHD, although, since overweight persons are more likely to have elevated blood pressure and serum cholesterol, CHD and obesity are statistically associated (Levy, 1982).

Cigarette smoking, hypertension and heightened serum cholesterol are generally considered the major risk factors—at least they have been the targets of the major efforts to predict and prevent CHD, and feature most prominently in advice to patients once CHD has been diagnosed. This preoccupation has its limitations. For one, CHD is less closely linked to these "big three" risk factors than is sometimes supposed. Combining the data from eight major prospective studies of CHD in the United States, the 10-year incidence of new CHD was seven times higher among individuals with all three risk factors as compared to those with none of these risk factors (Marmot & Winkelstein, 1975). But this high risk group (which made up about 8% of the sample) had *only 17%* of the CHD experienced by the total sample. Widening the risk group to include everyone who had any *one* of the three risk factors encompassed 94% of the new CHD, but *90%* of this broadened risk group did *not* develop CHD in the 10-year study period. Clearly, additional variables, not considered in this study, must play important roles in the etiology of CHD.

The same conclusion emerges from a 5-year prospective study of CHD in male railroad workers in the United States and Europe (Keys et al., 1972). Within each geographic sample CHD was associated with age, smoking, serum cholesterol, and blood pressure, and the two samples were about equal on these risk factors. Unaccountably, there was twice as much CHD in the United States men as compared to the European men. The same finding was obtained in a comparison of CHD in Massachusetts versus Honolulu and Puerto Rico (Gordon, Garcia-Dalmier, Kagan, Kennel, & Schiffman, 1974).

There must be other critical forces at work in CHD.

Stress and Coronary Heart Disease

The first clear evidence that stress contributes to coronary heart disease, independently of the traditional risk factors, was provided in a study of social stress in monkeys (Kaplan et al., 1983). The subjects were macaques, animals that are normally highly social, living in socially stable groups. Stress was created throughout the 21-month experiment by changing the social group membership of the stressed monkeys every few weeks. As a result, these monkeys were continually faced with a high degree of instability, competition, and social tension. Monkeys in the unstressed control condition lived in stable social groups throughout. All of the monkeys were maintained on a "prudent diet," based on recommendations of the American Heart Association, which was low in saturated fats and contained almost no cholesterol. The socially stressed monkeys developed considerably more coronary artery atherosclerosis as compared to the control monkeys. There are no comparable data available for humans, but it is obvious that these findings may help explain how atherosclerosis and CHD can develop in "low risk" members of human populations.

Perhaps the most intriguing perspective on stress and CHD in humans is a set of personality characteristics whose presence is a risk factor for CHD that is " . . . greater than that imposed by age, elevated values of systolic blood pressure and serum cholesterol, and smoking, and appears to be of the same order of magnitude as the relative risk associated with the latter three of these other factors" (Review Panel on Coronary-prone Behavior and Coronary Heart Disease, 1981). This psychophysiological risk factor is known as "type A coronary-prone behavior", or simply *type A behavior*.

One day in the 1950s, an upholsterer was called to repair the waiting room furniture in the office of two San Francisco physicians. The chairs looked peculiar to him, as if worn over the years by thousands of tense and impatient buttocks perched on their very front edges. At the time, these cardiologists, Meyer Friedman and Roy Rosenman, paid little attention to this astute observation they were embarrassed to recall much later (Friedman & Rosenman, 1974). In fact, their discovery of type A behavior happened a few years later during research on heart disease in Junior League women and their husbands. The women turned out to have much lower incidence of CHD as compared to their husbands. At that time conventional medical wisdom was that CHD was largely a matter of diet, yet the husbands and wives had essentially the same diets. Why did the men have so much heart disease? Discussions with the participants, their colleagues at work, and their personal physicians pointed toward an unsuspected risk factor in CHD, namely "excessive competitive drive and meeting deadlines" (Friedman & Rosenman, 1974).

The type A individual consistently manifests, as a way of life, the three personality elements described following. The type A person is located at one extreme of a personality continuum, with the type B individual, who very seldom shows any type A behaviors, located at the other. Although most of us would fall somewhere in between, one or more type A characteristics are estimated to be present in about 50% of all employed males in the United States (Waldron, 1978), and in well over 50% of the population of large United States cities (Friedman et al., 1982).

Type A is less prevalent among females, but the sex difference vanishes when occupational status is taken into account (Waldron, 1978). Women in managerial positions show just as many type A characteristics as men. For some reason, type A behavior has been studied mostly in men, perhaps because the incidence of CHD and of type A are both higher among males than females. But there is every indication that conclusions about type A and CHD apply equally to both sexes. One study has reported about twice as much CHD and three times as much angina pectoris among type A as compared to type B women (Haynes, Feinleib, & Kannel, 1980).

The type A person experiences *time urgency*. He or she feels the constant pressure of deadlines—not just ordinary and realistic deadlines such as handing in a term paper when it is due or being to work on time—but unnecessary, self-imposed deadlines like getting to the beach by one o'clock on Sunday afternoon or arriving in Pittsburgh by Wednesday on a cross country vacation. Waiting in line or being caught in a traffic jam is a stressful experience, because time is a precious commodity, to be "spent" not wasted. A type A person has some tricks for getting things moving more quickly, including finishing other people's sentences for them. The most common time-saving trick is "polyphasic behavior"—doing several things at once such as shaving and drinking morning coffee while driving to work.

Excessive competitiveness is the second distinctive type A behavior. The individual plays to win and prefers leisure time activities in which there are winners and losers. It is type A behavior to begin keeping score when casually hitting a pingpong ball back and forth at a party. The type A jogger is the one with a stopwatch. At a party, the type A emerges as a strong social personality and dominates conversations, but two type A's do not converse well since neither cares to listen. The type A is respectful of high status persons (such contacts can be useful in the game of life), but exploits or simply ignores low status persons. Lacking time for quiet contemplation, the type A individual has no guiding philosophy of life beyond "getting ahead."

The third characteristic, *diffuse hostility*, may be a consequence of the first two. Other persons are frequently viewed as competitors; those who are not may still be resented because of the time they make one waste due to their bumbling mistakes and inconsiderate interruptions. Hostility seems to be a potent CHD risk factor in its own right. A sample of physicians who had taken a global personality test when they were in medical school at Johns Hopkins were followed up 25 years later (Barefoot, Dahlstrom, & Williams, 1983). A retest indicated that hostility scores had remained highly stable over the intervening years. The physicians who had had the highest hostility scores in medical school showed five times as much angina pectoris and myocardial infarction later on.

Type A behavior is assessed either in a standard 15-minute structured interview (See Chesney, Eagleston, & Rosenman, 1981, for details) or with objectively-scored paper and pencil self-report inventories that enable speedy and inexpensive group administration; the most widely used of these is the Jenkins Activity Survey (Jenkins, Rosenman, & Friedman, 1967). Techniques have been developed for assessing type A children (Matthews & Angulo, 1980). The various testing instruments define type A somewhat differently (Matthews, 1982).

Following the seminal observations of Rosenman and Friedman, a series of more formal investigations have verified the connection between type A behavior and CHD. The risk of having severe atherosclerosis and of dying of CHD are both as much as six times greater for type A as compared to type B persons (Friedman, Rosenman, Straus, Wurm, & Kositcheck, 1968). This is partly because other CHD risk factors are associated with type A behavior—the type A person is more likely to smoke cigarettes, have higher blood pressure, and so on. But even when these other risk factors have been matched, there is twice as much CHD among type A's as compared to type B's (Rosenman, Brand, Jenkins, Friedman, Straus, & Wurm, 1975). Therefore, type A behavior does not lead to CHD simply by predisposing people to have the other risk factors, but makes some kind of independent contribution.

In attempting to explain the progression from type A behavior to CHD, it is commonly suggested that the intense psychophysiological response of the hard-driving type A to certain common environmental stressors (e.g., a traffic jam) includes sympathetic neuroendocrine and cardiovascular components that promote atherosclerosis or other physiological precipitators of CHD.

There is some empirical support for this line of reasoning because there is a special relationship between type A and atherosclerosis (reviewed by Williams, 1982). For example, fewer than 50% of heart patients having only mild coronary atherosclerosis were classified as type A, as compared to 71% of those with moderate and 93% of those with severe atherosclerosis (Blumenthal, Williams, Long, Schanberg, & Thompson, 1978). It has also been shown that type A individuals make greater cardiovascular responses to certain stressors as compared to other persons. Thus, type A heart patients showed larger increases in blood pressure during a confrontative and challenging interview than did other heart patients, even though they were taking SNS beta-blocking medication intended to control their blood pressure (Dembroski, MacDougall, & Lushene, 1979). Similar results have been reported with a non-patient population in which the stressor was a competitive video paddle game with a $5 prize at stake for the winner (Dembroski, MacDougall, Shields, Petitto, & Lushene, 1978); type A's had larger elevations in both blood pressure and heart rate as compared to type B's.

Individuals with type A behavior may compound the consequences of their overreaction to common stressors by actually seeking out those stressors. Byrne (1981) has proposed that type A's are more likely than other persons to place themselves in social situations, in occupational groups, or other circumstances in which they are liable to encounter significant stressors. Consistent with his hypothesis, Byrne (1981) found that type A patients, hospitalized for coronary artery bypass surgery, reported having had a greater number of stressful life events in the one year prior to their myocardial infarction as compared to the other bypass patients. As Byrne admits, this finding does not establish that the cause and effect relationships are as he has hypothesized.

A final, and possibly practical observation, is that type A behavior may increase the risk of CHD only in moderately or highly stressful environments—more precisely, only in those settings having the particular stressors to which the type A person is specially sensitized. If so, the type

B individual could tolerate time pressures and competition without increased risk of CHD. But the type A person may be able to live safely only in a protected environment where traffic never backs up at the bridge in rush hour and the supermarket checkout lines are always short.

Treatment

Crisis Care

The accepted treatment for a heart attack is to get the patient to a hospital coronary care unit as quickly as possible, monitor the EKG for complications, give oxygen to ease the demands on the heart, administer analgesics to diminish the angina pain, try to suppress dangerous disruptions of the cardiac rhythm with drugs, provide sedation to dampen emotional responding, and offer reassurance (Willerson, 1982a). But as of the early 1970s, most heart attack patients died without reaching a hospital. Mortality is greatly reduced among those who reach a coronary care unit, but still ranges from 3% to 30% depending on the patient population and the quality of the care provided. Survivors of a heart attack suffer a yearly mortality rate of 5% (under age 50) to 10% (if over age 50) thereafter. Of the patients who survive their initial heart attack, about 25% have another within five years (Willerson, 1982a).

Bypass Surgery

Coronary artery bypass surgery is presently a routine, but controversial, alternative to pharmacological treatment of CHD. In this procedure, sections of coronary arteries that have become partly plugged with plaque are bypassed surgically; the aim is to increase the blood supply to the heart muscle. In the United States in 1975, 110,000 bypass surgeries were performed at an average cost of $15,000 to each patient (Kolata, 1981). Considering the risk to the patient (approximately 1% to 4% die from the operation and another 1% suffer neurological impairment), and the great expense of the procedure, the benefits of bypass surgery are surprisingly meager.

Evidence, including a recent substantial randomized trial with extended follow-up (CASS principal investigators and their associates, 1983) fails to establish that the procedure generally offers an extension of life. The most consistent benefit compared to pharmacological treatment is reduction in angina pain (Kolata, 1981).

There is some concern that bypass surgery may be a placebo procedure, as was another heroic, "high-tech" intervention of the 1950s, internal mammary artery ligation (see chapter 4). Ross (1976) reported that bypass surgery relieves pain and improves the quality of life for about 90% of patients, yet the risk of subsequent myocardial infarction is not reduced, nor is life expectancy lengthened as compared to patients who receive no surgery. Furthermore, there is no clear connection between enhancement of cardiac function and decrease in symptoms. If bypass surgery is an elaborate placebo procedure, one would think that there must be a way to secure these limited benefits at less expense and risk to patients.

Dietary Management

The "diet-heart hypothesis" has been a dominant theme behind attempts to control CHD. This idea was popularized by Gofman and his colleagues in 1950 when they reviewed evidence that serum cholesterol and atherosclerosis were associated, and argued that cholesterol levels could be lowered by dietary restrictions (Gofman et al., 1950). Physicians urged heart patients to lower their intake of cholesterol by cutting down on animal fats. Mann (1977) has acidly characterized this as the " . . . lost generation of misguided and fruitless preoccupation with the diet-heart hypothesis" (p. 644). As discussed in chapter 3, it is apparent that serum cholesterol is not closely dependent on dietary cholesterol and so is not very sensitive to dietary manipulations. As Mann (1977) has pointed out, "Subsequent trials have failed to show more than a trivial effect of dietary cholesterolemia, and no one has been able to prove that dietary treatments either prevent or modify the behavior of coronary heart disease" (p. 644).

There have been several large-scale tests of CHD prevention through programs attempting to modify all three of the major risk factors in patients at high risk of CHD. The most extensive effort has been the National Multiple Risk Factor Intervention Trial (Multiple Risk Factor Intervention Trial Research Group, 1982). Over 360,000 men were screened to yield the 12,866 participants, each of whom was in the top 15% in CHD risk as defined by cigarette smoking, blood pressure and serum cholesterol levels, but had no evidence of existing CHD. About half of them were randomly assigned to "usual care" and referred back to personal physicians, accompanied by the risk factor information. The remainder were assigned to "special intervention" in which there were intensive efforts to modify the three risk factors for an average of seven years. Individualized treatment plans were devised by teams composed of behavioral scientists, nutritionists, physicians, nurses, and health counselors. Various behavior modification techniques were used as individually appropriate, and there were frequent meetings. An attempt was made to develop "lifelong shopping, cooking, and eating patterns" in line with dietary goals to reduce cholesterol and sodium intake. Hypertensives were given pharmacological stepped care with mild dietary sodium restriction. Special efforts were made to get smokers to quit; these efforts incorporated group sessions, aversion therapy, and hypnosis. Fewer than 10% of the participants dropped out.

The final results were disappointing. The overall mortality rate was actually a little higher in the special intervention condition, 41.2 per 1,000, as compared to the usual care condition, 40.4 per 1,000. The CHD mortality rates were 17.9 per 1,000 for special intervention as compared to 19.3 for usual care, a difference that is not useful considering the expenditure of effort and money. A curious finding was that the overall mortality in this large sample of men was only about half what had been expected, given the entering risk factor information and earlier epidemiological research, a phenomenon that the researchers were unable to explain. There is concern, based on the National Risk Factor Intervention Trial, and studies with similar results, that large-scale attempts to decrease CHD mortality by attempting to modify the smoking habits and diets of millions of people would represent a misguided investment of limited health resources.

Altering Type A Behavior

It has been estimated, based on the strength of association between type A behavior and CHD, that CHD mortality would be reduced by 31% if type A behavior could be eliminated in high risk groups (Brand, Rosenman, Sholtz, & Friedman, 1976). The possibility of altering type A behavior is certainly important, given the dismal record of existing CHD prevention amd treatment measures.

There have been seven small studies using type A individuals with no evidence of CHD (Suinn, 1982). In each case, the goal was to reduce type A behavior with relatively brief interventions (less than 15 sessions) composed of self-regulation methods or more comprehensive stress management procedures. The general finding was less type A behavior as measured by self-report questionnaires, and, in some cases, as noted by actual behavior in the natural setting. There is no evidence reflecting on the persistence of these changes across time, or their clinical implications for reducing the risk of CHD. Six studies of type A CHD patients have obtained similar results with similar methods, but, in addition, have reported what appear to be clinically useful reductions in blood pressure, serum cholesterol, and triglyceride levels; these trials have not been large enough to obtain meaningful CHD mortality data (Suinn, 1982).

A more extensive evaluation of type A intervention was initiated in 1977 (Friedman et al., 1984). Based on an earlier finding that existing CHD tended to progress in type A CHD patients, but not in type B CHD patients (Krantz, Sanmorco, Selvester, & Matthews, 1979), this study began to follow 1,035 post-myocardial infarction patients across a five-year period. Half of the patients were given standard cardiac care, whereas the others received a special type A intervention including intensive behavioral counseling, progressive relaxation, meditation, role-playing, attitude change techniques, behavior modification procedures, and psychotherapeutic methods intended to substitute affection for hostility. Among the behavioral methods were daily assignments to practice specific non-type A behaviors such as driving below the speed limit, smiling at others, and intentionally losing in competitive games.

After three years of the type A intervention program, the results are encouraging. Type A behavior had decreased for 44% of the special intervention patients, significantly more so than for those receiving standard cardiological counseling. Only about half as many of the intervention patients (7.2%) had recurrent hearts attacks in the follow-up period, as compared to the control patients (13.7%).

8 ANS Disorders: Raynaud's, Migraine, Asthma, and Ulcers

ANS disorders are health problems that involve dysfunctions of organs regulated neurally by the ANS—notably the organs of the cardiovascular, gastrointestinal, and respiratory systems. The previous chapter explored cardiovascular psychophysiology in the context of essential hypertension and coronary heart disease. There are many other disorders involving the ANS; however, this chapter is not an encyclopedic survey of these. Rather, in order to convey the complexity of these health problems and the richness of current psychophysiological thinking, a limited set of conditions is presented in some depth—Raynaud's disease, migraine headache, bronchial asthma, and peptic ulcers.

The psychophysiological approach to the ANS disorders is based on two very general observations: (a) the important role of the ANS-innervated systems in stress and emotions; and (b) the influence of self-regulation procedures on ANS functions, raising the possibility of alternatives and complements to drugs and surgery that are less risky and unpleasant, and, in some cases, more effective.

RAYNAUD'S DISEASE

Incidence and Characteristics

For most persons, it is only a nuisance when their hands become chilled when exposed to a cold environment without adequate protection. However, for a few individuals, cold hands are a serious chronic problem, as was first noted by the physician, Maurice Raynaud, in the early 1860s.

Raynaud described a group of his patients who suffered painful attacks of reduced circulation in their fingers, and, less often, in their toes. A typical attack, or vasospasm, progressed through three stages, each with its characteristic skin coloration: (a) initial whiteness caused by stoppage of circulation and drainage of blood from the affected digits; (b) blueness, as some blood leaked into the area, but was trapped and lost its oxygen; and (c) redness, produced by extreme vasodilation as blood surged back into the region at the end of the attack.

It is customary to distinguish between *Raynaud's phenomenon*, in which the vascular attacks are secondary to an underlying condition such as atherosclerosis, and *Raynaud's disease*, in which the attacks are seen in the absence of any evident underlying physiological problem. The latter is usually regarded as the more benign of the two diagnostic categories. Among the interesting hypotheses that have been advanced to explain Raynaud's disease are that the vasospasms are due to: (a) SNS hyperreactivity (by Raynaud himself), (b) localized dysregulation of circulation, or (c) unusually thick blood that tends to become clogged in the vessels. None of these ideas is comfortably supported by existing evidence. It may be that, like essential hypertension, Raynaud's disease has many contributing factors; perhaps these vary from person to person.

The restricted blood flow of Raynaud's can lead to serious complications including retarded healing of cuts and sores on the digits, and, less commonly, atrophy or "autoamputation" of the ends of the digits, and gangrene. Regardless of complications, one major impact of Raynaud's is that the patient must watch his or her behavior carefully in order to avoid, when possible, situations that predictably elicit attacks.

Physiology and Etiology

The most reliable initiator of a Raynaud's attack is cold. Peripheral vasoconstriction in a cold environment is a normal physiological adjustment, whose adaptive function is to conserve heat. However, for the Raynaud's sufferer, once this normal vascular response has been launched, it tends to develop progressively into a full vasospasm. The eliciting stimulus can be as mild as taking frozen food out of the freezer or holding a cold drink.

Emotional stress can also precipitate an attack. As with cold, stress is a normal cause of peripheral vasoconstriction, mediated primarily by activity in SNS pathways that exercise the major neural control over vasoconstriction/vasodilation. In a classic paper, Mittleman and Wolff (1939) provided an early demonstration of the effects of stress on finger temperature. A sample of adult subjects with chronically cold hands, five of them diagnosed with Raynaud's, discussed their personal problems with a physician, and in some cases were criticized for their performance on some tests; both of these situations were presumably stressful. Abrupt

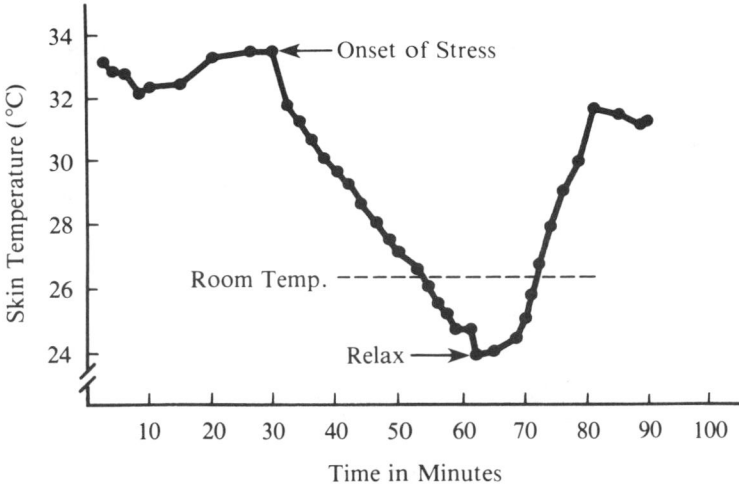

FIG. 8.1   Effects of stress on finger temperature in a patient with Raynaud's. Reprinted by permission of Elsevier Science Publishing Co., Inc. from Affective States and Skin Temperature: Experimental Study of Subjects with "Cold Hands" and Raynaud's Syndrome, by B. Mittelman and H. G. Wolff, *Psychosomatic Medicine, 1,* 274. Copyright 1939 by The American Psychosomatic Society, Inc.

decreases in finger temperature of about 10 degrees C were common. Typical results are shown in Fig. 8.1 for a single participant. At the first arrow the participant began working on a series of cognitive tasks, was "chided for her mistakes," and subjected to several loud noises in the room. Notice that her skin temperature actually dropped below room temperature, which is made possible by evaporative cooling of the skin by sweating. At the second arrow all of the stressors were terminated and she was asked to relax.

A right side *sympathectomy*, in which the SNS pathways to the right hand were surgically disconnected, was performed on one Raynaud's patient shortly after she had been tested and had shown vasospasms and cooling in the right hand in response to the stressors. She was retested after the operation. The results are shown in Fig. 8.2. The sympathectomized right hand now had only a modest vasoconstrictive reponse to stress, in contrast to the left hand where the response continued unabated. As a general observation, the authors note that stress and cold together are much more likely than cold alone to initiate a Raynaud's attack.

Treatment

Treatment of Raynaud's is typically limited to reassuring the patients and offering advice concerning how to behave, given their condition—to refrain from smoking, keep the extremities warm, apply heat during an attack, and perhaps consider moving to a warmer climate.

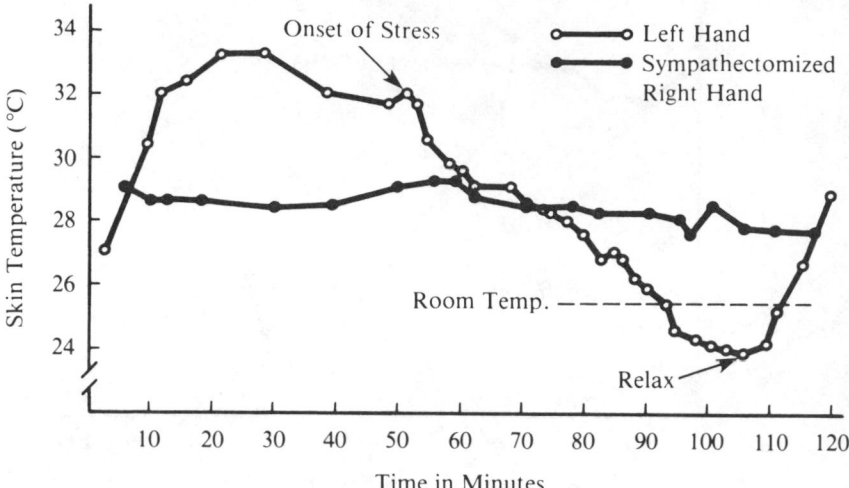

FIG. 8.2 Effects of stress on the finger temperatures of a normal and a sympathectomized hand in a patient having Raynaud's. Reprinted by permission of Elsevier Science Publishing Co., Inc. from Affective States and Skin Temperature: Experimental Study of Subjects with "Cold Hands" and Raynaud's Syndrome, by B. Mittelman and H. G. Wolff, *Psychosomatic Medicine, 1,* 290. Copyright 1939 by The American Psychosomatic Society, Inc.

Pharmacological and Surgical

Vasodilating drugs may be useful for some patients, but usage is restricted by their serious side effects that include tachycardia, nausea, ulcers, and, in the case of reserpine, depression. Somewhat surprisingly, sympathectomy frequently offers only partial and temporary relief from attacks, although the side effects of the surgery are permanent. In general, Raynaud's is not controlled very effectively by the traditional methods of drugs and surgery.

Self-Regulation

Skin temperature biofeedback, often combined with warmth-oriented autogenic phrases, seems to relate clearly and directly to the symptomology of Raynaud's. Because warm hands and vasospasms are physiologically incompatible, voluntarily increasing peripheral blood flow via hand warming should prevent attacks or abort them once the attacks are underway. Results of this approach have generally been quite encouraging (reviewed by Surwit, 1982). Therapeutic effects that equal or exceed the benefits that could be expected from drugs or surgery have been frequently reported. Significantly, the patients tested have been mainly treatment failures from earlier pharmacological therapy.

The promise and problems of self-regulation in Raynaud's disease are illustrated in an investigation by Surwit, Pilon, and Fenton (1978). Thirty adult patients suffering from Raynaud's disease were given a 4-week treatment period during which they attempted to warm their hands using either autogenic training or a combination of autogenic training and skin temperature biofeedback. Regardless of training condition, the treated patients improved in their ability to keep their hands warm in a cold environment, whereas the untreated control subjects actually became worse over the same time period. Regardless of treatment method, there were similar reductions in the frequency and intensity of Raynaud's attacks. A follow-up study reported that the therapeutic gains were sustained over a 1-year period (Keefe, Surwit, & Pilon, 1979). Curiously, although the therapeutic effects were maintained in the follow-up, self-regulation of hand temperature was not. This raises questions about the necessary role of enhanced peripheral blood flow in the treatment effect.

Another investigation has raised additional concerns about the nature of the treatment effect in self-regulation management of Raynaud's. Subjects with Raynaud's either practiced hand-warming biofeedback, EMG relaxation biofeedback, or were assigned to a control condition in which they simply monitored their condition by keeping detailed daily records (Guglielmo, Roberts, & Patterson, 1982). Only patients with no knowledge about clinical applications of biofeedback were included, and an elaborate double-blind design controlled for experimenter/therapist and patient expectations. Under these rigorous conditions, all of the patients reported substantial reductions in their attacks, but patients in the control condition improved as much as the treated patients. The authors conclude from this that physiologically non-specific placebo effects might be widespread in the self-regulation treatment of Raynaud's. This study must be interpreted with some caution for several reasons. As discussed in chapter 5, it may be impossible to adequately deliver biofeedback treatments in a double-blind arrangement. Also, as discussed in chapter 7, patients who simply monitored their blood pressure on a regular basis experienced clinically useful reductions in blood pressure compared to truly untreated controls (Engel, Glascow, & Gaarder, 1983). Therefore, the self-monitoring control condition of the study under discussion might actually have been an active treatment.

Not all of the therapeutic benefits of skin temperature biofeedback on Raynaud's can be explained by placebo. Freedman, Ianni, and Wenig (1983) randomly assigned 32 subjects having Raynaud's disease to experience 10 sessions of either: (a) the usual hand-warming biofeedback, (b) hand-warming biofeedback, but with the last half of training conducted during cold stress, (c) autogenic training ("my hands are warm and heavy"), or (d) EMG biofeedback (reduction of frontalis muscle tension). Half of the subjects in each self-regulation treatment also received stress management practice designed to foster self-control of thoughts associated with stressful experiences that led to attacks. All of the subjects were tested for voluntary hand-warming, including during the application of a cold stimulus, immediately before and after treatment. There was a 1-year follow-up.

The greatest reduction in attack frequency, by 92.5%, occurred after the hand-warming biofeedback during cold stress, followed by the standard hand-warming biofeedback training, which reduced attacks by 66.8%. The other treatments were much less helpful. After training, colder temperatures were needed to induce attacks in the skin temperature biofeedback-trained subjects, compared to the others, and these conditions also, in general, led to better control of hand temperature. While EMG biofeedback and autogenic training did seem to encourage psychophysiological relaxation, they had little effect on peripheral skin temperature (and presumably blood flow). The thrust of results, then, is that patients who were able to increase peripheral blood flow profited most from self-regulation training in Raynaud's.

In summary, while skin temperature biofeedback is a useful alternative to drugs or surgery for some Raynaud's victims, with the therapeutic effects sustained for clinically useful durations, there is some debate over the psychophysiological nature of the treatment effects. It is quite conceivable that the role of peripheral blood flow varies from patient to patient, and with different self-regulation treatment methods.

MIGRAINE HEADACHE

Incidence and Characteristics

Harold Wolff (1948) introduced his classic text on headache with the observation, "Since the human animal prides himself on 'using his head,' it is ironic and perhaps not without meaning that his head should be the source of so much discomfort" (p. ix). Headache is one of humankind's most pervasive health problems, as familiar as the common cold and tooth decay. Yet, the great majority of headache conditions are not linked to any underlying organic disease such as a brain tumor. Rather, as Wolff (1948) put it, a headache is more of a "biological reprimand than a threat" (p. ix). In this sense, headache is a prime example of a psychophysiological disorder.

About 20% of all headaches can be classed as migraine (summarized by Adams, Feuerstein, & Fowler, 1980). The National Migraine Foundation estimates that there are nearly 12 million "migraineurs" in the United States. Migraines most frequently emerge during adolescence, although onset can be later. Migraine is fairly common in children, and has been noted as early as 18 months; the reported prevalence of migraine headaches among 6-year-old school children is 4.5%.

Migraine is typically unilateral in onset but becomes generalized as the headache continues (Dalessio, 1980). At first the pain is pulsing or throbbing, in time with the pulse, but may become constant later in the headache. Usually there are associated gastrointestinal disturbances such as constipation or diarrhea, and especially nausea and vomiting during the actual headache. During an attack the migraineur looks very ill and feels very ill, often moaning or crying, with obviously distended blood vessels on the affected side of the skull; the face is pale and the extremities are cold. Frequently, sounds, and especially light, make the pain worse, so that the person is forced to withdraw from the world and go to bed. The duration of a migraine headache may vary from a few minutes to weeks, but typically ranges from 8 to 24 hours. Intensity may vary from mild attacks that hardly interfere with daily activities to incapacitating headaches that produce near coma.

In about 10% of migraine patients, painless, but distinctive pre-headache experiences anticipate the onset of headache by anywhere from a few minutes to one hour; these patients are said to have classic migraine as opposed to common migraine in which attacks are not heralded by such *prodromal* symptoms. The most familiar prodromal phenomena are visual and include blind spots, flashes, and geometric designs that tend to move around in the visual field contralateral to the side of the impending headache. The left portion of Figure 8.3 illustrates the development of a blind spot, or *scotoma*, during the onset of a migraine attack. Many classic

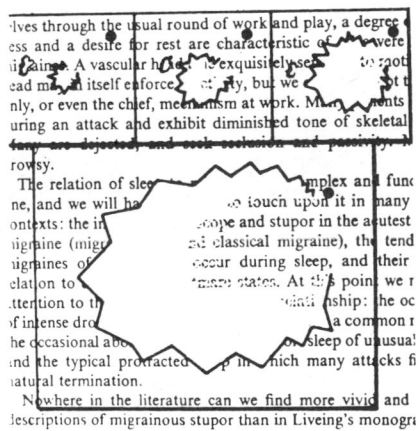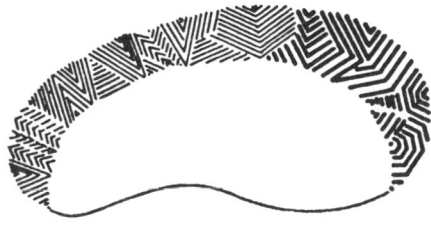

FIG. 8.3 Left: Development of a scotoma during the onset of a migraine attack. Right: The appearance of a fortification illusion at the border of a scotoma. From "The Pathogenesis of a Migraine Attack" by F. C. Rose, 1983, *Trends in Neurosciences, 6,* 248. Copyright 1983 by Elsevier Biomedical Press. Reprinted by permission.

migraine patients report that the scotoma is bordered by a "fortification illusion" as shown in the right portion of Figure 8.3; this particular one was drawn from introspection by the noted neuropsychologist, Karl Lashley (Lashley, 1941). Less often there may be dizziness, aphasia (language dysfunction), or mood alteration, particularly a buoyant feeling of well-being during the prodrome.

Physiology and Etiology

Physiology

A migraine headache attack progresses through two vascular phases. The first phase is vasoconstriction of the intracranial arteries supplying the brain. The nature of the prodromal experiences, if any, that precede a migraine headache depends on the brain areas whose blood supply is altered during vasoconstriction. The initial vasoconstriction threatens the blood supply to the brain, provoking the second vascular phase—a protective, but unfortunately painful, rebound vasodilation in which blood is rushed to the oxygen-starved brain cells. At the same time, the extracranial arteries dilate, creating the headache. The headache is located outside, not inside, the skull.

The common sense notion of why a migraine headache hurts is that it is painful for the arteries participating in the vasodilation to be stretched so excessively. Experiments on heroic volunteers have shown that mechanical distention of arteries from the inside does indeed hurt, and that pulsing pain like that of a migraine headache can be created by alternately stretching arteries and allowing them to passively constrict (Ray & Wolff, 1940). Furthermore, the analgesic effects of vasoconstrictive drugs (Wolff, 1948) and vasomotor biofeedback training (Allen & Mills, 1982) undertaken during migraine attacks, are dependent on the extent to which they diminish the pulse amplitude of the extracranial arteries.

There has been considerable interest in chemical changes that might underly the vascular events and pain of migraine. Many chemical suspects have been identified, but it has proven exceedingly difficult to establish any cause and effect relationships with regard to chemical regulation of migraine attacks. Histamine, neurokinin, and the prostaglandins have been implicated. It is intriguing that these are all vasodilators and stimulate pain receptors, as shown by experiments in which they have been injected under the skin (Guyton, 1982). Because migraine incidence appears to be related to menstruation and use of oral contraceptives, changes in estrogen and progesterone may be involved in some way. The neurotransmitter serotonin is also under suspicion (Sicuteri, Anselmi, & Fanciullacci, 1974) because it inhibits neural activity in certain pain pathways, influences cerebral circulation, changes in concentration during a migraine attack, and anti-serotonin drugs are sometimes useful in preventing migraine attacks.

Psychophysiology

Surveys of migraine patients have shown that most cite stress, worry, or emotional upset as prime precipitating factors in their headaches (e.g., Parnell & Cooperstock, 1979). From the psychophysiological perspective it is essential to work out how this relates to the chemical and vascular changes seen in migraine. One reasonable psychophysiological hypothesis, based on the concept of response specificity (see chapter 3), is that persons prone to migraine make exaggerated vascular responses to stressful stimulation (for some reason). Several experimental studies, in which the vasomotor responding of extracranial arteries during stress has been compared in normals and migraineurs, have supported this idea, but other carefully conducted studies have not (Andrasik, Blanchard, Arena, Saunders, & Baron, 1982; Feuerstein, Bush, & Corbisiero, 1982). A significant problem with this concept is that many migraine sufferers may experience a considerable delay of hours or even days between stress and headache—at least this phenomenon is mentioned frequently in the clinical literature on migraine (e.g., Graham, 1981). If it is true, then the critical psychophysiological process may be *recovery* from stress.

One of the more interesting, but speculative, psychophysiological hypotheses concerning migraine is that the vasoconstriction-vasodilation sequence represents a vascular "fail-safe reaction to 'information overload'" (Crisp, 1981, p. 72). Given that the information processing capacities of the left and right hemispheres are somewhat specialized (see chapter 2), then the side of a unilateral attack should depend on the type of information overload—verbal versus visuospatial—that initiated the attack. Furthermore, the disposition to fall prey to particular types of information overloads would depend on specific cognitive abilities and emotional characteristics of the person. As yet little evidence has been collected that speaks to this hypothesis.

There is an impression of the "typical migraine personality" that can be traced to psychoanalytic theory, bolstered primarily by clinical interviews:

Patients with migraine headaches are anxious, striving, perfectionistic, order-loving, rigid persons who, during periods of threat or conflict, become progressively more tense, resentful and fatigued. The person with migraine often attempts to gain approval by doing more and better than his fellows and to gain security by holding to a stable environment and a given system of excellent performance, even at a high cost of energy. This pattern brings increasing responsibility and admiration, but little love, so that he feels greater and greater resentment at the pace he feels obligated to maintain. Then tension associated with repeated frustration, sustained resentment and anxiety, often followed by fatigue and prostration, become the setting in which the migraine attack occurs. (Plum, 1971, p. 158)

The early clinical research that led to this view has many weaknesses, including vague diagnostic criteria of headache classifications, lack of comparison groups against which to compare the personalities of migraine patients, and impressionistic personality assessment techniques. Also, it seems possible that, because only about 50% of migraine sufferers are thought to seek treatment (Dalessio, 1980), those who do may be strongly achievement-oriented individuals whose incapacitating headaches are interfering with their ambitions. Later research on large samples of migraine patients, using objective personality assessment techniques and carefully selected matched comparison groups of other patients and "normal" controls, have not found migraineurs to be exceptionally perfectionistic and hostile, and especially have not supported the idea that such personality factors in some way cause migraine, rather than the other way around (e.g., Andrasik, Blanchard, Arena, Teders, Teevan, & Rodichok, 1982).

Treatment

Pharmacological

Treatment may be prevention-oriented or address the migraine attacks themselves. In treating migraine attacks, the patient is often advised to rest in a darkened room and apply ice to the area of extracranial vasodilation. Analgesics may also help diminish the pain. The vasoconstrictor, ergotamine tartrate—an adrenergic blocking agent—may be administered to patients who can tolerate this drug without excessive nausea, but drug dependence sometimes develops. Oral administration is useful only in the case of classic migraine, otherwise more rapid routes of administration— inhalation, suppositories, or injection—must be used (Plum, 1982).

Methysergide, an anti-serotonin agent that blocks vasodilation, is often prescribed prophylactically, but has serious side effects including vascular insufficiency and thickening of the heart valves. Maintenance on methysergide requires periodically discontinuing medication every few months in enforced "drug holidays" (Plum, 1982). Propranolol, which blocks beta-adrenergic receptors and, hence, may interfere with the initial vasoconstrictive stage of the constriction-dilation sequence in migraine, is also used for prevention (Posner, 1985); although propranolol has fewer side effects than methysergide, it also appears to be less effective. Such drugs seldom result in complete remission, but appear to reduce the intensity and frequency of migraine attacks in something over one-half of all patients so treated (summarized by Feuerstein & Gainer, 1982).

Self-Regulation

The great majority of migraine patients are initially treated pharmacologically. Therefore, those who eventually explore alternative procedures are individuals whose headaches are resistant to drug treatment. A variety of self-regulation methods and combinations of them, have been used. They appear to be roughly as effective as anti-migraine drugs, and, of course, lack the undesirable and sometimes dangerous side-effects of drugs; however, follow-up data is limited (see Ford, 1982).

Placebo is an important consideration in evaluating treatments of migraine. For example, Kewman and Roberts (1980) have reported clinically useful reductions in frequency and duration of migraine attacks, and self-reports of impairment due to migraine as a function of both hand-warming and hand-cooling biofeedback training. The efficacy of these apparently physiologically "opposite" manipulations would seem to rest, at least in part, in physiologically non-specific placebo effects. Similarly, Cohen, McArthur, and Rickles (1980) assigned migraineurs to 24 sessions of one of four types of biofeedback training: frontalis EMG reduction, EEG alpha increase, hand-warming relative to forehead temperature, and temporal artery vasoconstriction. There was no difference between the groups, each experiencing an approximate 20% reduction in migraine headaches per week. Although it is possible that each of the treatments may have engendered psychophysiological relaxation, physiological changes were small and independent of the therapeutic effects observed. Again, placebo is a likely explanation; the authors speculate about the possible placebo-like benefits of strengthening perceived self-control as a function of successful biofeedback training, regardless of the physiological response involved.

To help put matters in perspective, placebo appears to be just as pervasive in pharmacological treatment of migraine. Lance (1974) found that about 20% to 30% of migraine patients could be treated successfully using only chemically inert tablets, a figure that rose to 60% when relaxation training was added. One early, but extensive, study that included 2,511 migraine patients, found that prophylactic drugs and placebo medications were equally effective, each reducing headache symptoms in about 50% of the patients treated (Friedman & Merritt, 1957).

The treatment of migraine by self-regulation procedures is not totally explained by placebo, and this has certainly not been the rationale behind the self-regulation approaches. Biofeedback treatment of migraine may be traced to a chance observation at the Menninger Foundation Clinic in which an abrupt increase in finger temperature of about 10 degrees F in only two minutes was noted during the spontaneous termination of a migraine headache attack (Sargent, Green, & Walters, 1973). Based on this phenomenon, the Menninger group went on to treat 75 migraineurs using hand-warming skin temperature biofeedback facilitated by the autogenic phrase, "My hands are warm." Approximately 35% of the subjects were reported to be clearly improved (Sargent, Green, & Walters, 1973). Even though this was only a clinical trial with no controls of any sort, and the results were reported rather anecdotally, this research proved to be extremely influential and led to the widespread use of skin temperature biofeedback with migraine headache.

Although it has been supposed that hand-warming might diminish the flow of blood through the extra-cranial arteries by virtue of routing a greater share of the blood supply to the peripheral areas of the body, it has been known since the first Menninger study that this is probably not the case. Fig. 8.4 shows the skin temperature data from one of their initial

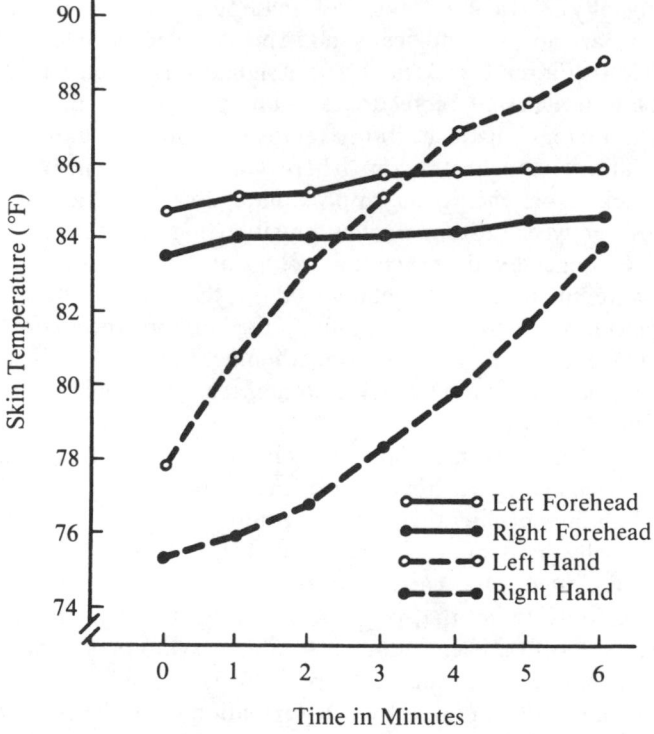

FIG. 8.4   Skin temperature of the forehead and hands during hand-warming biofeedback in a migraine patient. From "Psychosomatic Self-Regulation of Migraine Headache" (p. 65) by J. D. Sargent et al., 1973, in L. Birk (Ed.), *Biofeedback: Behavioral Medicine*, New York: Grune & Stratton. Copyright 1973 by Grune & Stratton. Adapted by permission.

patients during a biofeedback training session in which she happened to experience a migraine headache that was "partially relieved by hand warming" (Sargent, Walters, & Green, 1973). As can be seen, hand warming was not accompanied by forehead cooling as would be expected during a rerouting of blood flow—if anything, the skin temperature of the forehead increased slightly over time. It is more likely that hand warming exerts its therapeutic effect on migraine via reduction in SNS activity. Similarly, the efficacy of self-regulation procedures such as progressive relaxation, that probably have little direct effect on the vascular events implicated in the migraine attack, may be due to reduced SNS activity.

There is also some evidence to support the specific efficacy of techniques that address the vascular changes of migraine more or less directly, by reducing extra-cranial blood flow. For example, Friar and Beatty (1976) trained one group of migraine patients in vasoconstriction of the temporal artery, which was expected to be efficacious, and a second group in finger vasoconstriction, which was predicted not to be useful. The results were as expected.

Some of the strongest evidence in support of the therapeutic benefits of reducing extra-cranial blood flow has been provided by Allen and Mills (1982), who trained eight migraine patients to increase and decrease the pulse amplitude at the superficial temporal artery and at the finger. All of the patients had classic migraine, and were to come in to the lab at the first sign of the prodrome. Thus, these patients could be studied regularly *during* migraine attacks as they engaged in these self-regulation tasks. The subjects were able to learn to alter pulse volume at both locations during migraine attacks. Their head pain was significantly reduced during temporal artery vasoconstriction, but was not influenced by finger vasoconstriction versus vasodilation. For every patient, the greater the vasoconstriction (or the less the vasodilation), the less the pain. Not only does the study provide particularly strong evidence linking the alleviation of migraine to diminution of extra-cranial blood flow, but it is the first systematic examination of the utility of self-regulation procedures during a migraine attack.

The effects of biofeedback on migraine appear to be complex indeed. We have seen evidence implicating placebo, reduction in SNS activity, and specific localized reductions in extra-cranial blood flow. Given this state of affairs, it would seem important to learn to maximize these effects, combine them, and/or learn to route particular patients to particular treatment methods. There are some choices to be made between self-regulation methods. One patient may be especially responsive to placebo, another adept at reducing SNS activity, and still another at self-regulation of extra-cranial blood flow. It is perhaps worth repeating a point made in chapter 5—that several treatments may have roughly the same efficacy when averaged across a large patient population, but may differ in efficacy for an individual patient. If patients and treatments can be paired appropriately, then efficacy, as averaged across the treatments, will be increased.

BRONCHIAL ASTHMA

Incidence and Characteristics

It is estimated that of all persons now living in the United States, approximately 15 million either have had, currently have, or will have asthma (Young, 1980). Most asthmatics are less than 15 years old. Asthma is the leading cause of illness and disability among children ages 2 to 17 years (Daniele, 1985), and accounts for 25% of the days lost from school due to chronic illness. As children grow older, 40% of them show either complete remission or substantial improvement. "Occupational asthma" linked to specific allergens is a significant problem in adults, particularly among occupational groups such as meat wrappers, textile workers, bakers, farmers, and among persons who work in lumber mills, or with detergents or laboratory animals (Frazier, 1980). The direct costs of asthma for physicians' services, hospitalization, nursing home care, and drugs is about $1 billion each year, with about the same amount lost in wages due to absenteeism (Young, 1980).

Asthma is a chronic obstructive lung disease; others include emphysema and chronic bronchitis. It is characterized by intermittent, variable, and reversible obstruction of bronchial airways (Chai, 1975). Asthma is intermittent because the asthmatic suffers episodes or attacks of labored breathing, shortness of breath, coughing, wheezing, and watery eyes; variable in that the attacks can be so mild as to be merely a nuisance or so severe as to be life-threatening, and the intervals between attacks may vary widely; reversible because, unlike a condition such as emphysema, there is no irreversible damage to lung tissue. During an attack there is inadequate air exchange by the lungs, and the individual experiences *dyspnea*, or "air hunger." Oxygen and carbon dioxide levels in blood and tissue are altered during severe attacks.

Physiology and Etiology

Physiology

During an asthma attack there is excessive secretion of thick mucus into the bronchioles, inflammation of the bronchiole walls, and contraction of the smooth muscles in the walls of the bronchioles. The net effect is to narrow the diameter of the bronchiole airways with an increase in airway resistance. During the normal respiration cycle, the diameter of the bronchioles is smallest during expiration. Therefore the asthma patient has particular difficulty in breathing out during an attack.

For some patients, asthma attacks are consistently precipitated by particular allergens such as animal hairs or pollens. The specific immunological mechanism appears to be the presence of large quantities of antibodies, sensitive to particular antigens, causing the release of several chemicals that trigger the bronchial responses described previously (Guyton, 1982). For other patients there is no discernible link to allergens. However, the majority of asthma conditions fall somewhere in between with regard to degree of involvement of allergens. For these patients, some of their asthma attacks seem to be allergen related while others do not. Exercise and respiratory infection, as well as antigen-antibody reactions, are known to contribute to asthma attacks.

Psychophysiology

Stress and Asthma Attacks.   Many asthma patients report that their attacks occur in the presence of stress, anxiety, or other strong emotions, and in some cases indicate that these psychophysiological states precipitate asthma episodes. Nonetheless, attempts to elicit full-blown asthma attacks using experimental stressors in controlled laboratory settings have been generally unsuccessful (Alexander, 1981). Although on occasion there are statistically significant effects on important respiratory measures such as airway resistance, the changes in respiration do not approach an actual asthma attack in severity.

Perhaps emotional responses help intensify or prolong asthma episodes once they are underway. Creer (1979) has discussed a possible "vicious cycle of asthma" where the onset of an attack causes anxiety that exacerbates the major symptom (difficulty in breathing) that leads to greater anxiety, and so on. Because it is indisputable that asthma attacks are often accompanied by anxiety, this phenomenon deserves further study. Another reason for clarifying the role of stress and emotions in the asthma attack is that this forms the basic rationale for using relaxation training in hopes of ameliorating the condition.

Learning and Asthma Attacks.   Nearly 100 years ago MacKenzie (1886) reported an interesting incident with an asthma patient for whom roses were a specific allergen—presentation of an artificial flower, with the suggestion that it was a real rose, was sufficient to initiate an attack. The role of suggestion in asthma episodes has been examined more systematically since that time. One technique has been to administer a neutral gas to asthmatic subjects while leading them to believe that they are inhaling their allergen or some other "bronchospastic" agent. This procedure resulted in significant increases in airway resistance for 19 of 40 patients; of these, 12 responded with full-blown asthma attacks. Their attacks could be reversed by administering a saline placebo (Luparello, Lyons, Bleecker, & McFadden, 1968). A follow-up investigation using the same subjects replicated the findings of the first study in that the reactors continued to respond to suggestion with asthma attacks, while the nonreactors did not (McFadden, Luparello, Lyons, & Bleecker, 1969). Significantly, the response to suggestion was abolished by an injection of atropine, which blocks the activity of the vagus nerve, the parasympathetic pathway to the lungs.

Closely related to, and perhaps underlying, the effects of suggestion, is the possibility that asthmatic responses may be subject to classical conditioning. In *classical conditioning* a neutral stimulus (fire siren) acquires the capacity to elicit a reflex response (asthma attack) through its association in time with an effective eliciting stimulus (pollen). Thus, if a fire siren happened to be wailing in the distance during the onset of a severe pollen-initiated attack, perhaps in the future the sound of a fire siren, or maybe even the sight of a fire truck, would be sufficient to precipitate an attack. Many investigators have suggested that asthma attacks are initiated in the absence of allergens via this mechanism (reviewed by Purcell & Weiss, 1970). Several elaborate and carefully conducted series of studies using large numbers of subjects have obtained essentially negative findings regarding classical conditioning of asthma-like responses. This question should be examined further, given that bronchial dilation/constriction is regulated by the ANS, and ANS responses are eminently conditionable. Furthermore, we would expect asthma-like responses to follow the laws of classical conditioning, from the growing literature on successful classical conditioning of many other components of immunological responding (reviewed by Ader, 1981).

Respiratory disorders, including asthma, could be influenced by instrumental learning. In chapter 3 it was suggested how particular stress-related symptoms could be strengthened by selective rewards. Along the same lines, Creer (1979) has described a case in which the asthma attacks of an 8-year-old boy always occurred about half an hour after his father arrived home from work, no matter what the actual time of day. Careful observations revealed that the father tended not to spend time with his son except when the boy was having difficulty with his asthma, so that the "sole way the son had of receiving his father's attention was by having an asthma attack" (p. 199). As the father began to spend more time with his son when the boy was free from attacks, the number of attacks decreased, while at the same time the father/son relationship developed more appropriately.

Turnbull (1962) has speculated about a somewhat different role of instrumental learning in asthma. Perhaps the asthma attack functions as an avoidance response that serves to get the individual out of unpleasant circumstances and thereby reduce anxiety. Evidence for any role of instrumental learning in asthma is limited to informal observations such as the case report previously mentioned. However, it might be added that a convincing asthma "wheeze" can easily be produced voluntarily by an asthmatic, and research to be presented shortly indicates that changes in airway resistance can be trained using biofeedback procedures.

To summarize, an important role for stress and emotions in the precipitation of asthma attacks is widely assumed, but has not been demonstrated. Psychophysiological influences are seen in: (a) the possible exacerbating role of anxiety elicited by the attack, (b) the apparent involvement of suggestion, perhaps via classical conditioning, in initiating attacks, (c) instrumental learning as a possible mechanism by which asthma symptoms, regardless of origin, might be strengthened and maintained, and (d) "psychomaintenance" of asthma (see below).

Treatment

For most patients asthma treatment is limited to an attempt at identifying any guilty allergens, urging the patient to avoid them, and the use of drug therapy.

Pharmacological

There are several possible approaches using drug treatment, and these may be used in combination. Because SNS activity dilates the bronchioles, sympathomimetics may be administered as bronchodilators during an attack in order to relax the airways. Other drugs are more prevention-oriented and address the immunological aspects of asthma. Among these are agents intended to interfere with the chemical action of mast cells in the early stages of the immune response. In severe cases, corticosteroids may be administered to suppress the immune system, and hence the localized allergic reaction of the lungs. Another avenue is to employ innoculation-type techniques in an attempt to desensitize the individual to troublesome allergens. In general, asthma treatment is among the more successful applications of pharmacological therapy, although the response of individual patients to specific drugs is quite variable and may be erratic within an individual over time. Common side effects include cardiac acceleration, vomiting, and tremor with SNS enhancing agents; cataracts and mood changes are problems with the corticosteroids.

Behavior Therapy

Behavior therapy is used occasionally as an adjunct to drug treatment of asthma, especially in children. Creer (1979) has presented many examples of behavior problems and behavioral approaches to treatment. Common problem behaviors in asthma include failing to take prescribed medication, reacting inappropriately to the early signs of a possible asthma attack, and using the illness as an opportunity to avoid responsibilities. Such behaviors are especially noteworthy in children because they may be carried over into adulthood. If this happens, these behaviors may prove to be more limiting in the long run than the asthma condition itself.

Self-Regulation

Even though a role for stress and emotional responding has not been clearly established for asthma, a variety of psychophysiological relaxation training procedures have been explored, based on the possibility that relaxation may abort a potential asthma attack or at least diminish its severity. A series of studies have examined the use of abbreviated forms of progressive relaxation with asthma in childhood (e.g., Alexander, Gerd, Cropp, & Chai, 1979). These investigations have typically obtained improvement in respiratory measures, and the effects of progressive relaxation have exceeded the effects of just sitting quietly. However, the therapeutic effects have not been great enough for abbreviated progressive relaxation to be a useful alternative to drug therapy.

There is at least one report of impressive results with autogenic training in adult asthmatics (Schaeffer & Freytag-Klinger, 1975). This study was conducted over the summer months, when asthma allergens are especially troublesome. Control subjects experienced the expected seasonal decline in expiratory flow over the period of the study, while the treated patients showed clinically significant improvement in expiratory air flow. Of the 41 persons given autogenic training, 35 had increased expiratory flow equal to or greater than that achieved by administration of novodrine, a bronchodilator. In the one year preceding treatment, the autogenic training patients lost 663 days of work, but in the one year following treatment they only lost 77 days of work.

EMG biofeedback-assisted relaxation training has also been tested (reviewed by Yates, 1980). The results of these studies have been variable, ranging from clinically significant improvement with reduction in medication to no therapeutic effects at all.

The idea that relaxation might help the asthmatic is, in one sense, paradoxical. The bronchial constriction of an attack is, after all, indicative of excessive PNS activity relative to the opposing SNS action—hence the relief provided by sympathomimetic bronchodilators during an attack. Therefore, to the extent that self-regulation training leads to generalized psychophysiological relaxation, the asthmatic may be *actually learning bronchoconstriction*! The danger of this surely varies across individuals and across relaxation training procedures in ways that are presently unpredictable. Also, recall that the hypothesized initiating role of stress and emotions has been elusive in the lab, yet there are many individual anecdotal reports. Perhaps this is because the stress-related factors are important in only a subset of asthmatic patients. Putting all of these speculations together, it becomes more understandable as to how the effects of relaxation training on asthma can be so variable. Persons with stress-related attacks who are able to learn to relax without, at the same time experiencing bronchial constriction, would obtain impressive benefits; others might not be helped, or could even be made worse. Should this speculation prove to be accurate, then it would become important to learn to pair up the right patients with the right treatments.

Harding and Maher (1982) reasoned that heart rate acceleration training might counter the excessive PNS relative to SNS action on the lungs during an asthma attack, and help asthma patients. The results of an initial study were promising. Potential subjects who responded substantially to a placebo inhalant were excluded. Experimental subjects were successful in learning to speed their heart rate, showed some increased post-session expiratory flow and significantly reduced their number of attacks and medication usage. The control subjects, who practiced keeping their heart rate steady, did not enhance expiratory flow and had no improvement on the therapeutic indices.

The most direct self-regulation strategy at present is to monitor and feed back a respiratory response that actually participates in the asthma attack. An investigation using four severely asthmatic children ages 10 to 16, and a non-asthmatic volunteer, illustrates this approach (Feldman, 1976). During a series of brief 5- to 10-minute sessions, the subjects breathed into a device that continuously measured respiratory resistance. The biofeedback was a tone whose pitch was proportional to respiratory resistance. The results are shown for a representative participant in Fig. 8.5. Each of the asthmatic children was able to reduce respiratory resistance during biofeedback. The magnitude of this self-regulation was roughly comparable to the respiratory effect of an inhalation treatment with the bronchodilator, isoproterinol. The single non-asthmatic subject was unsuccessful in controlling respiratory resistance, however, this is probably not an important finding because non-asthmatics have been able to control similar respiratory responses with the aid of biofeedback in other studies (e.g., Steptoe, Phillips, & Harling, 1981). The latter study is noteworthy because of large differences in the ability of different subjects

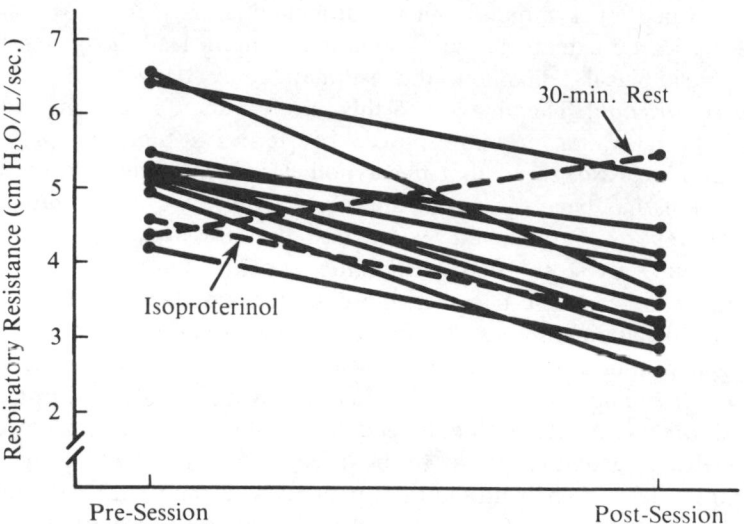

FIG. 8.5 Effects on airway resistance of respiratory biofeedback, a chemical bronchodilator (isoproterinol), and resting quietly for a single asthmatic child. Reprinted by permission of Elsevier Science Publishing Co., Inc. from The Effect of Biofeedback Training on Respiratory Resistance of Asthmatic Children, by G. M. Feldman, *Psychosomatic Medicine, 38,* 31. Copyright 1976 by The American Psychosomatic Society, Inc.

to achieve self-regulation of respiratory responses. As the authors suggest, this argues for careful patient selection for respiratory biofeedback treatment of asthma.

Psychomaintenance of Asthma

Psychological factors are important in the long-term maintenance of asthma. *Psychomaintenance* has been defined as the "perpetuation of physical illness or the defeat of medical treatment because of psychologic, as opposed to strictly physical reasons" (Dirks, Robinson, & Dirks, 1981, p. 64). An important recent innovation in asthma research has been the development of a practical procedure for predicting the odds of rehospitalization for asthma (Dirks, Robinson, & Moore, 1981). This instrument, the Battery of Asthma Illness Behavior (BAIB) screens for three psychological dimensions of asthma: (a) attitudes toward the illness and treatment of it, (b) several personality variables, and (c) subjective sensations of the patient during asthma attacks. Scores on the BAIB are not related to the objective severity of physical symptoms, such as airway resistance, but are related to certain features of recovery such as compliance/noncompliance with treatment, the amount of medication prescribed, the patient's report of asthma interference with normal life, and the physician's judgment of illness severity. Of the highest risk group, as identified by the BAIB during an initial hospitalization, 77.4% were rehospitalized for treatment of asthma, compared to less than 30% of the asthmatic patients with lower risk BAIB profiles. It may soon be possible to intervene, once high risk patients have been identified, to alter the factors contributing to psychomaintenance in order to reduce the need for further medical services.

PEPTIC ULCER

Incidence and Characteristics

An ulcer victim typically suffers from chronic peptic ulcer, "a sharply circumscribed loss of the tissue lining those parts of the digestive tract exposed to gastric juice containing acid and pepsin" (Grossman, 1982, p. 635). Simply, the person has digested a section of his or her gastrointestinal lining. The hallmark symptom is localized abdominal pain that flares up over a period of days or weeks, with pain free intervals in between (Walsh, 1982). The pain is usually absent first thing in the morning, when the digestive processes are relatively quiet, and immediately after meals, when the gastrointestinal lining is protected by food. Although the actual ulcer is sometimes located in the stomach (gastric ulcer), it is usually found in the upper few centimeters of the intestines (duodenal ulcer), and, less often, in the very bottom of the esophagus where it is exposed to digestive juices sloshing up from the stomach. There is usually only a single ulcer.

Peptic ulcer was a rare disorder prior to 1900, but increased sharply in the first part of this century. About 1955, hospitalizations and mortality due to peptic ulcer began to decline. As with the similar historical changes in coronary heart disease, the reasons are obscure. It is commonly estimated that 5% to 10% of all persons now living in the United States can expect to have an ulcer sometime during their lifetime. This may be a low estimate because many ulcers never cause enough discomfort or complications to lead to a diagnosis. A study of autopsies in England found ulcers in 27% of males and 15% of females between the ages of 45 and 65 (Grossman, 1982). In 1977 the cost of peptic ulcers in the United States was on the order of $1 to 2.5 billion (Kurata, Honda, & Frankl, 1982).

Although peptic ulcer is usually thought of as merely unpleasant and inconvenient, there were over 6,000 deaths associated with the condition in the United States in 1983 (National Center for Health Statistics, 1984). These deaths were due to complications, as when a major artery fails and there is considerable loss of blood, or when a hole is eaten all the way through the gastrointestinal wall.

Physiology and Etiology

Physiology

The immediate cause of a peptic ulcer is a disruption in the delicate balance between the level of acid-pepsin secretion, and the resistance of the gastrointestinal lining (the mucosa) to injury from the chemical action of these substances. Hydrochloric acid and the enzyme, pepsin, are secreted into the stomach for purposes of digestion. The acid breaks foods down into small particles after which the pepsin is able to digest the proteins found in meat and vegetables. Acid-pepsin secretion is stimulated by histamine, the hormone gastrin, and by neural impulses from the parasympathetic vagus nerve, which also increases blood flow in the mucosa and facilitates motility of the gastrointestinal smooth muscles in order to move food along. Activity in the sympathetic nerves has roughly the opposite effect of vagal action, inhibiting all these digestive activities. Highly alkaline substances are secreted at appropriate times and in sufficient quantities to neutralize excess digestive acids and thereby protect the mucosa. This process is aided by several reflexes that are supposed to inhibit acid-pepsin release and increase alkaline production between digestive periods. The mucus emitted by the mucosa, as well as lubricating the gastrointestinal passage, affords some protection against acid-pepsin injury. As a final protective measure, the surface cells of the mucosa are actually replaced every four to six days in the normal human (Grossman, 1982).

From the above, it can be seen that there are several ways in which the acid-pepsin/resistance balance could become disturbed, resulting in an ulcer. The gastric ulcer patient often has normal acid-pepsin secretion levels, indicating that the problem must be lowered mucosal resistance. In contrast, the duodenal ulcer patient may secrete 15 times the normal amount of hydrochloric acid overnight, when the digestive processes should be at rest (Guyton, 1982), which implicates hypersecretion of acid-pepsin in duodenal ulcers. This could be due to excessive vagal stimulation.

It is reasonable to suppose that the substances we introduce into the stomach might play some role in the development of ulcers. Surprisingly, there is no direct evidence that the types of food we eat contribute in any way to peptic ulcer, and this includes hot, spicy foods (Grossman, 1982). Of all the substances that regularly find their way into the human stomach, it is ironic that a pharmacological agent—aspirin—has been most definitely identified as a cause of peptic ulcers. Approximately 30% of all patients taking aspirin regularly for arthritis pain develop gastric ulcers (Grossman, 1982).

Psychophysiology

Although peptic ulcer is frequently offered as a prototypical example of a psychosomatic disorder, some of the more popular beliefs concerning the mind and the stomach appear to be medical folklore. One belief is the common image of the ulcer victim as a harried young business executive, saddled with great responsibilities. However, ulcers, as is the case with practically every health problem, are more prevalent among low status blue-collar workers than among executives and professionals (e.g., French, 1963; Smith, Colligan, & Hurrell, 1980).

Attempts to identify a hypothetical ulcer-prone personality have not been very successful. Alexander's (1950) psychoanalytic view of the ulcer patient was summarized in chapter 3. Others have maintained that ulcers are precipitated by chronic anxiety, but that the psychodynamic origin of the anxiety is unimportant in understanding ulcer development (e.g., Mahl, 1950). Alternatively, according to Graham's (1972) specific attitude hypothesis (chapter 3), the ulcer patient is a person who "felt deprived of what was due him and wanted to get even" (p. 857). None of the personality characteristics just reviewed seem to be associated with ulcers in any unique way (reviewed by Weiner, 1977). There are just too many ulcer patients whose personalities do not resemble the proposed configurations, as well as many ulcer-free individuals who do show the supposed ulcer-prone personality signs.

Despite the rather negative psychophysiological considerations introduced thus far, it is indisputable that stress and emotions contribute in some way to the development of ulcers. Unfortunately, the psychophysiological study of the stomach is made difficult by its location and the fact that, unlike the heart, it does not do anything that can be readily detected from the outside. Until very recently, firsthand knowledge of the behavior of the stomach during stress and emotions depended on the study of individuals with a gastric fistula. A *fistula* is an opening into the stomach through the abdomen, usually due to a puncture wound, or as a result of a surgical procedure carried out to provide a way to get food into the stomach when the esophagus is damaged. The first observed links between stomach events and emotions can be found in Beaumont's classic 1833 monograph describing what he saw through the fistula of his patient, Alexis St. Martin, who had suffered a gunshot wound to the stomach (Wolf, 1981). Beaumont was able to detect changes in the color and in the apparent secretions of the mucosa which were correlated with emotional activity in his cantankerous subject.

Subsequent experiments with animals have shown that a variety of experimental stressors can lead to peptic ulcers (Ader, 1971). Stomach ulcers were among the signs of the general adaptation syndrome noted by Selye (chapter 3). The stressors capable of inducing ulcers in animals include such psychological stressors as conflict resulting from competing, incompatible response tendencies, and the inability to control or predict aversive events (e.g., Weiss, 1972). These stressors are representative of the troublesome circumstances encountered by humans to varying degrees in their daily activities. Although ulcers cannot be produced intentionally in humans for ethical reasons, it has been shown that, for both animals and humans, the same types of stressful events that produce ulcers in animals result in heightened acid-pepsin secretion in humans (e.g., Mittelman & Wolff, 1942).

There are some important and interesting psychophysiological problems awaiting resolution. These include: (a) Determining the role of the vagus nerve in stress-related ulcers. Vagal neural activity stimulates acid-pepsin secretion, and conversely, vagotomy (see following) is helpful in some ulcer cases. Yet, the vagus nerve is part of the parasympathetic nervous system, whose action we associate, not with stress, but with psychophysiological relaxation. (b) Possibly related to the first problem—understanding the role of time factors in stress-related ulcers. Digestive processes are cyclic over time—bouts of intense activity alternate with periods of relative quiescence. In experiments with lower animals, the duration and scheduling of stress and rest have been critical variables in producing ulcers (e.g., Rice, 1963). It may be that in humans, the timing of stress, perhaps in relation to eating, and the psychophysiological state of the organism between digestive periods, will prove to be important factors in untangling the etiology of peptic ulcers. (c) Determining whether gastrointestinal behavior varies with different emotions. There is limited evidence that gastrointestinal activity, including acid secretion, intensifies during anger and fear, but may diminish during depression and related states characterized by withdrawal or turning inward from the environment (Gundry, Donaldson, Pinderhughes, & Barrabee, 1967). Should this emotional specificity be confirmed, then the risk of peptic ulcer might be partly determined by the individual's typical way of responding emotionally in stressful situations. (d) The ongoing controversy about the proper classification of peptic ulcer conditions (Weiner, 1977). Perhaps a number of clinically distinct entities having different etiology but with a final common path are being grouped together as "peptic ulcer." Some researchers make such a distinction between gastric and duodenal ulcers. Emotional factors may be more important in duodenal than in gastric ulcer (Yager & Weiner, 1971). Differentiation among ulcer conditions may be facilitated by the discovery of two types of pepsin, whose levels appear to be regulated independently and that seem to be related to the incidence of duodenal ulcers in different ways (Weiner, 1982).

Treatment

Pharmacological

Because peptic ulcers are sometimes accompanied by excessive acid secretion, antacids may be administered in an attempt to neutralize the suspected extra acid. The few adequate double-blind trials of antacids suggest that they accomplish more actual healing of ulcers than placebo, however, that they do not differ from placebo in their relief of pain (Isenberg, 1982). The popular over-the-counter antacids would have to be taken in enormous quantities—30 to 70 tablets at a time—to yield useful acid neutralization (Drake & Hollander, 1981).

Another pharmacological approach is to attempt to block the actual secretion of acid and pepsin. Anticholinergic agents are sometimes used to block vagal stimulation, but these have severe side effects and are currently not used widely. Histamine blocking agents, primarily cimetidine, are typically viewed as the treatment of choice, and, in the short run, heal ulcers in 80% to 90% of patients; unfortunately the relapse rate is estimated at 80%, once drug therapy is discontinued (Check, 1982). Possible side-effects include mental confusion, depression, immune failure, sexual dysfunction in males, as well as breast changes linked to suppression of androgen production in males (Altman, 1981).

Surgical

Surgery is performed in approximately 20% of the diagnosed cases of peptic ulcer (Walker & Sandman, 1981). In a *vagotomy*, the vagus nerve is surgically disconnected from the gastrointestinal tract which reduces acid-pepsin secretion, but also diminishes gastric motility, making it necessary to surgically enlarge the stomach exitway so that food may progress along the gastrointestinal passage. The therapeutic effects of vagotomy are sometimes temporary. Another procedure is to remove most of the stomach. This can be counted on to limit the reoccurence of gastric ulcers, but is not without its digestive complications.

Dietary

Ulcer patients are routinely urged to keep substances out of their gastrointestinal tracts that are thought to contribute to ulcers. Bland diets heavy on milk and cottage cheese are widely employed. Many studies have shown bland diets to be useless (Welsh, 1977). Milk, in fact, stimulates gastric acid secretion (Peterson, 1985), and the enormous quantities of animal fats in the form of dairy products consumed by some ulcer patients may contribute to heart disease (Altman, 1981). There is no specific diet that is of proven benefit for ulcer victims (Peterson, 1985).

Self-Regulation

Direct biofeedback training to address the gastrointestinal events that underlie peptic ulcers requires a practical method of continuous measurement of the responses in question. This presents some problems, and for this reason, there have been only a few biofeedback studies in this area. Several studies (Welgan, 1981) have been based on a method in which stomach juices are aspirated via a stomach tube that has been swallowed, enabling a feedback signal reflecting the volume or acidity of the gastric secretions. Both normals and ulcer patients are able to control acid secretion volume with this biofeedback arrangement, but therapeutic effects have not been demonstrated. Another approach involves measuring the electrogastrogram via electrodes installed on the skin of the the abdomen (see chapter 2), and providing feedback to the subject in the form of a meter reading. Healthy subjects have been able to control their gastrointestinal behavior with this setup, but again, it is not known whether such training might prove beneficial to ulcer patients (Walker & Sandman, 1981).

Psychotherapy

Psychotherapy may be a useful treatment approach to peptic ulcer, which is not surprising given the apparent involvement of stress and emotions in ulcer etiology. Perhaps the most promising of the psychological procedures is one combining assertiveness training and anxiety management (Brooks & Richardson, 1980). The anxiety management component is based on the possibility that ulcer victims may have difficulty in dealing with their anxieties, and involves therapist-directed exploration of cognitive sources of anxiety and introduction of methods of altering these cognitions. Assertiveness training is used to help the patients to better express and behave according to their feelings—skills in which ulcer patients may be deficient.

Brooks and Richardson (1980) administered the treatment just outlined to one group of ulcer patients over a 2-week period. A control group met with therapists but was not given the supposed active ingredients of the treatment. The treated patients improved more than the control patients on most of the indices used to assess treatment efficacy over the 60 days immediately following treatment. Specifically, they reported fewer ulcers symptoms, including pain, and consumed less antacids, an average of 63.2 ounces, compared to the control patients, who averaged 195.7 ounces. In a follow-up after 42 months, there was significantly less ulcer reoccurrence in the treated patients as compared to controls.

9 Brain Disorders: Epilepsy, Hyperactivity, and Alzheimer's Disease

In this chapter we consider disorders that affect the organ of thought and consciousness—the brain. These disorders are not responsible for as many deaths as the cardiovascular conditions reviewed in chapter 7, but they are, in some ways, more ominous and dreaded. With brain disorders, we face the possibility of changes in our *selves*, or in someone we love. Alzheimer's disease, for example, has been called "the disease that robs the mind of the victim and breaks the heart of the family" (Goldsmith, 1984, p. 1805).

As in the chapters on ANS disorders, only a subset of the health problems of the CNS will be introduced in order to consider these in appropriate depth. Most prominent among the topics not considered are the conditions that have traditionally been grouped under the heading of "mental illness." The psychophysiology of mental illness is an important topic, with many recent developments, especially in the neurochemical aspects of psychosis. However, this material is available in clinical psychology textbooks, and so will not be covered here. This chapter considers three very different CNS disorders—epilepsy, hyperactivity, and Alzheimer's disease.

EPILEPSY

Incidence and Characteristics

Epilepsy brings to mind a generalized convulsive attack. We envision an episode that begins with a peculiar outcry, and loss of consciousness. The entire body becomes rigid for up to a minute, followed by convulsive twitching and jerking of the extremities. During this phase the person may emit foamy saliva, lose bladder and bowel control, and bite his or her tongue severely. After a few minutes the seizure subsides, and consciousness returns, generally with an initial period of confusion. There is permanent amnesia for the time period surrounding the attack.

The attack just described is a *grand mal* or *tonic-clonic* epileptic seizure. This condition is dramatic and conspicuous, but it is seen in fewer than 20% of adult epileptics (Delgado-Escueta, 1985). The term *epilepsy* is broader and refers to "the many types of recurrent seizures produced by paroxysmal excessive neuronal discharges in different parts of the brain that can be due to a variety of cerebral and general bodily disorders" (Glaser, 1982, p. 2114). Not all epileptic seizures entail loss of consciousness, nor do they involve spasmodic movements of the skeletal muscles. In this chapter the common practice of writing "epilepsy" (singular) is followed; however, because the term refers to a broad and complex family of seizure conditions, it is best to think "the epilepsies" (plural).

It is estimated that 2% of the United States population has had more than one seizure, and hence would be considered epileptic (Epilepsy Foundation of America, 1975). The incidence among children may be higher. Children commonly outgrow their epilepsy before reaching adulthood, although certain seizure conditions grow worse with age. The frequency and severity of seizures varies greatly. There may be years between attacks or there may be hundreds of attacks in a single day; they may be barely noticeable or so debilitating as to require hospitalization. *Status epilepticus* refers to continuous seizures during which the patient remains unconscious, and is a medical emergency because of the high risk of brain damage and possible heart and kidney failure.

Physiology and Etiology

Physiology

In neural terms, an epileptic seizure is the repetitive synchronized or paroxysmal discharge of many neurons in the brain. The summated firing of these cells produces exaggerated "spikes" and slow wave activity in the EEG during a seizure, as shown in Fig. 9.1. It can be seen that in this particular attack the abnormal discharge was distributed throughout the cerebral cortex. This type of attack is considered a *generalized seizure*; the grand mal or tonic-clonic seizure, already described, is one example. A second generalized seizure type is the *petit mal* or *absence attack*. In such an attack the person stares blankly for a matter of seconds during which there is no awareness of the surroundings. The EEG record in Fig. 9.1 was taken during an absence attack. For children who have absence

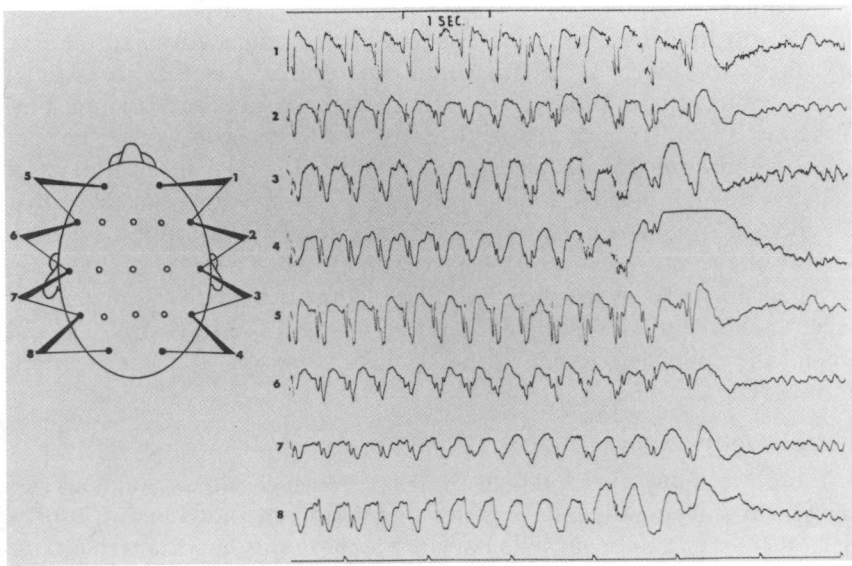

FIG. 9.1   EEG records from eight brain areas during a generalized seizure (petit mal) in a 10-year-old child, reverting to normal EEG on the right as the seizure ends. From *The Epilepsies: Modern Diagnosis and Treatment* (p. 63) by J. M. Sutherland et al., 1974, Edinburgh: Churchill Livingstone. Copyright 1974 by Churchill Livingstone Limited. Reprinted by permission.

attacks, the presenting problem may be difficulty in school with a complaint from the teacher that the child frequently "spaces out" in the classroom.

In about 67% of adults and 40% of children with seizures, the attacks are confined to a localized area of the brain, and are known as *partial* or *focal seizures* (Delgado-Escueta, 1985). Sometimes the seizure starts at a limited *epileptic focus* and then spreads rapidly to other brain areas, sometimes developing into a generalized seizure. The *Jacksonian seizure* is characterized by initial twitching at the end of an extremity which then "marches" up the limb to encompass the muscles of the entire limb. Another partial epilepsy is the *sensory seizure*, which, as the name suggests, occurs in the sensory areas of the cortex—depending on the location, there may be anything from itching to foul odors to visual hallucinations. There are many other types of epileptic seizures. The general rule is that the behavioral and experimental manifestations are determined by the location of the abnormal neural discharge. There will be convulsive movements of the skeletal muscles only if neurons in the motor cortex participate in the attack.

A variety of brain abnormalities predispose toward seizures. They include: (a) hereditary brain defects, (b) birth trauma, (c) head injuries, (d) allergic reactions, as to bee stings, (e) cerebral vascular disease, (f) brain tumors, (g) infections, (h) neural degenerative diseases, such as Alzheimer's, and (i) metabolic and toxic imbalances such as lead poisoning or withdrawal from alcohol (Engel, 1985). However, in most cases of epilepsy, it is not possible to implicate any of the previous causes, so that the etiology is unknown. Any given seizure probably has multiple causes. Several of the previous factors may combine, along with a precipitating event, such as a stress situation, flickering lights, or repetitive sounds. It is widely believed that there are chemical metabolic disturbances in and around the epileptic neurons in the brain of a person who has recurrent seizures (Glaser, 1982).

Psychophysiology

There are many anecdotal case reports in which stress situations are thought to somehow initiate seizures in prediposed individuals. Surprisingly, there seems to be no systematic research on this important question.

Attempts to specify a general epileptic personality type have yielded descriptions that are no more illuminating than global characterizations of Californians. This approach has been largely replaced by efforts to correlate particular psychophysiological qualities of the individual with specific seizure locations, based on the known specializations of function in various brain areas. Perhaps the most intensive research effort along these lines has been prompted by the hypothesis that schizophrenia is associated with left temporal lobe seizures, and manic-depressive psychosis with right temporal lobe seizures (Flor-Henry, 1974). In one study, 82 of 100 cases were classified correctly as right or left hemisphere focus by neuropsychological tests (Flor-Henry, 1976). However, the bulk of evidence by other researchers has not supported this theory (e.g., Rodin, Katz, & Lennox, 1976).

One important psychophysiological consideration is that the epileptic individual may have to contend with health problems beyond the seizures themselves. Not only is the condition itself highly stressful, but there is a continuing centuries-old social stigma attached to epilepsy—perhaps because during a seizure the person exhibits such a threatening loss of control over his or her actions. Thus, the patient may suffer anxiety, depression, or shame about the condition. Epilepsy has a relatively early onset—77% of persons who will have recurrent seizures in their lifetime have begun to do so by the end of adolescence (Epilepsy Society of America, 1975)—and with long duration. Any disorder with these characteristics can potentially have marked impact on the development of the person. For example, a child who has seizures may develop limiting dependencies created by well-meaning but overly-protective parents. Adequate treatment of epilepsy must take into account possible adjustment problems.

Treatment

Pharmacological

Epilepsy is almost always initially treated using anticonvulsant or antiepileptic drugs. Effects of drug treatment are difficult to predict (Glaser, 1982), and there is no single drug of choice. Thus, drug treatment involves experimentation—introducing the first choice drug and gradually building up dosages, then trying another anticonvulsant if necessary, and so on, perhaps exploring drug combinations if needed. Throughout, the goal must be a balance between seizure reduction and toxic side effects which must be monitored closely (Delgado-Escueta, 1985). Among the most common of these side effects are sedation and drowsiness, nausea, loss of appetite, rashes, and hyperactivity in children; the most drastic side effect is fatal liver failure. Antiepileptic drugs in common use include valproic acid (Depakene), carbamazepine (Tegretol), phenytoin (Dilantin), primidone (Mysoline), and phenobarbital (Luminal).

The prognosis, given antiepileptic drug treatment, varies somewhat with seizure types. It appears that most cases of epilepsy can be controlled reasonably well with a carefully planned and closely monitored drug program. The seizures are greatly reduced or totally eliminated, and the side effects of the medication are not debilitating. Unfortunately, a sizable minority of patients do not respond well to drug treatment. For example, it has been reported that 25% of epileptic children are not helped by antiepileptic drugs and another 25% continue to have some seizures despite drug maintenance (Carter & Gold, 1968). Also, the ultimate goal of withdrawing the antiepileptic drugs usually cannot be achieved without the return of seizures, even after the individual has been seizure-free with antiepileptic drugs for years (Glaser, 1982).

Surgical

Surgery is seldom a useful option; seizures often persist after removal of damaged brain tissue. The "split brain" operation to prevent spread of seizures between the left and right hemispheres in cases of intractible epilepsy, is well known, because of the splitting of consciousness that ensues. However, the original procedure—complete corpus callosum section—was performed on fewer than 100 patients before it was abandoned, partly because of the remarkable psychophysiological phenomena that had made it so fascinating to psychologists, philosophers, and neuroscientists. Partial corpus callosum section is still performed.

For the reasons just outlined, treatment alternatives to antiepileptic drugs and surgery have been developed. Although none of these alternatives have been universally beneficial, all have been useful with some patients. The major alternatives to the traditional medical treatments are: (a) behavior therapy procedures based on classical and operant learning principles, and (b) EEG biofeedback. Relaxation training and stress management techniques are sometimes used in instances where the onset of seizures is thought to be stress-related (reviewed by Mostofsky & Balaschak, 1976).

Behavior Therapy

A variety of methods based on classical conditioning have been used to prevent seizures. Efron (1957) discussed a professional singer whose seizures were consistently preceded by a complex anticipatory aura. Immediately before a seizure, she felt as if she were going to smell something, and experienced a voice in her right ear imploring her to look in that direction; if she complied, the seizure followed. Although she dreaded her attacks, she was unable to resist this action—so much so that at home she adopted the strategy of moving aside the furniture, lying down on the floor, and then looking over her shoulder to go into the inevitable seizure. After much experimentation, it was discovered that the smell of jasmine, if presented when she anticipated an odor, was able to prevent the seizure. Efron then systematically paired the sight of a bracelet with the smell of jasmine. The patient was able to abort her attacks by looking at her bracelet at the strategic moment. Eventually, she could control her seizures just by imagining the bracelet.

Forster (1977) has introduced an arsenal of classical conditioning-based techniques for controlling *reflex epilepsy*, in which attacks are consistently elicited by a specific simple stimulus like a flashing light, or a particular movement, or by more complex situations, such as reading, or even hearing a certain musical instrument or a particular melody. Among the successful procedures are: (a) counterconditioning techniques along the lines of the case study just mentioned; (b) presenting seizure-eliciting stimuli at gradually increasing, but subseizure threshold intensities; and (c) conditioning procedures introduced to help the patient detect the early signals of an impending seizure.

Operant interventions are based on the idea that seizure initiation is strengthened or weakened depending on the consequences of the seizure. This suggests that seizures, like pain behaviors (see chapter 4), might be maintained by their consequences, and that is indeed the case. This may be as obvious as a mentally retarded child who flashes his fingers back and forth across his eyes to produce a self-initiated seizure, or as subtle as the parental attention that can help sustain seizures. Both punishment and positive contingencies have been used successfully (reviewed by Pinkerton, Hughes, & Weinrich, 1982) with children and adults who are of normal intelligence or mentally retarded, and in settings including the home, the school, or an institution. The methods have been used successfully by professional behavior therapists and by parents and teachers who have been trained to use operant methods in the home or school.

Rewards or positive reinforcement have been used to reduce the incidence of seizures when they are made contingent on a minimum period of seizure-free time (e.g., Balaschak, 1976). Reward paradigms have also been used profitably in a more behavior-specific way to interrupt chains of behaviors that lead up to a seizure. A good example is a 17-year-old mentally retarded girl who had a lifelong history of seizures (Zlutnick, Mayville, & Moffat, 1975). At the onset of the research, she had multiple generalized motor seizures daily, despite large doses of dilantin and phenobarbital. A uniform behavioral sequence was observed for every seizure episode: (a) her body became rigid, (b) her arms were raised, fists clenched, directly out to her side, (c) her head snapped back, and (d) the seizure invariably followed.

Whenever the patient raised her arms, they were immediately placed back at her side or in her lap, and, following a delay of five seconds (to decrease the likelihood of her learning to raise her arms to initiate a reward sequence), she was praised effusively for having her arms down and given an M & M candy. The reward scheme was implemented by one of the authors, but it was gradually transferred to student peers of the patient at the training center for retarded adolescents, where the study was conducted. The results are shown in Fig. 9.2.

After 16 seizures per day in the pretreatment baseline, the rate fell to zero during the first treatment period. When the treatment contingency was temporarily withdrawn, seizures increased immediately to about six per day, then decreased to zero when the treatment was reinstated. Over a nine-month follow-up period, she was virtually seizure-free without treatment.

EEG Biofeedback

The idea that epileptic seizures could be suppressed using biofeedback methods originated unexpectedly during basic electrophysiological research with cats conducted by M. Barry Sterman and his colleagues (Sterman, 1973). These studies involved an EEG pattern of 12 to 15 Hz localized over the central sulcus dividing the motor and somatosensory areas of the cerebral cortex. This *sensorimotor rhythm* (SMR) was especially evident when the cats assumed a quiet, motionless posture, and could be enhanced through operant procedures in which the cats were rewarded with a drink of milk for producing the SMR. Some of the

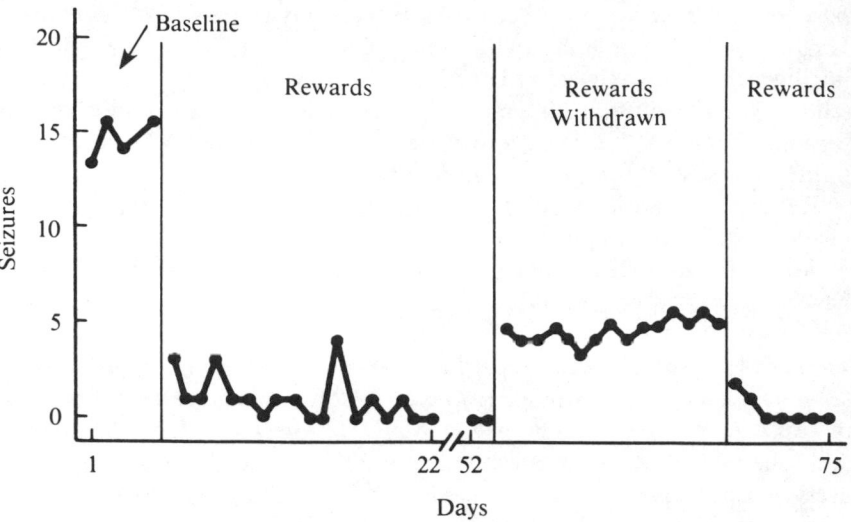

FIG. 9.2   The use of positive reinforcement to reduce the incidence of seizures in a 17-year-old mentally retarded girl. From "Modification of Seizure Disorders: The Interruption of Behavioral Chains" by S. Zlutnick et al., 1975, *Journal of Applied Behavior Analysis, 8,* 10. Copyright 1975 by the Society for the Experimental Analysis of Behavior. Adapted by permission.

SMR-trained cats were used in another experiment that required injection of a seizure-inducing drug. The SMR-trained cats did not have seizures at dosage levels that led to seizures in the other cats. Sterman hypothesized that their earlier SMR training had made these cats resistant to seizures; if so, SMR biofeedback might be a useful treatment for epilepsy in humans.

In an exploratory case study, Sterman and Friar (1972) worked with an adult female who had a seven-year history of generalized motor seizures. Her seizure frequency was about two per month in the year preceding treatment and she was taking two anti-convulsant drugs daily, which were continued during SMR training. There were about three 30-minute SMR biofeedback sessions per week in which she was to produce the SMR, assisted by light and tone feedback. Seizures decreased abruptly early in training and remained low over a five-year follow-up period. Later work from this and other labs (Finley, Smith, & Etherton, 1975; Lubar & Bahler, 1976) using SMR biofeedback with epilepsy has also been encouraging (Sterman & Shouse, 1980).

The most consistent effect of SMR training on the EEG is suppression of low frequency, high amplitude epileptiform activity. This is illustrated in the EEG data from a 6-year-old trainee shown in Fig. 9.3. Successively later stages of training are shown from top to bottom. Each panel displays

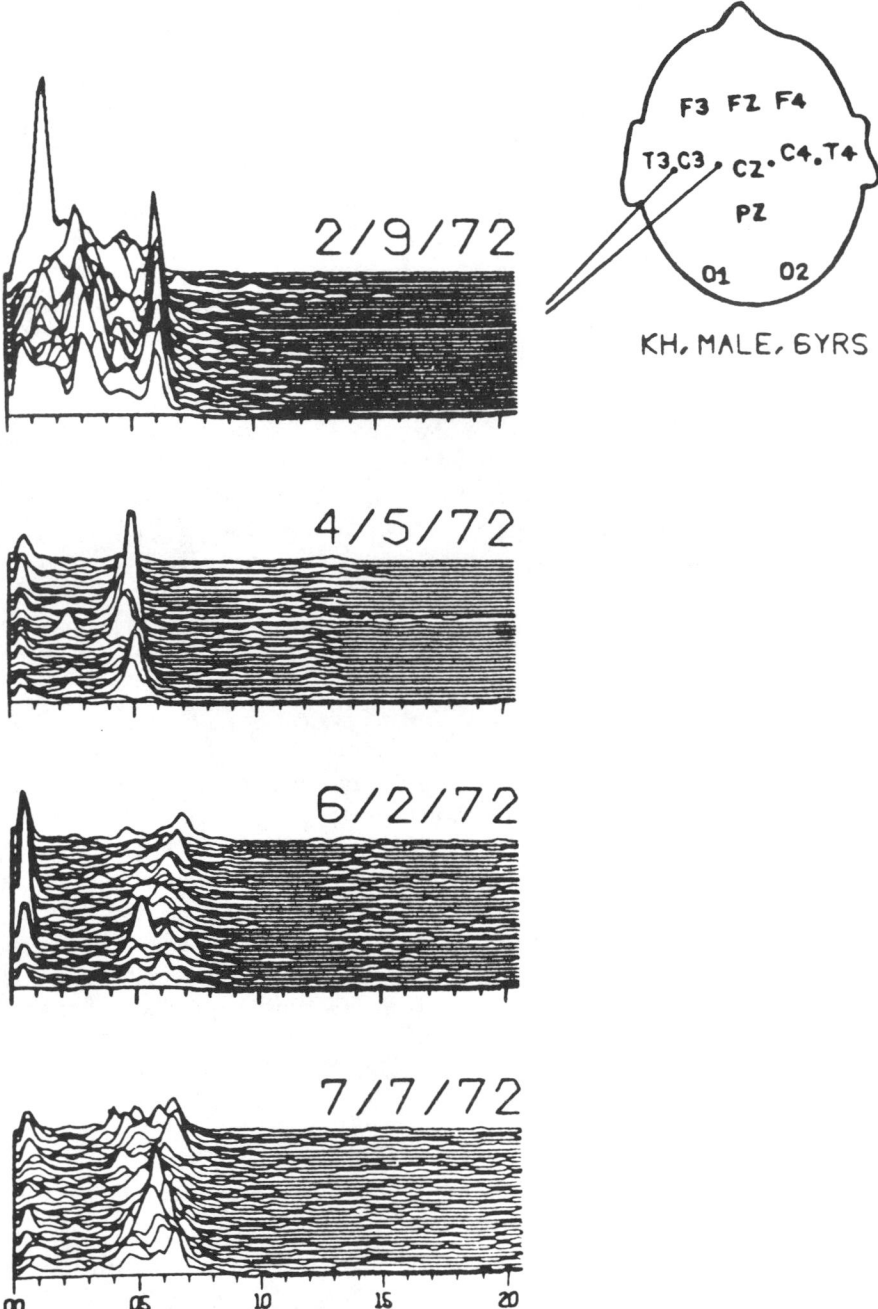

FIG. 9.3 Suppression of low frequency epileptiform EEG activity in a 6-year-old epileptic child by SMR biofeedback training. From "Biofeedback Training of the Sensorimotor Electroencephalogram Rhythm in Man: Effects of Epilepsy" by M. B. Sterman et al., 1974, *Epilepsia, 15*, 408. Copyright 1974 by Raven Press. Reprinted by permission.

the amount of EEG across frequency as the horizontal axis. Successive 17-second time periods are portrayed so that the third dimension, appearing to go into the page, is time. Notice the predominant slow wave activity at the beginning of training which disappeared as SMR biofeedback training progressed. The normalizing effect on the EEG is even seen during the sleep of SMR-trained patients (Sterman, 1977).

If SMR training is withdrawn, then seizures return, only to diminish if training is reinstated. Finley (1976), as an effective control for placebo, introduced false feedback for a seven-week period following SMR biofeedback training, and found that seizures increased significantly, but were then suppressed once again when SMR training was reintroduced.

The sum of available evidence indicates that some persons who have seizures that are poorly controlled by medication are able to learn *something* from EEG biofeedback training that enables them to suppress their seizures. It is suspected that SMR enhancement is not a necessary element of the treatment (Kuhlman & Kaplan, 1979). Seizure reductions have been reported many times following EEG biofeedback training of frequencies outside the SMR range (e.g., Kuhlman, 1978). Also, it may be significant that most EEG biofeedback methods for epilepsy—including the SMR work—have incorporated a "time out" contingency in which no feedback is available when low frequency epileptic-like patterns are detected electronically in the EEG. Maybe the trainees are sensitive to this contingency, and are learning to directly inhibit their epileptiform EEG. Consistent with this, seizure reductions have been obtained using this time out contingency alone (Cott, Pavloski, & Black, 1979). Perhaps any EEG biofeedback method that requires, for success, production of something other than epileptiform EEG activity, will be therapeutic. Because the EEG biofeedback methods offer hope for some patients whose prospects are bleak with pharmacological treatment, further research is badly needed to clarify the active ingredients in this procedure so as to maximize its benefits.

HYPERACTIVITY

Incidence and Characteristics

Jason is a restless 10-year-old. When he watches television, he squirms on the floor and absently kicks the furniture again and again; he aimlessly climbs up on things and slides off of them. Although he is of normal intelligence he is failing in school. He does not finish much of his work; the few assignments he does complete, he rushes through, making a great many careless errors—his teacher is convinced that he does not care about his work. The other children make fun of him because he is usually the first to blurt out an answer, but his answer is almost always incorrect. Jason jabs, pulls at, nudges and otherwise constantly annoys his classmates. He is easily frustrated when things do not go his way, which is often, and is prone to explosive temper tantrums. In sports and games his age-mates call him a quitter, a crybaby, and a poor sport. He cries easily and often. For obvious reasons, he is unpopular among his peers. Jason is in trouble at home, at school—wherever he goes. He sees himself as a failure, and his parents and his teacher are at their wits end. If Jason were a real child, he would be diagnosed as *hyperactive*, and prescribed daily doses of a CNS stimulant, probably methylphenidate hydrochloride (Ritalin).

Estimates of the prevalence of hyperactivity vary. Commonly cited figures range from 4% to 10% of United States elementary school-age children (Paternite & Loney, 1980). In contrast, a careful survey of the San Francisco Bay region produced an estimate of only 1% (Sandoval, Lambert, & Sassone, 1980). Boys are six to eight times as likely as girls to be diagnosed as hyperactive (Sandoval et al., 1980).

Hyperactive children are at increased risk of a number of difficulties in childhood: (a) *Academic deficiencies*. One study found that 50% of hyperactive children had failed two grades in school by adolescence (Huessy & Cohen, 1976). (b) *Poor social relationships*. Hyperactive children do not get along well with parents or teachers, partly because of disregarding commands, nor with their peers—they are more likely than other children to be disliked by their classmates (King & Young, 1982). (c) *Aggression and hostility*. Hyperactive children show more physical and verbal aggression in the classroom than do normal children (Abikoff, Gittelman-Klein, & Klein, 1977). (d) *Low self-esteem*. Hyperactive children tend to see themselves as failures rather than as competent, successful individuals (e.g., Weiss, Minde, Werry, Douglas, & Nemeth, 1971).

It was once supposed that hyperactive children outgrow their condition, to emerge none the worse for wear. But, as Ross and Pelham (1981) have observed, "Given the stormy, conflict-laden childhood and academic difficulties that are often associated with hyperactivity, it would be surprising if these youngsters' behavior were to be entirely unremarkable once they reached their adolescent and adult years" (p. 249). Hyperactive children experience special difficulties with their personal well-being and social lives as they develop into late adolescence and early adulthood (Hechtman & Weiss, 1983). For example, in a five-year follow-up study of hyperactive children, 25% showed significant antisocial behavior as teenagers (Weiss, Minde, Werry, Douglas, & Nemeth, 1971). Although some hyperactive children do not have special difficulties later on, from the perspective of 30 accumulated studies, the outlook is not good

(Amado & Lustman, 1982). Whereas the excessive movement diminishes across adolescent development, hyperactive children who showed conduct disturbances and poor peer relationships are at risk of carrying these problems into adulthood (Thorley, 1984). Hyperactive children, as adults, may show up with unusual frequency in other psychiatric classifications.

The Concept of the Hyperactive Child

No health concept has aroused more controversy and emotional debate than hyperactivity. The most vocal critics (e.g., Schrag & Divoky, 1975) charge that it has caused hundreds of thousands of children to become drug-dependent zombies at the hands of a coalition of incompetent teachers, psychologists and physicians, frustrated and ignorant parents, and greedy drug companies— all because they happen to display some of the more annoying traits of childhood. Proponents of stimulant treatment, who are often physicians, maintain that hyperactive children have a disease, and that this disease ought to be treated medically.

The concept of the hyperactive child was introduced by Laufer and Denhoff (1957), when they proposed a syndrome consisting of shortened attention span, distractability, and excessive purposeless physical activity. When this collection of symptoms was seen in the absence of severe mental retardation or evident brain damage, the child was said to be afflicted with the hyperkinetic impulse disorder.

The current formal designation of the condition by the American Psychiatric Association (1980) is *"attention deficit disorder with hyperactivity"* (ADDH). Diagnosis of ADDH requires the presence of each of the central symptoms shown in Table 9.1. Inattention and impulsivity, in the absence of actual behavioral hyperactivity, constitutes *"attention deficit disorder without hyperactivity"* (ADDNH). Thus, the official position of the American Psychiatric Association is that there is an attention syndrome that, in specific cases, may or may not be accompanied by excessive movement. In these pages, a hyperactive child is simply one who has been diagnosed as such and given the label. It is recognized that these children are a somewhat heterogeneous group, and that generalizations are risky.

Physiology and Etiology

Physiology

Hyperactivity is usually viewed by physicians as a disease syndrome—a set of associated symptoms presumed to have a common cause, so that it makes sense to think of an entity and give that entity a name.

TABLE 9.1
Diagnostic Criteria for Attention Deficit Disorder
with Hyperactivity (ADDH)

The child displays, for his or her mental and chronological age, signs of developmentally inappropriate inattention, impulsivity, and hyperactivity. The signs must be reported by adults in the child's environment, such as parents and teachers. Because the symptoms are typically variable, they may not be observed directly by the clinician. When the reports of teachers and parents conflict, primary consideration should be given to the teacher reports because of greater familiarity with age-appropriate norms. Symptoms typically worsen in situations that require self-application, as in the classroom. Signs of the disorder may be absent when the child is in a new or a one-to-one situation.

The number of symptoms specified is for children between the ages of eight and ten, the peak age range for referral. In younger children, more severe forms of the symptoms and a greater number of symptoms are usually present. The opposite is true of older children.

A. Inattention. At least three of the following:

(1) Often fails to finish things he or she starts
(2) Often doesn't seem to listen
(3) Easily distracted
(4) Has difficulty concentrating on schoolwork or other tasks requiring sustained attention
(5) Has difficulty sticking to a play activity

B. Impulsivity. At least three of the following:

(1) Often acts before thinking
(2) Shifts excessively from one activity to another
(3) Has difficulty organizing work (this not being due to cognitive impairment)
(4) Needs a lot of supervision
(5) Frequently calls out in class
(6) Has difficulty awaiting turn in games or group situations

C. Hyperactivity. At least two of the following:

(1) Runs about or climbs on things excessively
(2) Has difficulty sitting still or fidgets excessively
(3) Has difficulty staying seated
(4) Moves about excessively during sleep
(5) Is always "on the go" or acts as if "driven by a motor"

D. Onset before the age of seven.

E. Duration of at least six months.

F. Not due to Schizophrenia, Affective Disorder, or Severe or Profound Mental Retardation.

Note. From *Diagnostic and Statistical Manual of Mental Disorders* (3rd ed., pp. 43-44), 1980, Washington, DC: American Psychiatric Association. Copyright 1980 by the American Psychiatric Association. Reprinted by permission.

From this disease perspective, hyperactivity is considered to reflect an organic problem—a brain defect linked to hereditary factors, or possibly to events during pregnancy and birth. The term minimum brain damage has been associated with hyperactivity and other "learning disabilities" for years, and is commonly attached to individual children in sentences such as, "Jason is a minimum brain-damaged child." More recently, minimum brain dysfunction has gained ascendency. The message conveyed by these terms is that hyperactivity is caused by physical damage to the brain, or a disruption in the way it works, that cannot be seen in the usual clinical signs of brain damage, hence the "minimum." There is evidence that "subclinical" brain damage is not rare. But rather extensive subclinical damage is required for there to be recognizable cognitive or psychological effects, and these effects do not cluster together to form a distinct syndrome (Rutter, 1982). It is easy to overlook that the use of these terms explains nothing—they do not further our understanding of hyperactivity, or in any way suggest what to do about it—they are merely labels. They have been criticized for providing a means of *assuming* organic etiology when it cannot be proven, and for creating a false sense of understanding and order (Gallagher, 1966).

The response of hyperactive children to stimulants has been used to support the hypothesis of organic etiology. It was originally thought that the behaviorally calming and attention stabilizing effects of amphetamines on hyperactive children was paradoxical and distinguished them from normal children (Bradley, 1937). For this reason the response to stimulants was, and still is, sometimes used as an informal diagnostic criterion. If the child reponds well to amphetamines then he or she must be hyperactive; since 1978, evidence has been accumulating that this is a myth (Rapoport, Buchsbaum, Zahn, Weingartner, Ludlow, & Mikkelsen, 1978). Amphetamines reduce restlessness and help sustain attention in both normal and hyperactive children. The behavioral calming may well be secondary to the attention sustaining effect of the drugs, especially in the classroom setting. Amphetamines do not seem to consistently reduce motor activity outside of the classroom, and there are reports of increased activity with amphetamine use (reviewed by Solanto, 1984). A beneficial drug effect in no way verifies organic etiology. Unfortunately, many children continue to be maintained on amphetamines under the mistaken idea that the calming effect of the drug demonstrates that their brains must be abnormal.

Despite the widespread opinion that hyperactivity is a unitary syndrome, there are few studies to support this belief. This may seem remarkable, however, the existence of many thousands of real children who resemble our mythical Jason does not prove that the core symptoms are statistically associated. For example, Ullman, Barkley, and Brown

(1978) assessed the attentional processes and motor behaviors of a number of hyperactive children. They found that children with attentional problems were no more likely than any collection of children to be overly active; and the excessively active children were not unusually likely to have attention deficits.

The available evidence does not support a unitary hyperactivity syndrome, a common cause, or even a consistently impaired mediating process or processes. Children who are diagnosed as hyperactive are a heterogeneous group.

There have been attempts to map out subgroups of hyperactivity to lessen the confusion resulting from differing symptoms patterns, prognoses, etiology, mediating processes, and, perhaps, treatments of choice. The current American Psychiatric Association (1980) classification of hyperactivity into the ADDH and ADDNH types is a step toward subdividing the condition. In addition, evidence is emerging that hyperactivity may exist with and without associated conduct disturbances (Trites & Laprade, 1983). That is, some hyperactive children do not have antisocial behaviors, excessive aggression, and poor social relationships with peers and parents. Interestingly, August and Stewart (1983) studied the families of hyperactive children and found that hyperactive children with conduct disorders tended to have at least one parent with an antisocial diagnosis (antisocial behavior, drug or alcohol abuse, or hysteria). Conduct disorders were not present in hyperactive children whose parents themselves did not have such problems. Perhaps the hyperactive child is predisposed to conduct disorders, but whether these actually emerge is determined by social-environmental influences, especially parental behavior.

Etiology

There may be genetic involvement in hyperactivity. In one retrospective study, 16% of the fathers of hyperactive boys were found to have been hyperactive themselves as children, compared to 0% of the fathers of a control sample of boys (Cantwell, 1972). One could argue that, rather than supporting hereditary influence, this merely suggests that hyperactive boys grow up to be poor fathers. However, corresponding psychophysiological problems are more likely to show up in the biological parents of hyperactive children than in adoptive parents (Morrison & Stewart, 1973); siblings of hyperactive children are more likely to be hyperactive themselves than are more distant relatives (Safer, 1973). Information about the incidence of hyperactivity in twins reared together as compared to apart would help tease apart possible hereditary and environmental influences.

Certain events during pregnancy and birth cause subtle brain abnormalities. In particular, restriction of the oxygen supply during fetal development or birth results in brain lesions that can be detected using sophisticated neurological techniques (Towbin, 1970). Although it is often suggested that such perinatal factors underlie hyperactivity, several extensive studies (e.g., Rubin & Balow, 1977) have failed to detect any strong connections between pregnancy and birth complications and hyperactivity. On at least one occasion, a greater incidence of hyperactivity among the children of mothers who smoked during their pregnancy has been reported (Nichols & Chen, 1981). The present evidence indicates that perinatal events are, at most, weak predisposing factors for hyperactivity.

Others have emphasized the importance of social-environmental factors in hyperactivity (e.g., Thomas & Chess, 1977). According to this view, children who are constitutionally predisposed, react with hyperactivity when they must grow up in an environment whose demands exceed their capabilitites. Childrearing practices are thought to be especially important. Appropriate parenting may calm and nurture a difficult infant who would otherwise become hyperactive. But, it is more often the case that parents respond with frustration and resentment to a troublesome infant. This initiates an increasingly unhappy and stormy child-parent relationship, with each person reacting negatively against the demands of the other.

Many correlational studies have supported the social-environmental view in obtaining moderate statistical associations between hyperactivity and various parental behaviors and attitudes. For example, Paternite and Loney (1980) found that hyperactivity was associated with disharmony and hostility in child-parent relationships. Laboratory observations of interactions between hyperactive children and their parents are also consistent with the hypothesized importance of childrearing practices. During play and structured tasks, mothers of hyperactive children were more negative and directive toward the child, yet less responsive when the child initiated contact, as compared to the mothers of control children (Mash & Johnston, 1982). The difference was especially pronounced for younger (ages 2-6) as compared to older (ages 7-9) children. It is important to discover to what extent hyperactive children may be shaping parental behavior, rather than the other way around.

There are practical parenting "re-training" programs for the mothers and fathers of hyperactive children. One behaviorally- and cognitively-oriented program resulted in clinically useful gains for the children of the parents who were trained, which persisted over a 9-month follow-up period (Dubey, O'Leary, & Kaufman, 1983). It would be extremely helpful to develop predictive models that would identify children who are at increased risk of hyperactivity so that preventive environment-cushioning steps could be undertaken.

The ceaseless activity and erratic attention of the hyperactive child suggests an organism that is running too fast physiologically. Indeed, it was originally speculated that hyperactive children may suffer from too much autonomic arousal and activation of the cerebral cortex (Laufer & Denhoff, 1957). However, most studies have found no difference in autonomic and EEG activity between hyperactive and other children in the resting state. Interestingly, during various cognitive tasks, hyperactive children tend to be, if anything, *underaroused*, that is, indices such as heart rate and electrodermal activity are depressed and there is more EEG slow wave activity as compared to normal children (reviewed by Hastings & Barkley, 1978).

The possibility that hyperactive children are chronically underaroused has been the springboard for several psychophysiological theories of hyperactivity. Zentall and Zentall (1983) have elaborated on earlier theories to offer a model that cleverly integrates several diverse aspects of hyperactivity. According to their *optimal stimulation* analysis, when normal children are subjected to an environment with insufficient complex stimulation, they begin to behave as hyperactive children do in a normal environment. Anyone who has ridden 300 miles in a car containing an active 10-year old will immediately grasp the idea. The longer normal children are supposed to sit quietly with nothing of interest to do, the more restless they become. In the classroom setting, their behaviors would gradually earn descriptions such as "out of seat," "off task," and "disruptive"—the terms attached to the everyday actions of hyperactive children. According to the optimal stimulation model, such behaviors only *seem* purposeless. In fact, they represent attempts to increase the level of sensory stimulation to an optimal level. It is normal to engage in stimulus seeking behaviors when there is insufficient sensory stimulation. For most of us this happens only during infrequent periods of sensory deprivation; for the hyperactive child, stimulus seeking is a daily quest—a way of life. If stimulus seeking behaviors are unsuccessful and insufficient levels of stimulation continue, cognitive performance deteriorates—attention wanders, and so forth—another characteristic of the hyperactive child.

The optimal stimulation model suggests that CNS stimulants are behaviorally calming because, by increasing arousal level, they enable the child to make better use of existing stimulation, thereby requiring less "off-task" stimulus seeking. According to the model, hyperactive children would have the most difficulty in stimulus-poor environments, and there is evidence to this effect, even though for years it has been standard educational practice to place hyperactive children in extra quiet settings to minimize distractions. Zentall and Zentall (1983) suggest the opposite—that hyperactive children would benefit from a stimulus-rich environment;

although sensory enrichment is not seen as a cure for hyperactivity (no more so than is stimulant treatment), it might diminish self-created problems due to inappropriate (for the setting) stimulus-seeking behaviors. This possibility has not been adequately tested.

A final major theory of hyperactivity can be traced to Bradley's (1937) initial observation of the seemingly paradoxical calming effect of amphetamine on the behavior of children who would have been diagnosed as hyperactive today. Because amphetamine produces its effects by facilitating neural transmission at catecholamine synapses, it was hypothesized that hyperactive children have a disturbance in catecholamine metabolism that is specifically corrected by amphetamine. However, as indicated earlier, hyperactive children do not differ from other children in their behavioral response to amphetamine. Biochemical assay studies also fail to support the catecholamine-deficit view of hyperactivity (Solanto, 1984). Solanto (1984) suggests that amphetamines may lead to behavioral calming by narrowing the focus of attention.

Treatment

CNS Stimulants

There appears to be a consensus among practicing physicians that stimulant treatment of hyperactivity is desirable, efficacious in the short run, and free from serious side effects. A survey in Grand Rapids, Michigan found that over 85% of the hyperactive children in the sample had had CNS stimulants prescribed at one time or another (Bosco & Robin, 1980). About 75% of the children were taking, or had taken Ritalin and 8% Dexadrine (dextroamphetamine). On the order of 60% to 90% of hyperactive children who are treated with CNS stimulants are considered, by global judgments, to benefit (e.g., Whalen & Henker, 1980), but only 10% of the treated children fall within the normal range on social, behavioral, and cognitive variables (Sleator & von Neumann, 1974).

The technique of meta-analysis (which enables quantitative conclusions to be drawn from many studies that are not necessarily identical) was applied to 61 studies involving 1,972 hyperactive children treated mostly with Ritalin (Ottenbacher & Cooper, 1983). The treated children showed less excessive motor activity than 88.5% of the untreated control children. Overall, the most beneficial drug effects were for behavioral and social ratings, the least for academic achievement and tests of cognitive performance. It was estimated that about 30% of the positive changes were due to placebo rather than specific effects of the drugs.

Barkley and Cunningham (1978) have summarized the results of 17 studies of 2-6 week short-term experimental interventions with stimulants on varied samples of mainly hyperactive children. There were 52 different measures of academic achievement used altogether, with no improvement for 82.6% of these during the drug regimens. There was no discernible pattern or consistency among the achievement measures that showed improvement, which compounds reservations about the actual efficacy of the drug treatment.

Other reviews of research in this area lead to similar conclusions (e.g., Gadow, 1983). Improvement on reading, writing, spelling, and arithmetic is inconsistent. Gains on standard academic achievement tests are measurable, but not impressive. The academic and cognitive effects of stimulants are unpredictable across children and across time within a given child. As Whalen and Henker (1980) have concluded, "There is no conclusive evidence of improvement on standardized tests of achievement and considerable reason to doubt that such improvements occur with any consistency or durability" (p. 5).

Much less is known about the effects of stimulant treatment on the social behavior of hyperactive children. However, it appears that the drug effects in this domain are about as variable and uncertain as they are for academic performance (Pelham, 1982). Medicated hyperactive children do not consistently get along better with others as compared to hyperactive children without medication—they are not necessarily more compliant with teacher or parental requests, viewed more favorably by their peers, nor are their interactions more positive. Parental, peer, and teacher expectations and perceptions of the child when they are aware whether the child is medicated or not may be important in the natural setting, but are typically controlled in assessments of stimulant effects. Therefore, there may be social effects in the natural setting that are not linked to the drugs per se, but to the attitudes of others around the child.

Many studies have shown that extended stimulant regimens do not provide long-term academic or social gains (e.g., Weiss, Kruger, Danielson, & Elman, 1975). It is recognized, even among prescribing physicians, that stimulants are in no sense a cure for hyperactivity.

There are many known possible adverse side effects of stimulant treatment. One of the more common is suppression of growth. The growth of 86 previously untreated hyperactive children was traced for up to four years following the beginning of drug treatment, which averaged 40 mg per day of Ritalin (Mattes & Gittelman, 1983). Over successive years, their reduction in growth, expressed in percentile terms relative to age norms for height was: -1.4%, -8.1%, -13.4%, and -18.1%. It is not known whether hyperactive children may catch up with their lost growth if drug treatment is terminated while they are still in their growth years, nor whether their retarded growth is due to the known appetite suppressing effects of CNS stimulants. Before they were prohibited, amphetamines were widely used in weight loss formulas for adults.

A small percentage, estimated at 1.3% (Denckla, Bemporad, & MacKay, 1976), of children who take Ritalin develop *tics*—"a sudden rapid series of involuntary movements that are usually complex and coordinated" (Fahn, 1982, p. 2033). These tics usually disappear if medication is discontinued. However, if stimulant treatment is continued, the motor tics of some children gradually develop into the bizarre Gilles de la *Tourette's syndrome* (Lowe, Cohen, Detlor, Kremenitzen, & Shaywitz, 1982). In Tourette's there are *vocal tics*—involuntary and compulsive sounds such as barking, snorting, yelping, or words. For some reason the words are often obscene and may be accompanied by obscene gestures. Some of these symptoms could be confused with those of hyperactivity and could go ignored. Tourette's does not appear to subside when stimulants are withdrawn, and must be treated with antipsychotic drugs that have their own adverse side effects such as personality changes and tardive dyskinesia. Because there is a known hereditary factor in Tourette's, any tics or signs of the condition in relatives of the child are warning signals against stimulant treatment, as, of course, are the first hints of motor tics in the child under treatment.

There may be negative psychological side effects of being maintained on a drug. There has been concern that extended drug regimens may make children feel helpless and powerless, and that this may become integrated into their developing personalities (Whalen & Henker, 1976). Unfortunately, there has been very little systematic research, especially extended follow-up studies, to help us evaluate these concerns. One study found that hyperactive children felt less in control of their behavior— greater external locus of control—as compared to a normal sample of children, but not all of the hyperactive children were taking drugs (Linn & Hodge, 1982).

It is unlikely that there will be a moratorium on stimulant treatment of hyperactive children until the long-term psychological effects can be established. Given the continued extensive prescribing of stimulants to children, one constructive idea is to routinely employ a two-stage therapeutic strategy (Whalen & Henker, 1980). Before any drugs are introduced there should be an initial period of cognitive therapy aimed at reinforcing the child's self-control skills and strengthening his or her perception of personal causation. When the drug is introduced, it should be done in a way that casts the child, not the drug, as the origin of the therapeutic change: "Now remember, Chris, the medicine is like using a crutch when you have a bad ankle. It can help you, but it can't do the walking for you. You're the one that has to do the work" (Whalen & Henker, 1980, p. 26).

The Feingold Diet

In 1973, an allergist, Benjamin Feingold (1973) proposed that hyperactivity is the result of hypersensitivity to certain food additives and substances found naturally in foods. Specific preservatives and all food colorings, especially Red Dye #3, were singled out. Salicylates—chemicals found in aspirin and occurring naturally in foods such as tomatoes, apples, and almonds—were also proscribed against. When all of these substances were completely eliminated from the diet of hyperactive children, 30% to 50% were said to improve. The *Feingold diet* was introduced to the general public in a popular book, "Why Your Child is Hyperactive" (Feingold, 1975).

That something as prevalent, serious, and difficult to manage as hyperactivity could represent an allergic reaction was, and is, an intriguing idea. Feingold was saying that hyperactivity is a consequence of modern technology—that our diet, increasingly laden with highly processed unnatural foods, has led to an epidemic of hyperactivity. Local support organizations were formed. In 1982 the president of the Feingold Association of the United States reported 20,000 member families, and that 200,000 children were on the Feingold diet (Kolata, 1982).

The earliest forms of evidence reflecting on the Feingold hypothesis were anecdotal case reports, surveys, and dramatic testimonials from enthusiastic parents. For example, one mother described the consequences of the slightest deviation of her son from the diet like this: "A part of a slice of box cake produced a 72-hour marathon, with David sleeping only in snatches for the whole time. A spoonful of Jell-O at a relative's house had him up all night again and rambunctious during the day" (Kolata, 1982, p. 958).

The results of controlled experimental tests of the Feingold diet have not been nearly so supportive. A meta-analysis of 23 studies assessing the efficacy of the Feingold diet showed that hyperactive children on the diet were "better off" than only 55% of comparison hyperactive children who were not on the diet (Kavale & Forness, 1983).

It will be helpful to review one of the more elaborate investigations of the diet in detail to see how health care consumers and scientists could have reached such different conclusions about the Feingold diet. The diets of 36 hyperactive boys and their families were rigorously controlled over 6 to 8 week experimental periods (Harley, Ray, Tomasi, Eichman, Matthews, Chun, Cleeland, & Traisman, 1978). At the outset, all food supplies were removed from the home; thereafter, the researchers provided all food in weekly deliveries. To facilitate compliance, everyone in the family had the same diet. The substances proscribed by Feingold were present and absent from the diet in successive 3 to 4 week periods. These substances included: all foods with artificial flavor or color, all foods with salicylates, bologna, ham, frozen fish, all soft drinks except 7-Up, aspirin, cough drops, and toothpaste. Approved foods were supplied for special occasions such as a graduation dinner, as were the treats for the whole class whenever there was a birthday party at school. To disguise the dietary manipulations, many irrelevent items such as sweet potatoes and potato chips were introduced and removed at various points. Manufacturers provided candy and specialty cakes with and without artificial flavors and colors in identical packages. Parents and teachers periodically rated the children's behavior; the experimenters administered many objective tests of cognitive performance; academic achievement was monitored.

Positive dietary effects were seen mostly in the parents' ratings, and much less so in the teachers' ratings. Only 4 of the 36 boys were consistently judged as improved on the Feingold diet by both parents and teachers. There was no evidence that the diet facilitated cognitive performance or academic achievement.

Available research does not rule out the possiblity that there may be a subgroup of hyperactive children whose condition is of nutritional origin, as Feingold claimed. But if so, they are a tiny group and the beneficial nutritional effects of the diet are nowhere near as dramatic as would be supposed from the enthusiastic parent testimonials. The latter reflect nonspecific placebo effects, acting, not on the children, but on their parents. A "consensus development conference," sponsored by the National Institutes of Health, concluded that the evidence in the main did not support the efficacy of dietary control of hyperactivity, but that physicians and parents who believed in the diets should go ahead and try them (National Institutes of Health Consensus Development Panel, 1982).

Behavior Modification

Of the non-pharmacological treatments for hyperactivity under development, therapies based on operant learning principles are especially promising. Such alternatives are just beginning to be explored systematically.

One of the first investigations of behavior modification techniques with hyperactive children involved three children, ages 8 to 10, who were enrolled in special classes for learning disabled children (Ayllon, Layman, & Kandel, 1975). Each had been taking Ritalin for at least one year. Throughout the study, hyperactive behavior and academic performance were assessed every day in math and reading classes. Hyperactive behavior was scored every 25 seconds by an observer using a checklist, and included primarily gross motor behaviors (e.g., rocking in the chair, running around the room), disruptive noise with objects (e.g., excessively rustling book pages), and disturbing others (e.g., screaming, talking out, hitting classmates). Math performance was the number of correct answers on a different set of 10 arithmetic problems given daily; reading performance was the score on workbook comprehension tests based on material that had been read earlier.

The four phases of the study were: (a) a preliminary 17-day period during which baseline levels for hyperactive behavior and academics were established while medication continued, (b) a 3-day observation period following the withdrawal of Ritalin (which was withheld for the remainder of the study), (c) a 6-day period during which academic performance in math class was reinforced, and finally (d) a 6-day period during which reinforcement for reading was added, while math work continued to be reinforced. The reinforcement scheme was a token system in which the teacher added checks to a card for the goal math and reading behaviors. At the end of each day the accumulated check marks (from 0-75) were traded in for back-up reinforcers such as candy, school supplies, or free time. The results were quite similar for the three children, and are shown in Fig. 9.4 for one of them.

When Ritalin was withdrawn, hyperactive behavior increased in both math and reading class. This was a difficult period for the parents, teachers, and no doubt for the children themselves. It was only with some difficulty that the parents and teachers were persuaded to continue the experiment. When reinforcement for math work was introduced, math performance rose and hyperactive behavior during that class decreased to the level that had been seen under medication. Hyperactivity remained high and academic achievement low in reading class. When reading reinforcement was added, both of these problems were immediately corrected. Notice that at the end of the study, academic performances that were being reinforced were much higher as compared to during medication, *and* hyperactive behavior was about the same as had been present during medication. The same phenomena were seen with the other children.

More elaborate behavior modification programs can be instituted in which both parents and teachers are enlisted as therapists so that a system of beneficial contingencies can remain in effect 24 hours per day. Methods to encourage behavioral self-control, such as self-monitoring of target and undesirable behaviors, can be added (see Pelham, 1982, for a discussion and review of behavioral treatments of hyperactivity).

The authors of the study just presented suggest, based on their results, that stimulants be withdrawn periodically from hyperactive children so that alternative approaches can be tested (Ayllon et al, 1975). It seems rea-

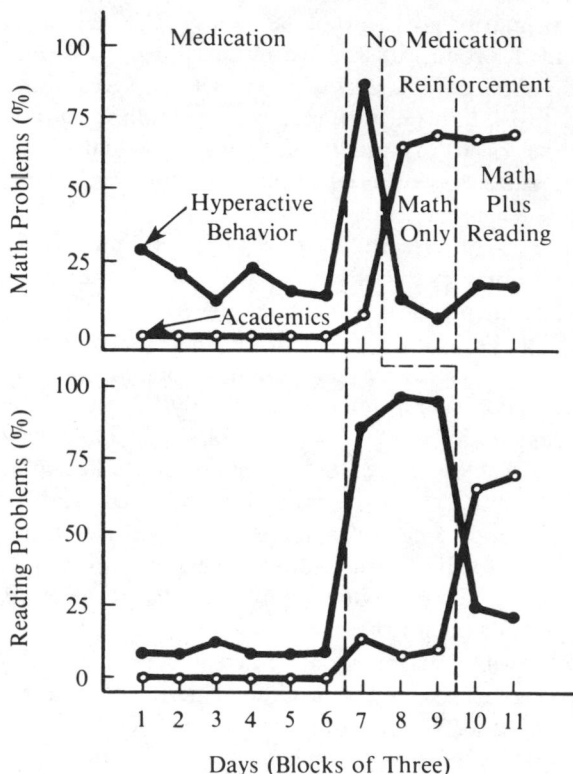

FIG. 9.4 Effects of a behavior modification procedure on the hyperactive behavior and academic performance of a learning disabled hyperactive child. From "A Behavioral-Educational Alternative to Drug Control of Hyperactive Children" by T. Ayllon et al., 1975, *Journal of Applied Behavior Analysis, 8*, 142. Copyright 1975 by the Society for the Experimental Analysis of Behavior. Adapted by permission.

sonable to go further and urge that no child be placed on a stimulant regimen without having explored the efficacy of a behavior modification program (Werry & Sprague, 1970).

Self-Regulation

It is likely that the fidgeting and excessive movement of the hyperactive child is accompanied by abundant electromyographic (EMG) activity. In fact, Braud (1978) has shown that EMG from the forehead (frontalis) muscles is elevated in hyperactive children as compared to normals when they are more or less at rest. Perhaps by learning to achieve and sustain low levels of EMG, hyperactive children can acquire self-control of their behavioral hyperactivity, and even experience enhanced attentional control. This reasoning is the basis for the scattered reports of muscle relaxation training, primarily using EMG biofeedback, with hyperactive children, dating to an early case report of successful treatment with an extremely hyperactive 6-year-old boy (Braud, Lupin, & Braud, 1975).

Most studies have involved only a few children, have lacked adequate controls to establish reduction in EMG activity as the active ingredient, and have not provided extended follow-up data. Given the limitations, the results have been positive. For example, Braud (1978) worked with 15 hyperactive children, 8 of whom had taken, or were taking, Ritalin. Equal sub-groups received, over 6 weeks, 12 sessions of frontalis muscle EMG biofeedback training, or modified progressive relaxation training, or no training at all. Home practice was encouraged. A sample of normal children were monitored, but not trained, for comparison purposes. Muscle tension decreased across sessions with both types of relaxation training, but not without training. The two types of training resulted in equivalent significant improvements in parent-rated distractability, behavioral hyperactivity, irritability, impulsivity, and, especially emotionality-aggression. The treated hyperactive children showed gains as compared to the untreated children on several cognitive tests. Medicated and non-medicated children improved equally. Because the parents were aware of whether or not the child was in an active treatment condition, at least some of the rated improvements must be due to parental expectation—placebo.

In an attempt to control for placebo, Omizo and Michael (1982) treated 16 control hyperactive children just the same as their 16 trained children, except the controls were connected to an inoperable biofeedback device and listened to stories, while the trained children received EMG biofeedback and heard a relaxation audio tape specially designed for children. Only the trained children lowered their muscle tension over the four sessions, and showed less behavioral impulsivity and greater attentional control as measured in a simple structured cognitive task.

If hyperactive children are underaroused (see aforementioned, Zentall & Zentall, 1983), and if muscle relaxation training should lead to generalized psychophysiological relaxation—still lower arousal—then this treatment would actually exacerbate hyperactivity. This important issue has not been addressed adequately. At a minimum it would seem essential to take steps to encourage feedback-specific physiological effects (see chapter 5) when EMG biofeedback is used with hyperactive children.

ALZHEIMER'S DISEASE

Incidence and Characteristics

Benjamin Franklin was 78 years old when he invented bifocals. Grandma Moses took up painting at the same age and was a productive artist until her death at 101. Picasso painted well into his 80s. Eubie Blake was still writing and playing ragtime music when he was 100. Some individuals retain their intellectual vigor as they age—senility is not the inevitable companion of aging. Unfortunately, many persons, as they enter their 60s and 70s, begin to have lapses of memory that become increasingly severe. They become disoriented and confused. A slow, relentless "death of the mind" follows as their original personality is gradually obliterated. Most of these individuals suffer from Alzheimer's disease—probably our most obscure major health problem.

Alzheimer's disease accounts for 50% to 60% of all cases of dementia, a severe impairment of cognitive functions whose symptoms were just outlined (Wolfson & Katzman, 1983). Simple tests such as naming the months of the year in reverse order are sensitive to the cognitive effects of dementia, but its symptoms are also evident in the tasks of everyday living. In the early stages of dementia, the effects may be seen in inability to balance a checkbook, carry out adequate grocery shopping, or travel without getting lost. In advanced cases, patients do not know where they are, and no long recognize their friends and family.

At least 5% of the United States population over age 65 have significant dementia (Coyle, Price, & DeLong, 1983); the figure is greater than 20% for those over 85 (Wolfson & Katzman, 1983). At least 55% of these patients are thought to have Alzheimer's. This means that over 650,000 persons are afflicted with Alzheimer's in the United States today. Alzheimer's is responsible for most confinements to nursing homes for the elderly, at an estimated yearly cost of $6 billion for institutional care (Coyle et al., 1983). The cost in human suffering is compounded by the stresses experienced by the family of the patient. As the percentage of elderly persons climbs, so will the prevalence and costs of Alzheimer's. Unless effective treatments are devised, this disorder may be our most serious chronic health problem by the year 2000.

Physiology and Etiology

Physiology

In 1907 a German neurologist, Alois Alzheimer, studied the brain of a 52-year-old patient who had suffered from premature dementia, and discovered a distinctive pattern of neural degeneration. The cerebral cortex was covered with an unusual number of *neural plaques*, which are enlarged masses of non-functional tissue that form at the end of axons. Plaques interfere with neural transmission. There were also many *neural tangles*—filaments growing within the cell bodies of cortical neurons. Later, it became evident that the same neuropathology was present in the brains of older patients who had shown dementia. Eventually, the same forms of neural degeneration were found in the cortex of deceased individuals with Down's syndrome. Most or all persons with Down's syndrome develop, and die of, progressive dementia in their 30s or 40s. From the evidence just presented, we can conclude that Alzheimer's disease is responsible for most cases of dementia in both normal persons and individuals with Down's syndrome, regardless of the age of onset. About 20% of the cases of dementia in the elderly are due to vascular diseases such as stroke which restrict the oxygen supply to brain areas, causing death of neurons.

The subsequent research elaborating on Alzheimer's original observations is an interesting story of scientific puzzle solving, the interplay between basic and applied research, and luck (reviewed by Coyle et al., 1983; Kolata, 1983). It soon became apparent that the neural plaques and tangles were not scattered randomly over the cerebral cortex, but concentrated on the frontal and temporal lobes and in the hippocampus, which is located within the temporal lobes. The affected parts were the brain areas most closely identified with memory and the higher order cognitive processes that are impaired in Alzheimer's. A major breakthrough occurred when several laboratories reported in the mid-1970s that brains from patients who had died of Alzheimer's had from 60% to 90% less choline acetyltranferase (CAT) activity in the cortex as compared to control brains from patients of the same age who had died of some other cause. This suggested that the disorder is somehow selective for acetylcholine (ACh) neurons, since CAT is the enzyme that manufactures the neurotransmitter ACh. Other research showed that the less CAT activity, the more plaques in the cortex. Acetylcholinesterase (AChE), the biochemical that breaks down excess ACh to clear ACh synapses, was also found to be greatly depleted in Alzheimer's victims. Normal memory processes are highly dependent on cholinergic activity. Alzheimer's is apparently caused by something that selectively destroys cholinergic neurons, leaving other systems intact (Bartus, Dean, Beer, & Lippa, 1982).

A second set of intially unrelated discoveries began to emerge at about the same time ACh was becoming implicated in Alzheimer's. This work eventually traced the cortical degeneration of Alzheimer's to a tiny, previously ignored area, deep in the brain, the *nucleus basalis of Maynert*. The nucleus basalis is situated right between the temples in the lower front portion of the brain—the basal forebrain—immediately above the optic chiasm. This area in rats was found to contain high levels of AChE activity, which is suggestive of a concentration of ACh neurons. Electrical recordings in monkeys showed that these cells were especially active during higher order behaviors; consistent with this, anatomists traced the axons of these cells directly to the cerebral cortex. When the nucleus basalis was destroyed in rats, ACh activity in the cortex was curtailed, just as in Alzheimer's disease. All of the evidence suggested that in Alzheimer's something must go wrong in the nucleus basalis of Maynert.

The final breakthrough occurred when Donald Price and his colleagues at the Johns Hopkins University School of Medicine were able to study the brain of a 74-year-old man who had died after a 14-year period of progressive dementia. The father, an aunt, and an uncle of the patient had shown the same symptoms. There was a profound loss of cells in the nucleus basalis. About 90% of the cells were dead. Adjacent brain areas were normal for an individual his age. The finding was confirmed by comparing the brains of deceased patients who had had Alzheimer's with the brains of control patients who had died of other causes. In addition, selec tive loss of nucleus basalis cells in the brains of patients with Down's syndrome was demonstrated.

It is not understood how the death of cells in the nucleus basalis leads to cortical plaqueing, although both the degeneration of the nucleus basalis and cortical plaque formation seem to be gradual processes, just like the slow progression of cognitive impairment in Alzheimer's. Perhaps healthy nucleus basalis neurons release some sort of trophic factor that is needed for normal cortical neural function (Coyle et al., 1983).

The neuropathology and the cognitive deterioration of Alzheimer's must be intimately connected. Plaques are known to disrupt the normal transmission of nerve impulses. The extent of cortical plaqueing and the severity of dementia are correlated. There are EEG changes associated with dementia. Many years ago, Romano and Engel (1944) studied 53 patients, some of whom would be diagnosed today as victims of Alzheimer's. Every patient who had disturbances in consciousness also had EEG abnormalities, almost always excessive slow wave activity. Consciousness and EEG characteristics varied together over time within patients—improvement in mental capacities was associated with EEG recovery. Patients with congestive heart failure, which diminishes the oxygen supply to the brain, had EEG slowing and cognitive deficits, both of which were temporarily corrected by administration of oxygen (Engel & Romano, 1944).

The 40 Hz EEG pattern (see chapter 10) may be selectively impaired in Alzheimer's. This rhythm seems to be associated with problem-solving or a state of "focused arousal." Patients with Alzheimer's and normal age-matched controls worked on a variety of cognitive tasks while 40 Hz activity was recorded (Spydell & Sheer, 1983). The normal participants had elevated 40 Hz EEG during the cognitive tasks, whereas the persons with Alzheimer's showed no such task-related increase. Other EEG frequencies must be monitored during cognitive tasks before we can confidently conclude that the 40 Hz rhythm is a special marker that distinguishes between Alzheimer's and normal aging.

Etiology

There has been great progress in clarifying the psychophysiological nature of Alzheimer's, but the etiological forces responsible for launching the neural degeneration and cognitive deterioration of the disorder are unknown. Several types of factors have been explored.

A hereditary factor has been well established for Alzheimer's, although the details of genetic transmission have not been worked out (Terry & Katzman, 1983). Alzheimer's tends to run in families so that relatives of a person with Alzheimer's are at increased risk of developing the disorder themselves. In a large sample of twin pairs over age 60, there was 42.8% concordance of dementia, including Alzheimer's, for monozygotic twins, 8.9% for dizygotic twins, 6.5% for other siblings, and 3.4% for parents (Kallman, 1956). There are reported cases of Alzheimer's when there is no family history of the disorder. The studies demonstrating genetic factors also suggest that other factors must be important, since the reported concordances for genetically identical individuals are not especially high. Alzheimer's is another example in which environmental factors must exploit genetically-determined vulnerabilities to result in the actual disorder.

The search for non-genetic factors has concentrated on toxic agents that might enter the vulnerable brain and initiate or accelerate neural degeneration. Some sort of (unknown) communicable virus has not been ruled out. Alzheimer's has also been construed as an autoimmune phenomenon.

Among the myriad toxic agents in the environment, aluminum has been singled out for special study, partly because it is ingested in fairly high levels due to aluminum cans, food wrap, and especially aluminum pots and pans. In some lower species, aluminum, when introduced directly into the brain in small amounts, results in neural tangles resembling those seen in Alzheimer's, accompanied by similar behavioral changes. There are reports of elevated aluminum levels in the brains of deceased Alzheimer's patients, but others have failed to find this relationship (reviewed by Terry & Katzman, 1983). One theory is that aluminum interferes with protein synthesis, to either depress normal activity or perhaps to initiate formation of abnormal proteins (Crapper, Karlik, & DeBoni, 1978).

Practically nothing is known about the possible role of psychological or experiential factors in Alzheimer's. Several studies indicate that personality variables do not predict subsequent Alzheimer's (e.g., Post, 1968). In the absence of evidence, one can speculate. My wife's 81-year-old grandfather seems to have suffered no diminution in intellectual vigor with his years. He begins each day with cognitive exercises in bed—puzzle-solving, memory tasks, and so on. It makes one wonder about a hypothetical disuse phenomenon whereby neurons living in less active brains might undergo damage due to lack of exercise.

Treatment

No effective methods have been discovered to prevent, reverse, or stop the biological ravages of Alzheimer's. "In caring for these patients and their families, one tries to help them as best one can while the disease runs its inexorable course" (Blass, 1984, p. 4). At present, the symptoms, and not the disease itself, are treated.

Management of Symptoms

There are many useful steps that can be taken to enhance the quality of life for patients and their families. For the patients, the interventions depend on the specific difficulties they are experiencing. Simple expedients, such as writing down anything that must be remembered, and always carrying one's address and phone number can be helpful. Behavior modification plans can be useful with patients who are aggressive, incontinent, or tend to wander. Many other interventions have been used to improve the lot of the victim of Alzheimer's (Eisdorfer, Cohen, & Preston, 1981).

There is a trend away from institutionalization of the elderly, including demented persons, toward home care, based on both economic and humanistic considerations. Community services such as adult day care, home delivered meals, counseling support groups, and a national Alzheimer's organization are available to assist families who choose this option. There are practical self-help guides to home care for the elderly (e.g., Trocchio, 1981). Nevertheless, caring for a person with Alzheimer's at home is a challenging and stressful undertaking. Training programs for home supporters of Alzheimer's patients are under development.

Levine, Dastoor, and Gendron (1983) analysed the common problems encountered when Alzheimer's patients live at home, and determined how the more effective supporters managed such problems. This became the basis for a coping skills training program for supporters incorporating: (a) motivation enhancement, through practice focusing on adaptive self-statements in stress situations; (b) assertiveness training, where appropriate, to assist the supporters in dealing effectively with family members who were not helpful; (c) stress reduction through self-regulation training and role-playing practice with stress situations; and (d) problem-solving training.

Health-oriented housing for elderly persons who require some health care and assistance, but not on a 24-hour basis, is an important innovation. In the Highland Heights experiment, about 200 aged patients were housed in a health-oriented apartment complex (Sherwood, Greer, Morris, & Mor, 1981). Over the study period from 1970 to 1976, these patients were healthier, happier, and fewer died as compared to age-matched controls. They were " . . . almost universally appreciative of the opportunity to live in Highland Heights" (Sherwood, et al., 1981, p. 5). The program was reasonably cost effective.

Pharmacological Treatment

Parallels between Parkinson's and Alzheimer's diseases offer a basis for hope in developing a pharmacological treatment that might arrest or even reverse the progression of Alzheimer's. Parkinson's, like Alzheimer's, involves selective destruction of an anatomically-localized and neurotransmitter-specific population of neurons. In the case of Parkinson's, dopamine neurons degenerate within a small brain area known as the substantia nigra. As with Alzheimer's, the factors that pre-cipitate this destructive process are unknown. But the course of Parkinson's has been slowed, at least for some patients, using methods that enhance the brain dopamine supply. Pharmacological agents, pri-marily Dopa (the precursor that crosses the blood-brain barrier and is converted to dopamine), are being used with some success, as are dietary manipulations intended to encourage absorption of Dopa and facilitate its passage through the blood-brain barrier (Calne, 1984).

Intensive efforts are underway to determine if there might be an effective way to bolster ACh activity in patients with Alzheimer's and combat their cognitive deterioration (reviewed by Bartus, Dean, Beer, & Lippa, 1982). These include implanting devices that provide extra ACh on a slow-release basis. Preliminary results suggest modest gains for some patients, especially early in the course of the disease. The idea of actually reversing cognitive impairments that have been created by permanent tis-sue damage is not as ridiculous as it might seem. If a given brain with structural damage could be made to operate with greater biochemical efficiency, this might compensate for the neural damage and even result in a net improvement with respect to a normal brain of the same age.

10 Wellness and Optimum Function

In this chapter we take up the neglected upper reaches of health. The first major section considers positive health as a long-term process, which will be referred to as *wellness*, the opposite of chronic illness. The second section deals with occasions on which congruence is established between ongoing psychophysiological processes and the demands of the setting to yield high levels of functioning. This will be called *optimum function*—a momentary, situation-specific glimpse of wellness.

The physiological, psychological, and behavioral headings used to divide the material should not be taken too seriously. The factors discussed under them overlap, interact, and, as health psychophysiology advances, will have to be integrated to fathom wellness.

WELLNESS

Everyone knows what it is to be ill. When a person speaks of dizziness, nausea, aching joints, or a sore throat, we immediately grasp these subjective qualities of illness. Similarly, there are familiar physiological dimensions of illness, such as fever, inflammation, or a runny nose, and predictable ways in which our behavior changes when we are sick—perhaps staying in bed all day rather than going to work or school. But what is it to be well? How does wellness feel? Does it have identifiable physiological markers? How does the well person behave? We know much less about wellness than illness.

272

The idea that wellness is not simply the absence of illness directed the selection of material for this chapter. This is in the spirit of a definition of health adopted long ago by the World Health Organization (1958): "Health is a state of complete physical, mental, and social well-being and is not merely the absence of disease and infirmity" (p. 3). Illness is a negative state, and wellness is a positive state, the two located at opposite ends of the health continuum.

The view that wellness lies beyond freedom from pathological processes is, at present, only a working hypothesis. This is sometimes overlooked, as is the fact that if wellness is not due to the absence of one thing, then it must be due to the presence of something else. Possible signatures of wellness, or even the antecendent conditions of wellness, have not been identified, although there is no shortage of advocates and believers for specific paths to wellness. The search for the stuff of wellness is one of the great challenges of contemporary science.

Physiological Aspects of Wellness

Wellness as Resistance to Disease

Wellness has been defined as heightened resistance to disease. Beyond not being ill, the well person is able to stay that way in the face of potentially unhealthy agents. The idea that a healthy person possesses corrective faculties that are poised to intervene when the normal state is somehow upset was introduced by Hippocrates with his *vis medicatrix naturae*—that disease is cured by natural powers (Cannon, 1939). Speaking in more general terms, Audy (1973) has defined positive health as the ability to rally after a challenge to adapt. Along the same lines, Selye (1976) considered wellness a state of optimum balance between forces requiring the organism to respond, and the ability of the organism to do so.

An optimally functioning immune system would be an essential element in wellness, according to the resistance-to-disease concept of wellness. However, the research examining variations in immunity has been almost exclusively concerned with suppression of immune function, that is, with the lower end of the health continuum. As indicated in chapter 3, it is clear that immunity is compromised during such disparate periods of stress as final exams, bereavement, and running a marathon. While we are beginning to grasp the circumstances under which immunity falls below normal, we do not have much idea how to cultivate super immunity.

Exploratory studies have begun to examine the effects of psychophysiological relaxation on immune function in normal individuals. For example, Peavey, Lawlis and Goven (1984) selected from an original population of 41 normal adult volunteers, 16 individuals who were under high stress, as indicated by self-report. A test of the vigor of phagocytosis revealed that the high stress subjects had lowered immunocompetence with respect to the total group. A later administration of the same test showed that a combination of verbal relaxation and muscle tension biofeedback led to greater phagocytic activity in a trained group as compared to an untreated control group. White blood cell counts were not influenced by the treatment. Further studies on this problem would be extremely valuable in order to discover if there are practical methods, perhaps involving psychophysiological self-regulation methods, to sufficiently strengthen the immunocompetence of normal individuals to increase resistance to disease.

Wellness as Homeostasis

The ideas just introduced are related to the concept of homeostasis, which itself could be considered a physiological doctrine of wellness. Claude Bernard, the 19th century French physiologist, proposed in 1879 that the stability of the *milieu interne*—the environment surrounding every cell of the body—is essential for survival of the organism. About 50 years later, Walter Cannon, in the United States, elaborated on this idea and introduced the term *homeostasis* to refer to the tendency toward constancy of the internal environment despite disturbances originating both inside and outside of the organism. For the body to function efficiently, various constituents of the extracellular fluid need to be kept within narrow tolerances although the cells of the body are continuously extracting nutrients from and discharging wastes into this fluid. Also, changes in cellular activity levels, as happen during physical exercise, alter the fluid matrix, as do stimuli outside the organism, such as a change in the weather or any event that requires a response from the organism. In the face of all this, the ingredients of the internal environment vary no more than a few percentage points in the healthy organism due to the complex regulating action of homeostasis. Wellness, from the physiological perspective, could be defined as the dynamic balance of the internal environment that results from homeostatic processes.

Psychological Aspects of Wellness

Many theorists have proposed that the healthy person is characterized by psychological growth. This unfolding of potential, has been identified with wellness. Freedom from psychopathology is not sufficient for wellness in the psychological domain.

Different theorists have emphasized particular aspects of psychological development. According to Kelly's (1955) "personal construct theory" each of us develops a set of concepts or ideas that we use to understand and interpret the world, including other people. For healthy individuals these constructs become progressively more complex over the lifespan, enabling more complex interactions with the world. Erikson (1963) emphasizes a succession of personal crises that everyone encounters across lifelong psychosocial development. The crisis of adolescence, for example, is to establish a personal identity. Other theories are more narrowly focused. Piaget (1970) addresses the intellectual development of children, and describes the emergence of adult-style logical thinking over a fixed set of stages. Kohlberg (1973) proposes that moral reasoning also develops across predictable stages, beginning with judgments on moral issues that are based strictly on self-interest, moving toward conventional conformity to rule-based morality, and eventually reaching, for some individuals, principles of conscience.

Each of the theories just mentioned speaks to some facet of the psychological growth of the healthy person. However, the most comprehensive, and probably the most influential growth-oriented concept is that of self-actualization, as formulated by the pioneering humanist, Kurt Goldstein, and later elaborated by the American psychologists, Carl Rogers and Abraham Maslow.

Kurt Goldstein and Self-Actualization

Goldstein (1940) reacted against prevailing negative formulations of human nature, in particular Freud's psychoanalytic theory. Freud's theory, and others like it, is negative insofar as the actions of a human being are said to be driven by "deficiency motivation." A human lifetime becomes nothing more than a series of struggles to escape a succession of deprivation states. According to Freudian theory, tenderness and affection are merely deflected sexuality; all of human culture has been created by sublimated repressed drives.

Goldstein conducted extensive studies of brain-injured patients during which he was able to catalogue a variety of impairments as a consequence of damage to the brain. Although different patients had their own patterns of limitations, Goldstein noticed a common thread linking the patients. They seemed to have an almost desparate need to cling to a psychological equilibrium by avoiding the unfamiliar and novel. The patients took pains to create and maintain an orderly, highly predictable world—a less-demanding, sheltered environment.

The behavior of his brain-injured patients made apparent, by contrast, what Goldstein came to believe was the fundamental urge of healthy human beings. What normal, healthy people had, but the patients lacked, is a joyful "coming to terms with the world," which is the "motive which sets the organism going." Goldstein gave the name, *self-actualization*, to this urge toward growth, understanding, and expression of creative powers.

Goldstein (1940) proposed that it was always an unhealthy sign when one's psychological resources were invested in maintenance of the status quo rather than movement toward self-actualization. Even individuals who are relatively well sometimes find themselves in this unfortunate state, wanting to "get away from it all" to regain their psychological equilibrium.

Carl Rogers and the Self

Rogers (1961) went on to conceive of self-actualization as "the directional trend which is evident in all organic and human life—the urge to expand, extend, develop, mature—the tendency to express and activate all the capacities of the organism or the self" (p. 351). This force motivates the individual to seek increased autonomy and self-sufficiency, to engage in creativity, and obtain an increasing range of experiences.

The *self* is the center of Roger's humanistic theories. We all have a self-image of what sort of person we are, and continuously monitor our experiences, thoughts, and actions against this self-perception. We also have an ideal self, an image of the kind of person we would like to be. The less distance between our actual self and our ideal self, the happier and more fulfilled we are, that is, the greater our psychological health.

Rogers' *client-centered therapy* is a product of his humanistic thinking. Here, the therapist is nondirective, functioning only as a mirror or sounding board to create the necessary circumstances within which the individual can find his or her own path toward self-development. Rogers believes that every person, no matter how troubled, is a valuable human being who is deserving of respect and dignity, and capable of self-healing when given an adequate opportunity.

Abraham Maslow and Self-Actualizers

One of Abraham Maslow's most valuable contributions to the psychology of positive health is his description of fully-functioning or self-actualizing individuals. Maslow screened thousands of persons in order to select a small sample who were then studied intensively using case study methods to yield in-depth portraits of individual personalities. A few historical figures, such as Albert Einstein and Eleanor Roosevelt, were included among his probable self-actualizing persons. Maslow concluded that self-actualizers shared a number of qualities that tended to set them apart from ordinary people (Maslow, 1970). Some of these are as follows.

Acceptance (self, others, nature). "a relative lack of overriding guilt, of crippling shame, and of extreme or severe anxiety . . . possible to accept themselves and their own nature without chagrin or complaint, or, for that matter, even thinking about the matter very much. . . . they can take the frailties and sins, weaknesses, and evils of human nature in the same unquestioning spirit with which one accepts the characteristics of nature" (p. 155).

Spontaneity; simplicity; naturalness. "relatively spontaneous in behavior and far more spontaneous than that in their inner life, thoughts, impulses, etc. Their behavior is marked by simplicity and naturalness, and by lack of artificiality or straining for effect. This does not necessarily mean consistently unconventional behavior. . . . conventionality is a cloak that rests lightly . . . and is easily cast aside . . . infrequently allows convention to hamper" (p. 157).

Freshness of appreciation. "the wonderful capacity to appreciate again and again, freshly and naively, the basic goods of life, with awe, pleasure, wonder, and even ecstasy . . . 'newness' . . . even the casual workaday, moment-to-moment business of living can be thrilling, exciting, and ecstatic . . . these intense feelings . . . come occasionally, rather than usually" (p. 163).

Democratic. "friendly with anyone of suitable character regardless of class, education, political belief, race, or color. . . . it often seems as if they are not even aware of these differences, which are for the average person so obvious and so important. . . . honestly respectful and even humble before people who can teach them something" (p. 167-168).

Strongly ethical. "Whether or not they could verbalize the matter, they rarely showed in their day-to-day living the chaos, the confusion, the inconsistencies, or the conflict that are so common in the average person's ethical dealings . . . they have definite moral standards, they do right and do not do wrong . . . their notions of right and wrong and of good and evil are often not the conventional ones. . . . If religion is defined only in social-behavioral terms, then these are all religious people, the atheists included" (p. 168-169).

Unhostile sense of humor. "they do not laugh at hostile humor (making people laugh by hurting someone) or superiority humor (laughing at someone else's inferiority) or authority-rebellion humor . . . (their humor) consists in large part of poking fun at human beings in general when they are foolish, or forget their place in the universe, or try to be big when they are actually small. . . . Probably Lincoln never made a joke that hurt anybody else" (p. 169-170).

Creativeness. "This is a universal characteristic . . . kin to the naive and universal creativeness of unspoiled children . . . projected out upon the world or touches whatever activity the person is engaged in. . . . Whatever one does can be done with a certain attitude, a certain spirit that arises out of the nature of the character of the person performing the act. If there were no choking-off of forces, we might expect that every human being would show this special type of creativeness" (p. 170-171).

Trancendence of enculturation. "they resist enculturation and maintain a certain inner detachment from the culture in which they are immersed . . . accept most states of affairs that they consider unimportant or unchangeable. . . . they are apt to elicit as a reaction only a shrug of the shoulders. These are not moral issues. But since this tolerant acceptance of harmless folkways is not warm approval with identification, this yielding to convention is apt to be rather casual and perfunctory" (p. 171-172).

Maslow also believed that self-actualizers were unusually astute in their perception of reality, tended to be quite problem-centered, had an affinity for solitude, were relatively autonomous of the culture in which they find themselves, have deep ties with few individuals, and tended to have more frequent mystical and peak experiences.

In his early research Maslow screened 3,000 college students and only found "one immediately usable subject and a dozen or two possible future subjects ('growing well')" (Maslow, 1970, p. 150). Most of us become side-tracked dealing with lower needs. Until these are satisfied self-actualization is not important. Feeling safe, accepted, loved, and respected, and having worked out one's philosophical bearings are prerequisites for self-actualization.

Facilitating Self-Actualization

According to Maslow (1967) there are certain behaviors that assist in the development of self-actualization. These behaviors, which are seen most clearly in people who are "growing well," are shown in Table 10.1. Attempting to rise above, or act independently from one's environment is a theme that runs through Maslow's suggestions for growth. Like Goldstein, Maslow had little use for the status quo; in fact, his rejection of it is even more emphatic. For Maslow, psychological health is not to be found in successful *adjustment to* one's circumstances, but in *transcendence of* them. The route to self-actualization is certainly not the path of least resistance.

Self-actualization may be the Western counterpart of the positive psychological changes that are major goals of meditation as elaborated in eastern writings. Although in the Western scientific literature meditation is discussed primarily as a means to decrease anxiety or to achieve psycho-

TABLE 10.1
Behaviors Leading to Self-Actualization

1. Experience life as a child does, with full absorption and concentration
2. Try something new rather than sticking to secure and safe ways
3. Listen to your own feelings in evaluating experiences rather than to the voice of tradition or authority or the majority
4. Be honest; avoid pretenses of "game playing"
5. Be prepared to be unpopular if your views do not coincide with those of most people
6. Assume responsibility
7. Work hard at whatever you decide to do
8. Try to identify your defenses and have the courage to give them up

Note. From "Self-actualization and Beyond" (pp. 281-285) by A. H. Maslow in *Challenges of Humanistic Psychology* edited by J. F. T. Bugental, 1967, New York: McGraw-Hill. Copyright 1967 by McGraw-Hill. Adapted by permission.

physiological relaxation, in the eastern literature the major theme is "optimization of mental health" (Compton & Becker, 1983). Both the humanistic and eastern mystical traditions maintain that every person possesses the potential for growth or perfection, they stress the importance of developing that potential, emphasize the path itself and not just the goal, advocate an "opening up" or giving up of neurotic defenses, and value positively alterations in consciousness. Meditation is sometimes undertaken specifically to cultivate peak experiences.

Several studies have shown that standard practice of Transcendental Meditation twice a day for several months results in reported increases in self-actualization (e.g., Nidich, Seeman, & Dreslin, 1973). For Zen meditation, which is more demanding, the first months of practice appear to be a period of confusion and anxiety arising from increased awareness of one's thoughts and emotions. Only after about 9 months do Zen meditators consistently report movement toward self-actualization (Compton & Becker, 1983).

Happiness

Simply feeling well must be an important aspect of wellness. Warden McDonald comes to mind. On a warm Spring afternoon, Mac is likely to be downtown in Berkeley, California chatting with passersby and occasionally selling a copy of his autobiography, *An Old Guy Who Feels Good* (McDonald, 1978).

Happiness is not used here to refer to a momentary mood, but to an extended overall sense of subjective well-being or satisfaction with life. The study of how and why people experience their lives in positive ways, like other topics in positive health, is not far advanced. However, there have been several consistent findings (reviewed by Diener, 1984). Many studies have shown that happy people are healthier, even when other variables such as age and wealth are kept constant. Happiness predicts longevity. Yet, large surveys have shown that happiness is not strongly associated with demographic variables such as income, education, age, race, or sex (Andrews & Wither, 1976). Although high socioeconomic status persons worry about different things as compared to low status persons, they worry about just as many things, and say that they would like to make as many changes in their lives. A study of persons who had won large sums of money in the Illinois State Lottery found that the lottery winners were not happier than a control sample of persons, and actually derived significantly less pleasure from everyday events in their lives (Brickman, Coates, & Janoff-Bulman, 1978). It is often assumed by normal persons that individuals with "defects" must enjoy their lives less and not be as happy, due to their special limitations. However, a study of persons with various conditions such as blindness, paralysis, malformed or missing limbs, and of mentally retarded children, found these "defective" persons were as happy as samples of ordinary comparison subjects (Cameron, Titus, Kostin, & Kostin, 1973). Findings such as these reveal that happiness does not reside in the objective quality of one's life.

Nonetheless, some people are happier than others—they experience their lives in a more positive way, both emotionally and in the cognitive judgments they make about their lives (Diener, 1984). If happiness is not the natural correlate of "the good life" as gauged by our society, what are its correlates? Happiness is found consistently in the presence of several psychological characteristics, especially high self-esteem, and extroversion leading to social activity. Happiness does not seem to be related to intelligence.

There is a successful happiness training program that shows, pleasantly, that normal individuals can set out to become happier. Fordyce (1977) first sifted through existing research to identify characteristics of very happy people which average persons could emulate. Pretesting isolated 14 of these elements which become the basis of the 14 Fundamentals Program (Fordyce, 1981). These are listed in Table 10.2.

The training program consists of two parts, and is routinely provided to groups in a classroom setting, although there is every reason to suppose that the method would work even better with individualized guidance and monitoring. The first part surveys research on happiness, the importance of happiness, and introduces the 14 fundamentals as "things you can do about your happiness." The second part is a detailed analysis of each of the 14 elements, including supporting research, the role of each in happiness, and specific cognitive and behavioral techniques designed to help

TABLE 10.2
Fourteen Fundamentals for Happiness

1. Keep busy and be more active
2. Spend more time socializing
3. Be productive in meaningful work
4. Get better organized and plan things out
5. Stop worrying
6. Lower your expectations and aspirations
7. Develop positive, optimistic thinking
8. Become present oriented
9. Work on a healthy personality
10. Develop an outgoing, social personality
11. Be yourself
12. Eliminate negative feelings and problems
13. Close relationships are the number one source of happiness
14. Put happiness as your most important activity

Note. From "A Program to Increase Happiness: Fourteen Fundamentals" by M. W. Fordyce, 1983, *Journal of Counseling Psychology, 30*, p. 484. Copyright 1983 by the American Psychological Association. Adapted by permission.

attain them. For example to stop worrying, trainees learn to keep a record each day of what they worry about, how much time is spent worrying, how many worries actually come true, and to use thought-substitution techniques to banish worrying thoughts.

The 14 Fundamentals Program has been evaluated in a series of seven studies involving community college students with a wide range of ages and backgrounds. The results thus far indicate that the program is a practical way for ordinary people to increase their personal happiness (Fordyce, 1977, 1983). There have been substantial gains in happiness as indicated on a variety of standard indices of happiness. Also, 81% of all the trainees say via global self-reports that they have become happier people as a consequence of the program; 39% say they are "much happier" or "extremely happy." Well over 90% of the participants exposed to the program report that they use some of the information; over 33% either use or think about the information on a daily basis. These figures are especially noteworthy since there were no extrinsic reasons to pay any attention whatsoever to anything in the program, much less incorporate features into one's life. Also, there was no effort to recruit as participants unhappy people, or individuals who expressly wished to become happier. Follow-up data show that increased happiness persists for at least 9 to 18 months, and limited follow-up results suggest that distinct benefits are present for 2 to 4 years after exposure to the 14 fundamentals.

Behavioral Aspects of Wellness

There are several behavioral definitions of wellness. For example, wellness has been defined as the level of "physical and mental well-being required to optimally perform activities usual for a person's age and social role" (O'Regan & Carlson, 1979). Along the same lines, Sorochan (1968, p. 675) has spoken of "optimal personal fitness for full, fruitful and creative lives." Wellness can be linked to behavior more clearly when the performance of specific activities is studied. Some of this research is reviewed later in the chapter. There has been considerable interest in the superior use of human potential. We will also discuss "peak performance" later in this chapter.

Competence

Robert White's (1959) concept of "competence" is relevant when we consider the behavioral dimensions of wellness. White was particularly struck by the behaviors of babies and infants, who spend much of their time in visual exploration, grasping, crawling, exploring novel objects and situations, and manipulating their surroundings. All of these activities, which are simply play to the developing organism, were seen by White as serving the process of learning to interact more effectively with the environment, which White called *competence*. There is a "feeling of efficacy" that accompanies increasing competence. The feeling of efficacy is an end in itself that motivates the individual to interact with the environment, learn to understand it, and control it. Thus, according to White, the healthy person develops in the direction of more and more competent behavior.

Self-Efficacy

What are the antecendents of competence? Certainly successful behavior in any task, whether it is playing a song on a harmonica or running a large corporation, will depend on many specific skills, but there is another element that is just as essential. Successful performance of any task is strongly dependent on the belief that one can indeed execute the required behaviors. This is the essence of Bandura's (1977) *self-efficacy theory*. As in the children's story, "The Little Engine That Could," success depends on task-specific self-confidence. In fact, according to Bandura, when sufficient incentives and the necessary skills are present, task performance is simply a function of one's belief in personal efficacy.

There are many types of evidence in support of the self-efficacy theory. Many studies have shown that experimental manipulations of self-efficacy can influence performance. For example, Weinberg and his colleagues have conducted a series of investigations using a staged leg endurance competitive task (e.g., Weinberg, Gould, Yukelson, & Jackson, 1981). Initial self-efficacy was manipulated by informing participants that they would be trying to exceed the performance level of a varsity athlete or a person recovering from a knee operation. Individuals reported higher self-efficacy and exerted more muscular effort when they believed they were being assessed against the performance level of the recovering patient.

If competence signifies behavioral wellness, and self-efficacy contributes to competence, strengthening self-efficacy should enhance well behavior. Some therapeutic interventions appear to enhance self-efficacy incidentally, by leading individuals to believe that they are capable of dealing with circumstances that would have been too formidable otherwise. Bandura and Adams (1977) found that modelling—watching others behave in a non-fearful manner with respect to snakes—and desensitization—learning to relax in the presence of snakes—both helped snake phobic individuals to deal with snakes. However, the interventions worked only when they increased self-efficacy. In the case of desensitization, it was as if relaxation around snakes helped only if it convinced the individual that he or she was no longer afraid of snakes. Bandura (1977) has argued that a variety of behavior change techniques actually operate through a common cognitive pathway—enhancement of self-efficacy.

There are many ways to nurture self-efficacy. These involve one of the four kinds of information that, according to Bandura (1977), shape the belief in self-efficacy: (a) one's task performance, (b) observation of others' behavior, (c) verbal persuasion—"Come on, you can do it!", and (d) emotional cues, for example those suggesting lack of fear. One practical approach derives from the circular relationship between performance and self-efficacy whereby success bolsters confidence, which strengthens performance, resulting in more success, and so on. But often we find ourselves engaged in tasks that require self-directedness to guide and sustain our activities over long periods. There are few signs of success and precious few external inducements to keep going. Setting up personal proximal goals provides accessible guides and incentives to help us along to more distant goals, building self-efficacy in the process. Establishing proximal goals ought to be especially helpful for children, who are less able than adults to divide up an extended task into a series of shorter tasks, each with an associated proximal goal.

In a test of the reasoning just developed, 40 children, ages 7 to 10, who had been identified by their teachers as having gross deficits in their arithmetic performance along with low interest in the subject, were studied (Bandura & Schunk, 1981). There were seven sessions of working arithmetic problems. The children were assigned to one of four conditions: (a) Proximal Goals: it was initially suggested to the children that they try to complete six pages of problems in each session, but not mentioned thereafter; (b) Distant Goals: it was suggested that they try to complete 42 pages of problems in the seven sessions; (c) No Goals: there was no mention of specific goals, although the children were instructed to try to complete as many problems as possible; and (d) Control: arithmetic performance was tested before and after the same time period with no intervening treatment. The measures of interest were: (a) arithmetic performance; (b) arithmetic self-efficacy, the child's private confidence rating on a 100-point scale of whether he or she would be able to do sample problems, having seen them briefly; and (c) intrinsic interest in arithmetic, as indicated by the number of arithmetic problems solved in a "free-choice" situation in which non-arithmetic cognitive problems could be chosen. The results are shown in Fig. 10.1. Proximal goals were clearly influential in engendering arithmetic competence, the perception of efficacy, and intrinsic interest in arithmetic. When there were attainable subgoals, children progressed rapidly in an activity that originally had held little attraction for them.

Overview of Wellness

We have been considering health as a continuum. Traditionally, the lower end, illness, has received the greatest attention, because it pertains to the very survival of the individual. The upper end of the health continuum, wellness, deals with the quality of existence, once survival has been assured. Living well depends on living at all. This leads us to consider the relationship of stability and change, a theme that runs through this chapter.

Homeostasis reflects stability, whereas the many growth processes discussed previously, represent change. These are opposing tendencies, yet growth can only occur when there is adequate stability to support it. This can be seen in primitive creatures that can only exist in extremely constant environments such as the depths of the sea or inside another organism ("stealing" homeostasis in the latter case). They are not only unprepared to profit from a complex environment, but find lethal, the change that a complex environment necessarily entails. Similarly, Goldstein's (1940) brain-damaged patients, with their limited neural resources, found it necessary to simplify their lives and concentrate on homeostasis rather than growth. Psychological change must be accompanied by stabilizing assimilation and integration for the process to consti-

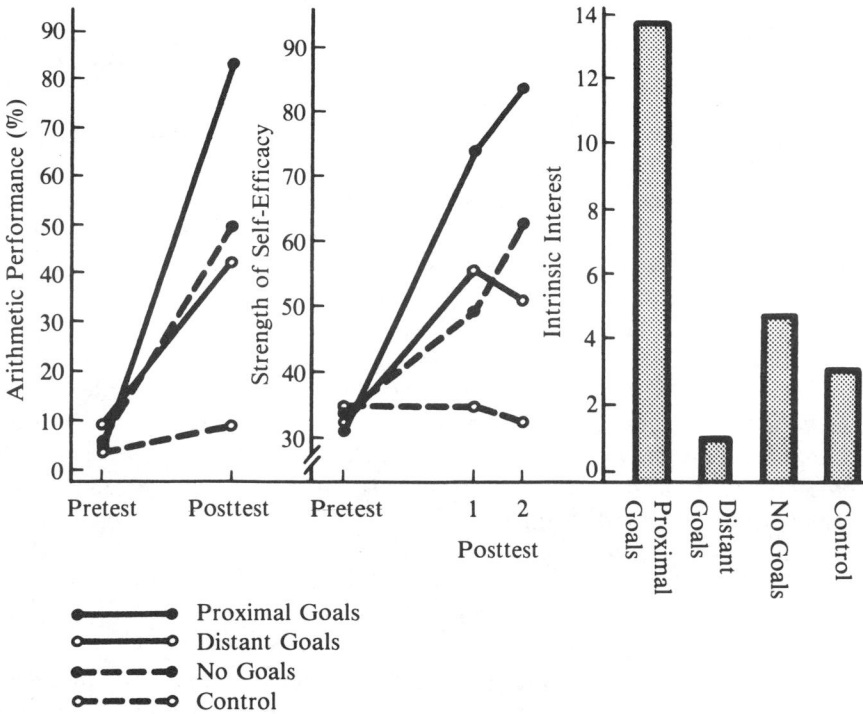

FIG. 10.1 Strengthening of arithmetic self-efficacy, actual performance, and intrinsic interest by proximal goals in children ages 7 to 10 years with low arithmetic interest and performance. From "Cultivating Competence, Self-Efficacy, and Intrinsic Interest through Proximal Self-Motivation" by A. Bandura and D. H. Schunk, 1981, *Journal of Personality and Social Psychology*, *41*, 592, 593. Copyright 1981 by the American Psychological Association. Adapted by permission.

tute growth; otherwise the change is chaotic and destructive—even lethal to the personality.

A holistic definition of wellness can be derived from the contents of this section: the simultaneous achievement of physiological homeostasis, psychological self-actualization, and behavioral competence.

OPTIMUM FUNCTION

In the section just concluded we discussed the possible qualities of wellness as an enduring chronic condition. Here, we turn to wellness as a momentary and situation-specific condition.

Physiological Aspects of Optimum Function

Arousal and Performance

In chapter 3 we considered the complex psychophysiological changes that mobilize the resources of the organism for action. At any moment the organism has a certain amount of this preparedness or *arousal*. There have been many variations on the idea that there is an intensity dimension to the overall psychophysiological status of the organism, a global "degree of excitement."

This way of thinking represents a greatly simplified view of a tangled situation. There is less than perfect correspondence at any given moment between the varied activities that figure into "degree of excitement," including: (a) behavioral activeness, (b) ANS mobilization, (c) neural activation such as cortical EEG desynchronization, (d) various chemical processes such as neurotransmitter and hormone production, and (e) a person's state of mind. Within the ANS, as was discussed in chapter 3, there are individually unique ANS stress profiles which, if nothing else, suggests difficulties in measuring arousal level for research purposes. Nonetheless, even considering these reservations, it is useful to analyse performance in relation to global arousal.

If we think about our daily activities, it is obvious that some of them are better performed under particular levels of arousal. Going to sleep is easier when arousal if low, but it is difficult to study during lowered arousal. Some behaviors require more arousal for optimum performance—a lifter struggling with a 500 pound weight or a sprinter coming out of the starting blocks needs all the arousal that can be mustered; other athletes such as a golfer crouching over a put, or a baseball player in the batter's box probably ought to have a more moderate arousal level. Intuitive notions such as these were formalized years ago in the *Yerkes-Dodson Law* (Yerkes & Dodson, 1908).

In contemporary language, the Yerkes-Dodson Law states that there is an inverted-U shaped relationship between arousal and task performance: up to a point, added arousal facilitates performance, but beyond a certain level, it begins to interfere. Furthermore, the more difficult the task, the lower the optimum level of arousal for that task. This generalization was inspired by the results of an experiment with mice in which the animals were required to always choose the brighter of two boxes (Yerkes & Dodson, 1908). The mice were punished for a mistake with an electric shock; the intensity of this shock was used to manipulate arousal. The learning task was either easy, moderate, or difficult depending on the brightness difference between the boxes. The joint effects of task difficulty and arousal on speed of learning are shown in Fig. 10.2. On the easy task, the

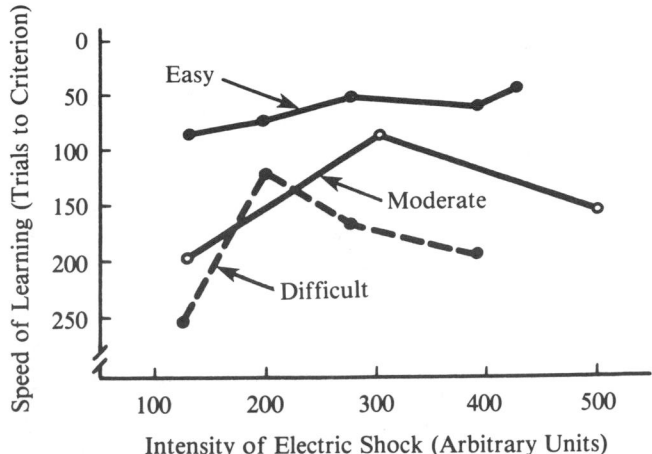

FIG. 10.2 Speed of learning for three levels of problem difficulty under different arousal levels induced by painful electric shock in mice. From "The Relation of Strength of Stimulus to Rapidity of Habit Formation" by R. M. Yerkes and J. D. Dodson, 1908, *Journal of Comparative Neurology and Psychology, 18,* 479. Copyright 1908 by Alan R. Liss, Inc. Adapted by permission.

more intense the shock, the quicker the mice learned; for the more difficult tasks, learning speed first increased, then decreased as shock intensity went up. The optimum shock, and presumably arousal level, was lower, the more difficult the task.

Later research has been generally supportive, considering that a great many factors, as well as arousal, influence performance of any task, and that in many laboratory studies only a narrow range of arousal levels is achieved (Duffy, 1972). Representative of later psychophysiological research, is an investigation in which voluntary muscle tension was used to alter physiological arousal, with heart rate used as an index of arousal (Wood & Hokanson, 1965). The participants exerted a specified force on a grip strength meter while they performed a cognitive task which required matching up numbers to geometric forms as quickly as possible. Their heart rate and performance data are shown in Fig. 10.3. Heart rate increased with greater induced tension, while performance peaked at a moderate arousal level, and then decreased with additional arousal.

Easterbrook (1959) has provided a useful elaboration and partial explanation of the Yerkes-Dodson law. According to Easterbrook, as arousal increases there is a progressive narrowing in the use of environmental cues. Depending on the requirements of the task, this may facilitate or interfere with performance. For the weight-lifter, restriction of irrelevant cues should facilitate performance; but, for a more complex multiple-cue

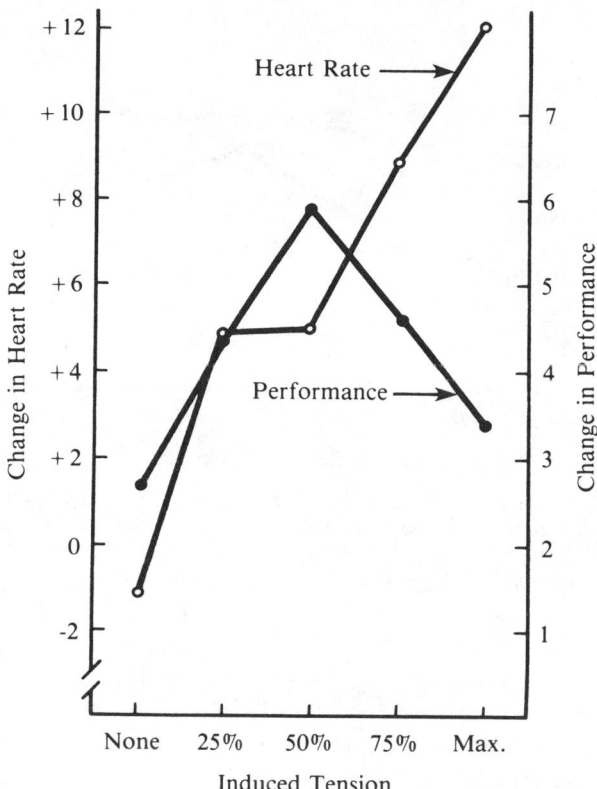

FIG. 10.3 Cognitive performance during five levels of arousal induced using a grip strength meter and indexed by heart rate. From "Effects of Induced Muscular Tension on Performance and the Inverted U Function" by C. G. Wood and J. E. Hokanson, 1965, *Journal of Personality and Social Psychology, 1*, 509. Copyright 1965 by the American Psychological Association. Adapted by permission.

activity, such as taking an exam, narrowing of cue utilization could prove disruptive. There is substantial empirical support for this idea (reviewed by Easterbrook, 1959), especially the selective narrowing of cue utilization as a result of stress-related arousal (reviewed by Hockey, 1979). We will return to the relationship among arousal, attentional processes, and performance later in this chapter in the context of athletics.

Theta and Vigilance

Slow EEG waves, in the theta (4 - 7 Hz) and alpha (8 - 13 Hz) ranges, from the visual processing areas of the cerebral cortex are associated with inattention to visual information in the normal, eyes open, individual. Drowsiness is known to accompany theta, in particular. Therefore, an optimum state for taking in and reacting to visual stimuli would involve little or no low frequency EEG; slow waves in the EEG from the back of the head signal trouble when monitoring a radar screen, driving a car, or reading a textbook. Following this reasoning, there have been several attempts to facilitate "vigilance" using EEG biofeedback procedures.

In one experiment, a realistic radar screen monitoring task was set up, complete with a rotating sweep line, random visual "noise" now and then, and an occasional target blip (Beatty, Greenberg, Deibler, & O'Hanlon, 1974). The participants were supposed to press a switch whenever a target was detected. The challenge was that there were only five targets every 15 minutes and the test ran on for two hours. Some of the participants were given biofeedback training in advance to suppress EEG theta, others to augment theta (to produce more of it). Then, during the radar monitoring task, each person watched the screen for two hours on two separate occasions—once while regulating his or her EEG as trained, and once while not attempting to control EEG theta (without feedback present). The EEG data indicated that the subjects were successful in EEG theta control including during the radar monitoring task. The blip detection results are shown in Fig. 10.4 for the four conditions across the two hours of the task. Better performance is indicated by fewer sweeps to detection, and the ordinate is upside down. The major findings are that the group trained to suppress EEG theta did significantly better while regulating theta than when not; in contrast, the theta augmenting group was significantly worse at detecting blips when regulating than when not. Individuals who have learned to suppress their EEG theta may show less of the performance decrements that occur over time during long boring tasks. Unfortunately, there have been no subsequent published studies following up this interesting possibility. In several experiments there have been difficulties in obtaining biofeedback control of EEG theta (reviewed by Rockstroh, Elbert, Birbaumer, & Lutzenberger, 1982).

40 Hz and Problem Solving

In certain species, including cats and humans, there is a narrow 36 - 44 Hz band of EEG activity that can be detected from implanted depth electrodes in lower animals and by ordinary surface electrodes in humans. This *40 Hz pattern* comes and goes relatively independently of high frequency beta EEG activity, which suggests that it may have some special functional significance. It has been proposed that 40 Hz EEG is associated with a state of "focused arousal" (Sheer, 1984). A neural model has been developed in which the 40 Hz pattern is represented as an optimum balance between sensitivity and stability of interacting assemblies of neurons (Freeman, 1975).

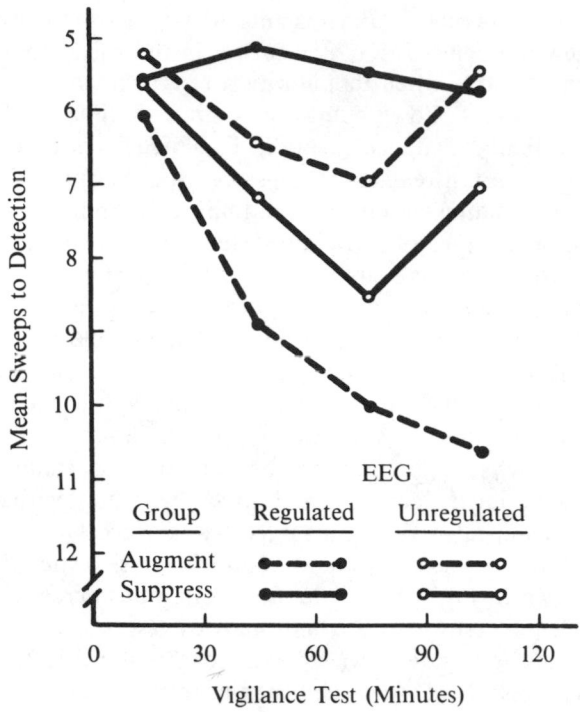

FIG. 10.4 Radar monitoring performance while biofeedback-trained subjects either augmented or suppressed EEG theta (Regulated conditions), or did not attempt to control EEG theta (Unregulated conditions). From "Operant Control of Occipital Theta Rhythm Affects Performance in a Radar Monitoring Task" by J. Beatty et al., 1974, *Science, 183,* 872. Copyright 1974 by the American Association for the Advancement of Science. Adapted by permission.

There are several lines of supporting evidence. Cats who were trained with rewards to increase 40 Hz in their visual cortex showed behavioral arousal and "fixed staring" when producing 40 Hz EEG (Bauer & Jones, 1976). Patients with Alzheimer's, as discussed in chapter 9, and children with learning disabilities, do not produce as much 40 Hz during problem solving as matched controls (Sheer, 1976; Spydell & Sheer, 1983). In several studies, biofeedback procedures have been used to both enhance and suppress 40 Hz EEG in normal adults (reviewed by Sheer, 1984). Trained individuals were unable to suppress the 40 Hz pattern when they were solving problems.

The 40 Hz pattern apparently supports successful cognition of the problem-solving kind. If this is so, individuals might be trained using 40 Hz biofeedback to enter a state of focused arousal and solve problems more effectively. Although Sheer and his colleagues have speculated along these lines as regards learning disabled children, they have brought forth no evidence on the possible cognitive benefits of 40 Hz training, including its possible utility for the average person who wishes to think more productively.

Slow potentials and Information Processing

"Coming events cast their shadows before" (Campbell, 1854). Imagine a musician in a major symphony orchestra in the moments leading up to an elaborate and difficult solo. What might we expect to see in the EEG? Figure 10.5 is an EEG record obtained by telemetry from a horn player in just such a situation. Notice that the entire EEG tracing gradually shifts upward (goes electrically negative), reaching its maximum deflection just before the solo begins. Many events that evoke preparation, attention, or expectancy "cast their shadows before" in the form of a distinct DC shift in the EEG, or what is more commonly called a *negative slow potential* (negative SP).

The negative SP was first described by Gray Walter (1964) who viewed the phenomenon as an expectancy or priming wave. Others have attributed the SP to attention, motivation, or preparation for a motor response (reviewed by Rockstroh, Elbert, Birbaumer, & Lutzenberger, 1982). According to a recent neuropsychological theory, the negative SP reflects neural energy mobilization, a kind of "cerebral potentiality" which is then

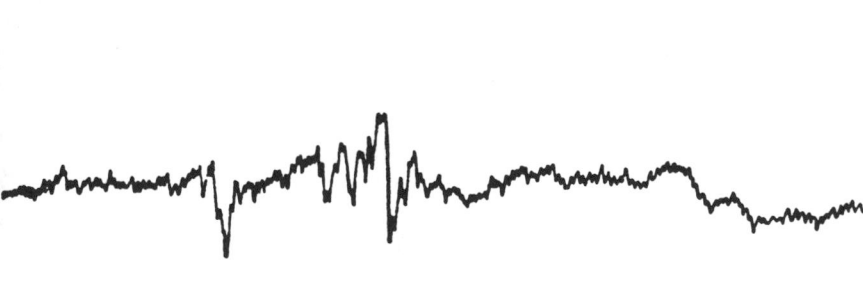

FIG. 10.5 Negative slow potential preceding a hornist's solo in a symphony orchestra. From "Psychophysiologische Untersuchungen uber die Belastung des Musikers in einem Symphonic Orchester" (p. 31) by V. M. Haider and E. Groll-Knapp, 1971, in M. Piperek (Ed.), *Stress and Kunst*, Stuttgart: Wilhelm Braumuller. Copyright 1971 by Wilhelm Braumuller. Adapted by permission.

consumed in the ensuing brain/cognitive activity (Rockstroh, Elbert, Birbaumer, & Lutzenberger, 1982).

SPs are distributed widely over the scalp and are usually of greatest amplitude when recorded from the top of the head (the vertex). Because SPs seemingly require the summated action of large numbers of neurons, lower brain structures must coordinate the formation of SPs. According to one model, the thalamus and reticular formation play important roles (Skinner & Yingling, 1977). Glial cells, the non-conducting units located in between and surrounding neurons, may participate in the generation of SPs.

The SP is thought to reflect preactivation or mobilization of the cortical regions that will be involved in the anticipated cognition (Rockstroh, Elbert, Lutzenberger, & Birbaumer, 1984). Cognition is superior when it has been ushered in by an SP. Facilitation of performance by SPs is shown most clearly using the "potential-related event" (Stamm, 1984) or the "brain trigger" paradigm (Bauer, 1984). Here, the EEG is monitored for a specific event of interest, say an SP; when that EEG event is detected, it triggers a cognitive task, such as presentation of a word to be memorized. This arrangement permits comparison of cognitive performance during distinctly contrasting EEG states.

Using a brain trigger paradigm, Stamm and his colleagues (reviewed by Stamm, 1984) found that monkeys who were allowed to attempt problems only after a negative SP, mastered a delayed choice task 5.8 times as quickly as yoked control monkeys who were given trials without respect to their EEG state. Parallel findings have been obtained with humans, who show better learning of concepts encoded in geometrical arrangements when stimulus presentation is triggered by a negative SP than a positive SP; the same was true for learning to associate pairs of words; negative SP triggers were superior to random triggers (reviewed by Bauer, 1984). The effects of a triggering negative SP obtained from a particular cortical location depends on the type of cognitive task that follows. In one experiment, participants were to choose as quickly as possible in a reaction time task between either two geometrical stimuli or two words. When presentation was initiated by negative SPs recorded from frontal lobe sites, reaction time was most facilitated for the geometrical task. However when parietal negative SPs triggered the trial, the participants were able to respond most rapidly to the linguistic task (reviewed by Stamm, 1984).

It is possible to train production of negative SPs using biofeedback. This has been explored most extensively by a group of German researchers led by Nils Bierbaumer (reviewed by Rockstroh et al., 1984). A little rocket ship on a video screen is the feedback display (see Fig. 10.6). The height of the rocket ship corresponds to the negativity-positivity of the SP. The task is to guide the ship during its 6-second flight across the screen so

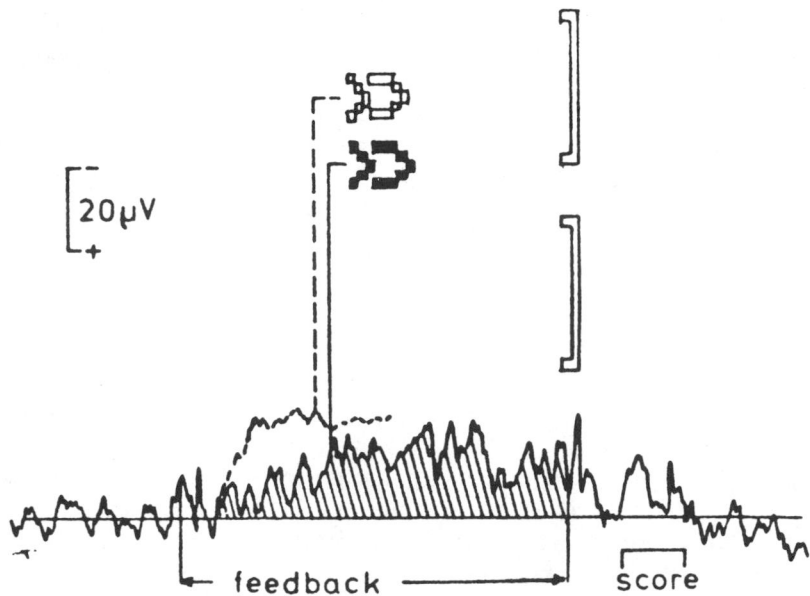

FIG. 10.6 Feedback display used to train voluntary control of negative slow potentials. (Greater negativity is indicated by the dotted line and higher rocket). From "Operant Control of Slow Brain Potentials" (p. 229) by B. Rockstroh et al., 1984, in T. Elbert et al. (Eds.), *Self-Regulation of the Brain and Behavior*, New York: Springer-Verlag. Copyright 1984 by Springer-Verlag Publishers. Reprinted by permission.

that it arrives at the specified goal on the right side of the screen. If the correct goal is reached, a point is added to the score displayed at the bottom right. Each point is worth about 40 cents. The dotted line and rocket show what would happen with increased negativity.

Using this procedure, participants were successfully trained to increase or decrease the negativity of SPs and to exercise this learned control in the absence of the feedback signal (Rockstroh, Elbert, Lutzenberger, & Birbaumer, 1982). Interspersed reaction time tests revealed faster button pushing to stop a hissing noise on negative SP trials for 17 of 20 participants. This study is a first step in exploring the use of negative SP biofeedback training to facilitate information processing.

It might be fruitful to combine negative SP biofeedback and the brain trigger paradigm. If successful, the individual would become adept at entering an optimum state for the task at hand, which would then automatically initiate the task. Presentation of the task should further reinforce the cortical self-regulation initiated by the biofeedback. The net result would be a type of automated "psychophysiological self-pacing."

A further refinement of optimum state training could incorporate the task performance X state data of a person to derive an individually tailored definition of optimum state. For example, the data might reveal that for a particular individual, SPs of a specific amplitude or slope are most highly associated with good performance; if so, only SPs fitting this description would be selected for biofeedback training and would become the brain triggers for stimulus presentation. The entire procedure could be automated.

Psychological Aspects of Optimum Function

A *peak experience* is like a momentary burst of wellness in the experiential domain, and, as such, may be the psychological signature of optimum function. Peak experiences may contribute to the development of self-actualization. Although, as Maslow observed, peak experiences occur more often for self-actualizers, most ordinary persons also peak. According to Maslow, an average person, during a peak experience, takes on many of the qualities found in self-actualizers on an extended basis. And, as a consequence of the peak experience, the person is changed, resulting in movement along the path of self-actualization.

Peak experiences are reported in varied circumstances. These valued moments would certainly include the types of experiences that come to mind when one is asked to name the "happiest moments of your life." Great creative moments, suddenly being "hit by" a piece of writing, an artwork, or some music, and moments of rapture associated with being in love are often mentioned. Religious persons sometimes ascribe the qualities of peak experiences to religious experiences, athletes to athletic experiences, and so on. The "runner's high" that is reported by some distance runners may be a type of peak experience. Peak experiences can also occur when their evocation cannot be linked to any distinct event, when a moment for unknown reasons, seems to just "come together." Peak experiences vary in emotional intensity from mildly exciting to the sorts of experiences Maslow believed an aged person could not safely endure very often.

What are the features that distinguish peak experiences from ordinary experiences? Maslow (1962) collected descriptions of peak experiences from personal interviews, written narratives, and pored over literature dealing with religion, mysticism, art, love, creativity, etc., to extract what he believed were the distinctive characteristics that set peak experiences apart from ordinary experiences. The following four qualities summarize his much more extensive descriptions of the phenomenon.

Completeness of the experience. The experience is apprehended as a complete unit, detached from any purpose or usefulness. It is fully attended to, indeed commanding total attention, fascination, and absorption. There is disorientation in time and space that often includes the perception of fusion with the world, and especially of existing in the here-now, or being immersed in the present.

Self-forgetfulness. Inhibitions vanish, and the person is more expressive, spontaneous, and innocently behaving. There may be Godlike total acceptance of the universe.

Feelings of goodness and wonder. The moment is experienced as good and desirable, never evil and undesirable. The person is full of wonder, awe, reverence, humility, and surrender. Afterward there is a feeling of having been fortunate or "graced."

Integration of the person. There is a total coming together of the person at all levels. The individual seems to be at the peak of his or her powers as everything "clicks" and is "in the groove." The person feels whole.

Somewhat different dimensions were obtained in a study of self-reports of peak experiences in art and music (Panzarella, 1980). Volunteers recruited at galleries and concerts were to describe an "intense, joyous experience of listening to music or looking at visual art." The experiences described had four major distinguishing features, each of which was a kind of ecstasy: (a) "renewal"—feeling refreshed and with a new view of the world as better and more beautiful, (b) "motor-sensory"—floating, tingling sensations, a faster heart beat, (c) "withdrawal"—loss of contact with the physical and social environment; and (d) "fusion-emotional"—happiness, joy, contentment.

The terms attached to peak experiences resemble those used to describe the mystical states that can be achieved through alterations in consciousness connected with the use of psychoactive drugs or the practice of contemplative meditation (see chapter 6). Maslow and others suggest that this is because there is only a single fundamental mystical transcendental experience, whether it is triggered chemically by LSD, nurtured patiently through pursuit of a meditative discipline, or stumbled upon by happenstance during everyday activities. It may also be that the apparent similarities of these experiences are more a measure of our limited understanding of them.

If peak experiences are a type of mystical experience, then practical directions for their cultivation can be found among the formal writings of Eastern meditative disciplines, and in more accessible form in the works of Western students of meditation such as Deikman (e.g., 1966). Some basics were introduced in chapter 6. It may be possible to pursue the peak experience in a more casual and light-hearted spirit, as suggested by Csikszentmihalyi's (1975) concept of "flow" in play (see following).

Behavioral Aspects of Optimum Function

Peak Performance

In the 1968 Mexico City Olympics Bob Beaman long-jumped more than 29 feet for a world record. At the time no jumper, including Beaman, had jumped even 28 feet. In 16 subsequent years of competition, no athlete has approached Beaman's 29' 2-1/2" record. Jesse Owens is best known for his performance at the 1936 Olympics in Germany because of its social and political impact. However, his greatest athletic accomplishment was the previous year when, in an Ohio State versus Michigan track meet, he broke six world records in the space in two hours.

Famous athletic achievements are associated with gifted athletes like Owens and Beaman, but ordinary human beings occasionally transcend their normal or average behavior, and do something that is, for them, remarkable. As far as one can tell, this potential is universal. A timid soul may save someone's life by performing an act of great heroism. An ordinary person may write a wonderful poem, paint a beautiful picture, or compose a moving piece of music. Everyone can think of an occasion when we "outdid ourselves," behaving in a way that we "didn't know we had in us." A young man who described himself as an enthusiastic, but not "first string" athlete, related the following:

> During one particular swim meet which was close, I was delegated to swim "third leg" or slow spot on a freestyle relay team. While I stood on the side of the pool, waiting my turn, I vividly remember telling myself that *this time* I was going to make my coach proud of me, that I was tired of being "behind," that *this was it*! Well, I hit the water, and I remember nothing else about the race except my coach's ecstatic face when I lifted my head. Somehow, I had come in ahead of everyone and put our team out in front. Our fast "anchor man" went on to win. We also won the meet. I was so excited and pleased with myself. To this day I can never remember doing well in another swim meet. It definitely was *not* my usual level of functioning. (Privette, 1981, p. 60)

These episodes of superior functioning are examples of *peak performance,* which has been defined as any "behavior that goes beyond the level at which a person normally functions" (Privette & Landsman, 1983, p. 195).

Not surprisingly, individuals describe their peak performances in varied human activities in terms that are similar to Maslow's (1962) analysis of peak experiences. Privette and Landsman (1983) developed 40 questionnaire items from content analyses of narrative accounts of " . . . one time you did something that you didn't know you were capable of doing" (p. 196). A new sample of college students then used the items to describe a personal peak performance as well as an occasion on which their behavior was average in the same situation. Behaviors included such diverse activities as a saxophone recital, saving farm animals from a burning barn, and bowling a game far above the respondent's typical score. The six items with the greatest mean difference between ordinary and peak performances were, in descending order: (a) "Must continue until finished," (b) "Left with fulfillment," (c) "All of me working together," (d) "Action just came out of me," (e) "Experience its own reward," and (f) "Situation demanded from me."

Other research indicates that there are three common elements of high level performance that cut across varied activities such as scientific discoveries, acts of invention, artistic creation, and athletic performance (Privette, 1981). These are : (a) "absorption and clarity"—clear and intense focus upon the object of the activity and upon oneself, (b) "spontaneity"—the behavior seems to "come by itself," and (c) "expression of self"—a feeling of wholeness and fulfillment.

Flow

Csikszentmihalyi (1975) has proposed that peak performance and peak experience sometimes occur together. Self-reports were obtained from a varied sample of highly skilled rock-climbers, chess players, composers, basketball players, and professional dancers. From these he identified a state he called *flow*, which seems to combine the affective qualities of the peak experience and the superior behavior of peak performance. Flow is "the wholistic sensation present when we act with total involvement" (Csikszentmihalyi, 1975, p. 43).

Flow involves acting without conscious intervention and occurs only when an individual is engaged in some form of structured interaction with the environment. Flow is often seen in play—"people are most human, whole, free, and creative when they play" (Csikzentmihalyi, 1975, p. 42).

The flow experience is described in the following narrative from a rock-climber:

> The mystique of rock climbing is climbing; you get to the top of the rock glad it's over but really wish it would go forever. The justification of climbing is climbing like the justification of poetry is writing; you don't conquer anything except things in yourself . . . the act of writing justifies poetry. Climbing is the same; recognizing that you are a flow. The purpose of the flow is to keep on flowing, not looking for a peak or utopia but staying in the flow. It is not a moving up but a continuous flowing; you move up only to keep the flow going. There is no possible reason for climbing except the climbing itself; it is a self-communication. (Csikzentmihalyi, 1975, p. 54)

The state of flow can occur only when there is a balance betweeen the opportunities or challenges of the environment and the individual's capa-

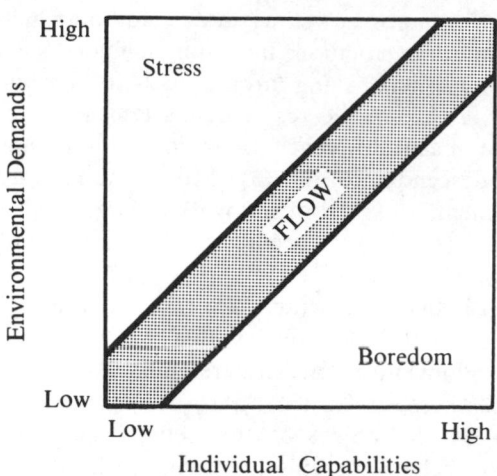

FIG. 10.7 Flow is possible when there is balance between opportunities (challenges) and individual capabilities. From *Beyond Boredom and Anxiety: The Experience of Play in Work and Games* (p. 49) by M. Csikszentmihalyi, 1975, San Francisco: Jossey-Bass. Copyright 1975 by Jossey-Bass, Inc. Adapted by permission.

bilities. This is illustrated in Fig. 10.7. Perhaps everyday settings such as work and school could be re-structured in order to increase flow experiences. Individualized "flow profiles" might be derived as diagnostic tools, in order to better match up individual abilities with environmental demands (Csiksentmihalyi, 1975).

Athletics

At the top of any sport is an elite group of genetically gifted, highly practiced, thoroughly conditioned, well coached athletes, all of whom are strongly motivated to excell. These performers have long since fully mastered all of the physical skills that are necessary for their chosen event. Yet, a few will consistently outperform the others. What is special about these exceptionally successful athletes? The Olympic decathlon gold medalist, Bruce Jenner, has said, "I always felt that my greatest asset was not my physical ability, it was my mental ability" (Garfield & Bennett, 1984, p. 9).

Many athletes and coaches have begun to suspect that, at every level, psychophysiological mastery is as essential for successful performance as command of the physical movements that must be executed. Even casual weekend athletes have been exposed to this view via popular books such as *The Inner Game of Tennis* (Gallwey, 1974) and *The Inner Athlete* (Nideffer, 1976b). The holistic approach to athletic performance has a longer history in Europe, especially in Eastern European countries, than in the United States where it has only recently become accepted. However, at present in the United States, sport psychology is one of the fastest growing psychology career fields.

The practice of sport psychology is long on enthusiasm and short on knowledge. There is no substantial body of research to support many of the techniques that are advocated by practitioners and accepted by athletes and coaches eager for an edge over the competition. Nonetheless, training programs based on some of the psychophysiological concepts discussed in this text have become commonplace. There are several structured programs available to the interested athlete, for example, a six-step "peak performance training" method developed by Garfield (Garfield & Bennett, 1984). The material that follows is a brief survey of current thinking in this field, organized around a holistic way of conceptualizing athletic performance that has been proposed by Suinn (1980). Athletic performance is assumed to be a function of natural aptitude plus acquisition of skill. Skill acquisition can be broken down into strengthening correct responses, eliminating incorrect responses, and transferring these skills to competition.

Strengthening Correct Responses

The sprinter must learn the proper pumping arm action to accelerate out of the starting blocks; the basketball player must be able to dribble competently with either hand; the batter must produce a smooth, level swing in baseball. Some of the ideas in this text can be applied, even in learning such specific motor skills. As discussed in chapter 5, Jacobson (1929) long ago pointed out that tension in muscles not used in a given task wastes energy. For example, an ultramarathoner, who may run 100 miles, will have more energy for running, if he or she can learn to minimize tension in all muscles that are not needed to produce each stride. Excess muscle tension may interfere with the smooth execution of a motor response. In chapter 5 a case was discussed involving a string player whose playing benefitted from biofeedback-based relaxation training of muscles opposing bowing action (Morasky, Reynolds, & Clarke, 1981). Athletes may have misplaced muscle tension, and not necessarily be aware of it. Careful diagnosis of the problem and muscle-specific biofeedback training should enable these athletes to improve activities such as putting in golf, serving in tennis, and free-throw shooting in basketball.

Sometimes an even more subtle analysis of motor skills can be fruitful, as illustrated in the relationship between shooting performance and several physiological variables (Daniels & Landers, 1981). Nationally ranked United States shooters with at least 7 years of competitive experience were studied. Pretesting revealed several heart and respiratory responses that negatively affected shooting performance. The problem varied from shooter to shooter: (a) shooting with heart rate greater than 100 BPM, (b) holding the breath too long before shooting, and (c) failing to shoot between heartbeats. Matched subjects were assigned to a biofeedback treatment group or a control group. The biofeedback subjects heard audio feedback of heart rate or respiration, depending on their specific problem, through a headset for five sessions of training involving 40 shots each. Depending on their disregulation, the shooters were to learn to keep their heart rate below 100 BPM when shooting, shoot before a warning signal indicated an extended breath hold, or shoot early in the cardiac cycle. Feedback was gradually phased out across training. The trained subjects improved significantly in both their physiological performance and their shooting performance, whereas the controls did not. This type of self-monitoring has many potential applications in athletics.

Some athletes attempt to sharpen their skills by systematically "practicing" them mentally, using imagery. *Visuo-motor behavior rehearsal* (VMBR) is the most widely used technique (Suinn, 1980). In VMBR, the athlete first learns to relax deeply using progressive relaxation, then, while relaxed, imagines a carefully pre-determined sequence of behaviors, thoughts, and emotions, attempting to experience them as realistically as possible. An individualized audio tape is usually used to facilitate home practice. The benefits should depend upon the athlete producing vivid, detailed images of correctly executed behaviors. Consistent with this, good imagers profit more from mental practice as compared to poor imagers (Ryan & Simons, 1982). And, as might be expected, athletes who already have a clear idea of how to properly perform the skill are at an advantage. Noel (1980) found that advanced amateur tennis players improved their serves in competition following a program of VMBR, whereas less adept players did not profit from their mental practice. Also, mental rehearsal is most helpful when there is a strong cognitive component to the athletic skills practiced, as in sequencing a complex string of movements (Feltz & Landers, 1983). Events such as gymnastics, figure skating, and slalom skiing, which require a smooth flow of movements from one behavior to the next, are prime candidates for VMBR.

Several types of preparatory activities may enhance athletic performance. Some steps are seemingly common sense, but often overlooked. For example, in team sports it is helpful to discuss with the team any anticipatory cognitive changes that are seen consistently in particular team members just before competing, such as withdrawing, becoming irritable, or giddy, so as to avoid misunderstandings and friction (Ravissa, 1984).

Appropriate psychophysiological warmup should become as routine a part of getting ready to perform as stretching and exercising the skeletal muscles. An important aspect of this is moving to the optimum arousal level for the event. As discussed earlier in this chapter, for certain events this may involve primarily "psyching up," for others "psyching down." Failure to perform at the optimum arousal level may explain why some athletes perform well in practice, only to "choke" in competition. This is particularly the case for athletes who suffer from "performance anxiety" (e.g., Landers, 1982), although some athletes perform best when they feel somewhat stressed. A variety of self-regulation techniques have been used successfully to increase or decrease arousal in preparation for competition (Suinn, 1980). The general importance of self-efficacy was discussed earlier in this chapter; strengthening the perception of self-efficacy is a useful element in preparation to perform.

The other view of the relationship between self-efficacy and athletics is also of interest—the effect of athletic participation on the athlete's self-concept. In one study, 5th and 6th graders ran a minimum of one mile at least three times per week for seven weeks (Percy, Dzuiban, & Martin, 1981). Their image of themselves, as measured by a self-concept scale for children, was more positive following the program, as compared to control children who did not participate. More generally, it appears that physical fitness strengthens the self-concept in a variety of settings, but does not affect other personality variables (reviewed by Folkins & Sime, 1981).

The ability to appropriately direct and control attention according to situational demands is a critical element of athletic performance. The attentional requirements of an athletic event vary along several dimensions including breadth of focus and the extent to which attention is directed to external environmental cues or inward (Nideffer, 1976a). For example, a running back in football must maintain broad attentional focus in order to notice patterns of blocking and shifting defensive alignments, but a sprinter in the starting blocks must attend very narrowly to the sound of the starter's pistol. A third attentional difference among athletic events is that for some events it is possible to maintain a fixed attentional style, but others may require frequent rapid shifts in orientation (Schmidt, 1984). A good example of the latter is the goalkeeper in soccer who must maintain a broad focus to follow the movements of many players, until there is a shot on the goal, at which time the goalie must instantly narrow his or her focus to the ball, and not be distracted by any other stimuli; following the save, the goalkeeper must broaden focus to assess the situation and decide what to do with the ball.

Many training techniques have been developed for strengthening control of the width, direction, and flexibility of attention in athletes. Some sport psychologists encourage their athletes to learn to think precisely the same thoughts in practice as in competition (Schmidt, 1984). In baseball and softball a good test for attentional narrowing is to play catch trying to hit, with each throw, one of six different targets on the torso. It is helpful to become "centered" periodically (Ravizza, 1984). The athlete briefly disengages from reacting to the demands of the event and returns to a known, practiced psychophysiological condition in which physiological and cognitive resources can be readied for continuation of the performance. The athlete usually practices centering to a specific behavioral cue if possible, such as the "ready" position adopted by an baseball infielder just before the pitch or a football lineman just before the ball is snapped. In sports with more continuous activity, "quick centering" may be taught, as whenever the ball goes out of bounds in field hockey (Ravizza, 1984). In general, the aim of these techniques is to get the mind involved with relevant aspects of the situation, but in a way that does not interfere with performance.

Transfer to Competition

The conditions of practice should approximate those of competition. Basketball coaches have their players practice free throws when they are tired, which is the condition in which they must attempt free throws in a game. Transfer is facilitated if in practice the athlete always attempts a quality performance with competition level concentration—"being there in the present" (Schmidt, 1984). Attention control and centering should be linked to cues that are present in the competitive situation. Athletes may be taught to explore a novel performance setting in order to establish a physical object to which the athlete can assign cue properties, such as by associating with it a positive suggestion—"Calm and strong." Normally negative aspects of competition can be made to facilitate performance by proper preparation. For example, athletes may welcome adverse weather conditions if they are better prepared for them than their competition; one athlete learned to look forward to pain because it indicated that he was putting forth his best effort (Suinn, 1980).

Eliminating Incorrect Responses

Athletes often execute motor skills incorrectly without being aware of it. The first step in correcting these problems is to bring them into awareness, so that the athlete can discriminate between correct and incorrect performance. The process may be aided by having the athlete deliberately practice the inappropriate responses.

Extended periods of poor performance, or "slumps," involve special psychological considerations. Athletes often randomly move from one attempted corrective measure to another, growing more frustrated with each unsuccessful attempt to break out of their slump, which further impairs their performance. Self-efficacy also suffers. Suinn (1980) suggests that these problems will be minimized if the athlete learns to perceive each unsuccessful adjustment as a positive step—information gained that helps narrow the field of possibilities. Also, the unreasonable goal of snapping out of the slump suddenly, should be replaced by the more modest goal of slow improvement.

Negative self-talk—"I hope I don't screw up!"—obviously undermines self-efficacy. It also involves a serious attentional error. A negatively stated goal, like "Don't fall off the balance beam!", is not useful in directing behavior because it does not indicate the correct response; and, by occupying the attention of the athlete, even briefly, it blocks the occurrence of relevant positive cognitions—all too often the fear is self-fulfilling. Thus, athletes must learn to think exclusively about what they want to make happen and not what they do *not* want to have happen. Several techniques may be helpful. The athlete who proceeds through a predetermined series of thoughts during a gymnastic routine will not engage in negative self-talk because consciousness is already occupied. Athletes can improve their skill in ignoring distractions and focussing on relevant cognitions by doing mental arithmetic problems while teammates try to distract them (Schmidt, 1984). Performers can learn to resist negative self-talk by practicing a relaxation procedure while playing an audio tape of negative self-talk (Ravissa, 1984).

References

Abbott, B. B., Schoen, L. S., & Badia, P. (1984). Predictable and unpredictable shock: Behavioral measures of aversion and physiological measures of stress. *Psychological Bulletin, 96*, 45-71.

Abikoff, H., Gittelman-Klein, R., & Klein, D. F. (1977). Validation of a classroom observation code for hyperactive children. *Journal of Consulting and Clinical Psychology, 45*, 772-783.

Abramson, L. Y., Seligman, M. E. P., & Teasdale, J. D. (1978). Learned helplessness in humans: Critique and reformulation. *Journal of Abnormal Psychology, 87*, 49-74.

Adams, H. E., Feuerstein, M., & Fowler, J. L. (1980). The migraine headache: A review of parameters, theories, and interventions. *Psychological Bulletin, 87*, 217-237.

Ader, R. (1971). Experimentally induced gastric lesions: Results and implications of studies in animals. *Advances in Psychosomatic Medicine, 6*, 1-39.

Ader, R. (1981). Behavioral influences on immune responses. In S. M. Weiss, J. A. Herd, & B. H. Fox (Eds.), *Perspectives on behavioral medicine* (pp. 163-182). New York: Academic Press.

Ahlquist, R. P. (1948). A study of the adrenergic receptors. *American Journal of Physiology, 153*, 586-600.

Akil, H., & Watson, S. J. (1980). The role of endogenous opiates in pain control. In H. W. Kosterlitz & L. Y. Terenius (Eds.), *Pain and society* (pp. 201-221). Weinheim: Verlag Chemie.

Alexander, A. B. (1981). Asthma. In S. N. Haynes & L. Gannon (Eds.), *Psychosomatic disorders: A psychophysiological approach to etiology and treatment* (pp. 320-358). New York: Praeger.

Alexander, A. B., Gerd, J., Cropp, A., & Chai, H. (1979). Effects of relaxation training on pulmonary mechanics in children with asthma. *Journal of Applied Behavior Analysis, 12*, 27-35.

Alexander, F. (1939). Emotional factors in essential hypertension. *Psychosomatic Medicine, 1*, 173-179.

Alexander, F. (1950). *Psychosomatic medicine: Its principles and applications.* New York: W. W. Norton.

Allen, R. A., & Mills, G. K. (1982). The effects of unilateral plethysmographic feedback of temporal artery activity during migraine head pain. *Journal of Psychosomatic Research, 26,* 133-140.

Altman, D. (1981). Peptic ulcer disease—The flowers that bloom in the spring—Medical Staff Converence, University of California, San Francisco. *Western Journal of Medicine, 135,* 201-207.

Amado, H., & Lustman, P. J. (1982). Attention deficit disorders persisting in adulthood: A review. *Comprehensive psychiatry, 23,* 300-314.

American Psychiatric Association. (1980). *Diagnostic and statistical manual of mental disorders* (3rd ed.) Washington, DC: American Psychiatric Association.

American Psychological Association. (1984). *Graduate study in psychology and related fields.* Washington, DC: American Psychological Association.

Anand, B. K., Chhina, G. S., & Singh, B. (1961). Some aspects of electroencephalographic studies in Yogis. *Electroencephalography & Clinical Neurophysiology, 13,* 452-456.

Anderson, D. E. (1981). Inhibitory behavioral stress effects upon blood pressure regulation. In S. M. Weiss, J. A. Herd, & B. H. Fox (Eds.), *Perspectives in behavioral medicine* (pp. 307-319). New York: Academic Press.

Anderson, D. E. (1984). Interactions of stress, salt, and blood pressure. *Annual Review of Physiology, 46,* 143-153.

Andrasik, F., Blanchard, E. B., Arena, J. G., Saunders, N. L., & Baron, K. D. (1982). Psychophysiology of recurrent headache: Methodological issues and new empirical findings. *Behavior Therapy, 13,* 407-429.

Andrasik, F., Blanchard, E. B., Arena, J. G., Teders, S. J., Teevan, R. C., & Rodichok, L. D. (1982). Psychological functioning in headache sufferers. *Psychosomatic Medicine, 44,* 171-182.

Andrews, F. M., & Withers, S. B. (1976). *Social indicators of well-being.* New York: Plenum.

Andrews, J. M. (1964). Neuromuscular re-education of the hemiplegic with the aid of the electromyograph. *Archives of Physical Medicine and Rehabilitation, 45,* 530-532.

Anliker, J. (1977). Biofeedback from the perspective of cybernetics and systems science. In J. Beatty & H. Legewie (Eds.), *Biofeedback and behavior* (pp. 21-45). New York: Plenum.

Aronoff, G. M., Evans, W. O., & Enders, P. L. (1983). A review of follow-up studies of multidisciplinary pain units. *Pain, 16,* 1-11.

Atkinson, R. L., Atkinson, R. C., & Hilgard, E. R. (1983). *Introduction to psychology* (8th ed.). New York: Harcourt, Brace, Jovanovich.

Audy, J. R. (1973). Health as a quantifiable property. *British Medical Journal, 4,* 486-487.

August, G. J., & Stewart, M. A. (1983). Familial subtypes of childhood hyperactivity. *Journal of Nervous and Mental Disease, 171,* 362-368.

Ayllon, T., Layman, D., & Kandel, H. J. (1975). A behavioral-educational alternative to drug control of hyperactive children. *Journal of Applied Behavior Analysis, 8,* 137-146.

Bagchi, B. K., & Wenger, M A. (1957). Electro-physiological correlates of some Yogi exercises. *Electroencephalography & Clinical Neurophysiology, Supplement 7,* 132-149.

Bakal, D. A. (1979). *Psychology and medicine.* New York: Springer.

Bakan, P. (1969). Hypnotizability, laterality of eye movement and functional brain asymmetry. *Perceptual and Motor Skills, 28,* 927-932.

Balaschak, B. A. (1976). Teacher-implemented behavior modification in a case of organically based epilepsy. *Journal of Consulting and Clinical Psychology, 44,* 218-223.

Bandura, A. (1977). Self-efficacy: Toward a unifying theory of behavioral change. *Psychological Review, 84,* 191-215.

Bandura, A., & Adams, N. E. (1977). Analysis of self-efficacy theory of behavioral change. *Cognitive Therapy and Research, 1*, 287-310.

Bandura, A., & Schunk, D. H. (1981). Cultivating competence, self-efficacy, and intrinsic interest through proximal self-motivation. *Journal of Personality and Social Psychology, 41*, 586-598.

Barber, J. (1977). Rapid induction analgesia: A clinical report. *The American Journal of Clinical Hypnosis, 19*, 138-147.

Barber, J. (1980). Hypnosis and the unhypnotizable. *The American Journal of Clinical Hypnosis, 23*, 4-9.

Barber, J., & Mayer, D. (1977). Evaluation of the efficacy and neural mechanism of a hypnotic analgesia procedure in experimental and clinical dental pain. *Pain, 4*, 41-48.

Barber, T. X. (1969). *Hypnosis: A scientific approach.* New York: Van Nostrand Reinhold.

Barchas, J. D., Akil, H., Elliott, G. R., Holman, R. B., Watson, S. J. (1978). Behavioral neurochemistry: Neuroregulation and behavioral states. *Science, 200*, 964-973.

Barefoot, J. C., Dahlstrom, W. G., & Williams, R. B., Jr. (1983). Hostility, CHD incidence, and total mortality: A 25-year follow-up study of 255 physicians. *Psychosomatic Medicine, 45*, 59-63.

Barkley, R. A., & Cunningham, C. E. (1978). Do stimulant drugs improve the academic performance of hyperkinetic children? *Clinical Pediatrics, 17*, 85-92.

Barofsky, I. (1981). Issues and approaches to the psychosocial assessment of the cancer patient. In C. K. Prokop & L. A. Bradley (Eds.), *Medical psychology: Contributions to behavioral medicine* (pp. 55-65). New York: Academic Press.

Bartus, R. T., Dean III, R. L., Beer, B. & Lippa, A. S. (1982). The cholinergic hypothesis of geriatric memory dysfunction. *Science, 217*, 408-417.

Basbaum, A. I. (1980). The anatomy of pain and pain modulation. In H. W. Kosterlitz & L. Y. Terenius (Eds.). *Pain and society* (pp. 93-122). Weinheim: Verlag Chemie.

Basmajian, J. V. (1963). Control and training of individual motor units. *Science, 141*, 440-441.

Basmajian, J. V. (1967). *Muscles alive.* Baltimore, MD: Williams & Wilkins.

Bassen, C. R. (1977). Immunosuppressive agents. In M. S. Thaler, R. D. Klausner, & H. J. Cohen (Eds.), *Medical immunology* (pp. 415-436). Philadelphia, PA: Lippincott.

Bauer, H. (1984). Regulation of slow brain potentials affects task performance. In T. Elbert, B. Rockstroh, W. Lutzenberger, & N. Birbaumer (Eds.), *Self-regulation of the brain and behavior* (pp. 216-226). New York: Springer-Verlag.

Bauer, R. H., & Jones, C. N. (1976). Feedback training of 36-45 Hz EEG activity in the visual cortex and hippocampus of cats: Evidence for sensory and motor involvement. *Physiology and Behavior, 17*, 885-890.

Beals, R. K., & Hickman, N. W. (1972). Industrial injuries of the back and extremities. *The Journal of Bone and Joint Surgery, 54-A*, 1593-1611.

Beary, J. F., & Benson, H. (1974). A simple psychophysiologic technique which elicits the hypometabolic changes of the relaxation response. *Psychosomatic Medicine, 36,* 115-120.

Beatty, J., Greenberg, A., Deibler, W. P., & O'Hanlon, J. F. (1974). Operant control of occipital theta rhythm affects performance in a radar monitoring task. *Science, 183*, 871-873.

Becker, D. E., & Shapiro, D. (1981). Physiological responses to clicks during Zen, Yoga, and TM meditation. *Psychophysiology, 18*, 694-699.

Becker, E. (1961). *Zen: A rational critique.* New York: W. W. Norton.

Beecher, H. K. (1956). Relationship of significance of wound to pain experienced. *Journal of the American Medical Association, 161*, 1609-1613.

Beecher, H. K. (1959). *Measurement of subjective responses: Quantitative effects of drugs.* New York: Oxford University Press.

Bennett, C. E., & Suter, S. (1980). Biofeedback-regulated asymmetries in facial skin temperature. *Psychological Reports, 46*, 29-30.

Benson, H., Arns, P. A., & Hoffman, J. W. (1981). The relaxation response and hypnosis. *The International Journal of Clinical and Experimental Hypnosis, 29,* 259-270.

Benson, H., Beary, J. F., & Carol, M. P. (1974). The relaxation response. *Psychiatry, 37,* 37-46.

Benson, H., Lehmann, J. W., Malhotra, M. S., Goldman, R. F., Hopkins, J., & Epstein, M. D. (1982). Body temperature changes during the practice of g Yum-mo yoga. *Nature, 295,* 234-236.

Berger, H. (1929). Uber das elektroenkephalogramm des Menschen. *Archiv fur Psychiatrie und Nervenkrankheiten, 87,* 527-580.

Berger, P. A., & Rexroth, K. (1980). Tardive dyskinesia: Clinical, biological, and pharmacological perspectives. *Schizophrenia Bulletin, 6,* 102-116.

Berkson, D. M., Stamler, J., Lindberg, H. A., Miller, W., Mathias, H., Lasky, H., & Hall, Y. (1960). Socioeconomic correlates of atherosclerotic and hypertensive heart disease. *Annals of the New York Academy of Sciences, 84,* 835-860.

Besson, J. M. R. (1980). Supraspinal modulation of the segmental transmission of pain. In H. W. Kosterlitz & L. Y. Terenius (Eds.). *Pain and society* (pp. 161-182). Weinheim: Verlag Chemie.

Black, A. H., Cott, A., & Pavloski, R. (1977). The operant learning theory approach to biofeedback training. In G. E. Schwartz & J. Beatty (Eds.), *Biofeedback: Theory and research* (pp. 89-127). New York: Academic Press.

Blanchard, E. B., Andrasik, F., Neff, D. F., Teders, S. J., Pallmeyer, T. P., Arena, J. G., Jurish, S. E., Saunders, N. L., & Ahles, T.A. (1982). Sequential comparisons of relaxation training and biofeedback in the treatment of three kinds of chronic headache or, the machines may be necessary some of the time. *Behavior Research & Therapy, 20,* 469-481.

Blanchard, E. B., & Young, L. D. (1973). Self-control of cardiac functioning: A promise as yet unfulfilled. *Psychological Bulletin, 79,* 145-163.

Blass, J. P. (1984). Stages of Alzheimer's disease. *Journal of the American Geriatrics Society, 32,* 4.

Blizard, D., Cowings, P., & Miller, N. E. (1975). Visceral responses to opposite types of autogenic training imagery. *Biological Psychology, 3,* 49-55.

Blumenthal, J. A., Williams, R. B., Long, Y., Schanberg, S. M., & Thompson, L. W. (1978). Type A behavior pattern and coronary atherosclerosis. *Circulation, 58,* 634-639.

Borkovec, T. D., & Sides, J. K. (1979). Critical procedural variables related to the physiological effects of progressive relaxation: A review. *Behaviour Research and Therapy, 17,* 119-125.

Bosco, J. J., & Robin, S. S. (1980). Hyperkinesis: Prevalence and treatment. In C. K. Whalen & B. Henker (Eds.), *Hyperactive children* (pp. 173-187). New York: Academic Press.

Brackett, N. C., Jr. (1983). Hypertension. In H. F. Conn (Ed.), *Current therapy: 1983* (pp. 197-205). Philadelphia, PA: W. B. Saunders.

Bradley, C. (1937). The behavior of children receiving Benzedrine. *American Journal of Psychiatry, 94,* 577-585.

Brady, J. (1958). Ulcers in executive monkeys. *Scientific American, 119,* 362-404.

Brand, R. J., Rosenman, R. H., Sholtz, R. I., & Friedman, M. (1976). Multivariate prediction of coronary heart disease in the Western Collaborative Group Study compared to the findings of the Framingham Study. *Circulation, 53,* 938-955.

Braud, L. W. (1978). The effects of frontal EMG biofeedback and progressive relaxation upon hyperactivity and its behavioral concomitants. *Biofeedback and Self-Regulation, 3,* 69-89.

Braud, L. W., Lupin, M. N., & Braud, W. G. (1975). The use of electromyographic biofeedback in the control of hyperactivity. *Journal of Learning Disabilities, 8,* 420-425.

Bregman, N. J., & McAllister, H. (1982). Motivation and skin temperature biofeedback: Yerkes-Dodson revisited. *Psychophysiology, 19,* 282-285.

Brener, J. (1974). A general model of voluntary control applied to the phenomena of learned cardiovascular change. In P. A. Obrist, A. H. Black, J. Brener, & L. V. DiCara (Eds.), *Cardiovascular psychophysiology* (pp. 365-391). Chicago, IL: Aldine-Atherton.

Brickman, P., Coates, D., & Janoff-Bulman, R. (1978). Lottery winners and accident victims: Is happiness relative? *Journal of Personality and Social Psychology, 36*, 917-927.

Brooks, G. R., & Richardson, F. C. (1980). Emotional skills training: A treatment program for duodenal ulcer. *Behavior Therapy, 11*, 198-207.

Brown, B. B. (1970). Awareness of EEG-subjective activity relationships detected within a closed feedback system. *Psychophysiology, 7*, 451-464.

Brown, B. B. (1974). *New mind, new body*. New York: Harper & Row.

Brownell, G. L., Budinger, T. F., Lauterbur, P. C., & McGeer, P. L. (1982). Positron tomography and nuclear magnetic resonance imaging. *Science, 215*, 619-626.

Buchsbaum, M. S., Davis, G. C., Coppola, R., & Naber, D. (1981). Opiate pharmacology and individual differences. II. Somatosensory evoked potentials. *Pain, 10*, 367-377.

Budzynski, T. H., & Stoyva, J. M. (1969). An instrument for producing deep muscle relaxation by means of analog information feedback. *Journal of Applied Behavior Analysis, 2*, 231-237.

Bunge, M. (1980). *The mind-body problem: A psychobiological approach*. New York: Pergamon Press.

Bureau of the Census. (1906). *Mortality statistics: 1900-1904*. Washington, DC: U.S. Government Printing Office.

Byrne, D. (1964). Repression-sensitization as a dimension of personality. In B. A. Maher (Ed.), *Progress in experimental personality research* (Vol. 1, pp. 169-220). New York: Academic Press.

Byrne, D. (1981). Type A behavior, life-events and myocardial infarction: Independent or related risk factors? *British Journal of Medical Psychology, 54*, 371-377.

Caldwell, J. R., Cobb, S., Dowling, M. D., & Jough, D. (1970). The dropout problem in antihypertension treatment. *Journal of Chronic Diseases, 22*, 579-592.

Calne, D. B. (1984). Progress in Parkinson's disease. *The New England Journal of Medicine, 310*, 523-524.

Cameron, P., Titus, D. G., Kostin, J., & Kostin, M. (1973). The life satisfaction of nonnormal persons. *Journal of Consulting and Clinical Psychology, 41*, 207-214.

Campbell, T. (1854). *The poetical works of Thomas Campbell* (W. A. Hill, Ed.). Boston: Little, Brown.

Cangello, V. W. (1961). The use of hypnotic suggestion for relief in malignant disease. *International Journal of Clinical and Experimental Hypnosis, 9*, 17-22.

Cangello, V. W. (1962). Hypnosis for the patient with cancer. *The American Journal of Clinical Hypnosis, 4*, 215-226.

Cannon, W. B. (1930). The autonomic nervous system: An interpretation. The Linacre lecture, 1930. *Lancet, II*, 1109-1115.

Cannon, W. B. (1939). *The wisdom of the body* (2nd ed.). New York: Norton.

Cannon, W. B. (1942). Voodoo death. *American Anthropologist, 44*, 169-181.

Cannon, W. B., & Britton, S. W. (1927). The influence of motion and emotion on medullia-drenal secretion. *American Journal of Physiology, 79*, 433-465.

Cannon, W. B., & Washburn, A. L. (1912). An explanation of hunger. *American Journal of Physiology, 29*, 441-454.

Cantwell, D. P. (1972). Psychiatric illness in the families of hyperactive children. *Archives of General Psychiatry, 27*, 414-417.

Carlson, N. R. (1980). *Physiology of behavior* (2nd ed.). Boston: Allyn and Bacon.

Carruthers, M. A. (1969). Aggression and atheroma. *Lancet, II*, 1170-1171.

Carter, B. D., Elkins, G. R., & Kraft, S. P. (1982). Hemispheric asymmetry as a model for hypnotic phenomena: A review and analysis. *The American Journal of Clinical Hypnosis, 24*, 204-210.

Carter, S., & Gold, A. (1968). Convulsions in children. *New England Journal of Medicine, 278*, 315-317.

CASS principal investigators and their associates. (1983). Coronary artery surgery study (CASS): A randomized trial of coronary artery bypass surgery: Survival data. *Circulation, 68*, 939-950.

Castelli, W. P., Abbott, R. D., & McNamara, P. M. (1983). Summary estimates of cholesterol used to predict coronary heart disease. *Circulation, 67*, 730-734.

Caton, R. (1875). The electric currents of the brain. *British Medical Journal, 2*, 278.

Chai, H. (1975). Management of severe chronic perennial asthma in children. *Advances in Asthma and Allergy, 2*, 1-12.

Chapman, C. R., Bendetti, C., Colpitts, Y. H., & Gerlach, R. (1983). Naloxone fails to reverse pain thresholds elevated by acupuncture: Acupuncture analgesia reconsidered. *Pain, 16*, 13-31.

Chapman, C. R., Chen, A. C., & Bonica, J. J. (1977). Effects of intrasegmental electrical acupuncture on dental pain: Evaluation by threshold estimation and sensory decision theory. *Pain, 3*, 213- 227.

Check, W. A. (1982). H2 antagonists: Long-term ulcer therapy? *Journal of the American Medical Association, 248*, 1683-1685.

Chesney, M. A., Eagleston, J. R., & Rosenman, R. H. (1981). Type A behavior: Assessment and intervention. In C. K. Prokop & L. A. Bradley (Eds.), *Medical psychology: Contributions to behavioral medicine* (pp. 19-36). New York: Academic Press.

Cinciripini, P. M., & Floreen, A. (1982). An evaluation of a behavioral program for chronic pain. *Journal of Behavioral Medicine, 5*, 375-389.

Cobb, L. A., Thomas, G. I., Dillard, D. H., Merendino, K. A., & Bruce, R. A. (1959). An evaluation of internal-mammary-artery ligation by a double-blind technic. *New England Journal of Medicine, 260*, 1115-1118.

Cobb, S., & Rose, R. M. (1973). Hypertension, peptic ulcer, and diabetes in air traffic controllers. *Journal of the American Medical Association, 224*, 489-492.

Cohen, D. (1972). Magnetoencephalography: Detection of the brain's electrical activity with a superconducting magnetometer. *Science, 175*, 664-666.

Cohen, F., & Lazarus, R. S. (1979). Coping with the stresses of illness. In G. C. Stone, F. Cohen, & N. E. Adler (Eds.), *Health psychology: A handbook* (pp. 217-254). San Francisco, CA: Jossey-Bass.

Cohen, M. J., McArthur, D. L., & Rickles, W. H. (1980). Comparison of four biofeedback treatments for migraine headache: Psychological and headache variables. *Psychosomatic medicine, 42*, 463-480.

Compton, W. C., & Becker, G. M. (1983). Self-actualization and experience with Zen meditation: Is a learning period necessary for meditation? *Journal of Clinical Psychology, 39*, 925-932.

Cott, A., Pavloski, R. P., & Black, A. H. (1979). Reducing epileptic seizures through operant conditioning of central nervous system activity: Procedural variables. *Science, 203*, 73-75.

Cowings, P. S., Billingham, J., & Toscano, W. B. (1977). Learned control of multiple autonomic responses to compensate for the debilitating effects of motion sickness. *Therapy in Psychosomatic Medicine, 4*, 318-323.

Coyle, J. T., Price, D. L., & DeLong, M. R. (1983). Alzheimer's disease: A disorder of cortical cholinergic innervation. *Science, 219*, 1184-1190.

Craib, A. R. & Perry, M. (1975). *EEG handbook* (2nd ed.). Fullerton, CA: Beckman Instruments.

Crapper, D. R., Karlik, S., & DeBoni, U. (1978). Aluminum and other metals in senile (Alzheimer) dementia. In R. Katzman, R. D. Terry & K. L. Bick (Eds.). *Alzheimer's disease: Senile dementia and related disorders* (pp. 471-485). New York: Raven Press.

Creer, T. L. (1979). *Asthma therapy: A behavioral health care system for respiratory disorders.* New York: Springer Publishing.

Creighton, C. (1891). *A history of epidemics in Britain* (Vol. 1). London: Cambridge University Press.

Crisp, A. H. (1981). Laterality of migraine and reported affect: The relavance of an hypothesis concerning the nature of migraine. *Journal of Affective Disorders, 3,* 71-75.

Critchley, M. (1970). *Aphasiology and other aspects of language.* London: Edward Arnold.

Cromwell, L., Weibell, F. J., Pfeiffer, E. A., & Usselman, L. B. (1973). *Biomedical instrumentation and measurements.* Englewood Cliffs, NJ: Prentice-Hall.

Csikszentmihalyi, M. (1975). *Beyond boredom and anxiety: The experience of play in work and games.* San Francisco, CA: Jossey-Bass.

Dalessio, D. J. (1980). *Wolff's headache and other head pain* (4th ed.). New York: Oxford University Press.

Daniele, R. P. (1985). Asthma. In J. B. Wyngaarden & L. H. Smith, Jr., (Eds.), *Cecil textbook of medicine* (17th ed., pp. 390-396). Philadelphia, PA: W. B. Saunders.

Daniels, F. S., & Landers, D. M. (1981). Biofeedback and shooting performance: A test of disregulation and systems theory. *Journal of Sport Psychology, 4,* 271-282.

Dass, B. R. (1979). Eastern and Western models of man. In D. Goleman and R. J. Davidson (Eds.), *Consciousness: Brain, states of awareness, and mysticism* (pp. 213-216). New York: Harper & Row.

D'Atri, D. (1975). Psychophysiological responses to crowding. *Environment and Behavior, 7,* 237-252.

Davidson, R. J., & Schwartz, G. E. (1977). Brain mechanisms subserving self-generated imagery: Electrophysiological specificity and patterning. *Psychophysiology, 14,* 598-602.

Davis, J. M. (1974). A two-factor theory of schizophrenia. *Journal of Psychiatric Research, 11,* 25-30.

Dawson, G. D. (1950). Cerebral responses to nerve stimulation in man. *British Medical Bulletin, 6,* 329.

Deikman, A. J. (1966). Deautomatization and the mystic experience. *Psychiatry, 29,* 324-328.

Delgado-Escueta, A. V. (1985). Epilepsy in adolescents and adults. In R. E. Rakel (Ed.). *Conn's Current therapy: 1985* (pp. 715-724). Philadelphia, PA: W. B. Saunders.

Dembroski, T. M., MacDougall, J. M., & Lushene, R. (1979). Interpersonal interaction and cardiovascular response in Type A subjects and coronary patients. *Journal of Human Stress, 5,* 28-36.

Dembroski, T. M., MacDougall, J. M., Shields, J., Petitto, J., & Lushene, R. (1978). Components of the Type A coronary-prone behavior pattern and cardiovascular responses to psychomotor performance challenge. *Journal of Behavioral Medicine, 1,* 159-176.

Denckla, M. B., Bemporad, J. R., & MacKay, M. C. (1976). Tics following methylphenidate administration. *Journal of the American Medical Association, 235,* 1349-1351.

Department of Health and Social Security. (1976). *Prevention and health: Everybody's business.* London: Her Majesty's Stationery Office.

Department of Health, Education, and Welfare. (1968). *Social forces and the nation's health.* Washington, DC: U.S. Government Printing Office.

Descartes, R. (1972). *Treatise of man* (T. S. Hall, Trans.). Cambridge, MA: Harvard University Press. (Original work published 1665).

DiCara, L. V., & Miller, N. E. (1968). Instrumental learning of vasomotor responses by rats: Learning to respond differentially in the two ears. *Science, 159,* 1485-1486.

Diener, E. (1984). Subjective well-being. *Psychological Bulletin, 95,* 542-575.

Dirks, J. F., Robinson, S. K., & Dirks, D. L. (1981). Alexisthymia and the psychomaintenance of bronchial asthma. *Psychotherapy and Psychosomatics, 36,* 63-71.

Dirks, J. F., Robinson, S. K., & Moore, P. N. (1981). The prediction of psychomaintenance in chronic asthma. *Psychotherapy and Psychosomatics, 36,* 105-115.

Dohrenwend, B. S., Krasnoff, L., Askenasy, A. R., & Dohrenwend, B. P. (1978). Exemplification of a method for scaling life events: The PERI life events scale. *Journal of Health and Social Behavior, 19*, 205-229.

Dollery, C. T. (1985). Arterial hypertension. In J. B. Wyngaarden & L. H. Smith, Jr. (Eds.), *Cecil textbook of medicine* (17th ed., pp. 266-284). Philadelphia, PA: W. B. Saunders.

Drake, D., & Hollander, D. (1981). Neutralizing capacity and cost effectiveness of antacids. *Annals of Internal Medicine, 94*, 215-217.

Dubey, D. R., O'Leary, S. G., & Kaufman, K. F. (1983). Training parents of hyperactive children in child management: A comparative outcome study. *Journal of Abnormal Child Psychology, 11*, 229-245.

Duffy, E. (1972). Activation. In N. S. Greenfield & R. A. Sternbach (Eds.), *Handbook of psychophysiology* (pp. 577-622). New York: Holt, Rinehart and Winston.

Easterbrook, J. A. (1959). The effect of emotion on cue utilization and the organization of behavior. *Psychological Review, 66*, 187-201.

Eberlin, P., & Mulholland, T. (1976). Bilateral differences in parietal-occipital EEG induced by contingent visual feedback. *Psychophysiology, 13*, 212-218.

Efron, R. (1957). The conditioned inhibition of uncinate fits. *Brain, 80*, 251-262.

Eisdorfer, C., Cohen, D., & Preston, C. (1981). Behavioral and psychological therapies for the older patient with cognitive impairment. In N. Miller & G. Cohen (Eds.). *Clinical aspects of Alzheimer's disease and senile dementia* (pp. 209-226). New York: Raven Press.

Elder, S. T., Geoffray, D. J., & McAfee, R. D. (1981). Essential hypertension: A behavioral perspective. In S. N. Haynes & L. Gannon (Eds.), *Psychosomatic disorders: A psychophysiological approach to etiology and treatment* (pp. 359-405). New York: Praeger.

Elson, B. D., Hauri, P., & Cunis, D. (1977). Physiological changes in Yoga meditation. *Psychophysiology, 14*, 52-57.

Engel, B. T. (1960). Stimulus-response and individual-response specificity. *Archives of General Psychiatry, 2*, 305-313.

Engel, B. T., & Bickford, A. F. (1961). Response specificity. *Archives of General Psychiatry, 5*, 478-489.

Engel, B. T., Gaarder, K. R., & Glascow, M. S. (1981). Behavioral treatment of high blood pressure: I. Analysis of intra- and interdaily variations of blood pressure during a one-month baseline period. *Psychosomatic Medicine, 43*, 255-270.

Engel, B. T., Glascow, M. S., & Gaarder, K. R. (1983). Behavioral treatment of high blood pressure: III. Follow-up results and treatment recommendation. *Psychosomatic Medicine, 45*, 23-29.

Engel, G. L. (1976). Psychologic factors in instantaneous cardiac death. *New England Journal of Medicine, 294*, 664-665.

Engel, G. L., & Romano, J. (1944). Delirium: II. Reversibility of the electroencephalogram with experimental procedures. *Archives of Neurology and Psychiatry, 51*, 378-392.

Engel, J. (1985). The epilepsies. In J. B. Wyngaarden & L. H. Smith (Eds.), *Cecil textbook of medicine* (17th ed, pp. 2149-2160). Philadelphia, PA: W. B. Saunders.

Engstrom, D. R. (1976). Hypnotic susceptibility, EEG-alpha, and self-regulation. In G. E. Schwartz and D. Shapiro (Eds.), *Consciousness and self-regulation* (Vol. 1, pp. 173-221). New York: Plenum.

Epilepsy Foundation of America. (1975). *Basic statistics on the epilepsies*. Philadelphia: F. A. Davis.

Eppinger, H., & Hess, L. (1917). *Vagotonia: A clinical study in vegatative neurology* (W. M. Kraus & S. E. Jelliffe, Trans.). New York: The Nervous and Mental Disease Publishing Company. (Original work published 1910)

Erickson, M. H. (1952). Deep hypnosis and its induction. In L. M. LeCron (Ed.), *Experimental hypnosis* (pp. 70-112). New York: Macmillan.

Erickson, M. H. (1964). The "surprise" and "My-Friend-John" techniques of hypnosis: Minimal cues and natural field experimentation. *The American Journal of Clinical Hypnosis, 6,* 293-307.

Erikson, E. H. (1963). *Childhood and society* (2nd ed.). New York: Norton.

Esdaile, J. (1977) Mesmerism in India. In Daniel N. Robinson (Ed.), *Significant contributions to the history of psychology: Series A—Orientations* (Vol. 10, pp. 1-272). Washington, DC: University Publications of America. (Original work published 1846)

Fahn, S. (1982). Tics (habit spasms, Tourette's syndrome). In J. B. Wyngaarden & L. H. Smith (Eds.), *Cecil textbook of medicine* (16th ed., p. 2033). Philadelphia, PA: W. B. Saunders.

Feingold, B. F. (1973). Food additives and child development. *Hospital Practice, 8,* 11-12.

Feingold, B. F. (1975). *Why your child is hyperactive.* New York: Random House.

Feldman, G. M. (1976). The effect of biofeedback training on respiratory resistance of asthmatic children. *Psychosomatic Medicine, 38,* 27-34.

Feltz, D. L., & Landers, D. M. (1983). The effects of mental practice on motor skill learning and performance: A meta-analysis. *Journal of Sport Psychology, 5,* 25-57.

Feuerstein, M., Bush, C., & Corbisiero, R. (1982). Stress and chronic headache: A psychophysiological analysis of mechanisms. *Journal of Psychosomatic Research, 26,* 167-182.

Feuerstein, M., & Gainer, J. (1982). Chronic headache: Etiology and management. In D. M. Doleys, R. L. Meredith, & A. R. Ciminero (Eds.), *Behavioral medicine: Assessment and treatment strategies (pp. 199-249).* New York: Plenum.

Finley, W. W. (1976). Effects of sham feedback following successful SMR training in an epileptic: Follow-up study. *Biofeedback and Self- Regulation, 1,* 227-235.

Finley, W. W., Niman, C. A., Standley, J., & Wansley, R. A. (1977). Electrophysiologic behavior modification of frontal EMG in cerebral-palsied children. *Biofeedback and Self-Regulation, 2,* 59-79.

Finley, W. W., Smith, H. A., & Etherton, M. D. (1975). Reduction of seizures and normalization of the EEG in a severe epileptic following sensorimotor biofeedback training: Preliminary study. *Biological Psychology, 2,* 189-203.

Flor-Henry, P. (1974). Psychosis, neurosis and epilepsy. *British Journal of Psychiatry, 124,* 144-150.

Flor-Henry, P. (1976). Lateralized temporal-limbic dysfunction and psychopathology. *Annals of the New York Academy of Sciences, 280,* 777-797.

Folkins, C. H., & Sime, W. E. (1981). Physical fitness training and mental health. *American Psychologist, 36,* 373-389.

Folkman, S., & Lazarus, R. S. (1980). An analysis of coping in a middle-aged community sample. *Journal of Health and Social Behavior, 21,* 219-239.

Ford, M. R. (1982). Biofeedback treatment for headaches, Raynaud's disease, essential hypertension, and irritable bowel syndrome: A review of the long-term follow-up literature. *Biofeedback and Self-Regulation, 7,* 521-536.

Fordyce, M. W. (1977). Development of a program to increase personal happiness. *Journal of Counseling Psychology, 24,* 511-521.

Fordyce, M. W. (1981). *The psychology of happiness: Fourteen fundamentals.* Fort Myers, FL: Cypress Lake Media.

Fordyce, M. W. (1983). A program to increase happiness: Further studies. *Journal of Counseling Psychology, 30,* 483-498.

Fordyce, W. E. (1976). *Behavioral methods for chronic pain and illness.* St Louis, MO: C. V. Mosby.

Forster, F. M. (1977). *Reflex epilepsy, behavioral therapy and conditional reflexes.* Springfield, IL: Charles C. Thomas.

Forsyth, R. P. (1969). Blood pressure responses to longterm avoidance schedules in the restrained rhesus monkey. *Psychosomatic Medicine, 31,* 300-309.

Forum on Hypertension in Minority Populations. (1982). *Proceedings of the 1980 Forum on Hypertension in Minority Populations.* Washington, DC: U. S. Government Printing Office.

Fowler, R. L., & Kimmel, H. D. (1962). Operant conditioning of the GSR. *Journal of Experimental Psychology, 63,* 563-567.

Frank, J. D. (1982). Biofeedback and the placebo effect. *Biofeedback and Self-Regulation, 7,* 449-460.

Frankl, V. E. (1969). Reductionism and nihilism. In A. Koestler & J. R. Smythies (Eds.), *Beyond reductionism* (pp. 396-408). London: Hutchinson.

Frazier, C. A. (Ed.). (1980). *Occupational asthma.* New York: Van Nostrand Reinhold.

Freedman, R. R., Ianni, P., & Wenig, P. (1983). Behavioral treatment of Raynaud's disease. *Journal of Consulting and Clinical Psychology, 51,* 539-549.

Freedman, R. R., Lynn, S. J., Ianni, P., & Hale, P. A. (1981). Biofeedback treatment of Raynaud's disease and phenomenon. *Biofeedback and Self-Regulation, 6,* 355-365.

Freeman, W. J. (1975). *Mass action in the nervous system.* New York: Academic Press.

French, J. R. P. (1963). The social environment and mental health. *Journal of Social Issues, 19*(4), 39-56.

Friar, L. R., & Beatty, J. (1976). Migraine: Management by trained control of vasoconstriction. *Journal of Consulting and Clinical Psychology, 44,* 46-53.

Friedman, A. P., & Merritt, H. H. (1957). Treatment of headache. *Journal of the American Medical Association, 163,* 1111-1117.

Friedman, M., & Rosenman, R. H. (1974). *Type A behavior and your heart.* New York: Alfred A. Knopf.

Friedman, M., Rosenman, R., & Carroll, V. (1958). Changes in the serum cholesterol and blood-clotting time in men subjected to cyclic variation of occupational stress. *Circulation, 17,* 852-861.

Friedman, M., Rosenman, R. H., Straus, R., Wurm, M., & Kositcheck, R. (1968). The relationship of behavior Pattern A to the state of the coronary vasculature: A study of fifty-one autopsy subjects. *American Journal of Medicine, 44,* 525-537.

Friedman, M., Thoresen, C. E., Gill, J. J., Powell, L. H., Ulmer, D., Thompson, L., Price, V. A., Rabin, D. D., Breall, W. S., Dixon, T., Levy, R., & Bourg, E. (1984). Alteration of type A behavior and reduction in cardiac recurrences in postmyocardial infarction patients. *American Heart Journal, 108,* 237-248.

Friedman, M., Thoresen, C. E., Gill, J. J., Ulmer, D., Thompson, L., Powell, L., Price, V., Elek, S. R., Rabin, D. D., Breall, W. S., Piaget, G., Dixon, T., Bourg, E., Levy, R. A., & Tasto, D. L. (1982). Feasibility of altering type A behavior pattern after myocardial infarction. *Circulation, 66,* 83-92.

Fromm, E., Brown, D. P., Hurt, S. W., Oberlander, J. Z., Boxer, A. M., & Pfeifer, G. (1981). The phenomena and characteristics of self-hypnosis. *International Journal of Clinical and Experimental Hypnosis, 29,* 189-246.

Gadow, K. D. (1983). Effects of stimulant drugs on academic performance in hyperactive and learning disabled children. *Journal of Child Development, 16,* 290-299.

Galin, D. (1974). Implications for psychiatry of left and right cerebral specialization. *Archives of General Psychiatry, 32,* 572-583.

Gallagher, J. J. (1966). Children with developmental imbalances: A psycho-educational definition. In W. M. Cruickshank (Ed.), *The teacher of brain-injured children* (pp. 21-43). Syracuse, NY: Syracuse University Press.

Gallwey, W. T. (1974). *The inner game of tennis.* New York: Random House.

Garfield, C. A., & Bennett, H. Z. (1984). *Peak performance.* Los Angeles, CA: Jeremy P. Tarcher.

Garwood, M., Engel, B. T., Capriotti, R. (1982). Autonomic nervous system function and aging: Response specificity. *Psychophysiology, 19,* 378-385.

Gellhorn, H. (1967). The tuning of the nervous system: Physiological foundations and implications for behavior. *Perspectives in Biology and Medicine, 10*, 559-619.

Gheorghiu, V. A., & Orleanu, P. (1982). Dental implant under hypnosis. *The American Journal of Clinical Hypnosis, 25*, 68-70.

Glascow, M. S., Gaarder, K. R., & Engel, B. T. (1982). Behavioral treatment of high blood pressure II. Acute and sustained effects of relaxation and systolic blood pressure biofeedback. *Psychosomatic Medicine, 44*, 155-170.

Glaser, G. H. (1982). The epilepsies. In J. B. Wyngaarden & L. H. Smith (Eds.), *Cecil textbook of medicine* (16th ed., pp. 2114-2124). Philadelphia, PA: W. B. Saunders.

Gloor, P. (1954). Autonomic functions of the diencephalon: A summary of the experimental work of Professor W. R. Hess. *Archives of Neurology and Psychiatry, 71*, 773-790.

Gofman, J. W., Lindgren, F., Elliott, H., Mantz, W., Hewitt, J., Strisower, B., & Herring, V. (1950). The role of lipids and lipoproteins in atherosclerosis. *Science, 111*, 166-171, 186.

Goldsmith, M. F. (1984). Attempts to vanquish Alzheimer's disease intensify, take new paths. *Journal of the American Medical Association, 251*, 1805-1807, 1811-1812.

Goldstein, I. B. (1981). Assessment of hypertension. In C. K. Prokop & L. A. Bradley (Eds.), *Medical psychology: Contributions to behavioral medicine* (pp. 37-54). New York: Academic Press.

Goldstein, K. (1940). *Human nature in the light of psychopathology.* Cambridge, MA: Harvard University Press.

Goodwin, J. S., Goodwin, J. M., & Vogel, A. V. (1979). Knowledge and use of placebos by house officers and nurses. *Annals of Internal Medicine, 91*, 106-110.

Gordon, T., Garcia-Palmier, M. R., Kagan, A., Kennel, W. B., & Schiffman, J. (1974). Differences in coronary heart disease in Framingham, Honolulu, and Puerto Rico. *Journal of Chronic Diseases, 27*, 329-344.

Graham, D. T. (1972). Psychosomatic medicine. In N. S. Greenfield & R. A. Sternbach (Eds.), *Handbook of psychophysiology* (pp. 839-924). New York: Holt.

Graham, D. T., Stern, J. A., & Winokur, G. (1958). Experimental investigation of the specificity of attitude hypothesis in psychosomatic disease. *Psychosomatic Medicine, 20*, 446-457.

Graham, J. R. (1981). Pathophysiology of headache for behavioral therapists. In R. S. Surwit, R. B. Williams, Jr., A. Steptoe, & R. Biersner (Eds.), *Behavioral treatment of disease* (pp. 259-271). New York: Plenum.

Green, E. E. (1973). Biofeedback for mind-body self-regulation: Healing and creativity. In D. Shapiro, T. X. Barber, L. V. DiCara, J. Kamiya, N. E. Miller, and J. Stoyva (Eds.), *Biofeedback & Self-control: 1972* (pp. 152-166). Chicago, IL: Aldine.

Green, E. E., Green, A. M., & Walters, E. D. (1970). Voluntary control of internal states: Psychological and physiological. *Journal of Transpersonal Psychology, 2*, 1-26.

Grevert, P., Albert, L. II., & Goldstein, A. (1983). Partial antagonism of placebo analgesia by naloxone. *Pain, 16*, 129-143.

Gribbin, B., Steptoe, A., & Sleight, P. (1976). Pulse wave velocity as a measure of blood pressure change. *Psychophysiology, 13*, 86-90.

Grossman, M. I. (1982). Peptic Ulcer: Pathogenesis and pathophysiology. In J. B. Wyngaarden & L. H. Smith, Jr. (Eds.), *Cecil textbook of medicine* (16th ed., pp. 635-640). Philadelphia, PA: W. B. Saunders.

Guglielmi, R. S., Roberts, A. H., & Patterson, R. (1982). Skin temperature biofeedback for Raynaud's disease: A double-blind study. *Biofeedback and Self-Regulation, 7*, 99-120.

Guglielmi, R. S., Roberts, A. H., Tellegen, A., & Zimmerman, R. L. (1981) Vasomotor lability and voluntary control of peripheral skin temperature. *Psychophysiology. 18*, 178. (Abstract)

Gundry, R. K., Donaldson, R. K., Finderhughes, C. A., & Barrabee, E. (1967). Patterns of gastric acid secretion in patients with duodenal ulcer: Correlations with clinical and personality features. *Gastroenterology, 52,* 176-184.

Gutmann, M. C., & Benson, H. (1971). Interaction of environmental factors and systemic arterial blood pressure: A review. *Medicine, 50,* 543-553.

Guyton, A. A. (1974). *Function of the human body* (4th ed.). Philadelphia, PA: W. B. Saunders.

Guyton, A. C. (1981). *Textbook of medical physiology* (16th ed.). Philadelphia, PA: W. B. Saunders.

Guyton, A. C. (1982). *Human physiology and mechanisms of disease.* Philadelphia, PA: W. B. Saunders.

Haider, V. M., & Groll-Knapp, E. (1971). Psychophysiologische untersuchungen uber die Belastung des Musikers in einem Symphonieorchester. In M. Piperek (Ed.), *Stress und kunst* (pp. 15-37). Stuttgart. Wilhelm Braumuller.

Hammond, E. C. (1966). Smoking in relation to death rates of 1 million men and women. In W. Haenszel (Ed.), *Epidemiological approaches to the study of cancer and other diseases* (pp. 127-204). Bethesda, MD: U.S. Public Health Service, National Cancer Institute Monograph No. 19.

Harano, K., Ogawa, K., & Naruse, G. (1965). A study of plethysmography and skin temperature during active concentration and autogenic exercise. In W. Luthe (Ed.), *Autogenic training: International edition* (pp. 55-58). New York: Grune & Stratton.

Harburg, E., Erfurt, J. C., Hauenstein, L. S., Chape, C., Schull, W. J., & Schork, M. A. (1973). Socio-ecologic stress, suppressed hostility, skin color, and Black-White male blood pressure: Detroit. *Psychosomatic Medicine, 35,* 276-296.

Harding, A. V., & Maher, K. R. (1982). Biofeedback training of cardiac acceleration: Effects on airway resistance in bronchial asthma. *Journal of Psychosomatic Research, 26,* 447-454.

Harley, J. P., Ray, R. S., Tomasi, L., Eichman, P. L., Matthews, C. G., Chun, R., Cleeland, C. S., & Traisman, E. (1978). Hyperkinesis and food additives: Testing the Feingold hypothesis. *Pediatrics, 61,* 818-828.

Harrison, V. F., & Mortenson, O. A. (1962). Identification and voluntary control of single motor unit activity in the tibialis anterior muscle. *Anatomical Record, 144,* 109-116.

Hastings, J. E., & Barkley, R. A. (1978). A review of psychophysiological research with hyperactive children. *Journal of Abnormal Child Psychology, 6,* 413-448.

Hatch, J. P. (1981). Voluntary control of sexual responding in men and women: Implications for the etiology and treatment of sexual dysfunctions. *Biofeedback and Self-Regulation, 6,* 191-205.

Havens, R. A. (1982). Approaching cosmic consciousness via hypnosis. *Journal of Humanistic Psychology, 22,* 105-116.

Hayes, R., Bennett, G. J., Newlon, P. G., & Mayer, D. J. (1978). Behavioral and physiological studies of non-narcotic analgesia in the rat, elicited by certain environmental stimuli. *Brain Research, 155,* 69-90.

Haynes, S. G., Feinleib, M., & Kannel, W. B. (1980). The relationship of psychosocial factors to coronary heart disease in the Framingham study. III. Eight-year incidence of coronary heart disease. *American Journal of Epidemiology, 111,* 37-58.

Head, H. (1893). On disturbances of sensation with special reference to the pain of visceral disease. *Brain, 16,* 1-133.

Hechtman, L., & Weiss, G. (1983). Long-term outcome of hyperactive children. *American Journal of Orthopsychiatry, 53,* 532-541.

Herberman, R. B., & Ortaldo, J. R. (1981). Natural killer cells: Their role in defenses against disease. *Science, 214,* 24-30.

Hilgard, E. R. (1965). *Hypnotic susceptibility.* New York: Harcourt, Brace and World.

Hilgard, E. R. (1973a). A neodissociation interpretation of pain reduction in hypnosis. *Psychological Review, 80,* 396-411.

Hilgard, E. R. (1973b). Dissociation revisited. In M. Henle, J. Jaynes, and J. Sullivan (Eds.). *Historical conceptions of psychology* (pp. 205-219). New York: Springer Publishing.

Hilgard, E. R. (1977). *Divided consciousness: Multiple controls in human thought and action.* New York: Wiley.

Hilgard, E. R., & Hilgard, J. R. (1975). *Hypnosis in the relief of pain.* Los Altos, CA: Kaufmann.

Hilgard, E. R., Weitzenhoffer, A. M., Landes, J., & Moore, R. K. (1961). The distribution of susceptibility to hypnosis in a student population. *Psychological Monographs, 75*(8, Whole No. 512).

Hillenberg, J. B., & Collins, F. L., Jr. (1982). A procedural analysis and review of relaxation training research. *Behaviour Research and Therapy, 20,* 251-260.

Hockey, R. (1979). Stress and the cognitive components of skilled performance. In V. Hamilton & D. M. Warburton (Eds.), *Human stress and cognition* (pp. 141-177). New York: Wiley.

Hokanson, J. E., & Burgess, M. (1962). The effects of three types of aggression on vascular processes. *Journal of Abnormal and Social Psychology, 64,* 446-449.

Holden, R. A., Ostfeld, A. M., Freeman, D. H., Hellenbrand, K. G., & D'Atri, D. A. (1983). Dietary salt intake and blood pressure. *Journal of the American Medical Association, 250,* 365-373.

Holmes, T. H., & Rahe, R. H. (1967). The Social Readjustment Rating Scale. *Journal of Psychosomatic Research, 11,* 213-218.

Holroyd, J. (1980). Hypnosis treatment for smoking: An evaluative review. *International Journal of Clinical and Experimental Hypnosis, 28,* 341-357.

Homick, J. L., Reschke, M. F., & Vanderploeg, J. M. (1984, May). *Space adaptation syndrome: Incidence and operational implications for the space transportation system program.* Paper presented at the NATO-AGARD Aerospace Medical Panel Symposium on Motion Sickness, Williamsburg, VA.

Horowitz, M. J., Simon, N., Holden, M., Connett, J. E., Billings, J. H., Borhani, N., & Benfari, R. (1983). The stressful impact of news of risk for premature heart disease. *Psychosomatic Medicine, 45,* 31-40.

Huessy, H. R., & Cohen, A. H. (1976). Hyperkinetic behaviors and learning disabilities followed over seven years. *Pediatrics, 57,* 4-10.

Hughes, J., Smith, T. W., Kosterlitz, H. W., Fothergill, L. A., Morgan, B. A., & Morris, H. R. (1975). Identification of two related pentapeptides from the brain with potent opiate agonist activity. *Nature, 8,* 145-149.

Hunchak, J. F. (1980). Hypnotic induction by entoptic phenomena. *American Journal of Clinical Hypnosis, 22,* 223-224.

Ikemi, Y., Nakagawa, S., Kimura, M., Dobeta, H., Ono Y., & Sugita, M. (1965). Bloodflow change by autogenic training—Including observations in a case of gastric fistula. In W. Luthe (Ed.), *Autogenic training: International Edition* (pp. 64-68). New York: Grune & Stratton.

Isenberg, J. I. (1982). Peptic ulcer: Medical treatment. In J. B. Wyngaarden & L. H. Smith, Jr. (Eds.), *Cecil textbook of medicine* (16th ed., pp. 646-650). Philadelphia, PA: W. B. Saunders.

Jacobson, E. (1929). *Progressive relaxation.* Chicago, IL: The University of Chicago Press.

Jacobson, E. (1954). Relaxation methods in labor. *American Journal of Obstetrics and Gynecology, 67,* 1035-1048.

Jacobson, E. (1978). *You must relax: Practical methods for reducing the tensions of modern living* (5th ed.). New York: McGraw-Hill.

Jenkins, C. D., Rosenman, R. H., & Friedman, M. (1967). Development of an objective psychological test for the determination of the coronary-prone behavior pattern in employed men. *Journal of Chronic Diseases, 20,* 371-379.

Jenkins, C. D., Tuthill, R. W., Tannenbaum, S. I., & Kirby, C. (1979). Social stressors and excess mortality from hypertensive diseases. *Journal of Human Stress, 5,* 29-40.

Jessell, T. M. (1982). Neurotransmitters and CNS disease: Pain. *Lancet, II,* 1084-1087.

Johnson, J. E., Kirchoff, K., & Endress, M. P. (1975). Altering children's distress behavior during orthopedic cast removal. *Nursing Research, 24,* 404-410.

Johnson, J. E., Morrissey, J. F., & Levanthal, H. (1973). Psychological preparation for an endoscopic examination. *Gastrointestinal Endoscopy, 19,* 180-182.

Johnson, J. H., & Sarason, I. G. (1979). Recent developments in research on life stress. In V. Hamilton & D. M. Warburton (Eds.), *Human stress and cognition* (pp. 205-233). Chichester, England: Wiley.

Johnson, L. S. (1979). Self-hypnosis: Behavioral and phenomenological comparisons with heterohypnosis. *International Journal of Clinical and Experimental Hypnosis, 27,* 240-264.

Jouvet, M. (1973). Telencephalic and rhombencephalic sleep in the cat. In W. B. Webb (Ed.), *Sleep: An active process* (pp. 12-25). Glenview, IL: Scott, Foresman.

Julien, R. M. (1981). *A primer of drug action* (3rd ed.). San Francisco, CA: W. H. Freeman.

Julius, S. (1977). Borderline hypertension: An overview. *Medical Clinics of North America, 61,* 495-511.

Kallmann, F. J. (1956). Genetic aspects of mental disorders in later life. In O. J. Kaplan (Ed.). *Mental disorders in later life* (2nd ed., pp. 26-46). Palo Alto, CA: Stanford University Press.

Kamiya, J. (1969). Operant control of the EEG alpha rhythm and some of its reported effects on consciousness. In Charles Tart (Ed.), *Altered states of consciousness* (507-517). New York: Wiley.

Kaplan, J. R., Manuck, S. B., Clarkson, T. B., Lusso, F. M., Taub, D. M., & Miller, E. W. (1983). Social stress and atherosclerosis in normocholesterolemic monkeys. *Science, 220,* 733-735.

Kapleau, P. (1965). *The three pillars of zen.* Salem, Massachusetts: John Weatherhill.

Kasamatsu, A., & Hirai, T. (1966). An electroencephalographic study of the Zen meditation (Zazen). *Folia Psychiatrica et Neurologica Japonica, 20,* 315-336.

Kasamatsu, A., & Hirai, T. (1969). An electroencephalographic study on the Zen meditation (Zazen). *Psychologia, 12,* 205-225.

Katkin, E. S., Morell, M. A., Goldband, S., Bernstein, G. L., & Wise, J. A. (1982). Individual differences in heartbeat discrimination. *Psychophysiology, 19,* 160-166.

Katz, N. W. (1980). Hypnosis and the addictions: A critical review. *Addictive Behaviors, 5,* 41-47.

Kavale, K. A., & Forness, S. R. (1983). Hyperactivity and diet treatment: A meta-analysis of the Feingold Hypothesis. *Journal of Learning Disabilities, 16,* 324-330.

Keefe, F. J., Surwit, R. S., & Pilon, R. N. (1979). Behavioral treatment of Raynaud's disease: A one-year follow-up. *Journal of Behavioral Medicine, 2,* 385-391.

Kelly, G. A. (1955). *The psychology of personal constructs* (Vol. 1). New York: Norton.

Kempner, W. (1948). Treatment of hypertensive vascular disease with rice diet. *American Journal of Medicine, 4,* 545-577.

Kewman, D., & Roberts, A. H. (1980). Skin temperature biofeedback and migraine headache: A double-blind study. *Biofeedback and Self-Regulation, 5,* 327-345.

Kewman, D. G., & Roberts, A. H. (1983). An alternative perspective on biofeedback efficacy studies: A reply to Steiner & Dince. *Biofeedback and Self-Regulation, 8,* 487-497.

Keys, A., Aravanis, C., Blackburn, H., van Muchem, F. S. P., Buzina, R., Djordjevic, B. S., Fidanza, F., Karvonen, M. J., Menotti, A., Puddu, V., & Taylor, H. L. (1972). Probability of middle-aged men developing coronary heart disease in five years. *Circulation, 45*, 815-828.

Kiecolt-Glaser, J. K., Garner, W., Speicher, C., Penn, G. M., Holliday, J., & Glaser, R. (1984). Psychosocial modifiers of immunocompetence in medical students. *Psychosomatic Medicine, 46*, 7-14.

Kiecolt-Glaser, J. K., Ricker, D., George, J., Messick, G., Speicher, C. E., Garner, W., & Glaser, R. (1984). Urinary cortisol levels, cellular immunocompetency, and loneliness in psychiatric inpatients. *Psychosomatic Medicine, 46*, 15-23.

Kimble, G. A. (1961). *Hilgard and Marquis' conditioning and learning* (2nd ed.). New York: Appleton-Century-Crofts.

King, C., & Young, R. D. (1982). Attentional deficits with and without hyperactivity: Teacher and peer perceptions. *Journal of Abnormal Child Psychology, 10*, 483-495.

Kiser, R. S., Khatami, M., Gatchel, R. J. Huang, X., Bhatia, K., & Altshuler, K. Z. (1983). Acupuncture relief of chronic pain syndrome correlates with increased plasma met-enkephalin concentrations. *Lancet, II*, 1394-1396.

Klumbies, G. (1983). *Psychotherapie in der inneren und allgemeinmedizin* (Vol. 4). Leipzig: Hirzel-Verlag.

Kobasa, S. C. (1979). Stressful life events, personality, and health: An inquiry into hardiness. *Journal of Personality and Social Psychology, 37*, 1-11.

Kobasa, S. C., Maddi, S. R., & Kahn, S. (1982). Hardiness and health: A prospective study. *Journal of Personality and Social Psychology, 42*, 168-177.

Kohlberg, L. (1973). Implications of developmental psychology for education: Examples from moral development. *Educational Psychologist, 10*, 2-14.

Kolata, G. (1983). Clues to Alzheimer's disease emerge. *Science, 219*, 941-942.

Kolata, G. (1981). Consensus on bypass surgery. *Science, 211*, 42-43.

Kolata, G. (1982). Consensus on diets and hyperactivity. *Science, 215*, 958.

Konorski, J., & Miller, S. (1937). On two types of conditioned reflex. *Journal of General Psychology, 16*, 264-272.

Kosambi, D. D. (1967). Living prehistory in India. *Scientific American, 216*(2), 105-114.

Kotses, H., & Glaus, K. D. (1981). Applications of biofeedback to the treatment of asthma: A crticial review. *Biofeedback and Self-Regulation, 6*, 573-593.

Kraft, W. A., & Rodolfa, E. R. (1982). The use of hypnosis among psychologists. *American Journal of Clinical Hypnosis, 24*, 249-257.

Krantz, D., Sanmorco, M., Selvester, R., & Matthews, K. (1979). Psychological correlates of progress of atherosclerosis in men. *Psychosomatic Medicine, 41*, 467-476.

Kraus, A. S., & Lilienfeld, A. M. (1959). Some epidemiological aspects of the high mortality rate in the young widowed group. *Journal of Chronic Diseases, 10*, 207-217.

Kroeber, A. L. (1948). *Anthropology*. New York: Harcourt.

Kuhlman, W. N. (1978). EEG feedback training of epileptic patients: Clinical and electroencephalographic analysis. *Electroencephalography and Clinical Neurophysiology, 45*, 699-710.

Kuhlman, W. N., & Kaplan, B. J. (1979). Clinical applications of EEG feedback training. In R. J. Gatchel & K. P. Price (Eds.). *Clinical applications of biofeedback: Appraisal and status* (pp. 65-96). New York: Pergamon.

Kuhn, T. S. (1962). *The structure of scientific revolutions*. Chicago, IL: University of Chicago Press.

Kurata, J. H., Honda, G. D., & Frankl, H. (1982). Hospitalization and mortality rates for peptic ulcers: A comparison of a large health maintenance organization and United States data. *Gastroenterology, 83*, 1008-1016.

Lacey, J. I., & Lacey, B. C. (1958). Verification and extension of the principle of autonomic response stereotypy. *American Journal of Psychology, 71*, 50-73.

Lance, J. W. (1974). The pathophysiology and treatment of migraine. *New Zealand Medical Journal, 79*, 954-960.

Landers, D. M. (1982). Arousal, attention, and skilled performance: Further considerations. *Quest, 33*, 271-283.

Lang, P. J. (1970). Autonomic control or learning to play the internal organs. *Psychology Today, 4*(5), 37-41, 86.

Lashley, K. S. (1941). Patterns of cerebral integration indicated by the scotomoas of migraine. *Archives of Neurology and Psychiatry, 46*, 331-339.

Lassen, N. A., Ingvar, D. H., & Skinh, E. (1978). Brain function and blood flow. *Scientific American, 239*, 62-71.

Laufer, M. W., & Denhoff, E. (1957). Hyperkinetic behavior syndrome in children. *Journal of Pediatrics, 50*, 463-474.

Lazarus, R. S. (1966). *Psychological stress and the coping process.* New York: McGraw-Hill.

Lazarus, R. S. (1981). The stress and coping paradigm. In C. Eisdorfer, D. Cohen, A. Kleinman, & P. Maxim (Eds.). *Models for clinical psychopathology* (pp. 177-214). New York: Spectrum.

Levene, H. I., Engel, B. T., & Pearsen, J. A. (1968). Differential operant conditioning of heart rate. *Psychosomatic Medicine, 30*, 837-845.

Levine, J. D., Gordon, N. C., & Fields, H. (1978). The mechanism of placebo analgesia. *Lancet, II*, 654-657.

Levine, J. D., Gordon, N. C., & Fields, H. L. (1982). Naloxone fails to antagonize nitrous oxide analgesia for clinical pain. *Pain, 13*, 165-170.

Levine, N. B., Dastoor, D. P., & Gendron, C. E. (1983). Coping with dementia: A pilot study. *Journal of the American Geriatrics Society, 31*, 12-18.

Levy, R. I. (1982). Prevalence and epidemiology of cardiovascular disease. In J. B. Wyngaarden & L. H. Smith, Jr. (Eds.), *Cecil textbook of medicine* (16th ed., pp. 98-101). Philadelphia, PA: W. B. Saunders.

Levy, R. I. (1985). Prevalence and epidemiology of cardiovascular disease. In J. B. Wyngaarden & L. H. Smith, Jr. (Eds.), *Cecil textbook of medicine* (17th ed., pp. 155-158). Philadelphia: W. B. Saunders.

Lewith, G. T., & Machin, D. (1983). On the evaluation of the clinical effects of acupuncture. *Pain, 6*, 111-127.

Light, K. C., Koepke, J. P., Obrist, P. A., & Willis, P. W., IV. (1983). Psychological stress induces sodium and fluid retention in men at high risk for hypertension. *Science, 220*, 429-431.

Linn, R. T., & Hodge, G. K. (1982). Locus of control in childhood hyperactivity. *Journal of Consulting and Clinical Psychology, 50*, 592-593.

Lipowski, Z. J. (1970). Physical illness, the individual and the coping process. *International Journal of Psychiatry in Medicine, 1*, 91-102.

Locke, S. E., Kraus, L., Leserman, J., Hurst, M. W., Heisel, J. S., & Williams, R. M. (1984). Life change stress, psychiatric symptoms, and natural killer cell activity. *Psychosomatic Medicine, 46*, 441-453.

London, M. D., & Schwartz, G. E. (1980). The interaction of instruction components with cybernetic feedback effects in the voluntary control of human heart rate. *Psychophysiology, 17*, 437-443.

Lowe, T. L., Cohen, D. J., Detlor, J., Kremenitzer, M. W., & Shaywitz, B. A. (1982). Stimulant medications precipitate Tourette's syndrome. *Journal of the American Medical Association, 247*, 1168-1169.

Lubar, J. F., & Bahler, W. W. (1976). Behavioral management of epileptic seizures following

EEG biofeedback training of the sensorimotor rhythm. *Biofeedback and Self-Regulation, 1,* 77-104.

Ludwig, A. M. (1966). Altered states of consciousness. *Archives of General Psychiatry, 15,* 225-234.

Luparello, T., Lyons, H. A., Bleecker, E. R., & McFadden, E. R., Jr. (1968). Influences of suggestion on airway reactivity in asthmatic subjects. *Psychosomatic Medicine, 30,* 819-825.

Luthe, W. (1963). Autogenic training: Method, research and application in medicine. *American Journal of Psychotherapy, 17,* 174-195.

Luthe, W. (1965a). Changes of iodine metabolism during autogenic therapy. In W. Luthe (Ed.), *Autogenic training: International edition* (pp. 71-78). New York: Grune and Stratton.

Luthe, W. (1965b). Lowering of serum cholesterol during autogenic therapy. In W. Luthe (Ed.), *Autogenic training: International edition* (pp. 88-91). New York: Grune and Stratton.

Luthe, W. (1970a). *Autogenic therapy: Dynamics of autogenic neutralization.* New York: Grune and Stratton.

Luthe, W. (1970b). *Autogenic therapy: Research and theory.* New York: Grune and Stratton.

Luthe, W. (1973). *Autogenic therapy: Treatment with autogenic neutralization.* New York: Grune and Stratton.

Luthe, W. (1979). About the methods of autogenic therapy. In E. Peper, S. Ancoli, & M. Quinn (Eds.), *Mind/body integration: Essential readings in biofeedback* (pp. 167-186). New York: Plenum.

Luthe, W., & Schultz, J. H. (1970a). *Autogenic therapy: Applications in psychotherapy.* New York: Grune and Stratton.

Luthe, W., & Schultz, J. H. (1970b). *Autogenic therapy: Medical applications.* New York: Grune and Stratton.

Lynch, W. C., Hama, H., Kohn, S., & Miller, N. E. (1976). Instrumental control of peripheral vasomotor responses in children. *Psychophysiology, 13,* 219-221.

MacGregor, G. A., Markandu, N. D., Best, F. E., Elder, D. M., Cam, J. M., Sagnella, G. A., & Squires, M. (1982). Double-blind randomized crossover trial of moderate sodium restriction in essential hypertension. *Lancet, 1,* 351-354.

MacKenzie, J. N. (1886). The production of "rose asthma" by an artificial rose. *American Journal of Medical Sciences, 91,* 45-57.

MacLeod-Morgan, C., & Lack, L. (1982). Hemisphere specificity: A physiological concomitant of hypnotizability. *Psychophysiology, 19,* 687-690.

Mahl, G. F. (1950). Anxiety, HCl secretion and peptic ulcer etiology. *Psychosomatic Medicine, 12,* 158-169.

Malmo, R. B., Shagass, C., & Davis, J. F. (1950). A method for the investigation of somatic response mechanisms in psychoneurosis. *Science, 112,* 325-328.

Mancia, G., Bertinieri, G., Grassi, G., Parati, G., Pomidossi, G., Ferrari, A., Gregorini, L., & Zanchetti, A. (1983). Effects of blood-pressure measurement by the doctor on patient's blood pressure and heart rate. *Lancet, II,* 695-697.

Mann, G. V. (1977). Diet-heart: End of an era. *New England Journal of Medicine, 297,* 644-650.

Mann, R. W. (1973). Prostheses control and feedback via noninvasive skin and invasive peripheral nerve techniques. In W. S. Fields & L. A. Leavitt (Eds.), *Neural organization and its relevance to prosthetics* (pp. 177-195) New York: Intercontinental Medical Book Corporation.

Manning, R. (1978). *A case study of muscle contraction headache.* Unpublished master's thesis, California State College, Bakersfield.

Margerison, J. H., St. John-Loe, P., & Binnie, C. D. (1967). Electroencephalography. In P. H. Venables & I. Martin (Eds.), *A manual of psychophysiological methods* (pp. 351-402). New York: Wiley.

Marinacci, A. A., & Horande, M. (1960). Electromyogram in neuromuscular reeducation. *Bulletin of the Los Angeles Neurological Society, 25,* 57-71.

Marmot, M., & Winkelstein, W. (1975). Epidemiological observations on intervention trials for prevention of coronary heart disease. *American Journal of Epidemiology, 101,* 177-181.

Marshall, M. S., & Bentler, P. M. (1976). The effects of deep physical relaxation and low-frequency-alpha brainwaves on alpha subjective reports. *Psychophysiology, 13,* 505-516.

Mash, E. J., & Johnston, C. (1982). A comparison of mother-child interactions of younger and older hyperactive and normal children. *Child Development, 53,* 1371-1381.

Maslow, A. H. (1962). *Toward a psychology of being.* New York: Van Nostrand.

Maslow, A. H. (1967). Self-actualization and beyond. In J. F. T. Bugental (Ed.), *Challenges of humanistic psychology* (pp. 279-286). New York: McGraw-Hill.

Maslow, A. H. (1970). *Motivation and personality* (2nd ed.). New York: Harper & Row.

Mattes, J. A., & Gittelman, R. (1983). Growth of hyperactive children on maintenance regimen of methylphenodate. *Archives of General Psychiatry, 40,* 317-321.

Matthews, K. A. (1982). Psychological perspectives on the type A behavior pattern. *Psychological Bulletin, 91,* 293-323.

Matthews, K. A., & Angulo, J. (1980). Measurement of the type A behavior pattern in children: Assessment of children's competitiveness, impatience-anger, and aggression. *Child Development, 51,* 466-475.

Matthysse, S. (1974). Dopamine and the pharmacology of schizophrenia: The state of the evidence. *Journal of Psychiatric Research, 11,* 107-113.

Mayer, D. J., Price, D. D., & Rafii, A. (1977). Antagonism of acupuncture analgesia in man by the narcotic antagonist naloxone. *Brain Research, 121,* 368-372.

McCarron , D. A., Morris, C. D., Henry, H. J., & Stanton, J. L. (1984). Blood pressure and nutrient intake in the United States. *Science, 224,* 1392-1398.

McDonald, W. (1978). *An old guy who feels good.* Berkley, CA: Ol' McDonald Press.

McFadden, E. R., Jr., Luparello, T., Lyons, H. A., & Bleecker, E. (1969). The mechanism of action of suggestion in the induction of acute asthma attacks. *Psychosomatic Medicine, 31,* 134-143.

Meares, A. (1982/83). A form of intensive meditation associated with the regression of cancer. *American Journal of Clinical Hypnosis, 25,* 114-121.

Melzack, R., & Wall, P. (1965). Pain mechanisms: A new theory. *Science, 150,* 971-979.

Melzack, R. (1973). *The puzzle of pain.* New York: Basic Books.

Meyers, A. W., Thackwray, D. E., Johnson, C. B., & Schlesser, R. (1983). A comparison of hypertensive individuals. *Behavior Therapy, 14,* 267-274.

Miller, M. P., Murphy, P. J., & Miller, T. P. (1978). Comparison of electromyographic feedback and progressive relaxation training in treating circumscribed anxiety stress reactions. *Journal of Consulting and Clinical Psychology, 46,* 1291-1298.

Miller, N. E. (1969). Learning of visceral and glandular responses. *Science, 163,* 434-445.

Miller, N. E., & Dworkin, B. R. (1977). Critical issues in therapeutic applications of biofeedback. In G. E. Schwartz & J. Beatty (Eds.), *Biofeedback: Theory and research* (pp. 129-161). New York: Academic Press.

Mittelman, B., & Wolff, H. G. (1939). Affective states and skin temperature: Experimental study of subjects with "cold hands" and Raynaud's syndrome. *Psychosomatic Medicine, 1,* 271-292.

Mittelman, B., & Wolff, H. G. (1942). Emotions and gastroduodenal function. *Psychosomatic Medicine, 4,* 5-61.

Mohapatra, S. N. (1981). *Non-invasive cardiovascular monitoring by electrical impedance technique.* London: Pitman Medical.

Moos, R. H. (1982). Coping with acute health crises. In T. Millon, C. Green, & R. Meagher (Eds.), *Handbook of clinical health psychology* (pp. 129-151). New York: Plenum.

Moos, R. H., & Engel, B. T. (1962). Psychophysiological reactions in hypertensive and arthritic patients. *Journal of Psychosomatic Research, 6,* 227-241.

Morasky, R. L., Reynolds, C., & Clarke, G. (1981). Using biofeedback to reduce left arm extensor EMG of string players during musical performance. *Biofeedback and Self-Regulation, 6,* 565-572.

Morgan, A. H., & Hilgard, E. R. (1973). Age differences in susceptibility to hypnosis. *International Journal of Clinical and Experimental Hypnosis, 21,* 78-85.

Morrison, F. R., & Paffenbarger, R. A., Jr. (1981). Epidemiological aspects of biobehavior in the etiology of cancer: A critical review. In S. M. Weiss, J. A. Herd, & B. H. Fox (Eds.), *Perspectives on behavioral medicine* (pp. 135-161). New York: Academic Press.

Morrison, J. R., & Stewart, M. A. (1973). *Archives of General Psychiatry, 28,* 888-891.

Morrow, G. R., & Morrell, C. (1982). Behavioral treatment for the anticipatory nausea and vomiting induced by cancer chemotherapy. *New England Journal of Medicine, 307,* 1476-1480.

Moss, C. S. (1965). *Hypnosis in perspective.* New York: Macmillan.

Mostofsky, D. I., & Balaschak, B. A. (1977). Psychobiological control of seizures. *Psychological Bulletin, 84,* 723-750.

Mulholland, T., & Runnals, S. (1962). A stimulus-brain feedback system for evaluation of alertness. *Journal of Psychology, 54,* 69-83.

Multiple Risk Factor Intervention Trial Research Group. (1982). Multiple risk factor intervention trial: Risk factor changes and mortality results. *Journal of the American Medical Association, 248,* 1465-1477.

Murray, J. B. (1982). What is meditation? Does it help? *Genetic Psychology Monographs, 106,* 85-115.

Nandi, S. (1978). Hormonal carcinogenesis: A novel hypothesis for the role of hormones. In M. A. Mehlman, R. E. Shapiro, M. F. Cranmer, & H. Norvell (Eds.), *Hazards from toxic chemicals* (pp. 13-20). Park Forest South, IL: Pathotox.

National Center for Health Statistics. (1984). Annual summary of births, deaths, marriages, and divorces: United States, 1983. *Monthly Vital Statistics Report, 32*(13).

National Institutes of Health Consensus Development Panel. (1982). Defined diets and childhood hyperactivity. *Journal of the American Medical Association, 248,* 290-292.

Nichols, P., & Chen, T. (1981). *Minimal brain dysfunction: A prospective study.* Hillsdale, NJ: Lawrence Erlbaum Associates.

Nideffer, R. M. (1976a). Tests of attentional and interpersonal style. *Journal of Personality and Social Psychology, 34,* 394-404.

Nideffer, R. M. (1976b). *The inner athlete: Mind plus muscle for winning.* New York: Crowell.

Nidich, S., Seeman, W., & Dreskin, T. (1973). Influence of Transcendental Meditation: A replication. *Journal of Counseling Psychology, 20,* 565-566.

Noback, C. R., & Demarest, R. J. (1975). *The human nervous system* (2nd ed.). New York: McGraw-Hill.

Noel, R. C. (1980). The effect of visuo-motor behavior rehearsal on tennis performance. *Journal of Sport Psychology, 2,* 221-226.

Olds, J. (1956). Pleasure centers in the brain. *Scientific American, 195,* 105-116.

Olds, J. (1973). The discovery of reward systems in the brain. In E. S. Valenstein (Ed.), *Brain stimulation and motivation* (pp. 81-99). Glenview, IL: Scott, Foresman.

Olds, J., & Milner, P. (1954). Positive reinforcement produced by electrical stimulation of septal area and other regions of rat brain. *Journal of Comparative and Physiological Psychology, 47,* 419-427.

Oman, C. M., Lichtenberg, B. K., & Money, K. E. (1984, May). *Space motion sickness monitoring experiment: Spacelab 1.* Paper presented at the NATO-AGARD Aerospace Medical Panel Symposium of Motion Sickness, Williamsburg, VA.

Omizo, M. M., & Michael, W. B. (1982). Biofeedback-induced relaxation training and impulsivity, attention to task, and locus of control among hyperactive boys. *Journal of Child Development, 15,* 414-416.

O'Regan, B., & Carlson, R. J. (1979). Defining health: The state of the art. *Holistic Health Review, 3,* 86-102.

Orne, M. T. (1959). The nature of hypnosis: Artifact and essence. *Journal of Abnormal and Social Psychology, 58,* 277-299.

Ornstein, R. E. (1972). *The psychology of consciousness.* New York: Viking Press.

Ottenbacher, K. J., & Cooper, H. M. (1983). Drug treatment of hyperactivity in children. *Developmental Medicine and Child Neurology, 25,* 358-366.

Overmier, J. B., & Seligman, M. E. P. (1967). Effects of inescapable shock upon subsequent escape and avoidance learning. *Journal of Comparative and Physiological Psychology, 63,* 23-33.

Pagano, R., Rose, R., Stivers, R., & Warrenburg, S. (1976). Sleep during Transcendental Meditation. *Science, 191,* 308-310.

Pagano, R. R., & Warrenburg, S. (1983). Meditation: In search of a unique effect. In R. J. Davidson, G. E. Schwartz, & D. Shapiro (Eds.), *Consciousness and self-regulation* (Vol. 3, pp. 153-210). New York: Plenum.

Page, L. B. (1979). Salt and hypertension: Epidemiology and mechanisms. In G. Onesti & C. R. Klimt (Eds.), *Hypertension: Determinants, complications, and intervention* (pp. 3-11). New York: Grune & Stratton.

Parnell, P., & Cooperstock, R. (1979). Tranquilizers and mood elevators in the treatment of migraine: An analysis of the Migraine Foundation Questionnaire. *Headache, 19,* 78-89.

Patel, C. H. (1975). Yoga and biofeedback in the management of hypertension. *Journal of Psychosomatic Research, 19,* 355-360.

Patel, C. H. (1977). Biofeedback-aided relaxation in the management of hypertension. *Biofeedback and Self-Regulation, 2,* 1-41.

Paternite, C. E., & Loney, J. (1980). Childhood hyperkinesis: Relationship between symptomology and home environment. In C. H. Whalen & B. Henker (Eds.), *Hyperactive children* (pp. 105-141). New York: Academic Press.

Panzarella, R. (1980). The phenomenology of aesthetic peak experiences. *Journal of Humanistic Psychology, 20,* 69-85.

Peavey, B. S., Lawlis, G. F., & Goven, A. (1984, August). *Biofeedback assisted relaxation: Effects on phagocytic immune functioning.* Paper presented at the meeting of the American Psychological Association, Toronto, Ontario, Canada.

Pelham, W. E. (1982). Childhood hyperactivity: Diagnosis, etiology, nature and treatment. In R. J. Gatchel, A. Baum, & J. E. Singer (Eds.), *Handbook of psychology and health* ((pp. 261-327). Hillsdale, NJ: Lawrence Erlbaum Associates.

Penfield, W. (1975). *The mystery of the mind.* Princeton, NJ: Princeton University Press.

Percy, L. E., Dzuiban, C. D., & Martin, J. B. (1981). Analysis of effects of distance running on self-concepts of elementary students. *Perceptual and Motor Skills, 52,* 42.

Pert, C. B., & Snyder, S. H. (1973). Opiate receptor: Demonstration in nervous tissue. *Science, 179,* 1011-1014.

Pervin, L. A. (1963). The need to predict and control under conditions of threat. *Journal of Personality, 31,* 570-587.

Pesut, N., & Kowalczyk, D. F. (1983). Considerations on the use of placebos in veterinary medicine. *Journal of the American Veterinary Medicine Association, 182,* 675-679.

Peterson, W. L. (1985). Peptic ulcer: Medical therapy. In J. B. Wyngaarden & L. H. Smith, Jr. (Eds.), *Cecil textbook of medicine* (17th ed., pp. 688-691). Philadelphia, PA: W. B. Saunders.

Pheasant, H. C. (1977). Backache—Its nature, incidence, and cost. *Western Journal of Medicine, 126,* 330-332.

Phillips, R. G. & Feeney, M. K. (1973). *The cardiac rhythms.* Philadelphia, PA: W. B. Saunders.

Piaget, J. (1970). Piaget's theory. In P. Mussen (Ed.), *Carmichael's manual of child psychology* (Vol. 1, pp. 703-732). New York: Wiley.

Pinkerton, S. S., Hughes, H., & Wenrich, W. W. (1982). *Behavioral Medicine: Clinical applications.* New York: Wiley.

Plotkin, W. B. (1977). On the social psychology of experiential states associated with EEG alpha biofeedback training. In J. Beatty & H. Legewie (Eds.), *Biofeedback and behavior* (pp. 121-134). New York: Plenum.

Plotkin, W. B. (1978). Long-term eyes-closed alpha-enhancement training: Effects on alpha amplitudes and on experiential state. *Psychophysiology, 15,* 40-52.

Plum, F. (1971). Headache. In P. B. Beeson & W. McDermott (Eds.), *Cecil-Loeb textbook of medicine* (13th ed., pp. 154-160). Philadelphia, PA: W. B. Saunder.

Plum, F. (1982). Headache. In J. B. Wyngaarden & L. H. Smith, Jr. (Eds.), *Cecil textbook of medicine* (16th ed., pp. 1948-1953). Philadelphia: W. B. Saunders.

Pooling Project Research Group. (1978). Relation of blood pressure, serum cholesterol, smoking habit, relative weight and ECG abnormalities to incidence of major coronary events: Final report of the Pooling Project. *Journal of Chronic Diseases, 31,* 201-306.

Posner, J. B. (1985). Disorders of sensation. In J. B. Wyngaarden & L. H. Smith, Jr. (Eds.), *Cecil textbook of medicine* (17th ed., pp. 2047-2064). Philadelphia, PA: W. B. Saunders.

Post, F. (1968). The development of progress of senile dementia in relationship to the functional psychiatric disorders of later life. In C. Muller & L. Ciompi (Eds.). *Senile dementia* (pp. 85-100). Baltimore, MD: Williams & Wilkins.

Privette, G. (1981). Dynamics of peak performance. *Journal of Humanistic Psychology, 21,* 57-67.

Privette, G. (1983). Peak experience, peak performance, and flow: A comparative analysis of positive human experiences. *Journal of Personality and Social Psychology, 45,* 1361-1368.

Privette, G., & Landsman, T. (1983). Factor analysis of peak performance: The full use of potential. *Journal of Personality and Social Psychology, 44,* 195-200.

Public Health Service. (1979). *Healthy people: The Surgeon General's report on health promotion and disease prevention* (DHEW Publication No. PHS 79-55071). Washington, DC: U.S. Government Printing Office.

Public Health Service. (1980). *Prooting health/preventing disease: Objectives for the nation.* Washington, DC: U.S. Government Printing Office.

Purcell, K., & Weiss, J. H. (1970). Asthma. In C. G. Costello (Ed.), *Symptoms of psychopathology: A handbook* (pp. 597-623). New York: Wiley.

Pykett, I. L. (1982). NMR imaging in medicine. *Scientific American, 246*(5), 78-88.

Rapoport, J. L., Buchsbaum, M. S., Zahn, T. P., Weingartner, H., Ludlow, C., & Mikkelsen, E. J. (1978). Dextroamphetamine: Cognitive and behavioral effects in normal prepubertal boys. *Science, 199,* 560-563.

Rausch, V. (1980). Cholecystectomy with self-hypnosis. *The American Journal of Clinical Hypnosis, 22,* 124-129.

Ravissa, K. (1984, March). *Teaching self-awareness and optimum arousal in athletes without instrumentation.* Paper presented at the meeting of the Biofeedback Society of America, Alququerque, NM.

Ray, B. S., & Wolff, H. G. (1940). Experimental studies on headache: Pain-sensitive structures of the head and their significance in headache. *Archives of Surgery, 41,* 813-856.

Ray, W. J. (1974). The relationship of locus of control, self-report measures and feedback to the voluntary control of heart rate. *Psychophsyiolgy, 11,* 527-534.

Ray, W. J., Frediani, A. W., & Harman, D. (1977). Self-regulation of hemispheric asymmetry. *Biofeedback and Self-Regulation, 2,* 195-199.

Razran, G. (1961). The observable unconscious and the inferable conscious in current Soviet psychophysiology: Interoceptive conditioning, semantic conditioning, and the orienting reflex. *Psychological Review, 68,* 81-147.

Reite, M., & Zimmerman, J. (1978). Magnetic phenomena of the central nervous system. *Annual Review of Biophysics and Bioengineering, 7,* 167-188.

Restrom, R. (1976). The teacher and the social worker in stimulant drug treatment of hyperactive children. *School Review, 85,* 97-108.

Review Panel on Coronary-prone Behavior and Coronary Heart Disease. (1981). Coronary-prone behavior and coronary heart disease: A critical review. *Circulation, 63,* 1199-1215.

Rice, H. K. (1963). The responding-rest ratio in the production of gastric ulcers in the rat. *The Psychological Record, 13,* 11-14.

Riley, V. (1981a). Psychoneuroendocrine influences on immunocompetence and neoplasia. *Science, 212,* 1100-1109

Riley, V. (1981b). Biobehavioral factors in animal work on tumorigenesis. In S. M. Weiss, J. A. Herd, & B. H. Fox (Eds.), *Perspectives on behavioral medicine* (pp. 183-214). New York: Academic Press.

Rockstroh, B., Elbert, T., Birbaumer, N., & Lutzenberger, W. (1982). *Slow brain potentials and behavior.* Baltimore, MD: Urban & Schwarzenberg.

Rockstroh, B., Elbert, T., Lutzenberger, W., & Birbaumer, N. (1982). The effects of slow cortical potentials on response speed. *Psychophysiology, 19,* 211-217.

Rockstroh, B., Elbert, T., Lutzenberger, W., & Birbaumer, N. (1984). Operant control of slow brain potentials: A tool in the intestigation of the potential's meaning and its relation to attentional dysfunction. In T. Elbert, B. Rockstroh, W. Lutzenberger, & N. Birbaumer (Eds.), *Self-regulation of the brain and behavior* (pp. 227-239). New York: Springer-Verlag.

Rodin, E. A., Katz, M., & Lennox, K. (1976). Differences between patients with temporal lobe seizures and those with other forms of epileptic attacks. *Epilepsia, 17,* 313-320.

Rogers, C. R. (1961). *On becoming a person: A therapist's view of psychotherapy.* Boston, MA: Houghton Mifflin

Rogers, M. P., Dubey, D., & Reich, P. (1979). The influence of the psyche and the brain on immunity and disease susceptibility: A critical review. *Psychosomatic Medicine, 41,* 147-164.

Romano, J., & Engel, G. L. (1944). Delirium: I. Electroencephalographic data. *Archives of Neurology and Psychiatry, 51,* 356-377.

Rose, F. C. (1983). The pathogenesis of a migraine attack. *Trends in Neurosciences, 6,* 247-248.

Rosenman, R. H., Brand, R. J., Jenkins, C. D., Friedman, M., Straus, R., & Wurm, M. (1975). Coronary heart disease in the Western Collaborative Group Study: Final follow-up experience of 8 1/2 years. *Journal of the American Medical Association, 233,* 872-877.

Ross, A. O., & Pelham, W. E. (1981). Child psychopathology. *Annual Review of Psychology, 32,* 243-278.

Ross, R. S. (1976). The problem of ischemic heart disease: Current approaches and implications. *The Johns Hopkins Medical Journal, 38,* 217-228.

Rowland, M., & Roberts, J. (1982). Blood pressure levels and hypertension in persons ages 6-74 years, U.S., 1976-80 (DHHS Publication No. PHS 82-1250). Washington, DC: U.S. Government Printing Office.

Rubin, R. A., & Balow, B. (1977). Perinatal influences on the behavior and learning problems of children. In B. Lahey & A. Kazdin (Eds.), *Advances in clinical child psychology* (Vol. 1, pp. 119-160). New York: Plenum.

Runnals, S., & Mulholland, T. (1965). Selected demonstrations of voluntary regulation of cortical activation. *Bedford Research, 11,* 26.

Rushmer, R. F. (1975). *Humanizing health care: Alternative futures for medicine.* Cambridge, MA: The MIT Press.

Russell, R., Sipich, J., & Knipe, J. (1976). Progressive relaxation training: A procedural note. *Behavior Therapy*, *7*, 566-567.

Rutter, M. (1982). Syndromes attributed to "minimal brain dysfunction" in childhood. *American Journal of Psychiatry*, *139*, 21-33.

Ryan, E. D., & Simons, J. (1983). What is learned in mental practice of motor skills: A test of the cognitive-motor hypothesis. *Journal of Sport Psychology*, *5*, 419-426.

Sabbagh, K. (Producer-Writer). (1973). *Mind over body* [Film]. New York: Time-Life Films.

Sacerdote, P. (1970). Theory and practice of pain control in malignancy and other protracted or recurring painful illnesses. *International Journal of Clinical and Experimental Hypnosis*, *18*, 160-180.

Sacerdote, P. (1981). Teaching self-hypnosis to adults. *International Journal of Clinical and Experimental Hypnosis*, *29*, 282-299.

Safer, D. J. (1973). A familial factor in minimal brain dysfunction. *Behavior Genetics*, *3*, 175-186.

Sandoval, J., Lambert, N. M., & Sassone, D. (1980). The identification and labelling of hyperactivity in children: An interactive model. In C. H. Whalen & B. Henker (Eds.), *Hyperactive children* (pp. 145-171). New York: Academic Press.

Sarason, I. G., Johnson, J. H., & Siegel, J. M. (1978). Assessing the impact of life changes: Development of the Life Experiences Survey. *Journal of Consulting and Clinical Psychology*, *46*, 932-946.

Sarason, I. G., Levine, H. M., & Sarason, B. R. (1982). Assessing the impact of life change. In T. Millon, C. Green, & R. Meagher (Eds.), *Handbook of clinical health psychology* (pp. 377-399). New York: Plenum.

Sarbin, T. R., & Coe, W. C. (1972). *Hypnosis: A social psychological analysis of influence communication*. New York: Holt, Rinehart, and Winston.

Sarbin, T. R., & Slagle, R. (1980). Psychophysiological outcomes of hypnosis. In G. D. Burrows and L. Dennerstein (Eds.), *Handbook of hypnosis and psychosomatic medicine* (pp. 53-65). New York: Elsevier/North-Holland.

Sargent, J. D., Green, E. E., & Walters, E. D. (1973). Preliminary report on the use of autogenic feedback training in the treatment of migraine and tension headaches. *Psychosomatic Medicine*, *35*, 129-135.

Sargent, J., Walters, E. D., & Green, E. E. (1973). Psychsomatic self-regulation of migraine headaches. In L. Birk (Ed.), *Biofeedback: Behavioral medicine* (pp. 55-68). New York: Grune & Stratton.

Sawynok, J., Pinsky, C., & LaBella, F. S. (1979). On the specificity of naloxone as an opiate antagonist. *Life Sciences*, *25*, 1621-1632.

Schachter, J. (1957). Pain, fear, and anger in hypertensives and normotensives. *Psychosomatic Medicine*, *19*, 17-29.

Schaeffer, G., & Freytag-Klinger, H. (1975). Objectifying the effect of autogenic training on disturbed ventilation in bronchial asthma. *Psychiatrie Neurologie und Medizinische Psycholgie*, *27*, 400-408.

Schmidt, A. (1984, March). *Developing concentration and consistency for performance*. Paper presented at the meeting of the Biofeedback Society of America, Albuquerque, NM.

Schrag, P., & Divoky, D. (1975). *The myth of the hyperactive child*. New York: Pantheon Books.

Schultz, J. H. (1932). *Das autogene training*. Stuttgart, Germany: Thieme Verlag.

Schultz, J. H., & Luthe, W. (1969). *Autogenic therapy: Methods*. New York: Grune and Stratton.

Schuster, M. M. (1974). Operant conditioning in gastrointestinal dysfunctions. *Hospital Practice*, *9*, 135-143.

Schwartz, G. E. (1972). Voluntary control of human cardiovascular integration and differentiation through feedback and reward. *Science*, *175*, 90-93.

Schwartz, G. E. (1976). Self-regulation of response patterning: Implications for psychophysiological research and therapy. *Biofeedback and Self-Regulation, 1,* 7-30.

Scribner, B. H. (1983). Editorial: Salt and hypertension. *Journal of the American Medical Association, 250,* 388-389.

Seer, P. (1979). Psychological control of hypertension: Review of the literature and methodological critique. *Psychological Bulletin, 86,* 1015-1043.

Segreto-Bures, J., & Kotses, H. (1982). Experimenter expectancy effects in frontal EMG conditioning. *Psychophysiology, 19,* 467-471.

Seligman, M. E. P. (1975). *Helplessness: On depression, development, and death.* San Francisco: W. H. Freeman.

Seligman, M. E. P., & Binik, Y. M. (1977). The safety signal hypothesis. In H. Davis & H. M. B. Hurwitz (Eds.), *Operant-Pavlovian interactions* (pp. 165-187). Hillsdale, NJ: Lawrence Erlbaum Associates.

Selye, H. (1936). A syndrome produced by diverse nocuous agents. *Nature, 138,* 32.

Selye, H. (1956). *The stress of life.* New York: McGraw-Hill.

Selye, H. (1976). *The stress of life* (rev. ed.). New York: McGraw-Hill.

Shapiro, A. K. (1960). Contribution to a history of the placebo effect. *Behavioral Science, 5,* 109-135.

Shapiro, D. H. (1982). Overview: Clinical and physiological comparison of meditation with other self-control strategies. *American Journal of Psychiatry, 139,* 267-274.

Shearn, D. W. (1962). Operant conditioning of heart rate. *Science, 137,* 530-531.

Sheer, D. E. (1976). Focused arousal and 40 Hz EEG. In R. M. Knight & D. J. Bakker (Eds.), *The neurophysiology of learning disorders* (pp. 71-87). Baltimore, MD: University Park Press.

Sheer, D. E. (1984). Focused arousal, 40-Hz EEG, and dysfunction. In T. Elbert, B. Rockstroh, W. Lutzenberger, & N. Birbaumer (Eds.), *Self-regulation of the brain and behavior* (pp. 64-84). New York: Springer-Verlag.

Shepherd, G. M. (1983). *Neurobiology.* New York: Oxford University Press.

Sherman, R. A. (1979). Successful treatment of one case of tardive dyskinesia with electrophysiographic feedback from the masseter muscle. *Biofeedback and Self-Regulation, 4,* 367-370.

Sherwood, S., Greer, D. S., Morris, J. N., & Mor, V. (1981). *An alternative to institutionalization.* Cambridge, MA: Ballinger.

Shirley, M. C., Burish, T. G., & Rowe, C. (1982). Effectiveness of multiple-site EMG biofeedback in the reduction of arousal. *Biofeedback and Self-Regulation, 7,* 167-184.

Sicuteri, F., Anselmi, B., & Fanciullacci, M. (1974). The serotonin theory of migraine. *Advances in Neurology, 4,* 383-399.

Simonton, O. C., Matthews-Simonton, S., & Creighton, J. (1978). *Getting well again.* Los Angeles, CA: J. P. Tarcher.

Singer, J. L., & Pope, K. S. (1981). Daydreaming and imagery skills as predisposing capacities for self-hypnosis. *International Journal of Clinical and Experimental Hypnosis, 29,* 271-281.

Sjolund, B. H., & Eriksson, M. B. E. (1980). Stimulation techniques in the management of pain. In H. W. Kosterlitz & L. Y. Terenius (Eds.), *Pain and society* (pp. 415-430). Weinheim: Verlag Chemie.

Skinner, B. F. (1937). Two types of conditioned reflex: A reply to Konorski and Miller. *Journal of General Psychology, 16,* 272-279.

Skinner, B. F. (1953). *Science and human behavior.* New York: Macmillan.

Skinner, J. E., & Yingling, C. D. (1977). Central gating mechanisms that regulate event-related potentials and behavior. In J. Desmedt (Ed.), *Attention, voluntary contraction and event-related cerebral potentials* (pp. 30-69). Basel: S. Karger.

Sleator, E., & von Neumann, A. (1974). Methylphenidate in the treatment of hyperkinetic children. *Clinical Pediatrics, 13,* 19-24.

Smith, M. J., Colligan, M. J., & Hurrell, J. J., Jr. (1980). A review of psychological stress research carried out by NIOSH, 1971 to 1976. In R. M. Schwartz (ed.), *New developments in occupational stress* (pp. 2-8) (DHHS Publication Number 81-102). Washington, DC: U. S. Government Printing Office.

Smith, R. E., Johnson, J. H., & Sarason, I. G. (1978). Life change, the sensation seeking motive, and psychological distress. *Journal of Consulting and Clinical Psychology, 46,* 348-349.

Smith, W. M. (1977). Treatment of mild hypertension: Results of a 10-year intervention trial. *Circulation Research, 40*(Supplement 1), 98-105.

Snyder, E. D., & Shor, R. E. (1983). Trance-inductive poetry: A brief communication. *The International Journal of Clinical and Experimental Hypnosis, 31,* 1-7.

Solanto, M. V. (1984). Neuropharmacological basis of stimulant drug action in attention deficit disorder with hyperactivity: A review and synthesis. *Psychological Bulletin, 95,* 387-409.

Sorochan, W. D. (1968). Health concepts as a basis for orthobiosis. *The Journal of School Health, 38,* 673-682.

Spiegel, H. (1970). A single-treatment method to stop smoking using ancillary hypnosis. *The International Journal of clinical and Experimental Hypnosis. 18,* 235-250.

Spiegel, H., & Spiegel, D. (1978). *Trance and treatment: Clinical use of hypnosis.* New York: Basic Books.

Spiegelberg, F. (1962). *Spiritual practices of India.* Secaucus, NJ: Citadel Press.

Spydell, J. D., & Sheer, D. E. (1983). Forty hertz EEG activity in Alzheimer's type dementia. *Psychophysiology, 20,* 313-319.

Stamler, J. (1981). Primary prevention of coronary heart disease: The last 20 years. *American Journal of Cardiology, 47,* 722-735.

Stamm, J. S. (1984). Performance enhancements with cortical negative slow potential shifts. In T. Elbert, B. Rockstroh, W. Lutzenberger, & N. Birbaumer (Eds.), *Self-regulation of the brain and behavior* (pp. 199-215). New York: Springer-Verlag.

Steptoe, A., Phillips, J., & Harling, J. (1981). Biofeedback and instructions in the modification of total respiratory resistance: An experimental study of asthmatic and non-asthmatic volunteers. *Journal of Psychosomatic Research, 6,* 541-551.

Sterman, M. B. (1973). Neurophysiologic and clinical studies of sensorimotor EEG biofeedback training: Some effects on epilepsy. In L. Birk (Ed.), *Biofeedback: Behavioral medicine* (pp. 147-165). New York: Grune & Stratton.

Sterman, M. B. (1977). Sensorimotor EEG operant conditioning: Experimental and clinical effects. *Pavlovian Journal of Biological Science, 12,* 63-92.

Sterman, M. B. (1981). EEG biofeedback: Physiological behavior modification. *Neuroscience and Biobehavioral Reviews, 5,* 405-412.

Sterman, M. B., & Friar, L. (1972). Suppression of seizures in an epileptic following sensorimotor EEG feedback training. *EEG and Clinical Neurophysiology, 33,* 89-95.

Sterman., M. B., Macdonald, L. R., & Stone, R. K. (1974). Biofeedback training of the sensorimotor electroencephalogram rhythm in man: Effects on epilepsy. *Epilepsia, 15,* 395-416.

Sterman, M. B., & Shouse, M. N. (1980). Quantitative analysis of training, sleep EEG and clinical response to EEG operant conditioning in epileptics. *EEG and Clinical Neurophysiology, 49,* 558-576.

Stern, R. M., & Ray, W. J. (1977). *Biofeedback.* Homewood, IL: Dow Jones-Irwin.

Stern, R. M., Ray, W. J., & Davis, C. M. (1980). *Psychophysiological recordings.* New York: Oxford University Press.

Sternbach, R. A. (1966). *Principles of psychophysiology,* New York: Academic Press.

Stiles, G. L., & Lefkowitz, R. J. (1984). Cardiac adrenergic receptors, *Annual Review of Medicine, 35,* 149-164.

Strand, F. L. (1978). *Physiology: A regulatory systems approach.* New York: Macmillan.

Stroebel, C. F., & Glueck, B. C. (1973). Biofeedback treatment in medicine and psychiatry: An ultimate placebo. In L. Birk (Ed.), *Biofeedback: Behavioral medicine* (pp. 19-33). New York: Grune & Stratton.

Suinn, R. M. (1980). Psychology and sports performance: Principles and applications. In R. M. Suinn (Ed.), *Psychology in sports: Methods and applications* (pp. 26-36). Minneapolis, MN: Burgess.

Suinn, R. M. (1982). Intervention with Type A behaviors. *Journal of Consulting and Clinical Psychology, 50,* 933-949.

Surwit, R. S. (1982). Behavioral approaches to Raynaud's disease. *Psychotherapy and Psychosomatics, 36,* 224-245.

Surwit, R. S., & Keefe, F. J. (1983). The blind leading the blind: Problems with the "double-blind" design in clinical biofeedback research. *Biofeedback and Self-Regulation, 8,* 1-2.

Surwit, R. S., Pilon, R. N., & Fenton, C. H. (1978). Behavioral treatment of Raynaud's disease. *Journal of Behavioral Medicine, 1,* 323-335.

Suter, S. (1977). Independent biofeedback self-regulation of EEG alpha and skin resistance. *Biofeedback and Self-Regulation, 2,* 255-258.

Suter, S., Fredericson, M., & Portuesi, L. (1983). Mediation of skin temperature biofeedback effects in children. *Biofeedback and Self-Regulation, 8,* 61-78.

Suter, S., Griffin, G., Smallhouse, P., & Whitlach, S. (1981). Biofeedback regulation of temporal EEG alpha asymmetries. *Biofeedback and Self-Regulation, 6,* 45-56.

Suter, S., & Naifeh, K. (1984, March). Autonomic changes during motion sickness. In J. Kamiya (Chair), *Autogenic feedback training for astronauts.* Symposium conducted at the meeting of the Biofeedback Society of America, Albuquerque, NM.

Suter, S., & Loughry-Machado, G. (1981). Skin temperature biofeedback in children and adults. *Journal of Experimental Child Psychology, 32,* 77-87.

Sutherland, J. M., Tait, H., & Eadie, M. J. (1974). *The epilepsies: Modern diagnosis and treatment.* Edinburgh: Churchill Livingstone.

Sutton, S., Braren, M., Zubin, J., & John, E. R. (1965). Evoked potential correlates of stimulus uncertainty. *Science, 150,* 1187-1188.

Takase, K. (1983). Revolutionary new pain theory and acupuncture treatment procedure based on new theory of acupuncture mechanism. *American Journal of Acupuncture, 11,* 305-323.

Tart, C. (1972). States of consciousness and state-specific sciences. *Science, 176,* 1203-1210.

Taub, E. (1977). Self-regulation of human tissue temperature. In G. E. Schwartz & J. Beatty (Eds.), *Biofeedback: Theory and research* (pp. 265-300). New York: Academic Press.

Tebecis, A. K., Ohno, Y., Matsubara, H., Sugano, H., Takeya, T., Ikemi, Y., & Takasaki, M. (1976/77). A longitudinal study of some physiological parameters and autogenic training. *Psychotherapy and Psychosomatics, 27,* 8-17.

Terry, R., & Katzman, R. (1983). Senile dementia of the Alzheimer type: Defining a disease. In R. Katzman & R. Terry (Eds.), *The neurology of aging* (pp. 51-84). Philadelphia: F. A. Davis.

Thomas, A., & Chess, S. (1977). *Temperament and development.* New York: Brunner/Mazel.

Thomas, C. B., & Murphy, E. A. (1958). Further studies on cholesterol levels in the Johns Hopkins medical students: The effects of stress at examination. *Journal of Chronic Diseases, 8,* 661-670.

Thorley, G. (1984). Review of follow-up and follow-back studies of childhood hyperactivity. *Psychological Bulletin, 96,* 116-132.

Tobian, L. (1979). Interrelationships of sodium and hypertension. In G. Onesti & C. R. Klimt (Eds.), *Hypertension: Determinants, complications, and intervention* (pp. 13-32). New York: Grune & Stratton.

Toguchi, M. (1974). *The complete guide to acupuncture.* New York: Frederick Fell.

Torrens, P. R., Breslow, L., & Fielding, J. E. (1982). The role of universities in personal health improvement. *Preventive Medicine, 11*, 477-484.

Toscano, W. B. (1984, March). Shuttle flight experiment 3AFT23: A test of autogenic training in space. In J. Kamiya (Chair), *Autogenic feedback training for astronauts.* Symposium conducted at the meeting of the Biofeedback Society of America, Albuquerque, NM.

Towbin, A. (1970). Central nervous system damage in the human fetus and newborn infant. *American Journal of Diseases of Children, 119*, 529-542.

Trachtman, J. N., Giambalvo, V., & Feldman, J. (1981). Biofeedback of accommodation to reduce functional myopia. *Biofeedback and Self-Regulation, 6*, 547-564.

Travis, T. A., Kondo, C. Y., & Knott, J. R. (1975). Subjective aspects of alpha enhancement. *British Journal of Psychiatry, 127*, 122-126.

Trites, R. L., & Laprade, K. (1983). Evidence for an independent syndrome of hyperactivity. *Journal of Child Psychology and Pediatrics and Allied Disciplines, 24*, 573-586.

Trocchio, J. (1981). *Home care for the elderly.* Boston, MA: CBI Publishing.

Turk, D. C., & Flor, H. (1984). Etiological theories and treatment for chronic back pain. II. Psychological models and interventions. *Pain, 19*, 209-233.

Turnbull, J. W. (1962). Asthma conceived as a learned response. *Journal of Psychosomatic Research, 6*, 59-70.

Tursky, B., Shapiro, D., & Schwartz, G. E. (1972). Automated constant cuff-pressure system to measure average systolic and diastolic blood pressure in man. *IEEE Transactions in Bio-Medical Engineering, 19*, 217-276.

Tyler, C. W. (1982). Assessment of visual function in infants by evoked potentials. *Developmental Medicine and Child Neurology, 24*, 853-856.

Tyson, P. D., & Audette, R. (1979). A multivariate approach to the relationship between alpha waves and experience during feedback. *Biofeedback and Self-Regulation, 4*, 63-79.

Ullman, D. G., Barkley, R. A., & Brown, H. W. (1978). The behavioral symptoms of hyperkinetic children who successfully responded to stimulant drug treatment. *American Journal of Orthopsychiatry, 48*, 425-437.

van Doornen, L. J. P., & Orlebeke, K. F. (1982). Stress, personality, and serum-cholesterol level. *Journal of Human Stress, 8*, 24-29.

Van Toller, C. (1979). *The nervous body.* New York: Wiley.

Veith, I. (1972). *The Yellow Emperor's classic of internal medicine.* Berkeley, CA: University of California Press.

Vonnegut, K. (1971). *The sirens of Titan: An original novel.* New York: Delacorte.

Wadden, T. A., & Anderton, C. H. (1982). The clinical use of hypnosis. *Psychological Bulletin, 91*, 215-243.

Wadden, T. A., & Penrod, J. H. (1981). Hypnosis in the treatment of alcoholism: A review. *American Journal of Clinical Hypnosis, 24*, 41-47.

Wain, H. J. (1980). Pain control through use of hypnosis. *American Journal of Clinical Hypnosis, 23*, 41-46.

Waldron, I. (1978). Sex differences in the coronary-prone behavior pattern. in T. Dembroski, S. Weiss, J. Shields, S. Haynes, & M. Feinleib (Eds.), *Coronary-prone behavior* (pp. 199-205). New York: Springer-Verlag.

Walker, B. B., & Sandman, C. A. (1981). Disregulation of the gastrointestinal system. In S. N. Haynes & L. Gannon (Eds.), *Psychosomatic disorders: A psychophysiological approach to etiology and treatment* (pp. 133-178). New York: Praeger.

Wallace, R. K. (1970). *The physiological effects of Transcendental Meditation.* Los Angeles: Maharishi International University Press.

Walsh, J. H. (1982). Peptic ulcer: Clinical and endocrine aspects. In J. B. Wyngaarden & L. H. Smith, Jr. (Eds.), *Cecil textbook of medicine* (16th ed., pp. 640-642). Philadelphia: W. B. Saunders.

Walsh, R. (1984). Journey beyond belief. *Journal of Humanistic Psychology, 24*, 30-65.

Walter, W. G. (1964). The contingent negative variation: An electrical sign of significance of association in the human brain. *Science, 146*, 434.

Watkins, L. R., & Mayer, D. J. (1982). Organization of endogenous opiate and nonopiate pain control systems. *Science, 216*, 1185-1192.

Weidman, W. H., Elveback, L. R., Nelson, R. A., Hodgson, P. A., & Ellefson, R. D. (1978). Nutrient intake and serum cholesterol level in normal children 6 to 16 years of age. *Pediatrics, 61*, 354-359.

Weinberg, R. S., Gould, D., Yukelson, D., & Jackson, A. (1981). The effect of preexisting and manipulated self-efficacy on a competitive muscular endurance task. *Journal of Sport Psychology, 3*, 345-354.

Weiner, H. (1977). *Psychobiology and human disease.* New York: Elsevier.

Weiner, H. (1982). The prospects for psychosomatic medicine: Selected topics. *Psychosomatic Medicine, 44*, 491-517.

Weiss, G., Kruger, E., Danielson, U., & Elman, M. (1975). Effect of long-term treatment of hyperactive children with methylphenidate. *Canadian Medical Association Journal, 112*, 159-165.

Weiss, G., Minde, K., Werry, J. S., Douglas, V. I., & Nemeth, E. (1971). Studies on the hyperactive child. VIII. Five-year follow-up. *Archives of General Psychiatry, 24*, 409-414.

Weiss, J. M. (1972). Psychological factors in stress and disease. *Scientific American, 226*(6), 104-113.

Welgan, P. R. (1981). Experimental modification of digestive pathology. *Neuroscience and Biobehavioral Reviews, 5*, 401-404.

Welsh, J. D. (1977). Diet therapy of peptic ulcer disease. *Gastroenterology, 72*, 740-745.

Wenger, M. A. (1941). The measurement of individual differences in autonomic balance. *Psychosomatic Medicine, 3*, 427-434.

Wenger, M. A. (1966). Studies of autonomic balance: A summary. *Psychophysiology, 2*, 173-186.

Wenger, M. A., Bagchi, B. K., & Anand, B. K. (1961). Experiments in India on "voluntary" control of the heart and pulse. *Circulation, 24*, 1319-1325.

Wenger, M. A., & Cullen, T. D. (1972). Studies of autonomic balance in children and adults. In N. S. Greenfield & R. A. Sternbach (Eds.), *Handbook of psychophysiology* (pp. 535-576). New York: Holt.

Werner, W. E. F., Schauble, P. G., & Knudson, M. S. (1982). *The American Journal of Clinical Hypnosis, 24*, 149-171.

Werry, J. S., & Sprague, R. L. (1970). Hyperactivity. In C. G. Costello (Ed.), *Symptoms of psychopathology* (pp. 397-417). New York: Wiley.

Whalen, C. K., & Henker, B. (1976). Psychostimulants and children: A review and analysis. *Psychological Bulletin, 83*, 1113-1130.

White, R. W. (1959). Motivation reconsidered: The concept of competence. *Psychological Review, 66*, 297-333.

Wildgruber, C., Lutzenburger, W., Elbert, T., & Birbaumer, N. (1977). Average pattern biofeedback: The method and a first step toward a clinical application. *Biofeedback and Self-Regulation, 2*, 326. (Abstract).

Willerson, J. T. (1982a). Acute myocardial infarction. In J. B. Wyngaarden & L H. Smith, Jr. (Eds.), *Cecil textbook of medicine* (16th ed., pp. 247-256). Philadelphia, PA: W. B. Saunders.

Willerson, J. T. (1982b). Sudden cardiac death. In J. B. Wyngaarden & L. H. Smith, Jr. (Eds.), *Cecil textbook of medicine* (16th ed., pp. 256-257). Philadelphia, PA: W. B. Saunders.

Williams, J. G. L., & Jones, J. R. (1968). Psychophysiological responses to anesthesia and operation. *Journal of the American Medical Association, 203*, 415-417.

Williams, R. B., Jr. (1982). Behavioral mechanisms in the pathophysiology of coronary heart disease. In R. S. Surwit, R. B. Williams, Jr., A. Steptoe, & R. Biersner (Eds.), *Behavioral treatment of disease* (pp. 5-21). New York: Plenum.

Winkelstein, L. B., & Levinson, J. (1959). Fulminating pre-eclampsia with caesarean section performed under hypnosis. *American Journal of Obstetrics and Gynecology, 78*, 420-423.

Winkler, J. K., & Bromberg, W. (1939). *Mind explorers.* New York: Reynal & Hitchcock.

Wittkower, E. P., & Dudek, S. Z. (1973). Psychosomatic medicine: The mind-body interaction. In B. B. Wolman (Ed.), *Handbook of general psychology* (pp. 242-272). Englewood Cliffs, NJ: Prentice-Hall.

Wolf, S. (1981). The psyche and the stomach: A historical vignette. *Gastroenterology, 80*, 605-614.

Wolf, S., & Wolff, H. G. (1948). Life situations, emotions, and gastric function: A summary. *American Practitioner, 3*, 1-14.

Wolff, H. G. (1948). *Headache and other head pain.* New York: Oxford University Press.

Wolfson, L. I., & Katzman, R. (1983). The neurologic consultation at age 80. In R. Katzman & R. Terry (Eds.), *The neurology of aging* (pp. 221-244). Philadelphia, PA: F. A. Davis.

Wolpe, J. (1958). *Psychotherapy by reciprocal inhibition.* Stanford, CA: Stanford University Press.

Wood, C. G., & Hokanson, J. E. (1965). Effects of induced muscular tension on performance and the inverted U function. *Journal of Personality and Social Psychology, 1*, 506-509.

Woolfolk, R. L., Carr-Kaffashan, L., McNulty, T. F., & Lehrer, P. (1976). Meditation training as a treatment for insomnia. *Behavior Therapy, 7*, 359-365.

World Health Organization. (1958). *Constitution: World Health Organization.* Geneva, Switzerland: World Health Organization.

World Health Organization. (1962). Arterial hypertension and ischaemic heart disease: Preventive aspects. *Technical Report Series, 231*, 4-7.

Yager, J., & Weiner, H. (1971). Observations in man. In J. Bastiaan, H. Freyberger, L. Levi, Z. J. Lipowski, J. C. Nemiah, E. Meyer, F. Reichman, P. Sainsbury, & H. Weiner (Eds.), *Advances in Psychosomatic Medicine* (Vol. 6, pp. 40-55). Basel: S. Karger.

Yamanaka, M., Greenberg, B., Johnson, L., Seilhamer, J., Brewer, M., Friedemann, T., Miller, J., Atlas, S., Laragh, J., Lewicki, J., & Fiddes, J. (1984). Cloning and sequence analysis of the cDNA for the rat atrial natriuretic factor precursor. *Nature, 309*, 719-722.

Yates, A. J. (1980). *Biofeedback and the modification of behavior.* New York: Plenum.

Yerkes, R. M., & Dodson, J. D. (1908). The relation of strength of stimulus to rapidity of habit formation. *Journal of Comparative Neurology and Psychology, 18*, 459-482.

Young, P. (1980). *Asthma and allergies: An optimistic future* (DHHS Publication No. NIH 80-388). Washington, DC: U.S. Government Printing Office.

Zentall, S. S., & Zentall, T. R. (1983). Optimal stimulation: A model of disordered activity and performance in normal and deviant children. *Psychological Bulletin, 94*, 446-471.

Zlutnick, S., Mayville, W. J., & Moffat, S. (1975). Modification of seizure disorders: The interruption of behavioral chains. *Journal of Applied Behavior Analysis, 8*, 1-12.

Author Index

Subject Index